THE OFFICIAL PRICE GUIDE TO Collectible RECORDS

BY
THE HOUSE OF COLLECTIBLES, INC.

We have compiled information herein through a *patented computerized process* which relies primarily on a nationwide sampling of information provided by noteworthy collectible experts, auction houses and specialized dealers. This sophisticated retrieval system enables us to provide the reader with the most current and accurate information available.

EDITOR
THOMAS E. HUDGEONS III

FIRST EDITION
THE HOUSE OF COLLECTIBLES, INC., ORLANDO, FLORIDA 32809

Published by: The House of Collectibles, Inc.
        Orlando Central Park
        1900 Premier Row
        Orlando, FL 32809
        Phone: (305) 857-9095

Printed in the United States of America

Library of Congress Catalog Card Number: 82-84652

ISBN: 0-87637-400-3

TABLE OF CONTENTS

PHOTO RECOGNITION

COVER — Marc Hudgeons, Orlando, FL 32809.

BECOME AN "OFFICIAL" CONTRIBUTOR TO THE WORLD'S LEADING PRICE GUIDES

Are you an experienced collector with access to information not covered in this guide? Do you possess knowledge, data, or ideas that should be included?

If so, The House of Collectibles invites you to **GET INVOLVED**.

The House of Collectibles continuously seeks to improve, expand, and update the material in the **THE OFFICIAL PRICE GUIDE SERIES.** The assistance and cooperation of numerous collectors, auction houses and dealers has added immeasurably to the success of the books in this series. If you think you qualify as a contributor, our editors would like to offer your expertise to the readers of the **OFFICIAL PRICE GUIDE SERIES.**

As the publishers of the most popular and authoritative Price Guides, The House of Collectibles can provide a far-reaching audience for your collecting accomplishments. *Help the hobby grow* by letting others benefit from the knowledge that you have discovered while building your collection.

If your contribution appears in the next edition, you'll become and **"OFFICIAL"** member of the world's largest hobby-publishing team. Your name will appear on the acknowledgement page, *plus you will receive a free complimentary copy.* Send a full outline of the type of material you wish to contribute. Please include your phone number. Write to: **THE HOUSE OF COLLECTIBLES, INC.** Editorial Department, 1900 Premier Row, Orlando, Florida, 32809.

SOLID GOLD

"Rock and Roll is Here to Stay" was the title of a 1950's chart buster, and it proved one of the most prophetic statements of the era. Though it's undergone numerous changes in the past two and a half decades, rock music is bigger than ever today. It now totally dominates the music scene, and some of the world's wealthiest individuals — Paul McCartney and Mick Jagger to name — are rock stars.

Almost everybody involved in the Birth of Rock is gone from the scene; even most of the Liverpool Sound people of the sixties have faded into oblivion. Their places have been taken by New Wavers, Punkers, and Acid Rockers. But music leaves a legacy, and those old discs are still being played and enjoyed. In fact they've spawned one of the most popular hobbies of our day — finding them, collecting them, and preserving them.

The rock record hobby goes much deeper than replaying the past. For one thing, many of these discs are genuinely scarce, especially in mint or near-mint condition. Most of these cuts have been repressed (on LP's or elsewhere), but a collector — as opposed to a listener — wants the original.

If you paid 79¢ for the original back in 1958 or 1959, and plucked it from a shelf harboring dozens of copies, you probably never imagined you were getting a "collectible." Neither did anyone else! As with all kinds of collector's items, time and circumstances can do funny things. Million-selling gold records were manufactured in such quantities that most of them HAVEN'T become scarce, though they're sought by collectors nevertheless. Discs that reached only as far as #35 or #40 on the charts were produced in far lower quantities . . . and the flops of yesteryear usually had miniscule output.

Collecting the forgotten sides by forgotten artists is one of the major facets of the rock hobby. Mostly these were one-shots. The artist cut a record which failed to get any airplay and was never heard from again. Musically some of these records were not bad; they just failed to click. Quite a few of the labels were one-shots, too; they pressed just that lone record and vanished for keeps. There were hundreds and hundreds of these hopeful discs by hopeful groups and singles during the '50's and '60's. Previously undiscovered ones still turn up from time to time. Some are worth a modest $8 to $12; others fall into the $20 to $40 category; but still others go for more than $100.

The early sides cut by Rock's Greats are likewise a favorite of collectors. These, too, can be scarce and costly. In this category is the most valuable single rock record, "My Bonnie" by Tony Sheridan and the Beat Brothers (later to be known as The Beatles, minus Tony Sheridan). The Elvis cuts on Sun Records, when he was under contract to Sam C. Phillips in Tennessee, are collector's items of the first rank. Unlike "My Bonnie," which didn't get far geographically, the Elvis Sun pressings were distributed all across the country in the mid 1950's. Today, thanks to the fact that Elvis fans can't be talked into parting with them, they're hard to get and far from cheap.

If you have vintage rock records, this book will help you to appraise them. If you're thinking of building a collection, it will tell you the prices you can expect to pay, when buying from "golden oldies" dealers. It will also help you identify some of the songs and artists that you've half remembered, half forgotten. In short, it's required reading for anyone for whom "Rock and Roll is Here to Stay."

HOW TO BEGIN A COLLECTION

If you're not already into Rock/Country record collecting, you might be wondering about how to begin. In a way this is a do-it-yourself hobby. There are no "beginners' kits" available, as for many other hobbies. But that's a plus, because it means that your collection will be uniquely your own — not somebody else's idea of what a collection should be. You'll need, of course, to follow certain guidelines, to keep from paying too much or getting records that aren't really worthwhile. And chances are you'll want to specialize in one direction or another, rather than skipping around and building up a miscellaneous collection. Beyond that — it's up to you, and you shouldn't hesitate for a moment to follow your instincts and collect the records and artists YOU find most appealing . . . regardless of whether they're trendy or valuable.

You might already have the foundation of a collection without even being aware of it. If you have certain favorite recording artists and have been buying their new releases for a few years, you've got the perfect springboard to a collection. You can go out and get the earlier records of those same artists, ones that were made before you started buying. If the artist(s) has been around for a while, you might have missed dozens of singles and LP's from the earlier part of their careers. Chances are, these are now all out-of-pirnt. You can't get them from your usual record source, but dealers in "old and scarce" records have them. They can be bought as a collection if you have the money and want to do it that way. Or you can go along getting one or two at a time and working gradually toward completion. If rare discs are involved, some patience and hunting may be necessary before locating them. But you WILL find them, and the sooner you get them, the less you'll probably have to pay. Values are constantly going up, so anything you buy next year is apt to be more expensive than it is this year.

A single-artist collection is appealing to many hobbyists. Of course if your favorite artist is a newcomer into the recording industry, there won't be much available. In that case you might want to open up a secondary collection devoted to some other artist, possibly someone whose music was an influence on your favorite star. There are all sorts of possibilities. Flipping through the listings in this book will give you many ideas.

If you want a target that's bigger in scope, you could try collecting a certain style of music (such as New Wave Rock) or recordings of a given time-period. These are more specialized pursuits. You'll run into quite a few high-priced rarities and it's entirely up to you, whether you want to include them in your collection or bypass them. You needn't worry about completion with this kind of collection. Nobody who concentrates on a broad category of recordings ever hopes for a complete collection. There's simply more material available than anyone could assemble in a lifetime. The goal is merely to build up an interesting collection and enjoy yourself along the way. At the same time you might be amassing a financial investment, even without planning to, considering the rate at which many records appreciate in value.

Most collectors who set their sights on a time-period choose the 1950's. This is the most appealing decade because it ushered in the 45 r.p.m. single. Rock was born in the fifties and scored its great successes because of the 45 vinyl disc. Country music, too, benefited enormously from the introduction of vinyl records. When you "collect the fifties" you're collecting these music forms at the most significant stages of development. Rather than tackling the entire decade, though, you could restrict yourself to certain artists. It all depends on whether you'd be more pleased with a representative collection — reflecting the works of many different artists with different styles — or a more highly specialized one.

If you want to build a collection around a Star Artist of the past, you'll be buying the hobby's Blue Chips . . . as these records tend to grow in demand and value faster than any others. Certain recording artists of the past (either deceased, or no longer actively making records) have become greater favorites of collectors than others. Buddy Holly is of course the prime example. During his brief lifetime Holly was unquestionably a star and his records sold very well. But after his untimely death, he became a "cult figure" and his songs became a source of influence to many later artists. Even before record collecting had emerged as an authentic hobby, with established market values, Buddy Holly's original recordings were selling for premium prices wherever they could be had. Today, if you want to make a Buddy Holly collection, there are a number of specialized dealers who stock ALL his singles and albums. But, as you will note in the listings in this book, some of them are quite expensive. Before you choose and artist to collect, decide whether or not you're determined to have a complete collection. Then decide whether your budget would allow it! If Buddy Holly, Elvis and the Beatles would be too costly for you (complete collections on any of these artists would cost well over $1,000), there are many "artists of the past" whose recordings are not quite so valuable. You might make a unique collection with any one of them, as you COULD be the only collector specializing in their records.

What it really boils down to is: what do you like? And WHO do you like? In any hobby — records or anything else — it's always best to follow your own personal tastes, rather than collect something because it's popular or because a book tells you to. If you grew up in the '50's and '60's, the music you liked the most in those days will probably be your favorite for collecting . . . even if you THINK your tastes have changed. Don't be concerned about getting out of the mainstream of the hobby, if you have an interest in artists who are not heavily collected at the moment. The truth is that there's no mainstream in the record hobby! It's simply composed of many individuals collecting what they want to collect. If the records that appeal to you are not particularly valuable at the present time, or seem to be lacking in general interest, this could easily change in time. The record hobby is never a closed book. Things that happen TODAY in the recording industry influence, to some extent, trends in collecting. And very often these go in cycles. "Punk rock" of the '80's is inspired by the leather-jacket, greased-hair look of the '50's. Very possibly the Liverpool Sound of the '60's will come back — in some altered form

— eventually. Who can say? There are just so many "new ideas," so themes and styles are frequently borrowed from the past. To young people they're entirely new. To the slightly older crowd they sometimes inspire a collecting enthusiasm!

Another possibility is to center your collection around rare recordings, regardless of the artist or the particular style of music. Although such a collection has a miscellaneous, catch-all nature, the rarity and value of each record binds them together and provides a very fascinating focal point. The rare records are of course the expensive ones, so you might have to go slow if this is your chosen line of specializing — adding perhaps one record every month or so to your collection. Whether this is satisfactory to you depends on your personality and your outlook toward the hobby. Some collectors are content to save up, and add nothing to their holdings until they can get a really desirable item. They don't mind going a long while without buying; they fill in the void by reading the collector publications, corresponding with other hobbyists, and doing plenty of planning about what they'll be buying in the future. Others, however, aren't happy unless they can go out record shopping every week or two. They would rather buy records constantly, spending a few dollars per disc, than own individual records worth $100 or more. Once again this is totally up to you and nobody will say you're wrong, no mater how you choose to go about it.

Looking at things from the strictly financial side of the fence, you would have very little to be shaky about, in buying expensive records. Chances are, if you pay $100 for a record, you'll run into someone who chuckles and claims you've thrown your money away — that the hobby is a passing fad and the record will be worthless in the future. Maybe YOU have some hidden doubts yourself. If so, you should be reassured by the fact that values have STEADILY increased, as a result of more and more collectors coming into the hobby, and that the outlook for the future is definitely positive. Of course there's no way of knowing how big a hobby this will become. But its potential is boundless, and even a person who isn't overly optimistic would have to admit that just the surface has been scratched so far. In stamp and coin collecting, the major rarities fetch well over $100,000 — in some cases close to $1,000,000. These are older hobbies and the values have been building for many, many years. It COULD be that the rarest, most sought-for Rock/Country discs will eventually grow into that kind of value category. In any event, one thing is sure. As the hobby continues to expand, there will be greater and greater demand for the scarcest discs, more competition, and an inevitable decline of supply, as some records become lost or damaged . . . or go into museum collections (there are already many museum collections of records in this country, most notably at the Library of Congress in Washington, D.C.). All this *has to* add up to rising prices.

But this isn't to say that you couldn't do just as well, financially, buying records that are inexpensive today. The $5 and $6 records of today might increase in value even more sharply than those which are already expensive. This will almost certainly be the case, for little-known records by artists who are coming into big popularity right now.

There is very little danger that you could lose money by collecting records, no matter what direction your collection takes. If you buy right — that is, don't overpay, and get records in the best possible condition — and hold your records for a reasonable length of time after buying them, you should have no trouble selling them at a profit when the time comes. Collectors who take losses on their records are the ones who switch around from one artist or type of music to another. They build up a collection or start to build one, then get another idea and sell the collection after a few months. Since a dealer will discount from the market value when he buys records, you will nearly always lose money by selling your records this quickly, but this is true of other hobby collections, too. No hobby market goes up fast enough . . . except in very rare instances . . . to return a profit in just several months.

Want some more suggestions? Here are a few:

GOLDEN DISCS. Build a collection of records that sold one million copies each. You might be surprised but well over 1,000 such records exist. None of them (unless you get into 78's) are rare and valuable; you'll never be spending even as much as $10 on a record.

LABEL COLLECTION. Choose a label that specialized in the kind of music that appeals to you, and restrict your collecting to records of that company.

DEBUT RECORDS. Collect a variety of artists in the FIRST record they cut.

PICTURE SLEEVE RECORDS. Many 45's have been issued with picture sleeves. These sleeves are collectors' items, too, and a collection of the records in their original sleeves has extra value.

TWO-WAY HITS. Records that were big in both the Pop and Country fields.

WHERE TO BUY AND SELL

There are many, many sources for out-of-print, collectible records. If you have the time to visit flea markets and garage sales you'll find old records by the score, many of them selling well below their actual collector value and occasionally, ABOVE their collector value — which make it imperative that you know the market prices. They turn up at thrift shops, charity bazaars, the Salvation Army, Goodwill Industries, and just about everywhere that you could find second-hand merchandise. Finding specific records that you need in this fashion is difficult, though . . . and when they do turn up, they might not be in the best of condition. This is why advanced collectors, or anyone who wants to have a choice collection with a minimum of inconvenience, do most of their buying from specialist dealers. Until a few years ago, you had to live in a large city to be near a "Golden Oldies" shop — or do your buying by mail-order. Today, with hundreds of such shops dotted across the country, most collectors are within easy reach of one (or more). Also, the Old Records shows and conventions held in different parts of the country bring the dealers and their stocks to you.

It's hard to convince the general public that some people actually make a living — and a good one — buying and selling out-of-print records. But they indeed do, which shows the popularlity of the record collecting hobby. Golden Oldie dealers operate in the same fashion as stamp and coin dealers. They try to keep comprehensive stocks of the most popular, in-demand artists, as well as scarce records by lesser-known performers. They buy from the public and sell to the public, and, like all other businessmen, their profit comes from selling at a higher price than they buy. But for those in the out-of-print record business, it's like no other business at all. Nearly all the dealers are former collectors or are still collecting. They gained their knowledge of the hobby, and many of their "contacts," from years of active collecting. They saw that they could, as collectors, make money selling or swapping their duplicates. Why not do it as a business? You'll find that they're a very helpful group of individuals. They perfectly understand your collecting passion for Conway Twitty or Brenda Lee or whoever you're collecting. These are the people you should get to know. Visit their shops. Get on their mailing lists. When you get to be a steady customer, the dealers will put aside records for you as they come in, so you don't miss an item that you were waiting months to buy.

Of course, all the shops selling collector records are not alike. Some are much larger than others. Some are slanted more to Rock, some to Pop, and others to Country; while others attempt to maintain a general stock in all fields. Certain dealers have "specialties," just like collectors; you'll find some shops with an absolutely complete showing of every Elvis Presley record, including the scarce Sun label releases. This is considered a big plus for the dealers because it draws specialist customers to them, who can count on getting just the record they need at the moment without having to shop around. As you can probably guess, specialist dealers who "highlight" Presley or the Beatles or Buddy Holly in their shops charge slightly higher prices than the rest of the trade. You will generally find that the condition of records handled by specialists is the best obtainable.

In most out-of-print record shops the 45's are arranged on wall shelves, filed alphabetically by artist. Albums will either be on wall shelves, too, or in file cartons. Duplicate copies (which every shop has, of most of its discs — sometimes a dozen of them) will either be in the regular file or kept in a back room where only the proprietor can get to them. When a record is sold, he goes in the back and gets another copy to replace it. This method is preferred by many dealers, because when just a single copy is on the shelf it tends to give customers the feeling that they should buy NOW. Also, when duplicates are displayed of a scarce record, some customers might think the record isn't really scarce. Don't feel that way! Some shops have duplicates of the Presley Sun label recordings. They're STILL very scarce and valuable — the dealer has simply done a very good job (and probably went to considerable expense) in assembling his stock of them.

At nearly all shops, the record's price is stated on the sleeve. There may or may not be a statement of condition. If the condition is not stated, you should ask to play the record, as it may be difficult to judge the condition from a mere visual examination. Don't forget that condition is important . . . even if it isn't especially important to YOU. Some collectors are just as happy to get a long-sought-for record in used condition, as if the condition was mint. That's okay, but NOT if you're paying a "mint" price for a "used" record! You'll find that records are priced in line with condition most of the time, but any dealer can slip up. Once you take the record home it may no longer be accepted back for a refund, so do your investigating in the shop and satisfy yourself that the price reflects the condition.

If you can't get to a shop, you can buy from the shops by mail. Most of them do mail-order business, either by the "wantlist" or "sale list" method (or both). The wantlist method means that you send the dealer a list of the records you're interested in buying. A wantlist should state the artist, label, and song selections — and the label serial numbers if you know them (all the serial numbers are given for records listed in this book). Don't state the prices you're willing to pay. The dealers already have their stock priced, record by record, and will let you know their selling prices on the discs you want.

Don't send out the same wantlist to more than one dealer at a time. Wait until you get a report from one dealer before contacting someone else. Unless the records you're seeking are very obscure, you'll find most times that the dealers have a high batting average on wantlists. Don't list more records on your wantlist than you're prepared to buy. In other words, show the dealers that you're serious and dedicated about the hobby. In that way you'll always get fast service and a lot of little "preferred customer" extras along the way.

Maybe you're asking: Will a dealer charge me more for a record on my wantlist, because he knows I want it, than if I just found it on his shelf? The answer is NO in most cases. The dealers have 90% of the stock priced according to the current retail market, and the price is the same whether you "walk in" or "send in." The dealers are very well informed on values. They either KNOW the value, or look it up, on every record they handle. They don't wait until a customer requests the record before putting a price on it.

The other method of buying by mail is via Sale Lists. These are lists issued by the dealers, sent out either free or for some nominal charge. Dealers who issue sale lists put them out every two or three months. The list is arranged alphabetically by artist, but might be broken up into categories if the dealer sells Rock, Country, and other types of music. The important thing to realize about Sale Lists is that they don't cover the shop's whole stock. No list is an effort to reflect everything the dealer has on hand. Usually, each list is comprised of the "cream" of recent purchases, made since the previous list was circulated. Either that, or the dealer will select certain artists from his stock to spotlight on the list. If you don't see what you want on the list, this is not necessarily an indication that the shop doesn't have it. The dealers never try to put out a list of everything in their stock, as this would not only be very time-consuming but it would also make each list very similar in content.

The condition of each record will be stated in the list. Sometimes there will be several copies of the same disc in different grades of condition — at different prices of course. The customer usually has to pay the shipping charges on records ordered by mail. Don't worry about whether they'll be packed well. The dealers send out records constantly and are experts at packing them safely.

Selling Records. The dealers are always prepared to buy records. This is how they acquire most of their stock, by buying from the public (collectors, as well as people who've come across old records in the attic). They'll be more than happy to buy from you IF you have collectible records to sell. A dealer won't buy something he can't sell, or has doubts about whether he can sell it. For your records to be salable to a dealer, they must be out-of-print (no longer obtainable from distributors) and in good condition. Records of fairly recent vintage, from about 1970 on, are usually NOT salable to a dealer unless the condition is *mint* . . . that is, showing no signs whatsoever of having ever been played. If you're selling LP's they must be in original sleeves, and the sleeves cannot be torn or stained. Of course you will do much better selling your records if you have material in hot demand by collectors. If a record is from the 1970's or later, you can be almost certain that the dealer already has copies of it. Postage stamp dealers buy commemorative stamps at the Post Office as they come out, and Golden Oldie dealers do just about the same thing: they get current records from distributors at the wholesale prices and put them away to "mature." If a dealer has five or six copies of a record in stock, for each of which he paid just the WHOLESALE price, he won't be too anxious to pay you a premium over the RETAIL price for yours. You cannot count on doing too well when selling such records as there is no scarcity factor behind them. With the older discs it's of course a very different story, because the dealers weren't in business back in the 1950's and '60's and weren't getting these records at wholesale. They have to pay you a good price for them, because there's no other source for early records. If a dealer buys his records from other dealers, he's paying even more!

Prices paid by different dealers are not always the same, but they will be approximately the same on MOST records. Naturally you will never get the full retail price (as shown in this book) when selling to a dealer, since he must allow himself a working margin to meet expenses and leave a reasonable profit. So it becomes a matter of what proportion of the retail value will you receive? A third? Half? Two thirds? Normally you will get the largest proportion of retail value for *very scarce* records in *mint* condition, such as a Triple-D Buddy Knox with no signs of use. For discs of that class, you will be paid around 70% of the retail value, with a possible variation up or down depending on circumstances. A dealer will always pay a little more for a record he doesn't already have in stock, than one which he has in two or three specimens. Unfortunately, you're not likely to know what he has in stock when you take records to sell to him!

Seventy percent of retail value means you would get $70 for a record listed at $100.

If a record is somewhat less scarce, but still in mint condition, the dealer will pay around 60% of retail value — or $6 for a record that he sells for $10.

When the condition is *less than mint,* a somewhat larger deduction is taken from the retail price, simply because the dealer is more interested in building up his stock of mint records than his stock of Very Fine or Fine. Taking the above example, of $70 for a $100 record in mint condition, we'll assume that this same disc has a retail value of $40 in Very Fine (used) condition. The dealer would perhaps pay you $20 for a Very Fine specimen, which means 50% of the retail value. It's the same record, but the difference in condition make it less desirable for the dealer to handle.

For a record that sells at $2 in mint condition, the dealer may offer you only 50¢. There's no incentive for him to add to his already large stock of such records unless he can get them very inexpensively.

Of course there are other possibilities for selling, such as contacting collectors by placing a classified newspaper ad. In this way you could get the full retail prices, just as charged by the dealers, but it might take much longer to sell your records.

If you do decide to sell to a dealer, here are some things you should do:

1. Check out the values first (in this book), so you can compare them against the dealer's offer. Be candid about the condition. If you've played the records a great deal they aren't mint, even though they may look perfect.

2. Clean them with a record brush or cloth and place each record in a sleeve, if they aren't already in sleeves.

3. Get to the shop when it isn't too busy, as a purchase takes more of the proprietor's time than a sale. Early in the day is usually best.

4. If the dealer asks how much you want for your records, name a price about 10% higher than you'd consider satisfactory. But don't ask for the full retail value or anything even close to it.

As you get further into record collecting, the ins and outs of buying and selling will become second nature. The dealers will become your friends and the ways of the record business will not seem mysterious anymore. Don't get down on yourself if you make a few mistakes buying or selling at the beginning. Most hobbyists do when they get into a new hobby. Your on-target deals later on will more than compensate for these early blunders. You'll be surprised how quickly you accumulate just as much expertise as the professionals.

GRADING THE CONDITION

Every record that's ever been made . . . from Caruso to the Beatles . . . was intended to be played and enjoyed. No records have been created as museum pieces. But record collectors, like most other hobbyists, are very influenced by condition. They want their records in the best obtainable condition and are willing to pay premium sums for it. If you're new to record collecting, one of the important points to be recognized at the outset is that CONDITION COUNTS, and the value of any record is DIRECTLY RELATED to its state of preservation. In fact — odd as this sounds — the condition is really more important than the record! A disc in mint condition that sells for $50 might sell for just $2 if worn or scratched. Therefore, the condition accounts for $48 of the value and the artist and song account for just $2!

You have to be aware of condition when you buy and when you sell . . . and when you make trades. You have to not only be aware of it, but aware of the effect it has on values.

As you'll see, all the records listed in this book are priced in MINT and VERY GOOD condition — the two highest grades of condition for collectible records. There is a very noticeable difference in value between Mint and Very Fine, sometimes as much as 100%, even though a casual glance at the records would fail to distinguish between a "Mint" and a "Very Good" copy.

It isn't difficult to grade records correctly. Grading is not a matter of personal opinion. A standard approach is used by all collectors and dealers, which makes for the fewest arguments and disappointments. Of course there will always be some isolated cases in which one party believes a record's condition to be different than another party.

To grade a record's condition properly it should be played, as a visual grading is "iffy." Most experienced collectors and dealers can make very accurate visual gradings, but there will always be a slip-up here and there even among the best experts. The simple fact is that some records look pristine but don't sound that way. The "golden oldie" shops have phonos on hand and don't object to you playing a record that you intend you buy . . . so long as you don't go along aimlessly playing one record after another.

Sleeve grading is also important. Beginning in the late 1960's, many 45 r.p.m. singles were sold in picture sleeves. They were intended as advertising devices, not collectors' items, they've become just that. When such records are still in the original sleeves they have a premium value, and this value is governed of course by the sleeve's condition. A mint condition sleeve could double the value of the record. One in poor condition might add just 10% to the value. Sleeve grading enters the picture with EP's and LP's, too. These MUST be in the original sleeves to be considered "collectible." EP and LP sleeves tend to be preserved in a higher grade of condition because they were printed on heavier stock than 45 single sleeves, which are nothing more than thin paper. Still, there are differences, as some will be found with soiling or stains while occasionally an albun 25 or 30 years old turns up with an absolutely perfect mint sleeve. Collectors want the optimum condition they can get, in both the record and the sleeve!

Sleeve grading is very simple because you need only look at it. An EP or LP sleeve should not have bent corners, tears, stains, scribbling, or anything else that mars the appearance. A 45 r.p.m. single sleeve should not be torn or stained — it inevitably will be a little bent at the corners from ordinary handling. This is not considered a fault.

As an aid to readers and particularly beginners, the COMPLETE guidelines for grading records in ALL levels of condition are given here. But we hasten to point out that records in the lower grades of condition (less than Very Good) are not considered collectible by most hobbyists. If you have any — don't throw them out! Play them. Enjoy them. They can be your "playing copies," while you seek out better-grade specimens for your collection.

MINT. A record in fresh unused condition just as it came from the factory, shows no signs of wear or handling. The vinyl is bright, the label has no scratches or marks or any kind; the record when played has no surface noise that could be attributable to wear even if played on sensitive equipment. But remember that the technical quality of 45 r.p.m. records from the 1950's was not equal to today's. Even a perfectly Mint specimen may not sound "clean" when played on sensitive equipment. What you're hearing is not surface noise from WEAR, but noise that was in the master used for pressing. Some experience will be needed to distinguish between the two. Also, *dust particles* can create surface noise on a Mint record. Be sure records are clean before you give them a test playing. This is true of the needle, too.

VERY GOOD. A record in Very Good condition has been played a number of times, which is evident by SLIGHT surface noise caused by minor wear to the vinyl coating. The record is not scratched or nicked and the label is not marred in any way.

GOOD. Shows more wear than a record in Very Good condition. Surface noise is apparent from the beginning to end of the "hit" side of the record, and is more pronounced than on a Very Good disc.

FAIR. The record has obviously been played a great deal on the "hit" side or possibly on both sides. There may be minor scratches, noticeable when the record is held at a slant to the light — but they do not cause the needle to jump. Label may be scratched or soiled.

POOR. The record is nicked and badly scratched, to the point where the needle jumps when playing it. May also be out of shape as a result of exposure to exteme heat, thereby creating a "wavy" sound when played. Whenever a record is wavy it automatically grades Poor, even if there are no other defects.

The usual differences in value for records in the different grades are as follows, but these are approximate only and can vary (see the listings section for specific examples):

RECORD WORTH $100 IN MINT CONDITION

Value in "Very Good"	$40-50
Value in "Good"	15-20
Value in "Fair"	4-6
Value in "Poor"	0

RECORD WORTH $50 IN MINT CONDITION

Value in "Very Good"	$20-25
Value in "Good"	6-9
Value in "Fair"	1-2
Value in "Poor"	0

RECORD WORTH $10 IN MINT CONDITION

Value in "Very Good"	$4-5
Value in "Good"	1-2
Value in "Fair"	0
Value in "Poor"	0

Whenever you find records that are stored in a box without sleeves — just jumbled together — there is no hope of any of them being in Mint condition. As the surfaces of records rub against each other, they cause scratches and wear.

Obviously, the number of Mint specimens that exist of any given record is much smaller than those in other grades of condition. With older records there is an even greater discrepancy between existing "Mints" and used copies. In the case of 45 r.p.m. singles from the 1950's, there may be only one mint specimen for every 20 or 30 used copies (which would include every grade from Very Good down to Poor). It should be easy to see, therefore, why these Mint discs are worth the stiff premium prices at which they sell. The record is the same but the SCARCITY FACTOR is much different between Mint and Used condition.

Extended Play recordings and Long Play albums tend to be preserved in better condition, on the whole, than singles. This is naturally because the average owner placed these records back in their sleeves after playing them, and the sleeve afforded good protection. Also, LP's are not played as much as singles because of the longer playing time. Someone might play their favorite single over and over again, dozens of playings at a time, but it's rare for albums to be played more than once at a single listening. Consequently, AN ALBUM IN MINT CONDITION IS NOT — USUALLY — WORTH AS MUCH OF A PREMIUM AS A SINGLE RECORD IN MINT CONDITION.

Judging from the relatively low grade of condition in which so many records of the 1950's and '60's are found, you'd naturally assume that record owners were very lax in those days, throwing them around like frisbees. That's partly true. But it isn't just the fault of private owners. Some of these heavily worn, battered records of yesteryear are jukebox copies. They were played to death in the jukeboxes of the land. Others are discards from the record libraries of radio stations, where they were also heavily played.

Learn to correctly grade your records, and you'll do better in buying and selling.

CARE AND STORAGE

Care and storage of vinyl records is fairly simple compared to the old 78 r.p.m.s, which easily cracked and shattered. Still they do require some attention if you want to keep them in the best possible condition.

The first step of course is to *buy* records in well-preserved condition, and strive to keep up the standard of your collection. You might occasionally let a "filler" slip in, if the disc is very scarce and hard to get in Very Good or Mint condition. But if you're serious about record collecting, and especially if you have any plans of possibly using your collection as a financial investment, you'll want to have the majority of specimens in mint condition.

The main thing you want to accomplish in storage is to protect your records against scratching, nicks, and warping. Records have to be kept in sleeves of some kind — that's a must. For best protection the sleeves should not be the light flimsy kind in which records are normally sold. These are printed from cheap stock for the purpose of saving money. They're fine for the record shops but as a collector you can't keep your records in them year after year. They're so thin that the record could be scratched right THROUGH the sleeve. You can get good-quality protective sleeves from most of the dealers who sell out-of-print records. These are several times the weight of "record shop" sleeves and do the job very well. They carry no printing whatsoever, and if you like you can make notations on them (date the record was purchased, from whom, price, and so on) — but remember to make your notations when the sleeve is EMPTY. They aren't cheap but are well worth the money. Buy them in quantity and save.

After your records are properly sleeved, you'll need some method of storing them. Boxes are sold by record dealers, in corrugated and plastic, in which records can be filed. These come in two sizes, for 7-inchers (45 r.p.m. singles and EP's) and 12-inchers (LP's). The filing arrangement in these boxes is the same as in a file cabinet. Your records are filed alphabetically by the artist and letter boards are used so you can locate any particular letter of the alphabet easily.

There are other possibilities for storage but they aren't quite as satisfactory. Because records are flat and no taller than books, some beginning collectors line them up on bookcase shelves. After all, they say, this is what the dealers do in their shops — which is perfectly true. Shelf storage is not recommended, however. It seems convenient at the outset but as your collection expands it won't be. For one thing, you have to do a lot of pushing and pulling to get the records off the shelf, and this invites damage. If the shelf is tightly packed, matters are worse. If the shelf is partly empty, the records are sure to flop over and land in a pile, just as books do. For dealers this isn't a bad arrangement because their stock moves in and out and no record is on the shelves for ages.

Albums are made with sets of paper pockets into which records can be inserted. These may be acceptable for a collector's use IF the records are also protected by sleeves.

Make sure that your records are not stored in an area of the home where heat and humidity are likely to build up. Vinyl records will warp if they're too near a fireplace, stove, or any other source of heat — including direct sunlight on a hot summer's day. Many collectors are not aware of the dangers of heat. Vinyl is a plastic and plastic melts!

You'll need to clean your records occasionally. When you first acquire a record, it may not have been cleaned in years. The best thing is to wipe it gently with a rag that's been moistened with rubbing alcohol (but don't use this approach with 78's, as alcohol will turn the surface white). If the record is merely a little dusty it can be cleaned with an ordinary record cleaning cloth, available at any record shop. Because of static electricity, dust particles are attracted to records and it's a good idea to wipe them clean before and after each playing.

Sometimes you'll encounter an old record with a sticker on the label. Usually these records have come from department stores, which have the habit (or did, in the past) of labeling them like all other merchandise in the store. If it's a peel-away sticker it can be removed without much difficulty, though not quite as easily as when the sticker was new. Over the years the gum hardens somewhat and the label could tear when peeled off, or leave some remnants behind. If the label was glued on, peeling won't work. You'll have to moisten it with water and rub — gently — with a rag. There's always a danger of damaging the label when you do this, so it may be wiser to leave well enough alone.

To the perennial question of whether warping can be corrected, the answer is, sadly, no. Once a record has been warped you can't bring it back to the original condition. You might be able to straighten out the record somewhat by leaving it under a heavy weight for a few days, but it will always be slightly warped — meaning "no value" as a collectors' item.

Nor can you do anything to remove scratches or nicks in a record. But don't jump to conclusions about them. When you give a record a test playing and the needle sticks or jumps, this is sometimes the needle's fault and not the record's. Make sure the needle is clean and not worn out. Dust accumulates on needles rapidly. You might play five or six records with no problem, then have the needle suddenly jump. "It can't be the needle," you're apt to think, because it was fine on the previous records. But it was gradually picking up dust, and reached the point where enough had accumulated to make it scratch or skip. Don't condemn the record until you've checked out the equipment!

When playing records that have collector value, always play them one at a time. Don't stack them in an automatic machine, as tempting as this may be. Stacking leads to damage. Vinyl records won't crack when they fall on top of each other, but they get rubbed and scratched by being stacked. Many collectors prefer not to play their records AT ALL, especially if they were in mint condition when acquired. You can always record your favorite selections on a cassette and play the cassette instead — or get lower-grade copies for playing.

Take along a plastic bag when shopping for records, just in case your purchases get caught in the rain on the way home.

Don't leave records in the glove compartment or trunk of a car on a very hot day, as this could cause warping.

If you carry records in a suitcase with other items, make sure the other items won't damage them. Place heavy cardboards on both sides of the records for protection.

When mailing records, cut out two pieces of heavy cardboard, each about 2" wider on all sides than the record. Place the record(s) between them like a sandwich and tape up the edges, then wrap securely in paper. This procedure is suitable for all vinyl records but not for 78's, which, because of the fragility, must be more protectively packed. The best way to send 78's is in a tin canister used for motion picture film.

HOW TO USE THIS BOOK

All the artists covered in this book are listed alphabetically. Solo performers are alphabetized under their last name — Johnny Cash under "C," Paul Anka under "A." Groups are alphabetized by the first word in the group name, except when the first work is "The."

For Example:

BUFFALO SPRINGFIELD is listed under "B" for BUFFALO

THE MAMAS AND THE PAPAS is listed under "M" for MAMAS

Records are listed under the artist's name that appears on the label. If an artist recorded under two or more different names (such as Tom & Jerry/Simon & Garfunkel), LOOK UNDER BOTH NAMES TO FIND THE LISTINGS.

Each artist's listing begins with his (or her) 45 r.p.m. singles. These are arranged sequentially by the issue numbers on the labels, shown on the left column of the listings. Next to the issue numbers, the record label is stated. Then the selections on each side of the record are separated by a slash (/), such as:

MAGIC MOMENTS/FRIDAY IN THE RAIN

There are two price columns. The first indicates the value for a specimen in Very Good condition, showing very slight signs of use, and the second for a perfect Mint copy just as it came from the factory.

Beneath the listings for each artist's 45 r.p.m. singles are further listings for his Extended Play (EP) and Long Play (LP) recordings, if any. The same arrangement is followed for these as for the 45's, with the exception that CONDITION take into account the sleeve as well as the record. The designation for Mono (M) or Stereo (S) is given for each LP listed. If you have a mono album for one that is listed as stereo you can figure that its value could be up to 25% less than the stereo value.

It is not claimed that every recording of the listed artists is included. Very recent recordings are automatically excluded, because most of them are still obtainable at the issue price from ordinary record shops. Some older recordings may have been omitted because of lack of information, or, in some cases, a shortage of space in the book. The omission of a recording should not be taken to mean that it is any more or less valuable than those included.

When you use this book, don't think merely in terms of artist and selection. Quite often the SAME selections (front and back of the record) by the SAME artists were pressed on two or more labels, and the value is likely to be different depending on the label. Just compare the value of "Party Doll" by Buddy Knox on Triple-D with the same number on Roulette! The Roulette version was a Top Ten hit, pressed in probably more than a million copies. The Triple-D (which preceded it) has a very small pressing.

As far as condition goes, there are (of course) other grades of condition beyond the two for which prices are stated in this book. These are the two highest grades of condition. Records in lower grade condition, showing more wear than a Very Good copy, are usually not regarded as "collectible" unless the record is rare. In that case a collector might buy a well-used specimen as a space filler, with the intention of replacing it with a better copy when the opportunity comes along. The values of records in lower grades of condition are much, much less than shown. Even when a record is truly scarce and worth $100 in Mint condition, it might bring only $5 if heavily used — or even less. You will very seldom find dealers stocking such records, or offering to buy them.

A word or two about the prices. There are thousands of prices in this book and most readers are certain to be asking, "Where do they come from? How did we arrive at them?"

These are the average retail prices being charged by dealers at the time of compiling. Sale lists, advertisement, and other pricing data supplied by professional dealers were the basis for working out these "averages." We're quick to point out that prices DO vary in this hobby, as in most hobbies. Whenever something is out-of-print and can be obtained only secondhand, there is no standard retail value . . . no "list price." It becomes worth whatever the seller can get for it, and that's determined largely by what the customer is willing to pay. Some sales are made at very different prices than those indicated — higher and lower. Nevertheless these are the fair averages, taking account of all sales and all ups and downs. If past trends hold true, these average prices will rise during the year, and by the time the NEXT edition is published some of these records might be worth quite a bit more. Therefore if a dealer asks 10% or 20% above the stated prices for certain records, don't be too quick to conclude that he's overcharging.

For more information refer to the Official Price Guide to Records, published by The House of Collectibles.

— A —

ISSUE #	LABEL		PRICE RANGE	

ABBA

ISSUE #	LABEL			
☐ 3035	*ATLANTIC*	WATCH OUT/WATERLOO	1.50	3.00
☐ 3209		DANCE WHILE THE MUSIC STILL		
		GOES ON/HONEY HONEY	1.50	3.00
☐ 3240		RING RING/HASTA MANANA	1.50	3.00
☐ 3265		MAN IN THE MIDDLE/S.O.S.	1.50	3.00

ABBA—ALBUMS

☐ SD-18146 (S)				
	ATLANTIC	ABBA	3.50	10.00
☐ SD18207 (S)		ARRIVAL	3.50	10.00

JOHNNY ACE

☐ 1015	*FLAIR*	MIDNIGHT HOURS JOURNEY/		
		TROUBLE AND ME	16.00	45.00
☐ 102	*DUKE*	MY SONG/FOLLOW THE RULE	3.75	7.00
☐ 107		CROSS MY HEART/ANGEL	3.75	7.00
☐ 112		THE CLOCK/ACES WILD	3.75	7.00
☐ 118		SAVING MY LOVE FOR YOU/YES BABY	3.25	5.50
☐ 128		PLEASE FORGIVE ME/YOU'VE BEEN		
		GONE SO LONG	3.25	5.50
☐ 132		NEVER LET ME GO/BURLEY CUTIE	3.25	5.50
☐ 136		PLEDGING MY LOVE/NO MONEY	3.25	5.50
☐ 144		ANYMORE/HOW CAN YOU BE SO MEAN	3.25	5.50
☐ 148		SO LONELY/I'M CRAZY BABY	3.25	5.50
☐ 154		DON'T YOU KNOW/STILL LOVE YOU SO	3.25	5.50

JOHNNY ACE—EPs

☐ 80	*DUKE*	JOHNNY ACE	13.00	26.00

JOHNNY ACE—ALBUMS

☐ 70	*DUKE*	JOHNNY ACE MEMORIAL ALBUM	60.00	150.00
☐ 71 (S)		JOHNNY ACE MEMORIAL ALBUM	4.00	10.00

ALLMAN BROTHERS

☐ 56002	*LIBERTY*	HEARTBEAT/NOTHING BUT TEARS	4.00	9.00
☐ 8003	*CAPRICORN*	BLACK HEARTED WOMAN/		
		EVERY HUNGRY WOMAN	1.50	3.00
☐ 8011		REVIVAL/	1.50	3.00
☐ 8014		WHIPPING POST/MIDNIGHT RIDER	1.50	3.00
☐ 0003		MELISSA/AIN'T WASTIN' TIME NO MORE	1.50	3.00
☐ 0007		MELISSA/BLUE SKY	1.50	3.00

ISSUE #	LABEL		PRICE RANGE	
☐ 0014		STAND BACK/ONE WAY OUT	1.50	3.00
☐ 0027		PONY BOY/RAMBLIN' MAN	1.50	3.00
☐ 0036		JESSICA/COME & GO BLUES	1.50	3.00
☐ 0053		MIDNIGHT RIDER/		
		DON'T MESS UP A GOOD THING	1.50	3.00

ALLMAN BROTHERS—ALBUMS

☐ SD2-805 (S)	*ATCO*	BEGINNINGS	8.75	27.00
☐ SD33-308 (S)		THE ALLMAN BROTHERS	10.00	30.00
☐ SD33-342 (S)		IDLEWILD SOUTH	7.50	20.00
☐ CP-0156 (S)		WIN, LOSE OR DRAW	3.50	12.50
☐ 2CP-0164 (S)		ROAD GOES ON FOREVER	3.50	12.50
☐ CX4-0131 (QUAD)		AT FILLMORE EAST	4.75	16.50

ANGELS

☐ 107	*CAPRICE*	'TIL/A MOMENT AGO	2.00	3.50
☐ 112		CRY BABY CRY/THAT'S ALL I ASK OF YOU	2.00	3.50
☐ 116		EVERBODY LOVES A LOVER/BLOW, JOE	2.00	3.50
☐ 118		I'D BE GOOD FOR YOU/		
		YOU SHOULD HAVE TOLD ME	2.00	3.50
☐ 121		A MOMENT AGO/COTTON FIELDS	2.00	3.50
☐ 1834	*SMASH*	MY BOYFRIEND'S BACK/(LOVE ME) NOW	1.75	3.00
☐ 1854		I ADORE HIM/		
		THANK YOU AND GOODNIGHT	1.75	3.00
☐ 1870		WOW WOW WEE/		
		SNOWFLAKES AND TEARDROPS	1.75	3.00
☐ 1885		LITTLE BEATLE BOY/JAVA	1.75	3.00
☐ 1915		DREAM BOY/JAMAICA JOE	1.75	3.00
☐ 1931		THE BOY FROM 'CROSS TOWN/		
		A WORLD WITHOUT LOVE	1.75	3.00

ANGELS—ALBUMS

☐ 1001 (S)	*CAPRICE*	AND THE ANGELS SING	7.00	18.00
☐ 67039 (S)	*SMASH*	MY BOYFRIEND'S BACK	8.00	22.50
☐ 67048 (S)		A HALO TO YOU	8.00	22.50

ANIMALS

☐ 13242	*MGM*	GONNA SEND YOU BACK TO WALKER/		
		BABY LET ME TAKE YOU HOME	2.00	3.50
☐ 13264		HOUSE OF THE RISING SUN/		
		TALKING 'BOUT YOU	1.75	3.00
☐ 13274		I'M CRYING/TAKE IT EASY BABY	1.75	3.00
☐ 13298		BOOM BOOM/BLUE FEELING	1.75	3.00
☐ 13311		DON'T LET ME BE MISUNDERSTOOD/		
		CLUB A GO GO	1.75	3.00

PAUL ANKA

ISSUE #	LABEL		PRICE RANGE	
☐ 13339		BRING IT ON HOME/FOR MISS CAULKER	1.75	3.00
☐ 13382		WE GOTTA GET OUT OF THIS PLACE/		
		I CAN'T BELIEVE IT	1.75	3.00
☐ 13414		IT'S MY LIFE/		
		I'M GOING TO CHANGE THE WORLD	1.75	3.00
☐ 13468		INSIDE-LOOKING OUT/YOU'RE ON MY MIND	1.75	3.00
☐ 13514		DON'T BRING ME DOWN/CHEATING	1.75	3.00
☐ 13582		SEE SEE RIDER/SHE'LL RETURN IT	1.75	3.00
☐ 13636		HELP ME GIRL/THAT AIN'T WHERE IT'S AT	1.75	3.00
☐ 13721		WHEN I WAS YOUNG/		
		A GIRL NAMED SANDOZ	1.75	3.00
☐ 13769		SAN FRANCISCAN NIGHTS/GOOD TIMES	1.75	3.00
☐ 13868		MONTEREY/AIN'T THAT SO	1.75	3.00
☐ 13917		ANYTHING/IT'S ALL MEAT	1.75	3.00
☐ 13939		SKY PILOT (PT. 1)/(PT. 2)	1.75	3.00
☐ 14013		WHITE HOUSES/		
		RIVER DEEP-MOUNTAIN HIGH	1.75	3.00

ANIMALS—ALBUMS

☐ 4264 (S)	*MGM*	THE ANIMALS	8.00	22.50
☐ 4281 (S)		THE ANIMALS ON TOUR	7.00	18.00
☐ 4305 (S)		ANIMAL TRACKS	7.00	18.00
☐ 4324 (S)		THE BEST OF THE ANIMALS	6.00	15.00
☐ 4384 (S)		ANIMALIZATION	6.00	15.00
☐ 4414 (S)		ANIMALISM	6.00	15.00
☐ 4433 (S)		ERIC IS HERE	6.00	15.00
☐ 4454 (S)		BEST OF ERIC BURDON AND		
		THE ANIMALS, VOL. II	6.00	15.00
☐ 4484 (S)		WINDS OF CHANGE	4.00	10.00
☐ 4537 (S)		THE TWAIN SHALL MEET	4.00	10.00
☐ 4553 (S)		EVERY ONE OF US	4.00	10.00
☐ 4591 (S)		LOVE IS	4.00	10.00
☐ 4602 (S)		GREATEST HITS OF ERIC BURDON		
		AND THE ANIMALS	4.00	10.00

PAUL ANKA

☐ 472	*RPM*	I CONFESS/		
		BLAU-WILE DEVEEST FONTAINE	21.00	36.00
☐ 9831	*ABC-*			
	PARAMOUNT	DIANA/DON'T GAMBLE WITH LOVE	2.25	4.50
☐ 9855		I LOVE YOU BABY/		
		TELL ME THAT YOU LOVE ME	2.25	4.00
☐ 9880		YOU ARE MY DESTINY/		
		WHEN I STOP LOVING YOU	2.25	4.00

ISSUE #	LABEL		PRICE RANGE	
☐ 9907		CRAZY LOVE/		
		LET THE BELLS KEEP RINGING	2.25	4.00
☐ 9937		MIDNIGHT/VERBOTEN	2.25	4.00
☐ 9956		JUST YOUNG/SO IT'S GOODBYE	2.25	4.00
☐ 9987		MY HEART SINGS/THAT'S LOVE	2.25	4.00
☐ 10011		I MISS YOU SO/LATE LAST NIGHT	2.25	4.00
☐ 10022		LONELY BOY/YOUR WAY	2.25	4.00
☐ 10040		PUT YOUR HEAD ON MY SHOULDER/		
		DON'T EVER LEAVE ME	2.25	4.00
☐ 10064		IT'S TIME TO CRY/		
		SOMETHING HAS CHANGED ME	2.25	4.00
☐ 10082		PUPPY LOVE/ADAM AND EVE	2.25	4.00
☐ 10106		MY HOME TOWN/SOMETHING HAPPENED	2.25	4.00
☐ 10132		HELLO YOUNG LOVERS/		
		I LOVE YOU IN THE SAME OLD WAY	2.25	4.00
☐ 10147		SUMMER'S GONE/I'D HAVE TO SHARE	2.25	4.00
☐ 10163		I SAW MOMMY KISSING SANTA CLAUS/		
		RUDOLPH THE RED-NOSED REINDEER	2.75	4.50
☐ 7977	*RCA*	LOVE ME WARM AND TENDER/		
		I'D LIKE TO KNOW	1.75	3.00
☐ 8030		A STEEL GUITAR AND A GLASS OF WINE/		
		I NEVER KNEW YOUR NAME	1.75	3.00
☐ 8068		EVERY NIGHT/THERE YOU GO	1.75	3.00
☐ 8097		ESO BESO/GIVE ME BACK MY HEART	1.75	3.00
☐ 8115		LOVE/CRYING IN THE WIND	1.75	3.00
☐ 8170		REMEMBER DIANA/AT NIGHT	1.75	3.00
☐ 8195		HELLO JIM/YOU'VE GOT THE		
		NERVE TO CALL THIS LOVE	1.75	3.00
☐ 8237		WONDROUS ARE THE WAYS OF LOVE/		
		HURRY UP AND TELL ME	1.75	3.00
☐ 8272		DID YOU HAVE A HAPPY BIRTHDAY?/		
		FOR NO GOOD REASON AT ALL	1.75	3.00
☐ 8311		FROM ROCKING HORSE TO		
		ROCKING CHAIR/CHEER UP	1.75	3.00
☐ 8349		BABY'S COMING HOME/NO, NO	1.75	3.00
☐ 8396		IT'S EASY TO SAY/IN MY IMAGINATION	1.75	3.00
☐ 8441		CINDY GO HOME/OGNI VOLTA	1.75	3.00
☐ 0126		IN THE STILL OF THE NIGHT/		
		PICKIN' UP THE PIECES	1.75	3.00
☐ 0164		SINCERELY/NEXT YEAR	1.75	3.00

PAUL ANKA—EPs

☐ 296-1	*ABC-*			
	PARAMOUNT	MY HEART SINGS	7.25	12.00
☐ 296-2		MY HEART SINGS	7.25	12.00
☐ 296-3		MY HEART SINGS	7.25	12.00

ISSUE #	LABEL		PRICE RANGE	

PAUL ANKA—ALBUMS

☐ 240 (S)	**ABC-PARAMOUNT**	PAUL ANKA	20.00	50.00
☐ 296 (S)		MY HEART SINGS	17.50	42.50
☐ 323 (S)		PAUL ANKA SINGS HIS BIG 15	17.50	42.50
☐ 347 (S)		SWINGS FOR YOUNG LOVERS	15.00	35.00
☐ 353 (S)		ANKA AT THE COPA	12.50	30.00
☐ 360 (S)		IT'S CHRISTMAS EVERYWHERE	12.50	30.00
☐ 371 (S)		STRICTLY INSTRUMENTAL	10.00	25.00
☐ 390 (S)		PAUL ANKA SINGS HIS BIG 15, VOL. II	12.50	30.00
☐ 409 (S)		PAUL ANKA SINGS HIS BIG 15, VOL. III	12.50	30.00
☐ 420 (S)		DIANA	8.00	22.50
☐ 2502 (S)		YOUNG, ALIVE AND IN LOVE	8.00	22.50
☐ 2575 (S)		LET'S SIT THIS ONE OUT	8.00	22.50
☐ 2614 (S)		OUR MAN AROUND THE WORLD	7.00	18.00
☐ 2691 (S)		21 GOLDEN HITS	6.00	15.00
☐ 2744 (S)		SONGS I WISH I'D WRITTEN	7.00	18.00
☐ 2966 (S)		EXCITEMENT ON PARK AVENUE	7.00	18.00
☐ 3580 (S)		STRICTLY NASHVILLE	6.00	15.00
☐ 4142 (S)		GOODNIGHT MY LOVE	5.00	13.50
☐ 4250 (S)		LIFE GOES ON	5.00	13.50

ANNETTE

☐ 102	**DISNEYLAND**	HOW WILL I KNOW MY LOVE/ DON'T JUMP TO CONCLUSIONS	4.50	8.00
☐ 114		THAT CRAZY PLACE FROM OUTER SPACE/ GOLD DUBLOONS AND PIECES OF EIGHT	4.00	7.00
☐ 118		TALL PAUL/ MA, HE'S MAKING EYES AT ME	2.25	4.00
☐ 758		HOW WILL I KNOW MY LOVE/ANNETTE	3.25	5.50
☐ 786		THAT CRAZY PLACE IN OUTER SPACE/ HAPPY GLOW	4.00	7.00
☐ 336	**VISTA**	JO-JO THE DOG-FACED BOY/ LOVE ME FOREVER	2.25	4.00
☐ 339		LONELY GUITAR/WILD WILLIE	2.25	4.00
☐ 344		MY HEART BECAME OF AGE/ ESPECIALLY FOR YOU	2.25	4.00
☐ 349		FIRST NAME INITIAL/ MY HEART BECAME OF AGE	2.25	4.00
☐ 354		O DIO MIO/IT TOOK DREAMS	2.25	4.00
☐ 359		TRAIN OF LOVE/ TELL ME WHO'S THE GIRL	2.00	3.50
☐ 362		PINEAPPLE PRINCESS/ LUAU CHA CHA CHA	2.00	3.50

ISSUE #	LABEL		PRICE RANGE	
☐369		TALK TO ME BABY/I LOVE YOU BABY	2.00	3.50
☐374		DREAM BOY/PLEASE, PLEASE SIGNORE	2.00	3.50
☐375		INDIAN GIVER, MAMA, MAMA ROSA	2.00	3.50
☐384		HAWAIIAN LOVE TALK/ BLUE MUU MUU	2.00	3.50
☐388		DREAMIN' ABOUT YOU/ THE STRUMMIN' SONG	2.00	3.50
☐9828	*EPIC*	BABY NEEDS ME NOW/ MOMENT OF SILENCE	3.25	5.50
☐326	*TOWER*	WHAT'S A GIRL TO DO/ WHEN YOU GET WHAT YOU WANT	3.25	5.50

ANNETTE—EPs

☐04	*DISNEYLAND*	TALL PAUL	8.00	22.50
☐69		MICKEY MOUSE CLUB-ANNETTE	7.00	18.00
☐3301	*VISTA*	LONELY GUITAR	7.00	18.00

ANNETTE—ALBUMS

☐3301 (M)	*VISTA*	ANNETTE	17.50	45.00
☐3302 (M)		ANNETTE SINGS ANKA	10.00	25.00
☐3303 (M)		HAWAIIANETTE	10.00	25.00
☐3304 (M)		ITALIANETTE	10.00	25.00
☐3305 (M)		DANCE ANNETTE	8.00	22.50
☐3309 (M)		THE PARENT TRAP	8.00	22.50
☐3312 (M)		ANNETTE-THE STORY OF MY TEENS	8.00	22.50
☐3313 (M)		TEEN STREET	12.50	30.00
☐3314 (M)		MUSCLE BEACH PARTY	10.00	25.00
☐3316 (M)		ANNETTE'S BEACH PARTY	10.00	25.00
☐3320 (M)		ANNETTE ON CAMPUS	7.00	18.00
☐3324 (M)		ANNETTE AT BIKINI BEACH	8.00	12.50
☐3325 (S)		ANNETTE'S PAJAMA PARTY	8.00	22.50
☐3327 (M)		ANNETTE SINGS GOLDEN SURFIN' HITS	7.00	18.00
☐3328 (M)		SOMETHING BORROWED, SOMETHING BLUE	7.00	18.00
☐3906 (M)		SNOW WHITE AND THE SEVEN DWARFS	7.00	18.00
☐4037 (M)		ANNETTE FUNICELLO	7.00	18.00

FRANKIE AVALON

☐0006	*X*	TRUMPET SORRENTO/THE BOOK	8.00	15.00
☐0020		A VERY YOUNG MAN WITH A HORN	12.00	20.00
☐0026		TRUMPET TARANTELLA/DORMI, DORMI	8.00	15.00
☐1004	*CHANCELLOR*	CUPID/JIVIN' WITH THE SAINTS	5.00	9.00
☐1006		TEACHER'S PET/SHY GUY	4.00	7.50
☐1011		DEDE DINAH/OOH LA LA	2.00	4.00
☐1016		YOU EXCITE ME/DARLIN'	2.00	4.00

ISSUE #	LABEL		PRICE RANGE	
☐ 1021		GINGERBREAD/BLUE BETTY	2.25	4.00
☐ 1026		I'LL WAIT FOR YOU/WHAT LITTLE GIRL	2.00	3.50
☐ 1031		VENUS/I'M BROKE	2.00	3.50
☐ 1036		BOBBY SOX TO STOCKINGS/		
		A BOY WITHOUT A GIRL	2.00	3.50
☐ 1040		JUST ASK YOUR HEART/TWO FOOLS	2.00	3.50
☐ 1045		WHY/SWINGIN' ON A RAINBOW	2.00	3.50
☐ 1048		DON'T THROW AWAY ALL THOSE		
		TEARDROPS/TALK TALK TALK	2.00	3.50
☐ 1052		WHERE ARE YOU/TUXEDO JUNCTION	2.00	3.50
☐ 1056		TOGETHERNESS/		
		DON'T LET LOVE PASS ME BY	2.00	3.50
☐ 1065		A PERFECT LOVE/THE PUPPET SONG	2.00	3.50
☐ 0697	*REPRISE*	BUT I DO/DANCING ON THE STARS	1.75	3.00
☐ 0826		FOR YOU LOVE/		
		WHY DON'T THEY UNDERSTAND	1.75	3.00
☐ 728	*UNITED*			
	ARTISTS	AGAIN/DON'T MAKE FUN OF ME	1.75	3.00
☐ 748		MY LOVE IS HERE TO STAY/		
		NEW FANGLED JINGLE JANGLE		
		SWIMMING SUIT FROM PARIS	1.75	3.00
☐ 800		MOON RIVER/		
		EVERY GIRL SHOULD GET MARRIED	1.75	3.00
☐ 895		THERE'LL BE RAINBOWS AGAIN/		
		I'LL TAKE SWEDEN	1.75	3.00

FRANKIE AVALON—EPs

☐ 5001	*CHANCELLOR*	FRANKIE AVALON, VOL. I-II-III	5.00	9.00
☐ 5002		THE YOUNG FRANKIE AVALON	5.00	9.00
☐ 5004		SWINGIN' ON A RAINBOW	4.00	7.00
☐ 5011		SUMMER SCENE	6.00	11.00
☐ 5012		THE GOOD OLD SUMMERTIME	6.00	11.00
☐ 302		GUNS OF THE TIMBERLAND	7.25	12.00
☐ 303		BALLAD OF THE ALAMO	7.25	11.00

FRANKIE AVALON—ALBUMS

☐ 5001 (M)				
	CHANCELLOR	FRANKIE AVALON	12.50	30.00
☐ 5002 (M)		THE YOUNG FRANKIE AVALON	10.00	25.00
☐ 5004 (M)		SWINGIN' ON A RAINBOW	10.00	25.00
☐ 5009 (M)		AVALON AND FABIAN	10.00	25.00
☐ 5011 (M)		SUMMER SCENE	8.00	22.50
☐ 5018 (M)		A WHOLE LOTTA FRANKIE	8.00	22.50
☐ 5022 (S)		AND NOW, ABOUT MR. AVALON	10.00	25.00
☐ 5025 (S)		ITALIANO	10.00	25.00
☐ 5027 (S)		YOU ARE MINE	10.00	25.00

ISSUE #	LABEL		PRICE	RANGE
☐ 5031 (S)		FRANKIE AVALON'S CHRISTMAS ALBUM	10.00	25.00
☐ 5032 (S)		FRANKIE AVALON SINGS CLEOPATRA	7.00	18.00

— B —

BADFINGER

☐ 1815	*APPLE*	COME AND GET IT/ROCK OF ALL AGES	1.75	3.00
☐ 1822		NO MATTER WHAT/		
		CARRY ON UNTIL TOMORROW	1.75	3.00
☐ 1841		DAY AFTER DAY/MONEY	1.75	3.00
☐ 1844		BABY BLUE/FLYING	1.75	3.00
☐ 1864		APPLE OF MY EYE/BLIND OWL	2.00	3.50
☐ 7801	*WARNER BROTHERS*	I MISS YOU/SHINE ON	2.25	4.00

BADFINGER—ALBUMS

☐ 3364 (S)	*APPLE*	MAGIC CHRISTIAN MUSIC	7.00	18.00
☐ 3367 (S)		NO DICE	6.00	15.00
☐ 3387 (S)		STRAIGHT UP	6.00	15.00
☐ 2762 (S)	*WARNER BROTHERS*	BADFINGER	5.00	13.50
☐ 2827 (S)		WISH YOU WERE HERE	5.00	13.50

JOAN BAEZ

☐ 35012	*VANGUARD*	BANKS OF THE OHIO/OLD BLUE	2.50	5.50
☐ 35013		PAL OF MINE/LONESOME ROAD	2.00	4.50
☐ 35023		WE SHALL OVERCOME/		
		WHAT HAVE THEY DONE TO THE RAIN	1.50	3.50
☐ 35031		DADDY YOU BEEN ON MY MIND/		
		THERE BUT FOR FORTUNE	1.50	3.50
☐ 35040		SWALLOW SONG/		
		PACK UP YOUR SORROWS	1.50	3.50
☐ 35055		NORTH/BE NOT TOO HARD	1.50	3.50
☐ 35092		ROCK SALT & NAILS/IF I KNEW	1.25	3.00
☐ 35138		NIGHT THEY DROVE OLD DIXIE		
		DOWN/WHEN TIME IS STOLEN	1.25	3.00
☐ 35145		LET IT BE/POOR WAYFARING STRANGER	1.25	3.00
☐ 32890	*DECCA*	SILENT RUNNING/REJOICE IN THE SUN	1.25	3.00
☐ 1334	*A&M*	SONG OF BANGLADESH/PRISON TRILOGY	1.25	3.00
☐ 1362		IN THE QUIET MORNING/TO BOBBY	2.00	3.50
☐ 1393		LOVE SONG TO A STRANGER/		
		TUMBLEWEED	1.50	3.00

ISSUE #	LABEL		PRICE RANGE	
☐ 74-0568	*RCA*	BALLAD OF SACCO & VANZETTI/		
		HERE'S TO YOU	2.00	4.00
☐ 700006	*PORTRAIT*	ALTAR BOY & THE THIEF/		
		I'M BLOWIN' AWAY	1.25	3.00

JOAN BAEZ—ALBUMS

☐ VSD-2077 (S)				
	VANGUARD	JOAN BAEZ	10.00	32.00
☐ VSD7-9160 (S)		JOAN BAEZ	6.00	18.00
☐ VSD-2097 (S)		JOAN BAEZ, VOL. II	10.00	32.00
☐ VSD-2122 (S)		IN CONCERT, VOL. I	5.75	18.00
☐ VSD-2123 (S)		IN CONCERT, VOL. II	5.75	18.00
☐ VSD-49/50 (S)		COMTEMPORARY BALLAD BOOK	4.00	13.50
☐ VSD7-9230 (S)		NOEL	5.75	18.00
☐ VSD7-9310 (S)		ONE DAY AT A TIME	4.00	13.50
☐ VSD7-9320 (S)		MILAN	4.00	13.50
☐ VS-6560/61 (S)		THE FIRST 10 YEARS	8.00	28.00
☐ VD57-9313 (S)		CARRY IT ON	4.00	13.50
☐ VS-6570 (S)		BLESSED ARE	4.00	13.50
☐ VS07-9275 (S)		BAPTISM	3.25	12.50
☐ 5015 (M)	*FANTASY*	JOAN BAEZ IN SAN FRANCISCO	8.00	25.00
☐ SP-3614 (S)	*A&M*	GRACIAS A LA VIDA	4.00	13.50
☐ SP-3704 (S)		FROM EVERY STAGE	4.00	13.50
☐ SP-4339 (S)		COME FROM THE SHADOWS	4.00	13.50

HANK BALLARD
AND THE MIDNIGHTERS

☐ 5171	*KING*	THE TWIST/		
		TEARDROPS ON YOUR LETTER	2.25	4.00
☐ 5195		KANSAS CITY/I'LL KEEP YOU HAPPY	2.00	3.50
☐ 5215		SUGAREE/RAIN DOWN TEARS	2.00	3.50
☐ 5245		CUTE LITTLE WAYS/		
		HOUSE WITH NO WINDOWS	2.00	3.50
☐ 5275		NEVER KNEW/I COULD LOVE YOU	2.00	3.50
☐ 5289		LOOK AT LITTLE SISTER/		
		I SAID I WOULDN'T BEG	2.00	3.50
☐ 5312		THE COFFEE GRIND/WAITING	2.00	3.50
☐ 5341		FINGER POPPIN' TIME/		
		I LOVE YOU, I LOVE YOU SO-O-O	2.00	3.50

HANK BALLARD AND THE MIDNIGHTERS—EPs

☐ 435	*KING*	SINGIN' AND SWINGIN', VOL. I	7.00	18.00
☐ 451		SINGIN' AND SWINGIN', VOL. II	7.00	18.00
☐ 793		JUMPIN'	6.00	15.00

BEACH BOYS

ISSUE #	LABEL		PRICE RANGE	

HANK BALLARD
AND THE MIDNIGHTERS—ALBUMS

☐ 541 (M)	*KING*	THEIR GREATEST JUKE BOX HITS	17.50	45.00
☐ 581 (M)		HANK BALLARD AND THE MIDNIGHTERS	12.50	30.00
☐ 618 (M)		SINGIN' AND SWINGIN'	10.00	25.00
☐ 674 (M)		THE ONE AND ONLY	10.00	25.00
☐ 700 (M)		MR. RHYTHM AND BLUES	10.00	25.00
☐ 740 (M)		SPOTLIGHT ON HANK BALLARD	10.00	25.00
☐ 748 (M)		LET'S GO AGAIN	10.00	25.00
☐ 759 (M)		DANCE ALONG	8.00	22.50
☐ 781 (M)		THE TWISTIN' FOOLS	7.00	18.00
☐ 793 (M)		JUMPIN' HANK BALLARD AND THE MIDNIGHTERS	7.00	18.00
☐ 815 (M)		THE 1963 SOUND OF HANK BALLARD AND THE MIDNIGHTERS	6.00	15.00
☐ 867 (M)		BIGGEST HITS	6.00	15.00
☐ 896 (M)		A STAR IN YOUR EYES	6.00	15.00
☐ 913 (M)		THOSE LAZY, LAZY DAYS	6.00	15.00
☐ 927 (M)		GLAD SONGS, SAD SONGS	6.00	15.00
☐ 950 (M)		24 HIT TUNES	6.00	15.00

BAY CITY ROLLERS

☐ 45169	*BELL*	KEEP ON DANCING/ALRIGHT	2.00	3.50
☐ 120	*ARISTA*	BYE BYE BABY/IT'S FOR YOU	2.00	3.50
☐ 149		SATURDAY NIGHT/MARLINA	1.50	2.50
☐ 170		MONEY HONEY/MARYANNE	1.50	2.50
☐ 185		ROCK AND ROLL LOVE LETTER/SHANGHAI'D IN LOVE	1.50	2.50
☐ 193		DON'T STOP THE MUSIC/ DON'T STOP THE MUSIC	2.00	3.50

BEACH BOYS

☐ 301	*X*	SURFIN'/LUAU	75.00	125.00
☐ 301	*CANDIX*	SURFIN'/LUAU	30.00	50.00
☐ 331		SURFIN'/LUAU	30.00	50.00
☐ 4777	*CAPITOL*	SURFIN' SAFARI/409	2.75	4.50
☐ 4880		TEN LITTLE INDIANS/COUNTY FAIR	3.50	6.00
☐ 4932		SURFIN' U.S.A./SHUT DOWN	2.25	4.00
☐ 5009		SURFER GIRL/LITTLE DEUCE COUPE	2.25	4.00
☐ 5069		BE TRUE TO YOUR SCHOOL/IN MY ROOM	2.25	4.00
☐ 5096		LITTLE SAINT NICK/THE LORD'S PRAYER	4.50	9.00
☐ 5118		FUN, FUN, FUN/ WHY DO FOOLS FALL IN LOVE	2.00	3.50

ISSUE #	LABEL		PRICE RANGE	
☐ 5174		I GET AROUND/DON'T WORRY BABY	2.00	3.50
☐ 5245		WHEN I GROW UP/		
		SHE KNOWS ME TOO WELL	2.00	3.50
☐ 5306		DANCE, DANCE, DANCE/		
		THE WARMTH OF THE SUN	2.00	3.50
☐ 5312		THE MAN WITH ALL THE TOYS/		
		BLUE CHRISTMAS	4.00	7.00
☐ 5372		DO YOU WANNA DANCE?/		
		PLEASE LET ME WONDER	2.00	3.50
☐ 5395		HELP ME RHONDA/KISS ME BABY	2.00	3.50
☐ 5464		CALIFORNIA GIRLS/LET HIM RUN WILD	2.00	3.50
☐ 5540		THE LITTLE GIRL I ONCE KNEW/		
		THERE'S NO OTHER	2.00	3.50
☐ 5561		BARBARA ANN/GIRL DON'T TELL ME	2.00	3.50
☐ 5602		SLOOP JOHN B/YOU'RE SO GOOD TO ME	2.00	3.50
☐ 5676		GOOD VIBRATIONS/		
		LET'S GO AWAY FOR AWHILE	2.00	3.50
☐ 5706		WOULDN'T IT BE NICE/GOD ONLY KNOWS	2.00	3.50
☐ 2028		WILD HONEY/WIND CHIMES	2.00	3.50
☐ 2068		DARLIN'/HERE TODAY	2.00	3.50
☐ 2160		FRIENDS/LITTLE BIRD	2.25	4.00
☐ 2239		DO IT AGAIN/WAKE THE WORLD	2.25	4.00
☐ 2360		BLUEBIRDS OVER THE MOUNTAIN/		
		NEVER LEARN NOT TO LOVE	2.75	4.50
☐ 2432		I CAN HEAR MUSIC/ALL I WANT TO DO	2.25	4.00
☐ 2530		BREAK AWAY/CELEBRATE THE NEWS	5.00	10.00
☐ 2765		COTTON FIELDS/		
		THE NEAREST FARAWAY PLACE	8.50	15.00
☐ 0894	*REPRISE*	ADD SOME MUSIC TO YOUR DAY/		
		SUSIE CINCINATTI	2.25	4.00
☐ 0929		THIS WHOLE WORLD/SLIP ON THROUGH	2.75	4.50
☐ 0957		TEARS IN THE MORNING/		
		IT'S ABOUT TIME	2.15	4.50
☐ 0998		COOL, COOL WATER/FOREVER	2.15	4.50
☐ 1015		LONG PROMISED ROAD/DEIRDRE	2.15	4.50
☐ 1047		LONG PROMISED ROAD/TILL I DIE	2.25	4.00
☐ 1058		SURF'S UP/DON'T GO NEAR THE WATER	2.75	4.50
☐ 1091		CUDDLE UP/YOU NEED A MESS OF HELP		
		TO STAND ALONE	7.00	12.00
☐ 1101		MARCELLA/HOLD ON, DEAR BROTHER	3.50	6.00
☐ 1138		SAIL ON SAILOR/ONLY WITH YOU	3.50	6.00
☐ 1156		CALIFORNIA SAGA/FUNKY PRETTY	3.50	6.00
☐ 1321		CHILD OF WINTER/SUSIE CINCINATTI	7.00	12.00
☐ 1325		SAIL ON SAILOR/ONLY WITH YOU	2.25	4.00
☐ 66016	*ODE*	WOULDN'T IT BE NICE/		
		THE TIMES THEY ARE A-CHANGIN'	6.00	11.00

ISSUE #	LABEL		PRICE RANGE	

BEACH BOYS—EP

| ☐ 5267 | *CAPITOL* | FOUR BY THE BEACH BOYS | 10.00 | 18.00 |

BEACH BOYS—ALBUMS

☐ 1808 (M)	*CAPITOL*	SURFIN' SAFARI	7.00	18.00
☐ 1890 (M)		SURFIN' U.S.A.	6.00	15.00
☐ 1981 (M)		SURFER GIRL	6.00	15.00
☐ 1998 (M)		LITTLE DEUCE COUPE	6.00	15.00
☐ 2027 (M)		SHUT DOWN, VOL. II	6.00	15.00
☐ 2110 (M)		ALL SUMMER LONG	6.00	15.00
☐ 2164 (M)		THE BEACH BOYS' CHRISTMAS ALBUM	7.00	18.00
☐ 2198 (M)		THE BEACH BOYS' CONCERT	5.00	13.50
☐ 2269 (S)		THE BEACH BOYS TODAY!	5.00	13.50
☐ 2354 (S)		SUMMER DAYS (AND SUMMER NIGHTS)	5.00	13.50
☐ 2398 (S)		THE BEACH BOYS' PARTY	4.50	12.00
☐ 2458 (S)		PET SOUNDS	5.00	13.50
☐ 2545 (S)		BEST OF THE BEACH BOYS, VOL. I	4.00	11.50
☐ 2706 (S)		BEST OF THE BEACH BOYS, VOL. II	4.00	11.50
☐ 2859 (S)		WILD HONEY	6.00	15.00
☐ 2891 (S)		SMILEY SMILE	65.00	185.00
☐ 2893 (S)		STACK-O-TRACKS	30.00	75.00
☐ 2895 (S)		FRIENDS	5.00	13.50
☐ 2945 (S)		BEST OF THE BEACH BOYS, VOL. III	5.00	13.50

BEATLES

☐ 498	*VEE JAY*	PLEASE PLEASE ME/ASK ME WHY	65.00	150.00
☐ 522		FROM ME TO YOU/THANK YOU GIRL	18.00	40.00
☐ 581		FROM ME TO YOU/PLEASE PLEASE ME	3.50	6.00
☐ 587		DO YOU WANT TO KNOW A SECRET?/ THANK YOU GIRL	2.75	4.50
☐ 4152	*SWAN*	SHE LOVES YOU/I'LL GET YOU	25.00	60.00
☐ 4152		SHE LOVES YOU/I'LL GET YOU	2.25	4.00
☐ 4182		SIE LIEBT DICH/I'LL GET YOU	22.00	48.00
☐ 9001	*TOLLIE*	TWIST AND SHOUT/THERE'S A PLACE	3.50	6.00
☐ 9008		LOVE ME DO/P.S., I LOVE YOU	3.50	6.00
☐ 13213	*MGM*	MY BONNIE/THE SAINTS	3.50	6.00
☐ 13227		WHY/CRY FOR A SHADOW	8.50	15.00
☐ 6302	*ATCO*	SWEET GEORGIA BROWN/ TAKE OUT SOME INSURANCE ON ME	10.00	18.00
☐ 6308		AIN'T SHE SWEET/NOBODY'S CHILD	2.75	4.50
☐ 5112	*CAPITOL*	I WANT TO HOLD YOUR HAND/ I SAW HER STANDING THERE	2.75	4.50
☐ 5150		CAN'T BUY ME LOVE/ YOU CAN'T DO THAT	2.75	4.50

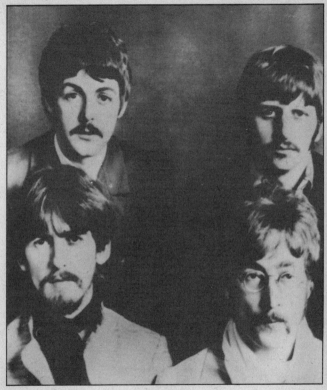

BEATLES

ISSUE #	LABEL		PRICE RANGE	
☐ 5222		A HARD DAY'S NIGHT/		
		I SHOULD HAVE KNOWN BETTER	2.75	4.50
☐ 5234		I'LL CRY INSTEAD/I'M HAPPY JUST TO		
		DANCE WITH YOU	2.75	4.50
☐ 5235		AND I LOVE HER/IF I FELL	2.75	4.50
☐ 5255		MATCHBOX/SLOW DOWN	2.75	4.50
☐ 5327		I FEEL FINE/SHE'S A WOMAN	2.75	4.50
☐ 5371		EIGHT DAYS A WEEK/I DON'T WANT		
		TO SPOIL THE PARTY	2.75	4.50
☐ 5407		TICKET TO RIDE/YES IT IS	2.75	4.50
☐ 5476		HELP/I'M DOWN	2.75	4.50
☐ 5498		YESTERDAY/ACT NATURALLY	2.75	4.50
☐ 5555		WE CAN WORK IT OUT/DAY TRIPPER	2.75	4.50
☐ 5587		NOWHERE MAN/WHAT GOES ON	2.25	4.00
☐ 5651		PAPERBACK WRITER/RAIN	2.25	4.00
☐ 5715		YELLOW SUBMARINE/ELEANOR RIGBY	2.25	4.00
☐ 5810		PENNY LANE/		
		STRAWBERRY FIELDS FOREVER	2.25	4.00
☐ 5964		ALL YOU NEED IS LOVE/		
		BABY YOU'RE A RICH MAN	2.25	4.00
☐ 2056		HELLO GOODBYE/I AM THE WALRUS	2.25	4.00
☐ 2138		LADY MADONNA/THE INNER LIGHT	2.25	4.00
☐ 2276	*APPLE*	HEY JUDE/REVOLUTION	1.75	3.00
☐ 2490		GET BACK/DON'T LET ME DOWN	1.75	3.00
☐ 2531		THE BALLAD OF JOHN AND YOKO/		
		OLD BROWN SHOE	1.75	3.00
☐ 2654		COME TOGETHER/SOMETHING	1.75	3.00
☐ 2764		LET IT BE/YOU KNOW MY NAME		
		(LOOK UP MY NUMBER)	1.75	3.00
☐ 2832		THE LONG AND WINDING ROAD/		
		FOR YOU BLUE	1.75	3.00

BEATLES—EPs

☐ 18901	*VEE JAY*	SOUVENIR OF THEIR VISIT TO AMERICA	17.50	45.00
☐ 2121	*CAPITOL*	FOUR BY THE BEATLES	30.00	75.00
☐ 5365		4 - BY THE BEATLES	20.00	50.00

BEATLES—ALBUMS

☐ DX 30 (S)	*VEE JAY*	BEATLES VS. THE FOUR SEASONS	50.00	135.00
☐ PRO 202 (M)		HEAR THE BEATLES TELL ALL	20.00	50.00
☐ 1062 (S)		INTRODUCING THE BEATLES	80.00	200.00
☐ 1062 (S)		INTRODUCING THE BEATLES	20.00	50.00
☐ 1062 (S)		INTRODUCING THE BEATLES	20.00	50.00
☐ 1085 (S)		JOLLY WHAT! THE BEATLES AND		
		FRANK IFIELD	350.00	900.00
☐ 1085 (S)		JOLLY WHAT! THE BEATLES AND		
		FRANK IFIELD	20.00	50.00

ISSUE #	LABEL		PRICE RANGE	
☐ 1092 (M)		SONGS, PICTURES AND STORIES		
		OF THE BEATLES	8.00	22.50
☐ 4215 (S)		THE BEATLES WITH TONY SHERIDAN		
		AND GUESTS	20.00	50.00
☐ 601 (S)		THE AMAZING BEATLES	12.50	30.00
☐ 69 (M)	*SAVAGE*	THE SAVAGE YOUNG BEATLES	10.00	25.00
☐ 563 (S)		THIS IS WHERE IT STARTED	7.00	18.00
☐ 2047 (S)	*CAPITOL*	MEET THE BEATLES	7.00	18.00
☐ 2080 (S)		THE BEATLES' SECOND ALBUM	7.00	18.00
☐ 2108 (S)		SOMETHING NEW	7.00	18.00
☐ 2222 (S)		THE BEATLES STORY	7.00	18.00
☐ 2228 (S)		BEATLES '65	7.00	18.00
☐ 2309 (S)		THE EARLY BEATLES	6.00	15.00
☐ 2358 (S)		BEATLES VI	7.00	18.00
☐ 2368 (S)		HELP!	7.00	18.00
☐ 2442 (S)		RUBBER SOUL	7.00	18.00
☐ 2553 (S)		YESTERDAY AND TODAY	350.00	900.00
☐ 2553 (S)		YESTERDAY AND TODAY	80.00	180.00
☐ 2576 (M)		REVOLVER	7.00	18.00
☐ 2653 (S)		SERGEANT PEPPER'S LONELY HEARTS		
		CLUB BAND	7.00	18.00
☐ 2835 (M)		MAGICAL MYSTERY TOUR	8.00	22.50
☐ 3366 (M)	*UNITED*			
	ARTISTS	A HARD DAY'S NIGHT	7.00	18.00
☐ 6366 (S)		A HARD DAY'S NIGHT	8.00	22.50
☐ 100 (S)	*APPLE*	CHRISTMAS FAN CLUB ALBUM	20.00	50.00
☐ 101 (S)		THE BEATLES	7.00	18.00
☐ 153 (S)		YELLOW SUBMARINE	7.00	18.00
☐ 383 (S)		ABBEY ROAD	7.00	18.00

BEAU BRUMMELS

☐ 8	*AUTUMN*	LAUGH LAUGH/STILL IN LOVE		
		WITH YOU BABY	2.00	3.50
☐ 10		JUST A LITTLE/THEY'LL MAKE YOU CRY	2.00	3.50
☐ 16		YOU TELL ME WHY/I WANT YOU	2.00	3.50
☐ 20		DON'T TALK TO STRANGERS/		
		IN GOOD TIME	2.00	3.50
☐ 24		GOOD TIME MUSIC/SAD LITTLE GIRL	2.00	3.50

BEAU BRUMMELS—ALBUMS

☐ 103 (M)	*AUTUMN*	INTRODUCING THE BEAU BRUMMELS	7.00	18.00
☐ 104 (M)		THE BEAU BRUMMELS, VOL. II	7.00	18.00

ISSUE #	LABEL		PRICE RANGE	

BEE GEES

☐6487	**ATCO**	NEW YORK MINING DISASTER-1941/		
		I CAN'T SEE NOBODY	1.75	3.00
☐6503		TO LOVE SOMEBODY/		
		CLOSE ANOTHER DOOR	1.75	3.00
☐6521		HOLIDAY/EVERY CHRISTIAN LION		
		HEARTED MAN WILL SHOW YOU	1.75	3.00
☐6532		(THE LIGHTS WENT OUT IN)		
		MASSACHUSETTS/SIR GEOFFREY		
		SAVED THE WORLD	1.75	3.00
☐6548		WORDS/SINKING SHIPS	1.75	3.00
☐6570		JUMBO/THE SINGER SANG HIS SONG	1.75	3.00
☐6603		I'VE GOTTA GET A MESSAGE TO YOU/		
		KITTY CAN	1.75	3.00
☐6639		I STARTED A JOKE/KILBURN TOWERS	1.75	3.00
☐6657		FIRST OF MAY/LAMPLIGHT	1.50	2.50
☐6682		TOMORROW TOMORROW/		
		SUN IN THE MORNING	1.50	2.50
☐6702		DON'T FORGET TO REMEMBER/THE LORD	1.50	2.50
☐6702		DON'T FORGET TO REMEMBER/		
		I LAY DOWN AND DIE	1.50	2.50
☐6741		IF I ONLY HAD MY MIND ON SOMETHING		
		ELSE/SWEETHEART	1.50	2.50
☐6752		I.O.I.O./THEN YOU LEFT ME	1.50	2.50
☐6795		LONELY DAYS/MAN FOR ALL SEASONS	1.50	2.50
☐6824		HOW CAN YOU MEND A BROKEN		
		HEART?/COUNTRY WOMAN	1.50	2.50
☐6847		DON'T WANT TO LIVE INSIDE MYSELF/		
		WALKING BACK TO WATERLOO	1.50	2.50
☐6871		MY WORLD/ON TIME	1.50	2.50
☐6896		RUN TO ME/ROAD TO ALASKA	1.50	2.50
☐6909		ALIVE/PAPER MACHE',		
		CABBAGES AND KINGS	1.50	2.50

BEE GEES—ALBUMS

☐223 (S)	**ATCO**	BEE GEES' 1ST	6.00	15.00
☐233 (S)		HORIZONTAL	6.00	15.00
☐253 (S)		IDEA	6.00	15.00
☐264 (S)		RARE, PRECIOUS AND BEAUTIFUL	7.00	18.00
☐292 (S)		BEST OF THE BEE GEES	6.00	15.00
☐321 (S)		RARE, PRECIOUS AND BEAUTIFUL,		
		VOL. II	7.00	18.00
☐327 (S)		CUCUMBER CASTLE	6.00	15.00
☐353 (S)		TWO YEARS ON	6.00	15.00
☐702 (S)		ODESSA	10.00	25.00
☐7003 (S)		TRAFALGAR	6.00	15.00

ISSUE #	LABEL		PRICE RANGE	

BELMONTS

☐3080	*LAURIE*	WE BELONG TOGETHER/ SUCH A LONG WAY	7.25	12.00
☐1000	*SURPRISE*	TELL ME WHY/ SMOKE FROM YOUR CIGARETTE	12.00	25.00
☐500	*SABRINA*	TELL ME WHY/ SMOKE FROM YOUR CIGARETTE	2.25	4.00
☐501		DON'T GET AROUND MUCH ANYMORE/ SEARCHING FOR A NEW LOVE	2.25	4.00
☐502	*SABINA*	I NEED SOMEONE/ THAT AMERICAN DANCE	2.25	4.00
☐503		I CONFESS/HOMBRE	2.25	4.00
☐505		COME ON LITTLE ANGEL/ HOW ABOUT ME?	2.25	4.00
☐507		DIDDLE-DEE-DUM/FAREWELL	2.25	4.00
☐509		ANN-MARIE/ACCENTUATE THE POSITIVE	2.25	4.00
☐513		WALK ON BY/LET'S CALL IT A DAY	2.25	4.00
☐517		MORE IMPORTANT THINGS TO DO/ LET'S CALL IT A DAY	2.25	4.00
☐519		C'MON EVERYBODY/WHY	7.25	12.00
☐521		NOTHING IN RETURN/SUMMERTIME TIME	7.25	12.00
☐809	*UNITED ARTISTS*	I DON'T KNOW WHY/SUMMERTIME	3.50	6.00
☐904		(THEN) I WALKED AWAY/TODAY MY LOVE HAS GONE AWAY	4.00	7.00
☐966		I GOT A FEELING/TO BE WITH YOU	4.00	7.00
☐5007		COME WITH ME/YOU'RE LIKE A MYSTERY	4.00	7.00
☐17173	*DOT*	SHE ONLY WANTS TO DO HER OWN THING/REMINISCENCES	3.00	4.50
☐17257		HAVE YOU HEARD/ANSWER ME, MY LOVE	3.00	4.50
☐17257		THE WORST THAT COULD HAPPEN/ ANSWER ME, MY LOVE	3.00	4.50

BELMONTS—ALBUMS

☐5001 (M)	*SABINA*	CARNIVAL OF HITS	12.50	30.00
☐25949 (S)	*DOT*	SUMMER LOVE	7.00	18.00
☐5123 (S)	*BUDDAH*	CIGARS, ACAPELLA AND CANDY	6.00	15.00

JESSE BELVIN

☐5115	*IMPERIAL*	ALL THAT WINE IS GONE/ DON'T CRY BABY	50.00	85.00
☐120	*HOLLYWOOD*	DREAM GIRL/ HANG YOUR TEARS OUT TO DRY	40.00	70.00
☐1059		DEAR HEART/BETTY MY DARLING	70.00	120.00

ISSUE #	LABEL		PRICE RANGE	
☐435	*SPECIALTY*	CONFUSIN' BLUES/BABY DON'T GO	8.50	15.00
☐447		DREAM GIRL/DADDY LOVES BABY	8.50	15.00
☐550		GONE/ONE LITTLE BLESSING	5.50	10.00
☐559		WHERE'S MY GIRL/		
		LOVE LOVE OF MY LIFE	5.50	10.00
☐12237	*FEDERAL*	SO FINE/SENTIMENTAL HEART	30.00	48.00
☐208	*MONEY*	I'M ONLY A FOOL/TROUBLE AND MISERY	9.00	18.00
☐1056	*CASH*	BEWARE/DRY YOUR EYES	6.00	11.00
☐987	*MODERN*	GIRL OF MY DREAMS/		
		I WANNA KNOW WHY	3.50	6.00
☐1005		GOODNIGHT MY LOVE/		
		I WANT YOU WITH ME CHRISTMAS	3.50	6.00
☐1005		GOODNIGHT MY LOVE/		
		LET ME LOVE YOU TONIGHT	3.50	6.00
☐1013		SENORITA/I NEED YOU SO	3.50	6.00
☐1015		DON'T CLOSE THE DOOR/BY MY SIDE	3.50	6.00

JESSE BELVIN—ALBUMS

☐2089 (S)	*RCA*	JUST JESSE BELVIN	17.50	45.00
☐2105 (S)		MR. EASY	15.00	35.00
☐5145 (M)	*CROWN*	THE CASUAL JESSE BELVIN	6.00	15.00
☐5187 (M)		THE UNFORGETTABLE JESSE BELVIN	6.00	15.00
☐1058 (M)	*CUSTOM*	GONE BUT NOT FORGOTTEN	6.00	15.00
☐960 (M)	*CAMDEN*	JESSE BELVIN'S BEST	6.00	15.00

CHUCK BERRY

☐1604	*CHESS*	MAYBELLENE/WEE WEE HOURS	4.00	7.00
☐1610		THIRTY DAYS/TOGETHER	5.00	9.00
☐1615		NO MONEY DOWN/		
		THE DOWNBOUND TRAIN	5.00	9.00
☐1626		ROLL OVER BEETHOVEN/DRIFTING HEART	4.00	7.00
☐1635		TOO MUCH MONKEY BUSINESS/		
		BROWN EYED HANDSOME MAN	5.00	9.00
☐1645		YOU CAN'T CATCH ME/HAVANA MOON	4.00	7.00
☐1653		SCHOOL DAY/DEEP FEELING	3.00	4.50
☐1664		OH BABY DOLL/LAJUNDA	3.00	4.50
☐1671		ROCK AND ROLL MUSIC/BLUE FEELING	3.00	5.00
☐1683		SWEET LITTLE SIXTEEN/		
		REELIN' AND ROCKIN'	3.00	5.00
☐1691		JOHNNY B. GOODE/AROUND AND AROUND	3.00	5.00
☐1697		BEAUTIFUL DELILAH/VACATION TIME	2.25	4.00
☐1700		CAROL/HEY PEDRO	2.25	4.00
☐1709		SWEET LITTLE ROCK AND ROLL/		
		JOE JOE GUN	2.25	4.00

ISSUE #	LABEL		PRICE RANGE	
☐ 1714		MERRY CHRISTMAS BABY/		
		RUN RUDOLPH RUN	2.25	4.00
☐ 1716		ANTHONY BOY/THAT'S MY DESIRE	2.25	4.00
☐ 1722		LITTLE QUEENIE/ALMOST GROWN	2.00	3.50
☐ 1729		BACK IN THE U.S.A./		
		MEMPHIS, TENNESSEE	2.00	3.50
☐ 1736		CHILDHOOD SWEETHEART/		
		BROKEN ARROW	2.00	3.50
☐ 1747		TOO POOPED TO POP/LET IT ROCK	2.00	3.50
☐ 1754		BYE BYE JOHNNY/WORRIED LIFE BLUES	2.00	3.50
☐ 1763		MAD LAD/I GOT TO FIND MY BABY	2.00	3.50

CHUCK BERRY—EPs

☐ 5118	*CHESS*	AFTER SCHOOL SESSION	8.50	15.00
☐ 5119		ROCK AND ROLL MUSIC	8.50	15.00
☐ 5121		SWEET LITTLE SIXTEEN	7.25	12.00
☐ 5124		PICKIN' BERRIES	7.25	12.00
☐ 5126		JOHNNY B. GOODE	7.25	12.00

CHUCK BERRY—ALBUMS

☐ 1426 (M)	*CHESS*	AFTER SCHOOL SESSION	12.50	30.00
☐ 1432 (M)		ONE DOZEN BERRYS	8.00	22.50
☐ 1435 (M)		CHUCK BERRY IS ON TOP	7.00	18.00
☐ 1448 (M)		ROCKIN' AT THE HOPS	7.00	18.00
☐ 1456 (M)		MORE JUKE BOX HITS	7.00	18.00
☐ 1465 (M)		MORE CHUCK BERRY	7.00	18.00
☐ 1485 (M)		CHUCK BERRY'S GREATEST HITS	7.00	18.00
☐ 1488 (M)		ST. LOUIS TO LIVERPOOL	7.00	18.00
☐ 1495 (M)		CHUCK BERRY IN LONDON	7.00	18.00
☐ 1498 (M)		FRESH BERRY'S	6.00	15.00
☐ 1514 (S)		CHUCK BERRY'S GOLDEN DECADE	4.50	9.00
☐ 1550 (S)		BACK HOME	4.50	9.00
☐ 21103 (S)				
	MERCURY	GOLDEN HITS	4.50	9.00
☐ 61123 (S)		IN MEMPHIS	4.50	9.00
☐ 61138 (S)		LIVE AT FILLMORE AUDITORIUM	4.50	9.00
☐ 61176 (S)		FROM ST. LOUIS TO FRISCO	4.50	8.00
☐ 61223 (S)		CONCERTO IN B. GOODE	4.50	9.00

BIG BOPPER

☐ 1008	*D*	CHANTILLY LACE/PURPLE PEOPLE EATER		
		MEETS THE WITCH DOCTOR	36.00	60.00
☐ 71343	*MERCURY*	CHANTILLY LACE/PURPLE PEOPLE EATER		
		MEETS THE WITCH DOCTOR	2.25	4.00

ISSUE #	LABEL		PRICE RANGE	
☐ 71375		BIG BOPPER'S WEDDING/		
		LITTLE RED RIDING HOOD	2.25	4.00
☐ 71416		WALKING THROUGH MY DREAMS/		
		SOMEONE WATCHING OVER YOU	4.00	7.00
☐ 71451		IT'S THE TRUTH, RUTH/		
		THAT'S WHAT I'M TALKING ABOUT	4.00	7.00
☐ 71482		PINK PETTICOATS/THE CLOCK	4.00	7.00

BIG BOPPER—ALBUM
☐ 20402 (M)

	MERCURY	CHANTILLY LACE	48.00	90.00

BIG BROTHER &
THE HOLDING COMPANY

☐ 657	*MAINSTREAM*	BLINDMAN/ALL IS LONLINESS	3.00	6.50
☐ 662		CALL ON ME/DOWN ON ME	3.00	6.50
☐ 666		INTRUDER/BYE BYE BABY	3.00	6.50
☐ 675		WOMEN IS LOSERS/		
		LIGHT IS FASTER THAN SOUND	3.00	6.50
☐ 678		LAST TIME/COO COO	3.00	6.50
☐ 44626	*COLUMBIA*	TURTLE BLUES/PIECE OF MY HEART	2.25	5.00
☐ 45502		NU BUGALOO JAM/BLACK WIDOW SPIDER	1.50	4.00

BIG BROTHER & THE HOLDING COMPANY—
ALBUM
☐ S-6099 (S)

	MAINSTREAM	BIG BROTHER & THE HOLDING COMPANY	6.50	20.00
☐ C-30631 (S)				
	COLUMBIA	BIG BROTHER & THE HOLDING COMPANY	5.00	15.00
☐ C-30222 (S)		BE A BROTHER	2.75	10.00
☐ C-30738 (S)		HOW HARD IT IS	3.75	11.00
☐ KCS-9700 (S)		CHEAP THRILLS	3.75	11.00

BLONDIE (WITH DEBBIE HARRY)

☐ 45097	*PRIVATE*			
	STOCK	X-OFFENDER/IN THE SUN	3.50	6.00
☐ 45141		IN THE FLESH/MAN OVERBOARD	3.50	6.00
☐ 2220	*CHRYSALIS*	DENIS/I'M ONE	2.00	3.50
☐ 2251		I'M GONNA LOVE YOU TOO/		
		JUST GO AWAY	2.25	4.00
☐ 2271		HANGING ON THE TELEPHONE/		
		FADE AWAY AND RADIATE	2.00	3.50

ISSUE #	LABEL		PRICE RANGE	

BLONDIE—ALBUM

☐ 2023 (S)	*PRIVATE STOCK*	BLONDIE	7.00	18.00

PAT BOONE

☐ 7062	*REPUBLIC*	REMEMBER TO ME MINE/		
		HALFWAY CHANCE WITH YOU	8.50	15.00
☐ 7084		I NEED SOMEONE/LOVING YOU MADLY	7.25	12.00
☐ 7119		I NEED SOMEONE/		
		MY HEART BELONGS TO YOU	4.50	9.00
☐ 15338	*DOT*	TWO HEARTS/TRA LA LA	2.25	4.00
☐ 15377		AIN'T THAT A SHAME/		
		TENNESSEE SATURDAY NIGHT	2.25	4.00
☐ 15422		AT MY FRONT DOOR/NO OTHER ARMS	2.25	4.00
☐ 15435		GEE WHITTAKERS/TAKE THE TIME	2.25	4.00
☐ 15443		TUTTI FRUITTI/I'LL BE HOME	2.25	4.00
☐ 15457		LONG TALL TALLY/		
		JUST AS LONG AS I'M WITH YOU	2.25	4.00
☐ 15472		I ALMOST LOST MY MIND/		
		I'M IN LOVE WITH YOU	2.00	3.50
☐ 15490		FRIENDLY PERSUASION/CHAINS OF LOVE	2.00	3.50
☐ 15521		DON'T FORBID ME/ANASTASIA	1.75	3.00
☐ 15545		WHY BABY WHY/		
		I'M WAITING JUST FOR YOU	1.75	3.00
☐ 15570		LOVE LETTERS IN THE SAND/BERNADINE	1.75	3.00
☐ 15602		REMEMBER YOU'RE MINE/		
		THERE'S A GOLD MINE IN THE SKY	1.75	3.00
☐ 15660		APRIL LOVE/WHEN THE SWALLOWS		
		COME BACK TO CAPISTRANO	1.75	3.00
☐ 15690		A WONDERFUL TIME UP THERE/		
		IT'S TOO SOON TO KNOW	1.75	3.00
☐ 15750		SUGAR MOON/CHERIE I LOVE YOU	1.75	3.00
☐ 15785		IF DREAMS CAME TRUE/		
		THAT'S HOW MUCH I LOVE YOU	1.75	3.00
☐ 15825		FOR MY GOOD FORTUNE/		
		GEE BUT IT'S LONELY	1.75	3.00
☐ 15840		I'LL REMEMBER TONIGHT/		
		THE MARDI GRAS MARCH	1.75	3.00
☐ 15888		WITH THE WIND AND THE RAIN IN YOUR		
		HAIR/GOOD ROCKIN' TONIGHT	1.75	3.00
☐ 15914		FOR A PENNY/		
		THE WANG DANG TAFFY APPLE TANGO	1.75	3.00

ISSUE #	LABEL		PRICE RANGE	

PAT BOONE—EPs

☐ 1049	*DOT*	PAT BOONE	4.00	8.00
☐ 1053		PAT ON MIKE	4.00	8.00
☐ 1054		FRIENDLY PERSUASION	4.00	8.00
☐ 1055		A DATE WITH PAT BOONE	3.50	6.00
☐ 1056		A CLOSER WALK WITH THEE	3.50	6.00
☐ 1057		FOUR BY PAT	3.50	6.00
☐ 1062		MERRY CHRISTMAS	3.50	6.00
☐ 1064		TUTTI FRUITTI	3.50	6.00
☐ 1069		STAR DUST	3.50	6.00
☐ 1075		MARDI GRAS	3.50	6.00
☐ 1076		SIDE BY SIDE	3.50	6.00
☐ 1082		TENDERLY	3.50	6.00
☐ 1083		PAT'S GREATEST HITS	3.50	6.00
☐ 1086		I'M IN THE MOOD FOR LOVE	3.00	5.00
☐ 1090		BEYOND THE SUNSET	3.00	5.00
☐ 1091		JOURNEY TO THE CENTER OF THE EARTH	3.00	5.00
☐ 1096		MOONGLOW	3.00	5.00

PAT BOONE—ALBUMS

☐ 3012 (M)	*DOT*	PAT BOONE	7.00	18.00
☐ 3030 (M)		HOWDY	6.00	15.00
☐ 3050 (M)		PAT	6.00	15.00
☐ 3068 (M)		HYMNS WE LOVE	6.00	15.00
☐ 3071 (M)		PAT'S GREAT HITS	4.00	12.00
☐ 25071 (S)		PAT'S GREAT HITS	6.00	15.00
☐ 25077 (S)		PAT BOONE SINGS IRVING BERLIN	6.00	15.00
☐ 25118 (S)		STAR DUST	6.00	15.00
☐ 25121 (S)		YES INDEED	6.00	15.00
☐ 25158 (S)		PAT BOONE SINGS	6.00	15.00
☐ 25180 (S)		TENDERLY	6.00	15.00
☐ 25181 (S)		GREAT MILLIONS	6.00	15.00
☐ 25222 (S)		WHITE CHRISTMAS	6.00	15.00
☐ 25261 (S)		PAT'S GREATEST HITS, VOL. II	6.00	15.00
☐ 25270 (S)		MOONGLOW	6.00	15.00
☐ 25285 (S)		THIS AND THAT	6.00	15.00
☐ 25346 (S)		GREAT, GREAT, GREAT	4.50	12.00
☐ 25384 (S)		MOODY RIVER	5.00	13.50
☐ 25399 (S)		I'LL SEE YOU IN MY DREAMS	4.50	12.00
☐ 25455 (S)		PAT BOONE GOLDEN HITS	4.50	12.00
☐ 25501 (S)		GUESS WHO	8.00	22.50

DAVID BOWIE

ISSUE #	LABEL		PRICE RANGE	

DAVID BOWIE

☐5815	WARNER BROTHERS	CAN'T HELP THINKING ABOUT ME/ AND I SAY TO MYSELF	18.00	30.00
☐85009	DERAM	RUBBER BAND/THE LONDON BOYS	12.00	22.00
☐85009		RUBBER BAND/THERE IS A HAPPY LAND	10.00	18.00
☐85016		LOVE YOU TILL TUESDAY/ DID YOU EVER HAVE A DREAM?	10.00	18.00
☐72949	MERCURY	SPACE ODDITY/ WILD-EYED BOY FROM FREECLOUD	7.25	12.00
☐73075		MEMORY OF A FREE FESTIVAL (PT. 1)/(PT. 2)	8.50	15.00
☐0605	RCA	CHANGES/ANDY WARHOL	2.00	3.50
☐0719		STARMAN/SUFFRAGETTE CITY	2.00	3.50
☐0838		THE JEAN GENIE/HANG ON TO YOURSELF	2.00	3.50
☐0876		SPACE ODDITY/THE MAN WHO SOLD THE WORLD	1.50	2.50

DAVID BOWIE—ALBUMS

☐16003 (M)	DERAM	DAVID BOWIE	20.00	50.00
☐18003 (S)		DAVID BOWIE	25.00	60.00
☐61246 (M)	MERCURY	MAN OF WORDS, MAN OF MUSIC	20.00	50.00
☐61325 (S)		THE MAN WHO SOLD THE WORLD	6.00	15.00
☐50007 (S)	LONDON	STARTING POINT	6.00	15.00
☐61829 (S)		IMAGES	6.00	15.00
☐4623 (S)	RCA	HUNKY DORY	6.00	15.00
☐4702 (S)		THE RISE AND FALL OF ZIGGY STARDUST AND THE SPIDERS FROM MARS	5.00	13.50
☐4813 (S)		SPACE ODDITY	4.50	12.00
☐4816 (S)		THE MAN WHO SOLD THE WORLD	4.00	10.00

BREAD

☐45365	ELEKTRA	CHANGE OF HEART/ LOST WITHOUT YOUR LOVE	1.50	3.00
☐45666		ANY WAY YOU WANT ME/DISMAL DAY	2.50	5.00
☐45668		COULD/I CAN'T MEASURE THE COST	2.50	5.00
☐45686		(I WANNA) MAKE IT WITH YOU/ WHY DO YOU KEEP ME WAITING	1.50	3.00
☐45701		IT DON'T MATTER TO ME/CALL ON ME	1.50	3.00
☐45711		TOO MUCH LOVE/LET YOUR LOVE GO	1.50	3.00
☐45720		IF/TAKE COMFORT	1.50	3.00
☐45740		LIVE IN YOUR LOVE/MOTHER FREEDOM	1.50	3.00
☐45751		BABY I'M-A WANT YOU/TRUCKIN'	1.50	3.00

ISSUE #	LABEL		PRICE RANGE	

BROOKLYN BRIDGE

☐ 60	*BUDDAH*	FROM MY WINDOW/		
		LITTLE RED BOAT BY THE RIVER	2.25	4.00
☐ 75		WORST THAT COULD HAPPEN/		
		YOUR KITE, MY KITE	1.75	3050
☐ 95		BLESSED IS THE RAIN/		
		WELCOME ME LOVE	1.75	3.00
☐ 126		YOUR HUSBAND - MY WIFE/		
		UPSIDE DOWN	1.75	3.00
☐ 139		YOU'LL NEVER WALK ALONE/		
		MINSTREL LADY	1.75	3.00
☐ 162		FREE AS THE WIND/		
		HE'S NOT A HAPPY MAN.............	1.75	3.00
☐ 179		DOWN BY THE RIVER/LOOK AGAIN	1.75	3.00
☐ 193		DAY IS DONE/OPPOSITES	1.75	3.00
☐ 199		NIGHTS IN WHITE SATIN/CYNTHIA	1.75	3.00
☐ 201		NEVER KNEW THIS KIND OF HURT		
		BEFORE/THEN RAIN CAME	1.75	3.00

BROOKLYN BRIDGE—ALBUMS

☐ 5034 (S)	*BUDDAH*	BROOKLYN BRIDGE	6.00	15.00
☐ 5042 (S)		SECOND	6.00	15.00
☐ 5065 (S)		THE BROOKLYN BRIDGE	6.00	15.00
☐ 5107 (S)		BRIDGE IN BLUE	6.00	15.00

JAMES BROWN

☐ 12258	*FEDERAL*	PLEASE PLEASE PLEASE/		
		WHY DO YOU DO ME	4.00	7.00
☐ 12277		HOLD MY BABY'S HAND/NO, NO, NO, NO	7.25	12.00
☐ 12289		JUST WON'T DO RIGHT/LET'S MAKE IT	7.25	12.00
☐ 12290		I WON'T PLEAD NO MORE/		
		CHONNIE ON CHON	7.25	12.00
☐ 12292		GONNA TRY/CAN'T BE THE SAME	7.25	12.00
☐ 12295		MESSING WITH THE BLUES/GONNA TRY	7.25	12.00
☐ 12300		I WALKED ALONE/		
		YOU'RE MINE, YOU'RE MINE	7.25	12.00
☐ 12311		THAT DOOD IT/		
		BABY CRIES OVER THE OCEAN	7.25	12.00
☐ 12316		BEGGING, BEGGING/		
		THAT'S WHEN I LOST MY HEART	7.25	12.00
☐ 12337		TRY ME/TELL ME WHAT I DID WRONG	3.00	5.00
☐ 12348		I WANT YOU SO BAD/		
		THERE MUST BE A REASON	3.00	5.00
☐ 12352		I'VE GOT TO CHANGE/		
		IT HURTS TO TELL YOU	3.00	5.00

ISSUE #	LABEL		PRICE RANGE	
☐ 12361		GOOD GOOD LOVIN'/		
		DON'T LET IT HAPPEN TO ME	3.00	5.00
☐ 12364		IT WAS YOU/GOT TO CRY	3.00	5.00
☐ 12369		I'LL GO CRAZY / I KNOW IT'S TRUE	3.00	5.00
☐ 12370		THINK/YOU'VE GOT THE POWER	3.00	5.00
☐ 12378		THIS OLD HEART/WONDER WHEN		
		YOU'RE COMING HOME	3.00	5.00
☐ 5423	*KING*	THE BELLS/AND I DO WHAT I WANT	3.00	5.00
☐ 5438		HOLD IT/THE SCRATCH	3.00	5.00
☐ 5442		BEWILDERED/IF YOU WANT ME	3.00	5.00
☐ 5466		I DON'T MIND/LOVE DON'T LOVE NOBODY	3.00	5.00
☐ 5485		STICKY SUDS(PT. 1)/PT. 2)	3.00	5.00
☐ 5524		BABY YOU'RE RIGHT/		
		I'LL NEVER LET YOU GO	3.00	5.00
☐ 5547		I LOVE YOU, YES I DO/		
		JUST YOU AND ME, DARLING	3.00	5.00
☐ 5573		LOST SOMEONE/CROSS FIRING	3.00	5.00
☐ 5614		NIGHT TRAIN/WHY DOES EVERYTHING		
		HAPPEN TO ME?	3.00	5.00
☐ 5657		SHOUT AND SHIMMY/COME OVER HERE	3.00	5.00
☐ 5672		MASHED POTATOES U.S.A./		
		YOU DON'T HAVE TO GO	3.00	5.00
☐ 5701		THREE HEARTS IN A TANGLE/		
		I'VE LOST MONEY	3.00	5.00
☐ 5710		EVERY BEAT OF MY HEART/LIKE A BABY	3.00	5.00
☐ 5739		PRISONER OF LOVE/CHOO-CHOO	3.00	5.00
☐ 5767		THESE FOOLISH THINGS/FEEL IT (PT. 1)	3.00	5.00
☐ 5803		SIGNED, SEALED AND DELIVERED/		
		WAITING IN VAIN	3.00	5.00

JAMES BROWN—EPs

☐ 430	*KING*	PLEASE, PLEASE, PLEASE	4.00	8.50
☐ 826		LIVE AT THE APOLLO	3.50	7.25

JAMES BROWN—ALBUMS

☐ 610 (M)	*KING*	PLEASE, PLEASE, PLEASE	15.00	35.00
☐ 635 (M)		TRY ME	12.50	30.00
☐ 683 (M)		THINK	12.50	30.00
☐ 743 (M)		THE ALWAYS AMAZING JAMES BROWN		
		AND THE FAMOUS FLAMES	10.00	25.00
☐ 771 (M)		JUMP AROUND	10.00	25.00
☐ 780 (M)		THE EXCITING JAMES BROWN	8.00	22.50
☐ 804 (M)		TOUR THE U.S.A.	8.00	22.50
☐ 826 (M)		THE JAMES BROWN SHOWN	8.00	22.50
☐ 851 (M)		PRISONER OF LOVE	8.00	22.50
☐ 883 (M)		PURE DYNAMITE	7.00	18.00
☐ 909 (M)		PLEASE, PLEASE, PLEASE	7.00	18.00

ISSUE #	LABEL		PRICE RANGE	
☐ 919 (M)		THE UNBEATABLE 16 HITS	7.00	18.00
☐ 938 (M)		PAPA'S GOT A BRAND NEW BAG	6.00	15.00
☐ 946 (M)		I GOT YOU (I FEEL GOOD)	6.00	15.00
☐ 985 (M)		SOUL BROTHER #1 (90)	5.00	13.50

BUCKINGHAMS

☐ 4618	SPECTRA-SOUND	SWEETS FOR MY SWEET/ BEGINNER'S LOVE	4.50	9.00
☐ 844	U.S.A.	DON'T WANT TO CRY/I'LL GO CRAZY	2.25	4.00
☐ 848		I CALL YOUR NAME/ MAKIN' UP AND BREAKIN' UP	2.25	4.00
☐ 860		KIND OF A DRAG/ YOU MAKE ME FEEL SO GOOD	1.75	3.00
☐ 869		LAWDY MISS CLAWDY/ MAKIN' UP AND BREAKIN' UP	1.75	3.00
☐ 44053	COLUMBIA	DON'T YOU CARE/ WHY DON'T YOU LOVE ME	1.75	3.00
☐ 44182		MERCY, MERCY, MERCY/YOU ARE GONE	1.75	3.00
☐ 44254		HEY BABY (THEY'RE PLAYING OUR SONG)/AND OUR LOVE	1.75	3.00
☐ 44378		SUSAN/FOREIGN POWER	1.75	3.00
☐ 44533		BACK IN LOVE AGAIN/ YOU MISUNDERSTAND ME	1.75	3.00
☐ 44672		WHERE DID YOU COME FROM/ SONG OF THE BREEZE	1.75	3.00
☐ 44923		IT'S A BEAUTIFUL DAY/ DIFFERENCE OF OPINION	1.75	3.00
☐ 3258	LAURIE	GONNA SAY GOODBYE/MANY TIMES	1.75	3.00

BUCKINGHAMS—ALBUM

☐ 107 (S)	U.S.A.	KIND OF A DRAG	7.00	18.00
☐ 9469 (S)		TIME AND CHARGES	6.00	15.00
☐ 9589 (S)		PORTRAITS	6.00	15.00
☐ 9703 (S)		IN ONE EAR AND GONE TOMORROW	6.00	18.00
☐ 9812 (S)		THE BUCKINGHAMS' GREATEST HITS	5.00	13.50

BUFFALO SPRINGFIELD

☐ 6428	ATCO	NOWADAYS CLANCY CAN'T EVEN SING/ GO AND SAY GOODBYE	2.00	3.50
☐ 6452		BURNED/EVERBODY'S WRONG	2.00	3.50
☐ 6459		FOR WHAT IT'S WORTH/DO I HAVE TO COME RIGHT OUT AND SAY IT	1.75	3.00
☐ 6499		BLUEBIRD/MR. SOUL	1.75	3.00

ISSUE #	LABEL		PRICE RANGE	
☐6519		ROCK 'N' ROLL WOMAN/		
		A CHILD'S CLAIM TO FAME	1.75	3.00
☐6545		EXPECTING TO FLY/EVERYDAYS	1.75	3.00
☐6572		UNO-MUNDO/MERRY-GO-ROUND	1.75	3.00
☐6602		KIND WOMAN/SPECIAL CARE	1.75	3.00
☐6615		ON THE WAY HOME/FOUR DAYS GONE	1.75	3.00

BUFFALO SPRINGFIELD—ALBUMS

☐200 (S)	ATCO	BUFFALO SPRINGFIELD	12.50	30.00
☐226 (S)		BUFFALO SPRINGFIELD AGAIN	6.00	15.00
☐256 (S)		LAST TIME AROUND	6.00	15.00
☐283 (S)		RETROSPECTIVE (THE BEST OF		
		BUFFALO SPRINGFIELD) (42)	5.00	13.50

JOHNNY BURNETTE

☐44001	FREEDOM	I'M RESTLESS/KISS ME	4.50	9.00
☐44011		GUMBO/ME AND THE BEAR	4.50	9.00
☐44017		SWEET BABY DOLL/		
		I'LL NEVER LOVE AGAIN	4.50	9.00
☐55222	LIBERTY	SETTIN' THE WOODS ON FIRE/		
		KENTUCKY WALTZ	2.25	4.00
☐55243		DON'T DO IT/PATRICK HENRY	2.25	4.00
☐55258		DREAMIN'/CINCINNATI FIREBALL	2.25	4.00
☐55285		YOU'RE SIXTEEN/I BEG YOUR PARDON	2.25	4.00
☐55298		LITTLE BOY SAD/		
		I GO DOWN TO THE RIVER	2.25	4.00
☐55318		BIG BIG WORLD/BALLAD OF THE		
		ONE-EYED JACKS	2.25	4.00
☐55345		GIRLS/I'VE GOT A LOT OF THINGS TO DO	2.25	4.00
☐55379		GOD, COUNTRY AND MY BABY/		
		HONESTLY I DO	2.25	4.00
☐55416		WHY AM I/CLOWN SHOES	2.25	4.00
☐55448		THE FOOL OF THE YEAR/		
		POOREST BOY IN TOWN	2.25	4.00
☐55489		DAMN THE DEFIANT/LONESOME WATERS	2.25	4.00
☐1116	CHANCELLOR	I WANNA THANK YOUR FOLKS/THE GIANT	2.25	4.00
☐1123		TAG ALONG/PARTY GIRL	2.25	4.00
☐1129		REMEMBER ME/TIME IS NOT ENOUGH	2.25	4.00

JOHNNY BURNETTE—EPs

☐1004	LIBERTY	DREAMIN'	9.00	18.00
☐1011		JOHNNY BURNETTE HITS	8.50	15.00

JOHNNY BURNETTE—ALBUMS

☐7179 (S)	LIBERTY	DREAMIN'	15.00	35.00
☐7183 (S)		JOHNNY BURNETTE	15.00	35.00

ISSUE #	LABEL		PRICE RANGE	
☐ 7190 (S)		JOHNNY BURNETTE SINGS	15.00	35.00
☐ 7206 (S)		HITS AND OTHER FAVORITES	15.00	35.00
☐ 7255 (S)		ROSES ARE RED	12.50	30.00
☐ 7389 (S)		THE JOHNNY BURNETTE STORY	12.50	30.00

JERRY BUTLER

☐ 1024	*ABNER*	ONE BY ONE/LOST	2.25	4.00
☐ 1028		HOLD ME MY DARLING/RAINBOW VALLEY	2.25	4.00
☐ 1030		I WAS WRONG/COULDN'T GO TO SLEEP	2.25	4.00
☐ 1035		A LONELY SOLDIER/I FOUND A LOVE	3.00	5.00
☐ 354	*VEE JAY*	HE WILL BREAK YOUR HEART/		
		THANKS TO YOU	2.00	3.50
☐ 371		O HOLY NIGHT/SILENT NIGHT	3.00	5.00
☐ 375		FIND ANOTHER GIRL/		
		WHEN TROUBLE CALLS	2.00	3.50
☐ 390		I'M A TELLING YOU/I SEE A FOOL	2.00	3.50
☐ 396		FOR YOUR PRECIOUS LOVE/		
		SWEET WAS THE WINE	2.00	3.50
☐ 405		MOON RIVER/AWARE OF LOVE	1.75	3.00
☐ 426		CHI TOWN/ISLE OF SIRENS	1.75	3.00
☐ 451		MAKE IT EASY ON YOURSELF/		
		IT'S TOO LATE	1.75	3.00
☐ 463		YOU CAN RUN/I'M THE ONE	1.75	3.00
☐ 475		WISHING STAR (TARUS BULBA THEME)/		
		YOU GO RIGHT THROUGH ME	1.75	3.00
☐ 486		WHATEVER YOU WANT/		
		YOU WON'T BE SORRY	1.75	3.00
☐ 526		I ALMOST LOST MY MIND/		
		STRAWBERRIES	1.75	3.00
☐ 534		WHERE'S THE GIRL/		
		HOW BEAUTIFUL YOU LIE	1.75	3.00
☐ 556		A WOMAN WITH SOUL/JUST A LITTLE BIT	1.75	3.00
☐ 567		NEED TO BELONG/GIVE ME YOUR LOVE	1.75	3.00
☐ 588		GIVING UP ON LOVE/I'VE BEEN TRYING	1.75	3.00
☐ 598		STAND ACCUSED/		
		I DON'T WANT TO HEAR ANYMORE	1.75	3.00

JERRY BUTLER—ALBUMS

☐ 2001 (M)	*ABNER*	JERRY BUTLER, ESQUIRE	15.00	35.00
☐ 1027 (M)	*VEE JAY*	JERRY BUTLER, ESQUIRE	10.00	25.00
☐ 1029 (M)		HE WILL BREAK YOUR HEART	8.00	22.50
☐ 1034 (M)		LOVE ME	8.00	22.50
☐ 1038 (M)		AWARE OF LOVE	8.00	22.50
☐ 1038 (S)		AWARE OF LOVE	12.50	30.00
☐ 1046 (S)		MOON RIVER	12.50	30.00

ISSUE #	LABEL		PRICE RANGE	
☐ 1057 (S)		FOLK SONGS	7.00	18.00
☐ 1075 (S)		FOR YOUR PRECIOUS LOVE	7.00	18.00
☐ 1076 (S)		GIVING UP ON LOVE	7.00	18.00
☐ 1099 (S)		DELICIOUS TOGETHER	7.00	18.00
☐ 1119 (S)		MORE OF THE BEST OF JERRY BUTLER	7.00	18.00

BYRDS

ISSUE #	LABEL		PRICE RANGE	
☐ 43271	*COLUMBIA*	MR. TAMBOURINE MAN/ I KNEW I'D WANT YOU	1.50	3.00
☐ 43332		ALL I REALLY WANT TO DO/ I'LL FEEL A WHOLE LOT BETTER	1.75	3.00
☐ 43424		TURN! TURN! TURN!/ SHE DON'T CARE ABOUT TIME	1.50	3.00
☐ 43501		IT WON'T BE WRONG/ SET YOU FREE THIS TIME	1.50	3.00
☐ 43578		EIGHT MILES HIGH/WHY	1.50	3.00
☐ 43702		5D (FIFTH DIMENSION)/CAPTAIN SOUL	1.50	3.00
☐ 43766		MR. SPACEMAN/WHAT'S HAPPENING	1.50	3.00
☐ 43987		SO YOU WANT TO BE A ROCK 'N' ROLL STAR/EVERYBODY'S BEEN BURNED	1.50	3.00
☐ 44054		MY BACK PAGES/RENAISSANCE FAIR	1.50	3.00
☐ 44157		HAVE YOU SEEN HER FACE/ DON'T MAKE WAVES	1.50	3.00
☐ 44230		LADY FRIEND/OLD JOHN ROBERTSON	1.50	3.00
☐ 44362		GOIN' BACK/CHANGE IS NOW	1.50	3.00
☐ 44499		YOU AIN'T GOIN' NOWHERE/ ARTIFICIAL ENERGY	1.50	3.00
☐ 44643		PRETTY BOY FLOYD/I AM A PILGRIM	1.50	3.00
☐ 44746		BAD NIGHT AT THE WHISKEY/ DRUG STORE TRUCK DRIVIN' MAN	1.50	3.00
☐ 44868		LAY LADY LAY/OLD BLUE	1.50	3.00
☐ 44990		BALLAD OF EASY RIDER/OIL IN MY LAMP . . .	2.00	3.50
☐ 44990		BALLAD OF EASY RIDER/ WASN'T BORN TO FOLLOW	1.75	3.00
☐ 45071		JESUS IS JUST ALRIGHT/ IT'S ALL OVER NIGHT, BABY BLUE	1.75	3.00
☐ 45259		CHESTNUT MARE/JUST A SEASON	1.75	3.00
☐ 45440		GLORY GLORY/CITIZEN KANE	1.75	3.00

BYRDS—ALBUMS

ISSUE #	LABEL		PRICE RANGE	
☐ 2372 (S)	*COLUMBIA*	MR. TAMBOURINE MAN	7.00	18.00
☐ 9254 (S)		TURN, TURN, TURN	7.00	18.00
☐ 9349 (S)		FIFTH DIMENSION	7.00	18.00
☐ 9442 (S)		YOUNGER THAN YESTERDAY	7.00	18.00
☐ 9516 (S)		THE BYRDS' GREATEST HITS	5.00	13.50

ISSUE #	LABEL		PRICE RANGE	
☐ 9670 (S)		SWEETHEART OF THE RODEO	5.00	13.50
☐ 9755 (S)		DR. BYRDS AND MR. HYDE	5.00	13.50
☐ 9942 (S)		BALLAD OF EASY RIDER	5.00	13.50

— C —

CADILLACS

☐ 765	*JOSIE*	GLORIA/I WONDER WHY	48.00	90.00
☐ 769		WISHING WELL/		
		I WANT TO KNOW ABOUT LOVE	60.00	110.00
☐ 773		NO CHANCE/SYMPATHY	24.00	42.00
☐ 778		DOWN THE ROAD/WIDOW LADY	15.00	24.00
☐ 785		SPEEDOO/LET ME EXPLAIN	4.00	7.00
☐ 792		ZOOM/YOU ARE	4.50	9.00
☐ 798		BETTY MY LOVE/WOE IS ME	4.50	9.00
☐ 805		THE GIRL I LOVE/THAT'S ALL I NEED	7.25	12.00
☐ 807		SHOCK-A-DOO/RUDOLPH THE		
		RED-NOSED REINDEER	3.50	6.00
☐ 812		SUGAR SUGAR/		
		ABOUT THAT GAL NAMED LOU	4.00	7.00
☐ 820		MY GIRL FRIEND/BROKEN HEART	7.25	12.00
☐ 821		LUCY/HURRY HOME	4.00	7.00
☐ 829		BUZZ BUZZ BUZZ/YEA YEA BABY	4.00	7.00
☐ 836		SPEEDO IS BACK/A LOOKA HERE	4.00	7.00
☐ 842		I WANT TO KNOW/HOLY SMOKE, BABY	2.25	4.00
☐ 846		PEEK-A-BOO/ OH OH LOLITA	2.25	4.00
☐ 857		JAY WALKER/COPY CAT	2.25	4.00
☐ 861		COOL IT FOOL/PLEASE MR. JOHNSON	2.25	4.00
☐ 866		ROMEO/ALWAYS MY DARLING	2.25	4.00
☐ 870		BAD DAN McGOON/DUMBELL	2.25	4.00
☐ 883		THE BOOGIE MAN/THAT'S WHY	2.25	4.00
☐ 915		I'LL NEVER LET YOU GO/		
		WAYWARD WANDERER	2.25	4.00

CADILLACS—ALBUMS

☐ 1045 (M)	*JUBILEE*	THE FABULOUS CADILLACS	35.00	90.00
☐ 1045 (M)		THE FABULOUS CADILLACS	20.00	50.00
☐ 1045 (M)		THE FABULOUS CADILLACS	12.50	30.00
☐ 1089 (M)		THE CRAZY CADILLACS	20.00	50.00
☐ 1089 (M)		THE CRAZY CADILLACS	8.00	18.00
☐ 5009 (M)		TWISTING WITH THE CADILLACS	10.00	25.00

ISSUE #	LABEL		PRICE RANGE	

GLEN CAMPBELL

☐ 1324	*CENECO*	DREAMS FOR SALE/I'VE GOT TO WIN	5.00	10.00
☐ 1087	*CREST*	TURN AROUND, LOOK AT ME/BRENDA	2.25	4.00
☐ 1096		MIRACLE OF LOVE/ONCE MORE	2.25	4.00
☐ 4783	*CAPITOL*	TOO LATE TO WORRY, TOO BLUE TO CRY	2.00	3.50
☐ 4856		LONG BLACK LIMOUSINE/HERE I AM	2.00	3.50
☐ 4867		KENTUCKY MEANS PARADISE/ TRUCK DRIVING MAN	2.00	3.50
☐ 4925		PRIMA DONNA/OH MY DARLING	2.00	3.50
☐ 4990		DARK AS A DUNGEON/DIVORCE ME C.O.D.	2.00	3.50
☐ 5037		AS FAR AS I'M CONCERNED/ SAME OLD PLACES	2.00	3.50
☐ 5172		THROUGH THE EYES OF A CHILD/ LET ME TELL YOU 'BOUT MARY	2.00	3.50
☐ 5279		SUMMER, WINTER, SPRING AND FALL/ HEARTACHES CAN BE FUN	2.00	3.50
☐ 5360		TOMORROW NEVER COMES/ WOMAN'S WORLD	2.00	3.50
☐ 5441		GUESS I'M DUMB/THAT'S ALL RIGHT	10.00	17.50
☐ 5504		THE UNIVERSAL SOLDIER/ SPANISH SOLDIER (45)	1.75	3.00
☐ 5545		LESS OF ME/PRIVATE JOHN Q.	2.00	3.00
☐ 5638		SATISFIED MIND/ CAN'T YOU SEE I'M TRYING?	2.00	3.00
☐ 5773		BURNING BRIDGES/ONLY THE LONELY	2.00	3.00
☐ 5854		I GOTTA HAVE MY BABY BACK/ JUST TO SATISFY YOU	2.00	3.00

GLEN CAMPBELL—ALBUMS

☐ 1810 (S)	*CAPITOL*	BIG BLUE GRASS SPECIAL	6.00	15.00
☐ 1881 (S)		TOO LATE TO WORRY - TOO BLUE TO CRY	6.00	15.00
☐ 2023 (S)		THE ASTOUNDING 12-STRING GUITAR OF GLEN CAMPBELL	4.50	12.00

CANNIBAL AND THE HEADHUNTERS

☐ 1001	*AIRES*	DANCE BY THE LIGHT/MEANS SO MUCH	3.50	6.00
☐ 642	*RAMPART*	LAND OF 1000 DANCES/ I'LL SHOW YOU HOW TO LOVE ME	2.00	3.50
☐ 644		HERE COMES LOVE/NAU NINNY NAU	2.00	3.50
☐ 646		FOLLOW THE MUSIC/I NEED YOUR LOVING	2.00	3.50
☐ 654		PLEASE BABY PLEASE/OUT OF SIGHT	2.00	3.50
☐ 1516	*DATE*	ZULU KING/LA BAMBA	2.00	3.50
☐ 1525		LAND OF 1000 DANCES/LOVE BIRD	1.75	3.00

GLENN CAMPBELL

ISSUE #	LABEL		PRICE RANGE	

CANNIBAL AND THE HEADHUNTERS—ALBUMS

☐ 3302 (S)	*RAMPART*	LAND OF 1000 DANCES	7.00	18.00
☐ 3001 (S)	*DATE*	LAND OF 1000 DANCES	6.00	15.00

FREDDY CANNON

☐ 4031	*SWAN*	TALLAHASSEE LASSIE/YOU KNOW	2.00	3.50
☐ 4038		OKEFENOKEE/KOOKIE HAT	2.25	4.00
☐ 4043		WAY DOWN YONDER IN NEW ORLEANS/ FRACTURED	2.00	3.50
☐ 4050		CHATTANOOGA SHOE SHINE BOY/BOSTON	2.00	3.50
☐ 4053		THE URGE/JUMP OVER	2.00	3.50
☐ 4057		HAPPY SHADES OF BLUE/ CUERNAVACA CHOO CHOO	2.00	3.50
☐ 4061		HUMDINGER/MY BLUE HEAVEN	2.00	3.50
☐ 4066		MUSKRAT RAMBLE/TWO THOUSAND-88	2.00	3.50
☐ 4071		BUZZ BUZZ A DIDDLE-IT/OPPORTUNITY	2.00	3.50
☐ 4078		TRANSISTOR SISTER/WALK ON THE MOON	2.00	3.50
☐ 4083		FOR ME AND MY GAL/ BLUE PLATE SPECIAL	2.00	3.50
☐ 4096		TEEN QUEEN OF THE WEEK/WILD GUY	2.00	3.50
☐ 4106		PALISADES PARK/ JUNE, JULY AND AUGUST	2.00	3.50
☐ 4117		WHAT'S GONNA HAPPEN WHEN SUMMER'S DONE/BROADWAY	2.00	3.50
☐ 4122		IF YOU WERE A ROCK AND ROLL RECORD/ THE TRUTH, RUTH	2.00	3.50
☐ 4132		FOUR LETTER MAN/ COME ON AND LOVE ME	2.00	3.50
☐ 4139		PATTY BABY/BETTY JEAN	2.00	3.50
☐ 4149		EVERYBODY MONKEY/OH GLORIA	2.00	3.50
☐ 4155		DO WHAT THE HIPPIES DO/ THAT'S THE WAY THE GIRLS ARE	2.00	3.50
☐ 4168		SWEET GEORGIA BROWN/WHAT A PARTY	2.00	3.50
☐ 4178		THE UPS AND DOWNS OF LOVE/ IT'S BEEN NICE	2.00	3.50
☐ 5409	*WARNER BROTHERS*	ABIGAIL BEECHER/ALL AMERICAN GIRL	2.00	3.50
☐ 5434		OK WHEELER THE USED CAR DEALER/ ODIE COLOGNE	2.00	3.50
☐ 5448		SUMMERTIME U.S.A./ GOTTA GOOD THING GOIN'	2.00	3.50
☐ 5487		TOO MUCH MONKEY BUSINESS/ LITTLE AUTOGRAPH SEEKER	2.00	3.50
☐ 5616		LITTLE MISS A-GO-GO/IN THE NIGHT	2.00	3.50

ISSUE #	LABEL		PRICE	RANGE
☐ 5645		ACTION/BEACHWOOD CITY	2.00	3.50
☐ 5666		LET ME SHOW YOU WHERE IT'S AT/		
		THE OLD RAG MAN	1.75	3.00
☐ 5673		SHE'S SOMETHIN' ELSE/		
		LITTLE BITTY CORRINE	1.75	3.00
☐ 5693		THE DEDICATION SONG/		
		COME ON, COME ON	1.75	3.00
☐ 5810		THE GREATEST SHOW ON EARTH/		
		HOKIE POKIE GAL	1.75	3.00
☐ 5832		NATALIE/THE LAUGHING SONG	1.75	3.00
☐ 5859		RUN FOR THE SUN/		
		USE YOUR IMAGINATION	1.75	3.00
☐ 5876		IN MY WILDEST DREAM/A HAPPY CLOWN	1.75	3.00
☐ 7019		MAVERICK'S FLATS/		
		RUN TO THE POET MAN	1.75	3.00
☐ 7075		20TH CENTURY FOX/CINCINNATI WOMAN	2.00	3.50

FREDDY CANNON—ALBUMS

☐ 502 (M)	SWAN	THE EXPLOSIVE FREDDY CANNON	20.00	50.00
☐ 504 (M)		HAPPY SHADES OF BLUE	15.00	35.00
☐ 505 (M)		SOLID GOLD HITS	15.00	35.00
☐ 507 (M)		PALISADES PARK	12.50	30.00
☐ 511 (S)		FREDDY CANNON STEPS OUT	15.00	35.00
☐ 1544 (S)	WARNER			
	BROTHERS	FREDDY CANNON	10.00	25.00
☐ 1612 (S)		ACTION!	8.00	22.50
☐ 1628 (S)		GREATEST HITS	8.00	22.50

CAPTAIN AND TENNILLE

☐ 001				
	BUTTERSCOTCH			
	CASTLE	THE WAY I WANT TO TOUCH YOU/		
		DISNEY GIRLS	24.00	42.00
☐ 101	JOYCE	THE WAY I WANT TO TOUCH YOU/		
		DISNEY GIRLS	8.50	15.00

KIM CARNES

☐ 166	AMOS	TO LOVE SOMEBODY/		
		I FELL IN LOVE WITH A POET	3.00	4.50
☐ 1902	A & M	LET YOU LOVE COME EASY/THE LAST		
		THING YOU EVER WANTED TO DO	2.00	3.50
☐ 1943		SAILIN'/HE'LL COME HOME	2.00	3.50

ISSUE #	LABEL		PRICE RANGE	

KIM CARNES—ALBUMS

☐7016 (S)	*AMOS*	REST ON ME	7.00	18.00
☐4548 (S)		KIM CARNES	6.00	15.00
☐4606 (S)		SAILIN'	6.00	15.00

JOHNNY CASH

☐221	*SUN*	HEY PORTER/CRY! CRY! CRY!	4.00	7.00
☐232		FOLSOM PRISON BLUES/ SO DOGGONE LONESOME	3.50	6.00
☐241		I WALK THE LINE/GET RHYTHM	2.25	3.75
☐258		TRAIN OF LOVE/THERE YOU GO	2.25	3.75
☐266		NEXT IN LINE/DON'T MAKE ME GO	2.25	3.75
☐279		HOME OF THE BLUES/ GIVE MY LOVE TO ROSE	2.25	3.75
☐283		BALLAD OF A TEENAGE QUEEN/BIG RIVER	2.00	3.50
☐295		GUESS THINGS HAPPEN THAT WAY/ COME IN STRANGER	2.00	3.50
☐302		THE WAYS OF A WOMAN IN LOVE/YOU'RE THE NEAREST THING TO HEAVEN	2.00	3.50
☐309		IT'S JUST ABOUT TIME/I JUST THOUGHT YOU'D LIKE TO KNOW	2.00	3.50
☐316		THANKS A LOT/ LUTHER PLAYED THE BOOGIE	2.00	3.50
☐321		KATY TOO/ I FORGOT TO REMEMBER TO FORGET	2.00	3.50
☐331		GOODBYE, LITTLE DARLING/YOU TELL ME	2.00	3.50
☐334		STRAIGHT A'S IN LOVE/ I LOVE YOU BECAUSE	2.00	3.50
☐343		DOWN THE STREET TO 301/ THE STORY OF A BROKEN HEART	2.00	3.50
☐347		MEAN EYED CAT/ PORT OF LONELY HEARTS	2.00	3.50
☐355		OH, LONESOME ME/LIFE GOES ON	2.00	3.50
☐363		MY TREASURE/SUGAR TIME	2.00	3.50
☐376		BLUE TRAIN/BORN TO LOSE	2.00	3.50
☐392		WIDE OPEN ROAD/BELSHAZAR	2.00	3.50

JOHNNY CASH—EPs

☐111	*SUN*	JOHNNY CASH SINGS HANK WILLIAMS	6.00	11.25
☐112		JOHNNY CASH	6.00	11.25
☐113		I WALK THE LINE	6.00	11.25
☐114		HIS TOP HITS	6.00	11.25
☐116		HOME OF THE BLUES	6.00	11.25
☐117		JOHNNY CASH	6.00	11.25

ISSUE #	LABEL		PRICE RANGE	

JOHNNY CASH—ALBUMS

☐ 1220 (M)	**SUN**	JOHNNY CASH WITH HIS HOT AND BLUE GUITAR	10.00	25.00
☐ 1235 (M)		JOHNNY CASH SINGS THE SONGS THAT MADE HIM FAMOUS	8.00	22.50
☐ 1240 (M)		JOHNNY CASH - GREATEST	8.00	22.50
☐ 1245 (M)		JOHNNY CASH SINGS HANK WILLIAMS	7.00	18.00
☐ 1255 (M)		NOW HERE'S JOHNNY CASH	7.00	18.00
☐ 1270 (M)		ALL ABOARD THE BLUE TRAIN	7.00	18.00
☐ 1275 (M)		THE ORIGINAL SUN SOUND OF JOHNNY CASH	7.00	18.00

CHAD AND JEREMY

☐ 1021	**WORLD ARTISTS**	YESTERDAY'S GONE/LEMON TREE	2.00	3.50
☐ 1027		A SUMMER SONG/NO TEARS FOR JOHNNY	2.00	3.50
☐ 1034		WILLOW WEEP FOR ME/IF SHE WAS MINE	2.00	3.50
☐ 1041		IF I LOVED YOU/DONNA DONNA	2.00	3.50
☐ 1052		WHAT DO YOU WANT WITH ME?/ VERY GOOD YEAR	2.00	3.50
☐ 1056		FROM A WINDOW/MY COLOURING BOOK	2.00	3.50
☐ 1060		SEPTEMBER IN THE RAIN/ ONLY FOR THE YOUNG	2.00	3.50
☐ 43277	**COLUMBIA**	BEFORE AND AFTER/FARE THEE WELL	1.75	3.00
☐ 43339		I DON'T WANNA LOSE YOU BABY/PENNIES	1.75	3.00
☐ 43414		I HAVE DREAMED/SHOULD I	1.75	3.00
☐ 43490		TEENAGE FAILURE/EARLY MORNING RAIN	1.75	3.00
☐ 43682		DISTANT SHORES/LAST NIGHT	1.75	3.00
☐ 43807		YOU ARE SHE/I WON'T CRY	1.75	3.00
☐ 44379		PAINTED DAYGLOW SMILE/EDITORIAL	1.75	3.00
☐ 44525		SISTER MARIE/REST IN PEACE	1.75	3.00
☐ 44660		PASTOR QUIGLEY/YOU NEED FEET	1.75	3.00

CHAD AND JEREMY—ALBUMS

☐ 2002 (S)	**WORLD ARTISTS**	YESTERDAY'S GONE	8.00	22.50
☐ 3005 (S)		CHAD AND JEREMY SING FOR YOU	8.00	22.50
☐ 9174 (S)		BEFORE AND AFTER	7.00	18.00
☐ 9198 (S)		I DON'T WANT TO LOSE YOU BABY	7.00	18.00
☐ 9364 (S)		DISTANT SHORES	7.00	18.00
☐ 9457 (S)		OF CABBAGES AND KINGS	7.00	18.00
☐ 9699 (S)		THE ARK	6.00	15.00
☐ 2470 (S)		THE BEST OF CHAD AND JEREMY	5.00	13.50
☐ 2546 (S)		MORE CHAD AND JEREMY	5.00	13.50

ISSUE #	LABEL		PRICE RANGE	

HARRY CHAPIN

☐ 45203	*ELEKTRA*	CAT'S IN THE CRADLE/VACANCY	1.75	3.25
☐ 45236		SHE SINGS SONGS/		
		I WANNA LEARN A LOVE SONG	1.75	3.25
☐ 45264		DREAMS GO BY/SANDY	1.50	3.00
☐ 45285		DIRT GETS UNDER THE FINGERNAILS/		
		TANGLED UP PUPPET	1.50	3.00
☐ 45327		BETTER PLACE TO BE (PT. 1)/PT. 2)	1.50	3.00
☐ 45368		COREY'S COMING	1.75	3.25
☐ 45426		I WONDER WHAT HAPPENED TO HIM/		
		DANCE BAND ON THE TITAC	1.75	3.25
☐ 45445		MY OLD LADY/I DO IT FOR YOU, JANE	1.75	3.25
☐ 45497		IF YOU WANT TO FEEL/		
		I WONDER WHAT WOULD HAPPEN	1.75	3.25
☐ 45770		TAXI/EMPTY	1.25	2.50
☐ 45792		ANY OLD KIND OF DAY/COULD YOU PUT		
		YOUR LIGHT ON, PLEASE	1.50	3.00
☐ 45811		SUNDAY MORNING SUNSHINE/		
		BURNING YOURSELF	1.25	2.50
☐ 45828		BETTER PLACE TO BE	1.25	2.50

RAY CHARLES

☐ 250	*SWING TIME*	BABY, LET ME HOLD YOUR HAND/		
		LONELY BOY	18.00	30.00
☐ 274		KISS ME, BABY/I'M GLAD FOR YOUR SAKE . . .	12.00	24.00
☐ 976	*ATLANTIC*	ROLL WITH MY BABY/		
		THE MIDNIGHT HOUR	15.00	24.00
☐ 984		THE SUN'S GONNA SHINE AGAIN/		
		JUMPIN' IN THE MORNIN'	12.00	20.00
☐ 999		MESS AROUND/FUNNY	12.00	20.00
☐ 1008		FEELIN' SAD/HEARTBREAKER	12.00	20.00
☐ 1021		IT SHOULD'VE BEEN ME/		
		SINNER'S PRAYER	10.00	18.00
☐ 1037		DON'T YOU KNOW?/LOSING HAND	10.00	18.00
☐ 1050		I'VE GOT A WOMAN/COME BACK	8.50	15.00
☐ 1063		THIS LITTLE GIRL OF MINE/		
		A FOOL FOR YOU	8.50	15.00
☐ 1076		GREENBACKS/BLACKJACK	7.25	12.00
☐ 1085		DROWN IN MY OWN TEARS/MARY ANN	3.75	6.50
☐ 1096		HALLELUJAH, I LOVE HER SO/		
		WHAT WOULD I DO WITHOUT YOU	3.75	6.50
☐ 1108		LONELY AVENUE/		
		LEAVE MY WOMAN ALONE	3.75	6.50
☐ 1124		AIN'T THAT LOVE/I WANT TO KNOW	3.75	6.50

ISSUE #	LABEL		PRICE RANGE	
☐ 1143		IT'S ALL RIGHT/		
		GET ON THE RIGHT TRACK BABY	3.75	6.50
☐ 1154		SWANEE RIVER ROCK/		
		I WANT A LITTLE GIRL	2.25	4.00
☐ 1172		TALKIN' 'BOUT YOU/		
		WHAT KIND OF MAN ARE YOU?	2.75	4.50
☐ 1180		YES INDEED/I HAD A DREAM	2.75	4.50
☐ 1196		YOU BE MY BABY/MY BONNIE	2.75	4.50
☐ 2006		ROCKHOUSE(PT. 1)/(PT. 2)	2.25	4.00
☐ 2010		THE RIGHT TIME/		
		TELL ALL THE WORLD ABOUT YOU . . .	2.25	4.00
☐ 2022		THAT'S ENOUGH/TELL ME HOW YOU FEEL . . .	2.25	4.00
☐ 2031		WHAT'D I SAY(PT. 1)/(PT. 2)	2.00	3.50
☐ 2043		I'M MOVIN' ON/I BELIEVE TO MY SOUL . . .	2.00	3.50
☐ 2047		LET THE GOOD TIMES ROLL/		
		DON'T LET THE SUN CATCH YOU CRYING . . .	2.25	4.00
☐ 2055		JUST FOR A THRILL/HEARTBREAKER	2.25	4.00
☐ 2068		TELL THE TRUTH/SWEET SIXTEEN	2.00	3.50
☐ 2084		COME RAIN OR COME SHINE/		
		TELL ME YOU'LL WAIT FOR ME	2.00	3.50

RAY CHARLES—EPs

☐ 587	*ATLANTIC*	RAY CHARLES	5.00	9.00
☐ 597		THE GREAT RAY CHARLES	4.50	9.00
☐ 607		ROCK WITH RAY CHARLES	4.50	9.00

RAY CHARLES—ALBUMS

☐ 8006 (M)	*ATLANTIC*	ROCK AND ROLL	15.00	35.00
☐ 8025 (M)		YES, INDEED!	12.50	30.00
☐ 8029 (M)		WHAT'D I SAY	12.50	30.00
☐ 8039 (M)		RAY CHARLES IN PERSON	10.00	25.00
☐ 8052 (M)		GENIUS SINGS THE BLUES	8.00	20.00
☐ 8054 (M)		DO THE TWIST WITH RAY CHARLES	7.00	18.00
☐ 8063 (M)		THE RAY CHARLES STORY, VOL. I	6.00	15.00
☐ 8064 (M)		THE RAY CHARLES STORY, VOL. II	6.00	15.00
☐ 8094 (S)		THE RAY CHARLES STORY, VOL. III	6.00	15.00
☐ 1256 (S)		THE GREAT RAY CHARLES	5.00	13.50
☐ 1279 (S)		SOUL BROTHERS	5.00	13.50
☐ 1289 (S)		RAY CHARLES AT NEWPORT	5.00	13.50
☐ 1312 (S)		THE GENIUS OF RAY CHARLES	4.50	12.00
☐ 1369 (S)		GENIUS AFTER HOURS	4.50	12.00

CHUBBY CHECKER

☐ 804	*PARKWAY*	THE CLASS/SCHOOLDAYS,		
		OH, SCHOOLDAYS	4.00	7.00

ISSUE #	LABEL		PRICE RANGE	
☐ 808		SAMSON AND DELILAH/		
		WHOLE LOTTA LAUGHIN'	7.25	12.00
☐ 810		DANCING DINOSAUR/		
		THOSE PRIVATE EYES	7.25	12.00
☐ 811		THE TWIST/TOOT	2.25	4.00
☐ 811		THE TWIST/TWISTIN' U.S.A.	2.00	3.50
☐ 813		THE HUCKLEBUCK/WHOLE LOTTA		
		SHAKING GOIN' ON	2.00	3.50
☐ 818		PONY TIME/OH, SUSANNAH	2.00	3.50
☐ 822		DANCE THE MESS AROUND/		
		GOOD, GOOD LOVIN'	2.00	3.50
☐ 824		LET'S TWIST AGAIN/		
		EVERYTHING'S GONNA BE ALL RIGHT	2.00	3.50
☐ 830		THE FLY/THAT'S THE WAY IT GOES	2.00	3.50
☐ 835		SLOW TWISTIN'/LA PALOMA TWIST	2.00	3.50
☐ 842		DANCIN' PARTY/		
		GOTTA GET MYSELF TOGETHER	2.00	3.50
☐ 849		LIMBO ROCK/POPEYE (THE HITCH-HIKER)	2.00	3.50
☐ 862		TWENTY MILES/LET'S LIMBO SOME MORE	2.00	3.50
☐ 873		BIRDLAND/BLACK CLOUD	1.75	3.00
☐ 879		TWIST IT UP/SURF PARTY	1.75	3.00
☐ 890		LODDY LO/HOOKA TOOKA	1.75	3.00
☐ 907		HEY BOBBA NEEDLE/SPREAD JOY	1.75	3.00
☐ 920		LAZY ELSIE MOLLY/ROSIE	1.75	3.00

CHUBBY CHECKER—ALBUMS

☐ 5001 (M)	*PARKWAY*	CHUBBY CHECKER	10.00	18.00
☐ 7001 (M)		TWIST WITH CHUBBY CHECKER	7.25	12.00
☐ 7002 (M)		FOR TWISTERS ONLY	7.25	12.00
☐ 7003 (M)		IT'S PONY TIME	7.25	12.00
☐ 7004 (M)		LET'S TWIST AGAIN	7.25	12.00
☐ 7007 (M)		YOUR TWIST PARTY	7.25	12.00
☐ 7008 (M)		TWISTIN' ROUND THE WORLD	7.25	12.00
☐ 7009 (M)		FOR TEEN TWISTERS ONLY	7.25	12.00
☐ 7011 (M)		DON'T KNOCK THE TWIST	7.25	12.00
☐ 7014 (M)		ALL THE HITS	7.25	12.00
☐ 7020 (S)		LIMBO PARTY	7.25	12.00
☐ 7022 (S)		BIGGEST HITS	7.25	12.00
☐ 7026 (S)		IN PERSON	7.25	12.00
☐ 7027 (S)		LET'S LIMBO SOME MORE	7.25	12.00
☐ 7030 (S)		BEACH PARTY	7.25	12.00
☐ 7040 (S)		CHUBBY'S FOLK ALBUM	7.25	12.00

ISSUE #	LABEL		PRICE RANGE	

CHER

☐ 66114	IMPERIAL	ALL I REALLY WANT TO DO/		
		I'M GONNA LOVE YOU	1.75	3.00
☐ 66136		WHERE DO YOU GO?/SEE SEE BLUES	1.75	3.00
☐ 66160		BANG BANG/OUR DAY WILL COME	1.75	3.00
☐ 66192		ALFIE/SHE'S NOT BETTER THAN ME	1.75	3.00
☐ 66217		BEHIND THE DOOR/MAGIC IN THE AIR	1.75	3.00
☐ 66223		DREAM BABY/MAMA		
		(WHEN MY DOLLIES HAVE BABIES)	1.75	3.00
☐ 66252		HEY JOE/OUR DAY WILL COME	1.75	3.00
☐ 66261		YOU BETTER SIT DOWN, KIDS/		
		ELUSIVE BUTTERFLY	1.75	3.00
☐ 66282		BUT I CAN'T LOVE YOU MORE/		
		CLICK SONG, NUMBER ONE	1.75	3.00
☐ 6658	ATCO	YOURS UNTIL TOMORROW/		
		THE THOUGHT OF LOVING YOU	1.50	2.50
☐ 6704		FOR WHAT IT'S WORTH/HANGIN' ON	1.50	2.50
☐ 6713		YOU MADE ME SO VERY HAPPY/		
		THE FIRST TIME	1.50	2.50
☐ 6793		SUPERSTAR/THE FIRST TIME	1.50	2.50

CHER—ALBUM

☐ 9292 (S)	IMPERIAL	ALL I REALLY WANT TO DO	7.25	12.00
☐ 12301 (S)		THE SONNY SIDE OF CHER	7.25	12.00
☐ 12320 (S)		CHER	7.25	12.00
☐ 12358 (S)		WITH LOVE	7.25	12.00
☐ 12373 (S)		BACKSTAGE	5.00	9.00
☐ 12406 (S)		GOLDEN GREATS	5.00	9.00

CHIFFONS

☐ 6003	BIG DEAL	TONIGHT'S THE NIGHT/DO YOU KNOW	7.25	12.00
☐ 20103	REPRISE	AFTER LAST NIGHT/DOCTOR OF HEARTS	4.00	7.00
☐ 3152	LAURIE	HE'S SO FINE/OH MY LOVER	2.00	3.50
☐ 3166		WHY AM I SO SHY/LUCKY ME	2.75	4.50
☐ 3179		ONE FINE DAY/WHY AM I SO SHY	2.00	3.50
☐ 3195		A LOVE SO FINE/ONLY MY FRIEND	2.00	3.50
☐ 3212		I HAVE A BOYFRIEND/		
		I'M GONNA DRY MY EYES	2.00	3.50
☐ 3224		TONIGHT I MET AN ANGEL/EASY TO LOVE	2.00	3.50
☐ 3262		SAILOR BOY/WHEN SUMMER IS THROUGH	2.00	3.50
☐ 3275		WHAT AM I GONNA DO WITH YOU, BABY/		
		STRANGE, STRANGE FEELING	2.00	3.50
☐ 3301		NOBODY KNOWS WHAT'S GOIN' ON/		
		THE REAL THING	2.00	3.50

ISSUE #	LABEL		PRICE RANGE	
☐ 3318		TONIGHT I'M GONNA DREAM/		
		HEAVENLY PLACE	2.00	3.50
☐ 3340		SWEET TALKIN' GUY/		
		DID YOU EVER GO STEADY	1.75	3.00
☐ 3350		OUT OF THIS WORLD/JUST A BOY	1.75	3.00
☐ 3357		STOP, LOOK, LISTEN/MARCH	1.75	3.00
☐ 3364		MY BOYFRIEND'S BACK/		
		I GOT PLENTY OF NUTTIN'	1.75	3.00
☐ 3377		KEEP THE BOY HAPPY/IF I KNEW THEN	1.75	3.00
☐ 3423		JUST FOR TONIGHT/TEACH ME HOW	1.75	3.00
☐ 3460		UP ON THE BRIDGE/MARCH	1.75	3.00
☐ 3497		LOVE ME LIKE YOU'RE GONNA LOSE ME/		
		THREE DIPS OF ICE CREAM	1.75	3.00
☐ 3630		MY SWEET LORD/MAIN NERVE	1.75	3.00
☐ 3648		DREAM, DREAM, DREAM/OH MY LOVER	1.75	3.00
☐ 558	*B. T. PUPPY*	MY SECRET LOVE/		
		STRANGE STRANGE FEELING	2.25	4.00
☐ 601	*WILD CAT*	NO MORE TOMORROWS/NEVER NEVER	2.25	4.00

CHIFFONS—ALBUMS

☐ 2018 (M)	*LAURIE*	HE'S SO FINE	12.00	20.00
☐ 2020 (M)		ONE FINE DAY	10.00	18.00
☐ 2036 (S)		SWEET TALKIN' GUY	10.00	18.00
☐ 1011 (S)	*B. T. PUPPY*	MY SECRET LOVE	8.50	12.00

LOU CHRISTIE

☐ 102	*C & C*	THE GYPSY CRIED/		
		RED SAILS IN THE SUNSET	20.00	35.00
☐ 4457	*ROULETTE*	THE GYPSY CRIED/		
		RED SAILS IN THE SUNSET	2.00	3.50
☐ 4481		TWO FACES HAVE I/		
		ALL THAT GLITTER ISN'T GOLD	2.00	3.50
☐ 4504		HOW MANY TEARDROPS?/YOU AND I	2.00	3.50
☐ 4527		SHY BOY/IT CAN HAPPEN	2.00	3.50
☐ 4545		STAY/THERE THEY GO	2.00	3.50
☐ 4554		WHEN YOU DANCE/		
		MAYBE YOU'LL BE THERE	2.00	3.50
☐ 13412	*MGM*	LIGHTNIN' STRIKES/		
		CRYIN' IN THE STREETS	1.75	3.00
☐ 13473		RHAPSODY IN THE RAIN/TRAPEZE	1.75	3.00
☐ 13533		PAINTER/DU RONDA	1.75	3.00
☐ 13576		IF MY CAR COULD ONLY TALK/		
		SONG OF LITA	1.75	3.00
☐ 13623		SINCE I DON'T HAVE YOU/		
		WILD LIFE'S IN SEASON	1.75	3.00

ISSUE #	LABEL		PRICE RANGE	
☐ 235	CO & CE	OUTSIDE THE GATES OF HEAVEN/		
		ALL THAT GLITTERS ISN'T GOLD	1.75	3.00
☐ 735	COLPIX	MERRY GO ROUND/GUITARS AND BONGOS	1.75	3.00
☐ 753		HAVE I SINNED?/POT OF GOLD	1.75	3.00
☐ 770		MAKE SUMMER LAST FOREVER/		
		WHY DID YOU DO IT, BABY?	1.75	3.00
☐ 778		A TEENAGER IN LOVE/BACKTRACK	1.75	3.00
☐ 799		BIG TIME/CRYIN' ON MY KNEES	1.75	3.00
☐ 44062	COLUMBIA	SHAKE HANDS AND WALK AWAY		
		CRYIN'/ESCAPE	1.75	3.00
☐ 44177		SELF EXPRESSION/		
		BACK TO THE DAYS OF THE ROMANS	1.75	3.00
☐ 44240		GINA/ESCAPE	1.75	3.00
☐ 44338		DON'T STOP ME/		
		BACK TO THE DAYS OF ROMANS	1.75	3.00

LOU CHRISTIE—ALBUMS

☐ 25208 (S)	ROULETTE	LOU CHRISTIE	10.00	25.00
☐ 25332 (S)		LOU CHRISTIE STRIKES AGAIN	8.00	22.50
☐ 4360 (S)		LIGHTNIN' STRIKES	7.00	18.00
☐ 4394 (S)		PAINTER OF HITS	7.00	18.00
☐ 1231 (S)		LOU CHRISTIE STRIKES BACK	7.00	18.00
☐ 4001 (S)		LOU CHRISTIE STRIKES AGAIN	7.00	18.00
☐ 5052 (S)	BUDDAH	I'M GONNA MAKE YOU MINE	5.00	13.50
☐ 5073 (S)		PAINT AMERICA LOVE	5.00	13.50
☐ 2000 (S)	THREE BROTHERS	LOU CHRISTIE	5.00	13.50

JIMMY CLANTON

☐ 537	ACE	I TRUSTED YOU/THAT'S YOU BABY	3.25	6.00
☐ 546		JUST A DREAM/YOU AIM TO PLEASE	2.25	4.00
☐ 551		A LETTER TO AN ANGEL/A PART OF ME	2.25	4.00
☐ 560		A SHIP ON A STORMY SEA/		
		MY LOVE IS STRONG	2.25	4.00
☐ 567		MY OWN TRUE LOVE/LITTLE BOY IN LOVE	2.25	4.00
☐ 575		GO JIMMY GO/I TRUSTED YOU	2.00	3.50
☐ 585		ANOTHER SLEEPLESS NIGHT/		
		I'M GONNA TRY	2.00	3.50
☐ 600		COME BACK/WAIT	2.00	3.50
☐ 607		WHAT AM I GONNA DO/IF I	2.00	3.50
☐ 616		DOWN THE AISLE/NO LONGER BLUE	2.00	3.50
☐ 622		I JUST WANNA MAKE LOVE/		
		DON'T LOOK AT ME	2.00	3.50

ISSUE #	LABEL		PRICE RANGE	
☐ 634		LUCKY IN LOVE WITH YOU/		
		NOT LIKE A BROTHER	2.00	3.50
☐ 641		TWIST ON LITTLE GIRL/WAYWARD LOVE	2.00	3.50
☐ 655		JUST A MOMENT/BECAUSE I DO	2.00	3.50
☐ 664		VENUS IN BLUE JEANS/HIGHWAY BOUND	3.50	6.00
☐ 668		HEART HOTEL/MANY DREAMS	2.00	3.50
☐ 8001		VENUS IN BLUE JEANS/HIGHWAY BOUND	2.00	3.50
☐ 8005		DARKEST STREET IN TOWN/		
		DREAMS OF A FOOL	2.00	3.50
☐ 8006		ENDLESS NIGHT/ANOTHER DAY,		
		ANOTHER HEARTACHE	2.00	3.50

JIMMY CLANTON—EPs

☐ 101 & 102	*ACE*	THINKING OF YOU	8.50	15.00
☐ 103		I'M ALWAYS CHASING RAINBOWS	8.50	15.00
☐ 642	*ACE*	TEENAGE MILLIONAIRE	7.25	12.00
☐ 10087	*TOP RANK*	JIMMY'S BIG FOUR	7.25	12.00

JIMMY CLANTON—ALBUMS

☐ 1001 (M)	*ACE*	JUST A DREAM	15.00	35.00
☐ 1007 (M)		JIMMY'S HAPPY	12.50	30.00
☐ 1008 (M)		JIMMY'S BLUE	12.50	30.00
☐ 1011 (M)		MY BEST TO YOU	12.50	30.00
☐ 1014 (M)		TEENAGE MILLIONAIRE	12.50	30.00
☐ 1026 (M)		VENUS IN BLUE JEANS	8.00	22.50
☐ 100 (M)	*PHILIPS*	JIMMY'S HAPPY/JIMMY'S BLUE	7.00	18.00
☐ 154 (S)		THE BEST OF JIMMY CLANTON	8.00	22.50

ERIC CLAPTON

☐ 6738	*ATCO*	TEASING/SOULING	1.75	4.00
☐ 15049	*POLYDOR*	EASY NOW/LET IT RAIN	1.75	4.00
☐ 15056		BELL BOTTOM BLUES/LITTLE WING	1.75	4.00
☐ 409	*RSO*	I SHOT THE SHERIFF/GIVE ME STRENGTH	1.50	3.00
☐ 500		I SHOT THE SHERIFF/GIVE ME STRENGTH	1.50	3.00
☐ 509		PRETTY BLUE EYES/		
		SWING LOW SWEET CHARIOT	1.50	3.00
☐ 513		KNOCKIN' ON HEAVEN'S DOOR/		
		SOMEONE LIKE YOU	1.50	3.00
☐ 861		ALL OUR PASTIMES/HELLO OLD FRIEND	1.50	3.00
☐ 868		HUNGRY/CARNIVAL	1.50	3.00
☐ 886		LAY DOWN SALLY/		
		NEXT TIME YOU SEE HER	1.50	3.00

ERIC CLAPTON—ALBUMS

☐ 1009 (S)	*RSO*	BACKLESS	12.50	42.00
☐ 035 (S)		SLOWHAND	12.50	42.00

ISSUE #	LABEL		PRICE RANGE	
☐ 3004 (S)		NO REASON TO CRY	3.75	10.00
☐ 3008 (S)		ERIC CLAPTON	5.00	15.00
☐ 3023 (S)		461 OCEAN BOULEVARD	2.75	9.00
☐ SO-877 (S)		RAINBOW CONCERT	2.75	9.00
☐ 4809 (S)		E. C. WAS HERE	2.75	9.00
☐ 803 (S)	*ATCO*	HISTORY OF ERIC CLAPTON	4.00	13.50

DAVE CLARK FIVE

☐ 212	*CONGRESS*	I KNEW IT ALL THE TIME/		
		THAT'S WHAT I SAID	3.50	6.00
☐ 5078	*RUST*	I WALK THE LINE/FIRST LOVE	4.50	9.00
☐ 3188	*LAURIE*	I WALK THE LINE/FIRST LOVE	4.50	9.00
☐ 5476	*JUBILEE*	CHAQUITA/IN YOUR HEART	4.00	7.00
☐ 9656	*EPIC*	GLAD ALL OVER/I KNOW YOU	2.00	3.50
☐ 9671		BITS AND PIECES/ALL OF THE TIME	2.00	3.50
☐ 9678		DO YOU LOVE ME/CHAQUITA	2.00	3.50
☐ 9692		CAN'T YOU SEE THAT SHE'S MINE/		
		NO TIME TO LOSE	2.00	3.50
☐ 9704		BECAUSE/THEME WITHOUT A NAME	2.00	3.50
☐ 9722		EVERYBODY KNOWS/OL' SOL	2.00	3.50
☐ 9739		ANY WAY YOU WANT IT/		
		CRYING OVER YOU	2.00	3.50
☐ 9763		COME HOME/YOUR TURN TO CRY	2.00	3.50
☐ 9786		REELIN' AND ROCKIN'/I'M THINKING	2.00	3.50
☐ 9811		I LIKE IT LIKE THAT/HURTIN' INSIDE	2.00	3.50
☐ 9833		CATCH US IF YOU CAN/ON THE MOVE	2.00	3.50
☐ 9863		OVER AND OVER/		
		I'LL BE YOURS (MY LOVE)	2.00	3.50
☐ 9882		AT THE SCENE/I MISS YOU	2.00	3.50
☐ 10004		TRY TOO HARD/ALL NIGHT LONG	2.00	3.50
☐ 10031		PLEASE TELL ME WHY/		
		LOOK BEFORE YOU LEAP	2.00	3.50
☐ 10053		SATISFIED WITH YOU/		
		DON'T LET ME DOWN	2.00	3.50
☐ 10076		NINETEEN DAYS/SITTING HERE BABY	2.00	3.50
☐ 10114		I'VE GOT TO HAVE A REASON/		
		GOOD TIME BABY	2.00	3.50
☐ 10144		YOU GOT WHAT IT TAKES/		
		DOCTOR RHYTHM	1.75	3.00

DAVE CLARK FIVE—ALBUMS

☐ 24093 (M)		GLAD ALL OVER	7.00	18.00
☐ 24104 (M)		THE DAVE CLARK FIVE RETURN	6.00	15.00
☐ 24117 (M)		AMERICAN TOUR	6.00	15.00
☐ 24128 (M)		COAST TO COAST	6.00	15.00

ISSUE #	LABEL		PRICE RANGE	
☐ 24139 (M)		WEEKEND IN LONDON	6.00	15.00
☐ 24162 (M)		HAVING A WILD WEEKEND	6.00	15.00
☐ 24178 (M)		I LIKE IT LIKE THAT	6.00	15.00
☐ 24185 (M)		DAVE CLARK FIVE'S GREATEST HITS	6.00	15.00
☐ 26198 (S)		TRY TOO HARD	5.00	13.50
☐ 26212 (S)		SATISFIED WITH YOU	5.00	13.50
☐ 26221 (S)		MORE GREATEST HITS	5.00	13.50
☐ 26236 (S)		5 X 5	5.00	13.50
☐ 26312 (S)		YOU GOT WHAT IT TAKES	5.00	13.50
☐ 26354 (S)		EVERYBODY KNOWS	5.00	13.50

PETULA CLARK

ISSUE #	LABEL		PRICE RANGE	
☐ 12049	**MGM**	THE PENDULUM SONG/ ROMANCE IN ROME	4.00	7.00
☐ 9142	**EPIC**	THERE IS NO CURE FOR L'AMOUR/ HOTTER 'N A PISTOL	4.00	7.00
☐ 10504	**LONDON**	WITH ALL MY LOVE/MY FRIEND THE SEA	2.75	4.50
☐ 10510		I'M COUNTING ON YOU/ SOME OTHER WORLD	2.75	4.50
☐ 10516		WHISTLIN' FOR THE MOON/TENDER LOVE	2.75	4.50
☐ 652	**WARWICK**	ROMEO/ISN'T THIS A LOVELY DAY	2.75	4.50
☐ 5582	**IMPERIAL**	BABY LOVER/EVER BEEN IN LOVE?	2.25	4.00
☐ 5655		WHERE ARE YOU (NOW THAT I NEED YOU?)/I LOVE A VIOLIN	2.25	4.00
☐ 3143	**LAURIE**	THE ROAD/JUMBLE SALE	2.75	4.50
☐ 3156		I WILL FOLLOW HIM/DARLING CHERI	2.00	3.50
☐ 3316		IN LOVE/DARLING CHERI	2.00	3.50
☐ 5494	**WARNER BROTHERS**	DOWNTOWN/YOU'D BETTER LOVE ME	1.75	3.00
☐ 5612		I KNOW A PLACE/JACK AND JOHN	1.75	3.00
☐ 5643		YOU'D BETTER COME HOME/HEART	1.75	3.00
☐ 5661		ROUND EVERY CORNER/TWO RIVERS	1.75	3.00
☐ 5684		MY LOVE/WHERE AM I GOING?	1.75	3.00
☐ 5802		A SIGN OF THE TIMES/TIME FOR LOVE	1.75	3.00
☐ 5835		I COULDN'T LIVE WITHOUT YOUR LOVE/ YOUR WAY OF LIFE	1.75	3.00
☐ 5863		WHO AM I/LOVE IS A LONG JOURNEY	1.75	3.00
☐ 5882		COLOR MY WORLD/TAKE ME HOME AGAIN . . .	1.75	3.00
☐ 7002		THIS IS MY SONG/HIGH	1.75	3.00
☐ 7049		DON'T SLEEP IN THE SUBWAY/ HERE COMES THE MORNING	1.75	3.00
☐ 7073		THE CAT IN THE WINDOW/ FANCY DANCIN' MAN	1.75	3.00
☐ 7097		THE OTHER MAN'S GRASS IS ALWAYS GREENER/ AT THE CROSSROADS	1.75	3.00

ISSUE #	LABEL		PRICE RANGE	
☐ 7216		DON'T GIVE UP/		
		EVERYTIME I SEE A RAINBOW	1.75	3.00
☐ 7244		AMERICAN BOYS/LOOK TO THE SKY	1.75	3.00
☐ 7275		HAPPY HEART/LOVE IS THE ONLY THING	1.75	3.00

PETULA CLARK—ALBUMS

☐ 2032 (S)	*LAURIE*	IN LOVE!	8.00	22.50
☐ 2043 (S)		PETULA CLARK SINGS FOR EVERYBODY	6.00	15.00
☐ 12027 (S)		PET CLARK	6.00	15.00
☐ 12281 (S)		UPTOWN WITH PET CLARK	7.00	18.00
☐ 1590 (M)	*WARNER BROTHERS*	DOWNTOWN	5.00	13.50
☐ 1590 (S)		DOWNTOWN	6.00	15.00
☐ 1598 (S)		I KNOW A PLACE	6.00	15.00
☐ 1608 (S)		THE WORLD'S GREATEST INTERNATIONAL		
		HITS	6.00	15.00
☐ 1630 (S)		MY LOVE	5.00	13.50
☐ 1645 (S)		I COULDN'T LIVE WITHOUT YOUR LOVE	5.00	13.50
☐ 1673 (S)		COLOR MY WORLD/WHO AM I?	5.00	13.50
☐ 1698 (S)		THESE ARE MY SONGS	5.00	13.50
☐ 1719 (S)		THE OTHER MAN'S GRASS		
		IS ALWAYS GREENER	5.00	13.50
☐ 1743 (S)		PETULA	4.00	10.00
☐ 1765 (S)		PETULA CLARK'S GREATEST HITS, VOL. I	4.00	10.00
☐ 1789 (S)		PORTRAIT OF PETULA	4.00	10.00
☐ 1823 (S)		JUST PET	4.00	10.00
☐ 1862 (S)		MEMPHIS	4.00	10.00
☐ 1885 (S)		WARM AND TENDER	4.00	10.00

CLEFTONES

☐ 1000	*GEE*	YOU BABY YOU/I WAS DREAMING	5.00	9.50
☐ 1011		LITTLE GIRL OF MINE/		
		YOU'RE DRIVING ME MAD	4.50	9.00
☐ 1016		CAN'T WE BE SWEETHEARTS?/		
		NIKI-HOKEY	4.00	7.00
☐ 1025		STRING AROUND MY HEART/		
		HAPPY MEMORIES	4.00	7.00
☐ 1031		I LIKE YOUR STYLE OF MAKING LOVE/		
		WHY DO YOU DO ME LIKE YOU DO?	4.00	7.00
☐ 1038		SEE YOU NEXT YEAR/TEN PAIRS OF SHOES ...	3.50	6.00
☐ 1041		HEY BABE/		
		WHAT DID I DO THAT WAS WRONG?	3.50	6.00
☐ 1048		LOVER BOY/BEGINNERS AT LOVE	3.50	6.00
☐ 1064		HEART AND SOUL/HOW DO YOU FEEL	2.25	4.00
☐ 1067		FOR SENTIMENTAL REASONS/DEED I DO	2.25	4.00

ISSUE #	LABEL		PRICE RANGE	
☐ 1074		EARTH ANGEL/BLUES IN THE NIGHT	2.25	4.00
☐ 1077		DO YOU/AGAIN	2.25	4.00
☐ 1079		LOVER COME BACK TO ME/		
		THERE SHE GOES	2.25	4.00
☐ 1080		HOW DEEP IS THE OCEAN/		
		SOME KIND OF BLUE	2.25	4.00

CLEFTONES—ALBUMS

☐ 705 (S)	*GEE*	HEART AND SOUL	15.00	35.00
☐ 707 (S)		FOR SENTIMENTAL REASONS	17.50	45.00

COASTERS

☐ 6064	*ATCO*	DOWN IN MEXICO/TURTLE DOVIN'	8.50	15.00
☐ 6073		ONE KISS LED TO ANOTHER/BRAZIL	7.25	12.00
☐ 6087		SEARCHIN'/YOUNG BLOOD	3.50	6.00
☐ 6087		SEARCHIN'/YOUNG BLOOD	2.25	4.00
☐ 6098		IDOL WITH THE GOLDEN HEAD/		
		MY BABY COMES TO ME	2.25	4.00
☐ 6104		SWEET GEORGIA BROWN/ WHAT'S		
		THE SECRET OF YOUR SUCCESS	2.25	4.00
☐ 6111		GEE GOLLY/DANCE	7.25	12.00
☐ 6116		YAKETY YAK/ZING! WENT THE		
		STRINGS OF MY HEART	2.25	4.00
☐ 6126		THE SHADOW KNOWS/		
		SORRY BUT I'M GONNA HAVE TO PASS	3.50	6.00
☐ 6132		CHARLIE BROWN/THREE COOL CATS	2.25	4.00
☐ 6141		ALONG CAME JONES/		
		THAT IS ROCK 'N' ROLL	2.25	4.00
☐ 6146		POISON IVY/I'M A HOG FOR YOU	2.25	4.00
☐ 6153		RUN RED RUN/WHAT ABOUT US	2.00	3.50
☐ 6163		BESAME MUCHO (PT. 1)/(PT. 2)	2.00	3.50
☐ 6168		WAKE ME, SHAKE ME/STEWBALL	2.00	3.50
☐ 6178		SHOPPIN' FOR CLOTHES/		
		SNAKE AND THE BOOKWORM	2.00	3.50
☐ 6186		WAIT A MINUTE/THUMBIN' A RIDE	2.00	3.50
☐ 6192		LITTLE EGYPT/KEEP ON ROLLING	2.00	3.50
☐ 6204		GIRLS, GIRLS, GIRLS (PT. 1)/(PT. 2)	2.00	3.50

COASTERS—EPs

☐ 4501	*ATCO*	ROCK AND ROLL WITH THE COASTERS	7.25	12.00
☐ 4502		KEEP ROCKIN' WITH THE COASTERS	7.25	12.00
☐ 4506		THE COASTERS	7.25	12.00
☐ 4507		TOP HITS	7.25	12.00

COASTERS—ALBUMS

☐ 101 (M)	*ATCO*	THE COASTERS	15.00	35.00

EDDIE COCHRAN

ISSUE #	LABEL		PRICE RANGE	
☐ 111 (M)		THE COASTERS' GREATEST HITS	12.50	30.00
☐ 123 (S)		ONE BY ONE	15.00	35.00
☐ 135 (S)		COAST ALONG WITH THE COASTERS	15.00	35.00

EDDIE COCHRAN

☐ 1026	CREST	SKINNY JIM/HALF LOVED	42.00	72.00
☐ 55056	LIBERTY	SITTIN' IN THE BALCONY/ DARK LONELY STREET	3.50	6.00
☐ 55070		MEAN WHEN I'M MAD/ONE KISS	4.50	9.00
☐ 55087		DRIVE-IN SHOW/AM I BLUE	4.00	7.00
☐ 55112		TWENTY FLIGHT ROCK/CRADLE BABY	4.00	7.00
☐ 55123		JEANNIE JEANNIE JEANNIE/ POCKETFUL OF HEARTACHES	4.00	7.00
☐ 55138		PRETTY GIRL/THERESA	4.00	7.00
☐ 55144		SUMMERTIME BLUES/LOVE AGAIN	2.25	4.00
☐ 55166		C'MON EVERYBODY/ DON'T EVER LET ME GO	2.25	4.00
☐ 55177		TEENAGE HEAVEN/I REMEMBER	3.50	6.00
☐ 55203		SOMETHIN' ELSE/BOLL WEEVIL SONG	2.75	4.50
☐ 55217		HALLELUJAH, I LOVE HER SO/ LITTLE ANGEL	4.00	7.00
☐ 55242		THREE STEPS TO HEAVEN/ CUT ACROSS SHORTY	4.00	7.00
☐ 55278		SWEETIE PIE/LONELY	3.50	6.00
☐ 55389		WEEKEND/LONELY	3.50	6.00

EDDIE COCHRAN—EPs

☐ 3061	LIBERTY	SINGIN' TO MY BABY, (PT. 1)	12.00	20.00
☐ 3061		SINGIN' TO MY BABY, (PT. 2)	12.00	20.00
☐ 3061		SINGIN' TO MY BABY, (PT. 3)	12.00	20.00

EDDIE COCHRAN—ABLUMS

☐ 3061 (M)	LIBERTY	SINGIN' TO MY BABY	35.00	90.00
☐ 3172 (M)		EDDIE COCHRAN	30.00	75.00
☐ 3220 (M)		NEVER TO BE FORGOTTEN	20.00	50.00
☐ 1123 (M)	SUNSET	SUMMERTIME BLUES	7.00	18.00

BOBBY COMSTOCK

☐ 602	TRIUMPH	JEALOUS FOOL/ZIG ZAG	3.50	6.00
☐ 349	BLAZE	TENNESSEE WALTZ/SWEET TALK	2.25	4.00
☐ 2051	ATLANTIC	JAMBALAYA/LET'S TALK IT OVER	2.00	3.50
☐ 124	MOHAWK	WAYWARD WIND/EVERYDAY BLUES	2.00	3.50
☐ 25000	FESTIVAL	GARDEN OF EDEN/A PIECE OF PAPER	2.00	3.50
☐ 5392	JUBILEE	BONY MARONIE/DO THAT LITTLE THING	2.00	3.50
☐ 5396		JEZEBEL/YOUR BIG BROWN EYES	2.00	3.50

ISSUE #	LABEL		PRICE RANGE	
☐ 202	*LAWN*	LET'S STOMP/I WANT TO DO IT	2.00	3.50
☐ 210		SUSIE BABY/TAKE A WALK	2.00	3.50
☐ 219		YOUR BOYFRIEND'S BACK/		
		THIS LITTLE LOVE OF MINE	2.00	3.50
☐ 224		I CAN'T HELP MYSELF/RUN MY HEART	2.00	3.50
☐ 229		THE BEATLE BOUNCE/		
		SINCE YOU'VE BEEN GONE	2.00	3.50
☐ 232		AIN'T THAT JUST LIKE ME/		
		CAN IT BE TRUE?	2.00	3.50
☐ 2164	*ASCOT*	RIGHT HAND MAN/ALWAYS	2.00	3.50
☐ 2175		I'M A MAN/I'LL MAKE YOU GLAD	2.00	3.50
☐ 2193		SHOT GUN SALLY/THIS MAGIC MOMENT	2.00	3.50
☐ 2216		OUT OF SIGHT/CAN'T JUDGE A BOOK	2.00	3.50

BOBBY COMSTOCK—ALBUMS

1000 (M)	*BLAZE*	ROCKIN' WITH BOBBY	12.50	30.00
16026 (S)	*ASCOT*	OUT OF SIGHT	8.00	22.50

SAM COOKE

☐ 596	*SPECIALTY*	LOVEABLE/FOREVER	3.50	6.00
☐ 619		I'LL COME RUNNING BACK TO YOU/		
		FOREVER	3.50	6.00
☐ 627		THAT'S ALL I NEED TO KNOW/		
		I DON'T WANT TO CRY	2.75	4.50
☐ 667		HAPPY IN LOVE/I NEED YOU NOW	2.75	4.50
☐ 4002	*KEEN*	FOR SENTIMENTAL REASONS/DESIRE ME	2.75	4.50
☐ 4009		LONELY ISLAND/YOU WERE MADE FOR ME . . .	2.75	4.50
☐ 4013		YOU SEND ME/SUMMERTIME	2.75	4.50
☐ 2003		FOR SENTIMENTAL REASONS/DESIRE ME	2.25	4.00
☐ 2005		ALL OF MY LIFE/STEALING KISSES	2.25	4.00
☐ 2006		WIN YOUR LOVE FOR ME/		
		LOVE SONG FROM "HOUSEBOAT"	2.25	4.00
☐ 2008		LOVE YOU MOST OF ALL/BLUE MOON	2.25	4.00
☐ 2018		EVERYBODY LIKES TO CHA-CHA-CHA/		
		LITTLE THINGS YOU DO	2.25	4.00
☐ 2022		ONLY SIXTEEN/LET'S GO STEADY AGAIN	2.25	4.00
☐ 2101		SUMMERTIME (PT. 1)/(PT. 2)	2.25	4.00
☐ 2105		THERE, I'VE SAID IT AGAIN/ONE HOUR		
		AHEAD OF THE POSSE	2.25	4.00
☐ 2111		NO ONE/IT AIN'T NOBODY'S BIZNESS	2.25	4.00
☐ 2112		WONDERFUL WORLD/		
		ALONG THE NAVAJO TRAIL	2.25	4.00
☐ 2117		WITH YOU/I THANK GOD	2.25	4.00
☐ 2118		STEAL AWAY/SO GLAMOROUS	2.25	4.00
☐ 2122		MARY, MARY LOU/EE-YI-EE-YI-OH	2.25	4.00

ISSUE #	LABEL		PRICE RANGE	
☐ 7701	*RCA*	TEENAGE SONATA/		
		IF YOU WERE THE ONLY GIRL	2.00	3.50
☐ 7730		YOU UNDERSTAND ME/		
		I BELONG TO YOUR HEART	2.00	3.50
☐ 7783		CHAIN GANG/I FALL IN LOVE EVERY DAY	2.00	3.50
☐ 7816		SAD MOOD/LOVE ME	2.00	3.50
☐ 7853		THAT'S IT, I QUIT, I'M MOVIN' ON/		
		DO WHAT YOU SAY	2.00	3.50
☐ 7883		CUPID/FAREWELL, MY DARLING	2.00	3.50
☐ 7927		FEEL IT/IT'S ALL RIGHT	2.00	3.50
☐ 7983		TWISTIN' THE NIGHT AWAY/		
		ONE MORE TIME	2.00	3.50
☐ 8036		BRING IT ON HOME TO ME/		
		HAVING A PARTY	2.00	3.50
☐ 8088		NOTHING CAN CHANGE THIS LOVE/		
		SOMEBODY HAVE MERCY	2.00	3.50
☐ 8129		SEND ME SOME LOVIN'/		
		BABY, BABY, BABY	2.00	3.50
☐ 8164		ANOTHER SATURDAY NIGHT/		
		LOVE WILL FIND A WAY	2.00	3.50
☐ 8215		FRANKIE AND JOHNNY/COOL TRAIN	2.00	3.50
☐ 8247		LITTLE RED ROOSTER/		
		YOU'VE GOTTA MOVE	2.00	3.50
☐ 8299		GOOD NEWS/BASIN STREET BLUES	2.00	3.50
☐ 8368		GOOD TIMES/TENNESSEE WALTZ	2.00	3.50

SAM COOKE—EPs

☐ 2001-3	*KEEN*	SAM COOKE	4.50	9.00
☐ 2006		ENCORE, VOL. I . . . . :	4.50	9.00
☐ 2007		ENCORE, VOL. II	4.50	9.00
☐ 2008		ENCORE, VOL. III	4.50	9.00
☐ 2012		TRIBUTE TO THE LADY, VOL. I	4.00	7.00
☐ 2013		TRIBUTE TO THE LADY, VOL. II	4.00	7.00
☐ 2014		TRIBUTE TO THE LADY, VOL. III	4.00	7.00
☐ 4372	*RCA*	ANOTHER SATURDAY NIGHT	4.00	7.00

SAM COOKE—ALBUMS

☐ 2001 (M)	*KEEN*	SAM COOKE	10.00	20.00
☐ 2003 (M)		ENCORE	8.50	15.00
☐ 2004 (M)		TRIBUTE TO THE LADY	8.50	15.00
☐ 86101 (M)		HIT KIT	8.50	15.00
☐ 86103 (M)		I THANK GOD	8.50	15.00
☐ 86106 (M)		WONDERFUL WORLD OF SAM COOKE	10.00	20.00
☐ 502 (M)	*FAMOUS*	SAM'S SONGS	7.25	12.00
☐ 505 (M)		ONLY SIXTEEN	7.25	12.00
☐ 508 (M)		SO WONDERFUL	7.25	12.00

ISSUE #	LABEL		PRICE RANGE	
☐ 512 (M)		CHA-CHA-CHA	7.25	12.00
☐ 2221 (M)	*RCA*	COOKE'S TOUR	8.50	15.00
☐ 2236 (M)		HITS OF THE 50'S	8.50	15.00
☐ 2293 (M)		SWING LOW	8.50	18.00
☐ 2392 (M)		MY KIND OF BLUES	7.00	18.00
☐ 2555 (M)		TWISTIN' THE NIGHT AWAY	6.00	15.00
☐ 2625 (M)		THE BEST OF SAM COOKE	6.00	15.00
☐ 2673 (M)		MR. SOUL	6.00	15.00
☐ 2709 (M)		NIGHT BEAT	6.00	15.00
☐ 2899 (M)		AIN'T THAT GOOD NEWS	6.00	15.00
☐ 2970 (M)		AT THE COPA	6.00	15.00
☐ 3367 (M)		SHAKE	6.00	15.00
☐ 3373 (M)		BEST OF SAM COOKE, VOL. II	6.00	15.00
☐ 3435 (M)		TRY A LITTLE LOVE	6.00	15.00
☐ 3517 (M)		UNFORGETTABLE SAM COOKE	6.00	15.00
☐ 3991 (M)		THE MAN WHO INVENTED SOUL	6.00	15.00
☐ 2110 (M)				
	SPECIALTY	TWO SIDES OF SAM COOKE	6.00	15.00
☐ 105 (M)	*SAR*	SOUL STIRRERS FEATURING SAM COOKE	6.00	15.00

RITA COOLIDGE

☐ 442	*PEPPER*	SECRET PLACES/RAINBOW CHILD	2.00	4.00
☐ 443		WALKIN' IN THE MORNIN'/		
		TURN AROUND & LOVE YOU	2.00	4.00
☐ 1256	*A&M*	MUD ISLAND/I BELIEVE IN YOU	1.50	2.50
☐ 1271		MOUNTAINS/CRAZY LOVE	1.50	2.50
☐ 1324		LAY MY BURDEN DOWN/NICE FEELIN'	1.50	2.50

ALICE COOPER

☐ 101	*STRAIGHT*	REFLECTED/LIVING	10.00	20.00
☐ 7141	*WARNER*			
	BROTHERS	EIGHTEEN/CAUGHT IN A DREAM	2.75	4.50
☐ 7398		RETURN OF THE SPIDERS/		
		SHOE SALESMAN	2.25	4.00
☐ 7449		EIGHTEEN/BODY	1.75	3.00
☐ 7490		CAUGHT IN A DREAM/		
		HALLOWED BE THY NAME	1.75	3.00
☐ 7529		UNDER MY WHEELS/DESPERADO	1.75	3.00
☐ 7568		BE MY LOVER/YEAH, YEAH, YEAH	1.75	3.00
☐ 7596		SCHOOL'S OUT/GUTTER CAT	1.50	2.50
☐ 7631		ELECTED/LUNEY TUNE	1.50	2.50
☐ 7673		HELLO HURRAY/GENERATION LANDSLIDE	1.50	2.50
☐ 7691		NO MORE MR. NICE GUY/		
		RAPED AND FREEZIN'	1.50	2.50

ISSUE #	LABEL		PRICE RANGE	
☐7724		BILLION DOLLAR BABIES/MARY ANN	1.50	2.50
☐7762		TEENAGE LAMENT '74/		
		HARD HEARTED ALICE	1.50	2.50
☐7783		MUSCLE OF LOVE/CRAZY LITTLE CHILD	1.75	3.00

ALICE COOPER—ALBUMS

☐1845 (S)	**STRAIGHT**	EASY ACTION	15.00	35.00
☐1051 (S)		PRETTIES FOR YOU	8.00	22.50
☐1883 (S)	**WARNER**			
	BROTHERS	LOVE IT TO DEATH...........	4.50	12.00
☐2567 (S)		KILLER	4.50	12.00
☐2623 (S)		SCHOOL'S OUT	4.00	10.00
☐2685 (S)		BILLION DOLLAR BABIES	4.00	10.00
☐2748 (S)		MUSCLE OF LOVE	4.00	10.00
☐2803 (S)		ALICE COOPER'S GREATEST HITS	4.00	10.00

CREAM

☐591-007	**POLYDOR**	WRAPPING PAPER/CAT'S SQUIRREL	4.50	9.00
☐6462	**ATCO**	I FEEL FREE/N.S.U.	2.25	4.00
☐6488		STRANGE BREW/		
		TALES OF BRAVE ULYSSES	2.25	4.00
☐6522		SPOONFUL (PT. 1)/(PT. 2)	2.25	4.00
☐6544		SUNSHINE OF YOUR LOVE/S.W.L.A.B.R....	1.75	3.00
☐6575		ANYONE FOR TENNIS?/		
		PRESSED RAT AND WARTHOG	1.75	3.00
☐6617		WHITE ROOM/THOSE WERE THE DAYS	1.75	3.00
☐6646		CROSSROADS/PASSING THE TIME........	1.75	3.00
☐6668		BADGE/WHAT A BRINGDOWN	1.75	3.00
☐6708		SWEET WINE/LAWDY MAMA	1.75	3.00

CREAM—ALBUMS

☐206 (S)	**ATCO**	FRESH CREAM	4.50	12.00
☐232 (S)		DISRAELI GEARS	4.50	12.00
☐700 (S)		WHEELS OF FIRE	4.50	12.00
☐7001 (S)		GOODBYE CREAM	4.50	12.00

CREEDENCE CLEARWATER REVIVAL

☐412	**SCORPIO**	PORTERVILLE/CALL IT PRETENDING	12.00	20.00
☐616	**FANTASY**	SUSIE Q (PT. 1)/(PT. 2)	2.00	3.50
☐617		I PUT A SPELL ON YOU/		
		WALK ON THE WATER	1.75	3.00
☐619		PROUD MARY/BORN ON THE BAYOU ...: ...	1.75	3.00
☐622		BAD MOON RISING/LODI	1.75	3.00
☐625		GREEN RIVER/COMMOTION	1.75	3.00
☐634		DOWN ON THE CORNER/FORTUNATE SON	1.75	3.00

ISSUE #	LABEL		PRICE RANGE	
☐637		TRAVELIN' BAND/		
		WHO'LL STOP THE RAIN?	1.75	3.00
☐641		UP AROUND THE BEND/		
		RUN THROUGH THE JUNGLE	1.75	3.00
☐645		LOOKIN' OUT MY BACK DOOR/		
		LONG AS I CAN SEE THE LIGHT	1.75	3.00
☐655		HAVE YOU EVER SEEN THE RAIN?/		
		HEY TONIGHT	1.75	3.00
☐665		SWEET HITCH-HIKER/DOOR TO DOOR	1.75	3.00
☐676		SOMEDAY NEVER COMES/		
		TEARIN' UP THE COUNTRY	1.75	3.00

CREEDENCE CLEARWATER REVIVAL—ALBUMS

☐8382 (S)	*FANTASY*	CREEDENCE CLEARWATER REVIVAL	5.00	13.50
☐8387 (S)		BAYOU COUNTRY	4.50	12.00
☐8393 (S)		GREEN RIVER	4.50	12.00
☐8397 (S)		WILLY AND THE POOR BOYS	4.50	12.00
☐8402 (S)		COSMO'S FACTORY	4.50	12.00
☐8410 (S)		PENDULUM	4.50	12.00
☐9404 (S)		MARDI GRAS	4.50	12.00
☐9418 (S)		CREEDENCE GOLD	4.00	10.00
☐9430 (S)		MORE CREEDENCE GOLD	4.00	10.00

CRESTS

☐103	*JOYCE*	SWEETEST ONE/MY JUANITA	18.00	30.00
☐105		NO ONE TO LOVE/WISH SHE WAS MINE	24.00	40.00
☐501	*COED*	SWEET LITTLE ANGEL/I THANK THE MOON	15.00	20.00
☐506		SIXTEEN CANDLES/BESIDE YOU	2.25	4.00
☐509		SIX NIGHTS A WEEK/I DO	2.25	4.00
☐511		FLOWER OF LOVE/MOLLY MAE	2.25	4.00
☐515		THE ANGELS LISTENED IN/		
		I THANK THE MOON	2.25	4.00
☐521		A YEAR AGO TONIGHT/PAPER CROWN	2.25	4.00
☐525		STEP BY STEP/GEE	2.25	4.00
☐531		TROUBLE IN PARADISE/ALWAYS YOU	2.25	4.00
☐535		JOURNEY OF LOVE/		
		IF MY HEART COULD WRITE A LETTER	2.25	4.00
☐537		ISN'T IT AMAZING/MOLLY ME	2.25	4.00
☐543		IN THE STILL OF THE NIGHT/		
		GOOD GOLLY MISS MOLLY	2.25	4.00
☐561		LITTLE MIRACLES/BABY I GOTTA KNOW	2.25	4.00
☐696	*TRANS ATLAS*	THE ACTOR/THREE TEARS IN A BUCKET	2.25	4.00
☐311	*SELMA*	GUILTY/NUMBER ONE WITH ME	2.25	4.00
☐400		TEARS WILL FALL/DID I REMEMBER	2.25	4.00
☐987	*PARKWAY*	TRY ME/HEARTBURN	2.25	4.00

ISSUE #	LABEL		PRICE RANGE	
☐ 999		I CARE ABOUT YOU/COME SEE ME	2.25	4.00
☐ 118		MY TIME/IS IT YOU?	2.25	4.00
☐ 2	*TIMES SQUARE*	NO ONE TO LOVE/WISH SHE WAS MINE	2.75	4.50
☐ 6		BABY/I LOVE YOU SO	2.75	4.50
☐ 97		BABY/I LOVE YOU SO	2.25	4.00
☐ 12112	*SCEPTER*	I'M STEPPING OUT OF THE PICTURE/ AFRAID OF LOVE	2.25	4.00
☐ 62403	*CORAL*	YOU BLEW OUT THE CANDLES/ A LOVE TO LAST A LIFETIME	2.75	4.50
☐ 256	*CAMEO*	I'LL BE TRUE/OVER THE WEEKEND	2.25	4.00
☐ 305		LEAN ON ME/MAKE UP MY MIND	2.25	4.00

CRESTS—EP

☐ 101	*COED*	THE ANGELS LISTENED IN	18.00	30.00

CRESTS—ALBUMS

☐ 901 (M)	*COED*	THE CRESTS SING ALL BIGGIES	30.00	75.00
☐ 904 (S)		THE BEST OF THE CRESTS	50.00	120.00

CREW CUTS

☐ 70341	*MERCURY*	CRAZY 'BOUT YOU, BABY/ANGELA MIA	2.25	4.00
☐ 70404		SH BOOM/I SPOKE TOO SOON	2.25	4.00
☐ 70443		OOP SHOOP/DO ME GOOD BABY	2.25	4.00
☐ 70490		ALL I WANNA DO/THE BARKING DOG	2.25	4.00
☐ 70491		DANCE MR. SNOWMAN DANCE/ TWINKLE TOES	2.25	4.00
☐ 70494		THE WHIFFENPOOF SONG/VARSITY DRAG	2.25	4.00
☐ 70527		EARTH ANGEL/KO KO MO	2.00	3.50
☐ 70597		DON'T BE ANGRY/CHOP CHOP BOOM	2.00	3.50
☐ 70598		UNCHAINED MELODY/ TWO HEARTS, TWO KISSES	2.00	3.50
☐ 70634		A STORY UNTOLD/CARMEN'S BOOGIE	2.00	3.50
☐ 70668		GUM DROP/SONG OF THE FOOL	2.00	3.50
☐ 70668		GUM DROP/PRESENT ARMS	2.00	3.50
☐ 70710		SLAM BAM/ARE YOU HAVING ANY FUN?	2.00	3.50
☐ 70741		ANGELS IN THE SKY/MOSTLY MARTHA	1.75	3.00
☐ 70782		SEVEN DAYS/THAT'S YOUR MISTAKE	1.75	3.00
☐ 70840		OUT OF THE PICTURE/HONEY HAIR, SUGAR LIPS, EYES OF BLUE	1.75	3.00

CREW CUTS—EPs

☐ 13261	*MERCURY*	CRAZY 'BOUT YOU BABY	5.00	10.00
☐ 13274		THREE CHEERS FOR THE CREW CUTS	5.00	10.00
☐ 13275		THREE CHEERS FOR THE CREW CUTS	5.00	10.00
☐ 13290		TOPS IN POPS	5.00	10.00
☐ 13325		THE CREW CUTS GO LONGHAIR	4.50	9.00

ISSUE #	LABEL		PRICE RANGE	
☐ 13326		LONGHAIR SWING WITH THE CREW CUTS	4.50	9.00
☐ 13327		SWING THE MASTERS	4.50	9.00

CREW CUTS—ALBUMS

☐ 20067 (M)				
	MERCURY	THE CREW CUTS GO LONGHAIR	8.00	22.50
☐ 20140 (M)		ON THE CAMPUS	8.00	22.50
☐ 20143 (M)		CREW CUT CAPERS	8.00	22.50
☐ 21044 (M)		ROCK AND ROLL BASH	8.00	22.50
☐ 20199 (M)		MUSIC ALA CARTE	7.00	18.00

CRICKETS

☐ 55009	*BRUNSWICK*	THAT'LL BE THE DAY/		
		I'M LOOKING FOR SOMEONE TO LOVE......	4.50	9.00
☐ 55035		OH BOY!/NOT FADE AWAY	4.50	9.00
☐ 55053		MAYBE BABY/TELL ME HOW	4.50	9.00
☐ 55072		THINK IT OVER/FOOL'S PARADISE	4.50	9.00
☐ 55094		IT'S SO EASY/LONESOME TEARS	7.25	12.00

CRICKETS—EPs

☐ 71036	*BRUNSWICK*	THE "CHIRPING" CRICKETS	25.00	40.00
☐ 71038		THE SOUND OF THE CRICKETS	25.00	40.00

CRICKETS—ALBUM

☐ 54038	*BRUNSWICK*	THE "CHIRPING" CRICKETS	45.00	120.00

CRYSTALS

☐ 100	*PHILLES*	THERE'S NO OTHER/		
		OH YEAH, MAYBE BABY.............	3.50	6.00
☐ 102		UPTOWN/		
		WHAT A NICE WAY TO TURN SEVENTEEN ...	3.50	6.00
☐ 105		HE HIT ME (AND IT FELT LIKE A KISS)/		
		NO ONE EVER TELLS YOU...............	4.50	9.00
☐ 106		HE'S A REBEL/I LOVE YOU EDDIE	2.25	4.00
☐ 109		HE'S SURE THE BOY I LOVE/		
		WALKIN' ALONG	2.25	4.00
☐ 112		DA DOO RON RON/GIT IT	2.25	4.00
☐ 115		THEN HE KISSED ME/BROTHER JULIUS	2.25	4.00
☐ 119		LITTLE BOY/HARRY AND MILT	2.75	4.70
☐ 122		ALL GROWN UP/IRVING.................	2.75	4.50
☐ 927	*UNITED ARTISTS*	MY PLACE/		
		YOU CAN'T TIE A GOOD GIRL DOWN	3.50	6.00
☐ 994		I GOT A MAN/ARE YOU		
		TRYING TO GET RID OF ME, BABY?	3.50	6.00

ISSUE #	LABEL		PRICE RANGE	

CRYSTALS—ALBUMS

☐ 4000 (M)	*PHILLES*	TWIST UPTOWN	25.00	60.00
☐ 4001 (M)		HE'S A REBEL	25.00	60.00
☐ 4003 (M)		THE CRYSTALS SING THE GREATEST HITS, VOL. I	20.00	50.00

— D —

ROGER DALTRY

☐ 066040	*ODE*	UNDERTURE/I'M FREE	1.25	2.50
☐ 40053	*TRACK*	GIVING IT ALL AWAY/WAY OF THE WORLD ...	1.25	2.50
☐ 40084		THINKING/	1.25	2.50
☐ 40453	*MCA-GOLDHAWKE*	HEART'S RIGHT/COME & GET YOUR LOVE	1.25	2.50
☐ 40512		FEELING/OCEANS AWAY	1.25	2.50
☐ 40765		SAY IT AIN'T SO, JOE/SATIN & LACE	1.25	2.50
☐ 40800		THE PRISONER/AVENGING ANNIE	1.25	2.50

ROGER DALTRY—ALBUMS

| ☐ 328 (S) | *MCA* | DALTRY .... | 5.00 | 15.00 |
| ☐ 2147 (S) | | RIDE A ROCK HORSE .... | 3.50 | 10.00 |

DANNY AND THE JUNIORS

☐ 711	*SINGULAR*	AT THE HOP/SOMETIMES	30.00	45.00
☐ 9871	*ABC-PARAMOUNT*	AT THE HOP/SOMETIMES	2.25	4.00
☐ 9888		ROCK AND ROLL IS HERE TO STAY/ SCHOOL BOY ROMANCE	2.25	4.00
☐ 9926		DOTTIE/IN THE MEANTIME	2.25	4.00
☐ 9953		CRAZY CAVE/A THIEF	2.25	4.00
☐ 9978		I FEEL SO LONELY/SASSY FRAN	2.25	4.00
☐ 10004		DO YOU LOVE ME?/ SOMEHOW I CAN'T FORGET	2.25	4.00
☐ 10052		PLAYING HARD TO GET/OF LOVE	2.25	4.00
☐ 4060	*SWAN*	TWISTIN' U.S.A./ A THOUSAND MILES AWAY	2.00	3.50
☐ 4064		O HOLY NIGHT/ CANDY CANE, SUGARY PLUM	2.75	4.50
☐ 4068		PONY EXPRESS/DAY DREAMER	2.00	3.50
☐ 4072		CHA CHA GO-GO/MR. WHISPER	2.00	3.50
☐ 4082		BACK TO THE HOP/CHARLESTON FISH	2.00	3.50

ISSUE #	LABEL		PRICE RANGE	
☐ 4092		TWISTIN' ALL NIGHT LONG/		
		SOME KIND OF NUT	2.00	3.50
☐ 4100		DOIN' THE CONTINENTAL WALK/		
		DO THE MASHED POTATO	2.00	3.50
☐ 4113		WE GOT SOUL/FUNNY	2.00	3.50

DANNY AND THE JUNIORS—EP

☐ 11	ABC-PARAMOUNT	AT THE HOP	18.00	30.00

DANNY AND THE JUNIORS—ALBUM

☐ 506 (M)	SWAN	TWISTIN' ALL NIGHT LONG	25.00	60.00

BOBBY DARIN

☐ 29883	DECCA	ROCK ISLAND LINE/TIMBER	12.00	20.00
☐ 29922		SILLY WILLIE/BLUE EYED MERMAID	8.50	15.00
☐ 30031		HEAR THEM BELLS/		
		THE GREATEST BUILDER	8.50	15.00
☐ 30225		DEALER IN DREAMS/HELP ME	8.50	15.00
☐ 30737		SILLY WILLIE/DEALER IN DREAMS	6.00	11.00
☐ 6092	ATCO	I FOUND A MILLION DOLLAR BABY/		
		TALK TO ME	2.75	4.50
☐ 6103		PRETTY BABY/DON'T CALL MY NAME	2.75	4.50
☐ 6109		JUST IN CASE YOU CHANGE YOUR MIND/		
		SO MEAN	2.75	4.50
☐ 6117		SPLISH SPLASH/JUDY, DON'T BE MOODY	2.25	4.00
☐ 6127		QUEEN OF THE HOP/LOST LOVE	2.25	4.00
☐ 6133		PLAIN JANE/WHILE I'M GONE	2.25	4.00
☐ 6140		DREAM LOVER/BULL MOOSE	2.25	4.00
☐ 6147		MACK THE KNIFE/		
		WAS THERE A CALL FOR ME	2.00	3.50
☐ 6158		BEYOND THE SEA/		
		THAT'S THE WAY LOVE IS	2.00	3.50
☐ 6161		CLEMENTINE/TALL STORY	2.00	3.50
☐ 6167		WON'T YOU COME HOME BILL BAILEY/		
		I'LL BE THERE	2.00	3.50
☐ 6173		BEACHCOMBER/AUTUMN BLUES	2.00	3.50
☐ 6179		ARTIFICIAL FLOWERS/		
		SOMEBODY TO LOVE	2.00	3.50
☐ 6183		CHRISTMAS AULD LANG SYNE/		
		CHILD OF GOD	2.00	3.50
☐ 6188		LAZY RIVER/OO-EE-TRAIN	2.00	3.50
☐ 6196		NATURE BOY/LOOK FOR MY TRUE LOVE	2.00	3.50
☐ 6200		COME SEPTEMBER/WALK BACK WITH ME	2.00	3.50
☐ 6206		YOU MUST HAVE BEEN A BEAUTIFUL BABY/SORROW TOMORROW	2.00	3.50

ISSUE #	LABEL		PRICE	RANGE
☐ 6211		AVE MARIA/O COME, ALL YE FAITHFUL	2.00	3.50
☐ 6214		IRRESISTABLE YOU/MULTIPLICATION	2.00	3.50
☐ 6221		WHAT'D I SAY (PT. 1)/(PT. 2)	2.00	3.50
☐ 6229		THINGS/JAILER, BRING ME WATER	2.00	3.50
☐ 6236		BABY FACE/YOU KNOW HOW	2.00	3.50
☐ 6244		I FOUND A NEW BABY/KEEP A WALKIN'	2.00	3.50
☐ 6297		MILORD/GOLDEN EARRINGS	2.00	3.50
☐ 6316		SWING LOW, SWEET CHARIOT/SIMILAU	2.00	3.50
☐ 6334		HARD HEARTED HANNAH/		
		MINNIE THE MOOCHER	2.00	3.50
☐ 4837	*CAPITOL*	IF A MAN ANSWERS/TRUE TRUE LOVE	1.75	3.00
☐ 4897		YOU'RE THE REASON I'M LIVING/		
		NOW YOU'RE GONE	1.75	3.00
☐ 4970		EIGHTEEN YELLOW ROSES/NOT FOR ME	1.75	3.00
☐ 5019		TREAT MY BABY GOOD/DOWN SO LONG	1.75	3.00
☐ 5079		BE MAD LITTLE GIRL/		
		SINCE YOU'VE BEEN GONE	1.75	3.00
☐ 5126		I WONDER WHO'S KISSING HER NOW/		
		AS LONG AS I'M SINGING	1.75	3.00
☐ 5257		THE THINGS IN THIS HOUSE/		
		WAIT BY THE WATER	1.75	3.00
☐ 5359		HELLO, DOLLY!/GOLDEN EARRINGS	1.75	3.00
☐ 5399		A WORLD WITHOUT YOU/VENICE	1.75	3.00
☐ 5443		WHEN I GET HOME/LONELY ROAD	1.75	3.00
☐ 5481		THAT FUNNY FEELING/GYP THE CAT	1.75	3.00

BOBBY DARIN—EPs

☐ 2676	*DECCA*	BOBBY DARIN	18.00	30.00
☐ 4502	*ATCO*	BOBBY DARIN	7.25	12.00
☐ 4504		THAT'S ALL	6.00	11.00
☐ 4505		BOBBY DARIN	6.00	11.00
☐ 4508		THIS IS DARIN	5.00	10.00
☐ 4512		DARIN AT THE COPA	5.00	10.00
☐ 4513		FOR TEENAGERS ONLY	5.00	10.00

BOBBY DARIN—ALBUMS

☐ 102 (M)	*ATCO*	BOBBY DARIN	17.50	45.00
☐ 104 (S)		THAT'S ALL	15.00	35.00
☐ 115 (S)		THIS IS DARIN	15.00	35.00
☐ 122 (S)		DARIN AT THE COPA	12.50	30.00
☐ 125 (S)		25TH DAY OF DECEMBER	12.50	30.00
☐ 126 (S)		TWO OF A KIND	12.50	30.00
☐ 131 (S)		THE BOBBY DARIN STORY	12.50	30.00
☐ 134 (S)		LOVE SWINGS	8.00	22.50
☐ 138 (S)		TWIST WITH BOBBY DARIN	8.00	22.50
☐ 140 (S)		BOBBY DARIN SINGS RAY CHARLES	8.00	22.50

ISSUE #	LABEL		PRICE RANGE	
☐ 146 (S)		THINGS AND OTHER THINGS	8.00	22.50
☐ 167 (S)		BOBBY DARIN WINNERS	7.00	18.00
☐ 1001 (M)		FOR TEENAGERS ONLY	10.00	25.00
☐ 1791 (S)	*CAPITOL*	OH! LOOK AT ME NOW	7.00	18.00
☐ 1826 (S)		EARTHY	7.00	18.00
☐ 1866 (S)		YOU'RE THE REASON I'M LIVING	7.00	18.00
☐ 1942 (S)		18 YELLOW ROSES	7.00	18.00
☐ 2007 (S)		GOLDEN FOLK HITS	7.00	18.00
☐ 2194 (S)		FROM HELLO DOLLY TO GOODBYE CHARLIE	7.00	18.00
☐ 2322 (S)		VENICE BLUE	7.00	18.00
☐ 2571 (S)		BEST OF BOBBY DARIN	7.00	18.00
☐ 8121 (S)		THE SHADOW OF YOUR SMILE	6.00	15.00
☐ 8126 (S)		IN A BROADWAY BAG	6.00	15.00
☐ 8135 (S)		IF I WERE A CARPENTER	5.00	13.50
☐ 8142 (S)		INSIDE OUT	5.00	13.50
☐ 8154 (S)		BOBBY DARIN SINGS DOCTOR DOLITTLE	5.00	13.50
☐ 1936 (S)	*DIRECTION*	BOBBY DARIN	4.00	10.00
☐ 1937 (S)		COMMITMENT	4.00	10.00
☐ 753 (S)	*MOTOWN*	BOBBY DARIN	4.00	10.00
☐ 813 (S)		DARIN: 1936-1973	4.00	10.00

JAMES DARREN

☐ 102	*COLPIX*	THERE'S NO SUCH THING/ MIGHTY PRETTY TERRITORY	2.75	4.50
☐ 113		GIDGET/YOU	2.25	4.00
☐ 119		ANGEL FACE/I DON'T WANNA LOSE YA	2.25	4.00
☐ 128		LOVE AMONG THE YOUNG/ I AIN'T SHARIN' SHARON	2.00	3.50
☐ 130		TEENAGE TEARS/LET THERE BE LOVE	2.00	3.50
☐ 138		YOU ARE MY DREAM/YOUR SMILE	2.00	3.50
☐ 142		BECAUSE THEY'RE YOUNG/ TEARS IN MY EYES	2.00	3.50
☐ 145		TRAVELING DOWN A LONESOME ROAD/ P.S., I LOVE YOU	2.00	3.50
☐ 168		MAN ABOUT TOWN/COME ON MY LOVE	2.00	3.50
☐ 189		GIDGET GOES HAWAIIAN/ WILD ABOUT THAT GIRL	2.00	3.50
☐ 609		GOODBYE CRUEL WORLD/VALERIE	1.75	3.00
☐ 622		HER ROYAL MAJESTY/ IF I COULD ONLY TELL YOU	1.75	3.00
☐ 630		CONSCIENCE/DREAM BIG	1.75	3.00
☐ 644		MARY'S LITTLE LAMB/ THE LIFE OF THE PARTY	1.75	3.00

ISSUE #	LABEL		PRICE RANGE	
☐ 655		HAIL TO THE CONQUERING HERO/		
		TOO YOUNG TO GO STEADY	1.75	3.00
☐ 664		HEAR WHAT I WANT TO HEAR/		
		I'LL BE LOVING YOU	1.75	3.00
☐ 672		PIN A MEDAL ON JOEY/DIAMOND HEAD	1.75	3.00
☐ 685		THEY SHOULD HAVE GIVEN YOU THE		
		OSCAR/BLAME IT ON MY YOUTH	1.75	3.00
☐ 696		GEGETTA/GRANDE LUNA, ITALIANO	1.75	3.00
☐ 708		UNDER THE YUM YUM TREE/BACKSTAGE	1.75	3.00
☐ 758		JUST THINK OF TONIGHT/		
		PUNCH AND JUDY	1.75	3.00
☐ 765		A MARRIED MAN/BABY, TALK TO ME	1.75	3.00
☐ 5648	*WARNER*			
	BROTHERS	BECAUSE YOU'RE MINE/		
		MILLIONS OF ROSES	1.75	3.00
☐ 5689		I WANT TO BE LONELY/TOMMY HAWK	1.75	3.00
☐ 5812		WHERE DID WE GO WRONG?/		
		COUNTING THE CRACKS	1.75	3.00
☐ 5838		CRAZY ME/THEY DON'T KNOW	1.75	3.00
☐ 5874		ALL/MISTY MORNING EYES	1.75	3.00
☐ 7071		THE HOUSE SONG/THEY DON'T KNOW	1.75	3.00
☐ 7152		CHERIE/WAIT UNTIL DARK	1.75	3.00

JAMES DARREN—ALBUMS

ISSUE #	LABEL		PRICE RANGE	
☐ 406 (M)	*COLPIX*	ALBUM NO. 1	8.00	22.50
☐ 418 (S)		GIDGET GOES HAWAIIAN	7.00	18.00
☐ 424 (M)		JAMES DARREN SINGS FOR ALL SIZES	6.00	15.00
☐ 428 (M)		LOVE AMONG THE YOUNG	6.00	15.00
☐ 1688 (S)	*WARNER*			
	BROTHERS	ALL	6.00	15.00

ANDREA DAVIS (MINNIE RIPERTON)

ISSUE #	LABEL		PRICE RANGE	
☐ 1980	*CHESS*	LONELY GIRL/YOU GAVE ME SOUL	3.50	6.00

SPENCER DAVIS GROUP

ISSUE #	LABEL		PRICE RANGE	
☐ 6400	*ATCO*	KEEP ON RUNNIN'/HIGH TIME BABY	2.00	3.50
☐ 6416		SOMEBODY HELP ME/STEVIE'S BLUES	2.00	3.50
☐ 50108	*UNITED*			
	ARTISTS	GIMMIE SOME LOVIN'/BLUES IN F	1.75	3.00
☐ 50144		I'M A MAN/CAN'T GET ENOUGH OF IT	1.75	3.00
☐ 50162		SOMEBODY HELP ME/		
		ON THE GREEN LIGHT	1.75	3.00
☐ 50202		TIME SELLER/DON'T WANT YOU NO MORE	1.75	3.00
☐ 50286		AFTER TEA/LOOKING BACK	1.75	3.00

ISSUE #	LABEL		PRICE RANGE	

SPENCER DAVIS GROUP—ALBUMS

☐6578 (S)	*UNITED ARTISTS*	GIMMIE SOME LOVIN'	8.00	22.50
☐6589 (S)		I'M A MAN	8.00	22.50
☐6641 (S)		SPENCER DAVIS GREATEST HITS	7.00	18.00
☐6652 (S)		WITH THEIR NEW FACE ON	7.00	18.00
☐6691 (S)		HEAVIES	5.00	13.50

JOEY DEE AND THE STARLITERS

☐5539	*JUBILEE*	DANCIN' ON THE BEACH/GOOD LITTLE YOU . . .	3.50	6.00
☐5554		SHE'S SO EXCEPTIONAL/IT'S GOT YOU	3.50	6.00
☐5566		YOU CAN'T SIT DOWN/ PUT YOUR HEART IN IT	3.50	6.00
☐4401	*ROULETTE*	PEPPERMINT TWIST (PT. 1)/(PT. 2)	2.00	3.50
☐4408		HEY, LET'S TWIST/ROLY POLY	2.00	3.50
☐4416		SHOUT (PT. 1)/(PT. 2)	2.00	3.50
☐4431		EVERYTIME (PT. 1)/(PT. 2)	2.00	3.50
☐4438		WHAT KIND OF LOVE IS THIS?/WING DING	2.00	3.50
☐4456		I LOST MY BABY/KEEP YOUR MIND ON WHAT YOU'RE DOIN'	2.00	3.50
☐4467		BABY, YOU'RE DRIVING ME CRAZY/ HELP ME PICK UP THE PIECES	2.00	3.50
☐4488		HOT PASTRAMI WITH MASHED POTATOES (PT. 1)/(PT. 2)	2.00	3.50
☐4503		DANCE, DANCE, DANCE/ LET'S HAVE A PARTY	2.00	3.50
☐4525		FANNIE MAE/YA YA	2.00	3.50
☐4539		DOWN BY THE RIVERSIDE/ GETTING NEARER	2.00	3.50

JOEY DEE AND THE STARLITERS—ALBUMS

☐503 (M)	*SCEPTER*	PEPPERMINT TWISTERS	8.00	22.50
☐25166 (S)	*ROULETTE*	DOIN' THE TWIST AT THE PEPPERMINT LOUNGE	8.00	22.50
☐25168 (S)		HEY, LET'S TWIST	8.00	22.50
☐25171 (S)		ALL THE WORLD IS TWISTIN'	7.00	18.00
☐25173 (S)		BACK AT THE PEPPERMINT LOUNGE	7.00	18.00
☐25182 (S)		TWO TICKETS TO PARIS	8.00	22.50
☐25197 (S)		JOEY DEE	7.00	18.00
☐25221 (S)		DANCE, DANCE, DANCE	7.00	18.00

ISSUE #	LABEL		PRICE RANGE	

DEEP PURPLE

☐ 1503	*TETRA-*			
	GRAMMATON	HUSH/ONE MORE RAINY DAY	1.75	3.00
☐ 1508		KENTUCKY WOMAN/HARD ROAD	1.75	3.00
☐ 1514		RIVER DEEP-MOUNTAIN HIGH/		
		LISTEN, LEARN, READ ON	1.75	3.00
☐ 1519		THE BIRD HAS FLOWN/EMMARETTA	1.75	3.00
☐ 1537		HALLELUJAH (I AM THE PREACHER)/		
		APRIL (PT. 1)	1.75	3.00
☐ 7504	*WARNER*			
	BROTHERS	BLACK NIGHT/INTO THE FIRE	2.00	3.50
☐ 7528		FIREBALL/I'M ALONE	2.00	3.50
☐ 7572		WHEN A BLIND MAN CRIES/		
		NEVER BEFORE	2.00	3.50
☐ 7595		STRANGE KIND OF WOMAN/I'M ALONE	2.00	3.50
☐ 7634		HIGHWAY STAR/HIGHWAY STAR	2.00	3.50
☐ 7672		WOMAN FROM TOKYO/SUPER TROUPER	1.75	3.00
☐ 7710		SMOKE ON THE WATER/		
		SMOKE ON THE WATER	1.50	2.50
☐ 7737		WOMAN FROM TOKYO/SUPER TROUPER	1.75	3.00
☐ 7784		MIGHT JUST TAKE YOUR LIFE/		
		CORONARIES REDIG	1.75	3.00
☐ 7809		BURN/CORONARIES REDIG	1.75	3.00
☐ 8049		HIGHBALL SHOOTER/		
		YOU CAN'T DO IT RIGHT	1.75	3.00
☐ 8069		STORMBRINGER/		
		LOVE DON'T MEAN A THING	1.75	3.00

DEEP PURPLE—ALBUMS

☐ 102 (S)	*TETRA-*			
	GRAMMATON	SHADES OF DEEP PURPLE	5.00	12.00
☐ 107 (S)		BOOK OF TALIESYN	5.00	12.00
☐ 119 (S)		DEEP PURPLE	5.00	12.00

DELLS

☐ 134	*VEE JAY*	TELL THE WORLD/FLIP BY COUNT MORRIS . . .	85.00	150.00
☐ 166		DREAMS ON CONTENTMENT/		
		ZING ZING ZING	36.00	60.00
☐ 204		OH WHAT A NITE/JO JO	7.25	12.00
☐ 230		MOVIN' ON/I WANNA GO HOME	7.25	12.00
☐ 236		WHY DO YOU HAVE TO GO?/		
		DANCE DANCE DANCE	7.25	12.00
☐ 251		A DISTANT LOVE/O-BOP SHE-BOP	7.25	12.00
☐ 258		PAIN IN MY HEART/		
		TIME MAKES YOU CHANGE	7.25	12.00

ISSUE #	LABEL		PRICE RANGE	
☐ 274		WHAT YOU SAY BABY/THE SPRINGER	7.25	12.00
☐ 292		I'M CALLING/JEEPERS CREEPERS	8.50	15.00
☐ 300		MY BEST GIRL/WEDDING DAY	8.50	15.00
☐ 324		DRY YOUR EYES/		
		BABY OPEN UP YOUR HEART	7.25	12.00
☐ 338		OH WHAT A NITE/I WANNA GO HOME	4.50	9.00
☐ 376		SWINGIN' TEENS/		
		HOLD ON TO WHAT YOU'VE GOT	4.50	9.00
☐ 595		SHY GIRL/WHAT DO WE PROVE?	4.00	7.00
☐ 615		OH WHAT A GOOD NIGHT/		
		WAIT 'TIL TOMORROW	4.00	7.00
☐ 674		STAY IN MY CORNER/IT'S NOT UNUSUAL	4.00	7.00
☐ 712		HEY SUGAR (DON'T GET SERIOUS)/		
		POOR LITTLE BOY	4.00	7.00
☐ 5415	ARGO	GOD BLESS THE CHILD/I'M GOING HOME	2.75	4.50
☐ 5428		THE (BOSSA NOVA) BIRD/ETERNALLY	2.75	4.50
☐ 5442		IF IT AIN'T ONE THING IT'S ANOTHER/		
		HI DIDDLEY DEE DUM DUM	2.75	4.50
☐ 5456		AFTER YOU/GOODBYE MARY ANN	2.75	4.50

DELLS—ALBUMS

☐ 1010 (M)	VEE JAY	OH WHAT A NITE	17.50	45.00
☐ 1141 (M)		IT'S NOT UNUSUAL	8.00	22.50

DELL-VIKINGS

☐ 106	LUNIVERSE	OVER THE RAINBOW/HEY SENORITA	15.00	25.00
☐ 205	FEE BEE	COME GO WITH ME/		
		HOW CAN I FIND TRUE LOVE	36.00	60.00
☐ 210		TRUE LOVE/UH UH BABY	7.25	12.00
☐ 214		WHISPERING BELLS/DON'T BE A FOOL	24.00	40.00
☐ 66	ALPINE	PISTOL PACKIN' MAMA/THE SUN	7.25	12.00
☐ 15538	DOT	COME GO WITH ME/		
		HOW CAN I FIND TRUE LOVE	2.75	4.50
☐ 15571		WHAT MADE MAGGIE RUN/		
		LITTLE BILLY BOY	2.75	4.50
☐ 15592		WHISPERING BELLS/DON'T BE A FOOL	2.75	4.50
☐ 15636		I'M SPINNING/WHEN I COME HOME	2.75	4.50
☐ 71132	MERCURY	COOL SHAKE/JITTERBUG MARY	2.25	4.00
☐ 71880		COME ALONG WITH ME/		
		WHAT 'CHA GOTTA LOSE	2.25	4.00
☐ 71241		YOUR BOOK OF LOVE/SNOWBOUND	2.75	4.00
☐ 71266		THE VOODOO MAN/CAN'T WAIT	2.75	4.00

DELL-VIKINGS—EPs

☐ 1058	DOT	COME GO WITH US	12.00	20.00
☐ 3362	MERCURY	THEY SING - THEY SWING	12.00	20.00

ISSUE #	LABEL		PRICE RANGE	

DELL-VIKINGS—ALBUMS

☐ 1000 (M)				
	LUNIVERSE	COME GO WITH THE DELL-VIKINGS	60.00	150.00
☐ 1003 (M)	**DOT**	BEST OF THE DELL-VIKINGS	40.00	110.00
☐ 20314 (M)				
	MERCURY	THEY SING - THEY SWING	50.00	135.00

DEMENSIONS

☐ 116	**MOHAWK**	OVER THE RAINBOW/		
		NURSERY RHYME ROCK...............	2.25	4.00
☐ 120		DON'T TAKE YOUR LOVE FROM ME/		
		ZING! WENT THE STRINGS OF MY HEART ...	2.25	4.00
☐ 121		AVE MARIA/GOD'S CHRISTMAS	2.25	4.00
☐ 123		A TEAR FELL/THERESA	2.25	4.00
☐ 62277	**CORAL**	COUNT YOUR BLESSINGS INSTEAD		
		OF SHEEP/AGAIN...................	2.00	3.50
☐ 62293		AS TIME GOES BY/SEVEN DAYS A WEEK	2.00	3.50
☐ 62323		YOUNG AT HEART/YOUR CHEATIN' HEART ...	2.00	3.50
☐ 62344		MY FOOLISH HEART/		
		JUST ONE MORE CHANCE	2.00	3.50
☐ 62359		FLY ME TO THE MOON/		
		YOU'LL NEVER KNOW	1.75	3.00
☐ 62382		JUST A SHOULDER TO CRY ON/		
		DON'T WORRY ABOUT BOBBY	1.75	3.00
☐ 62392		DON'T CRY PRETTY BABY/		
		— A LITTLE WHITE GARDENIA	1.75	3.00
☐ 62432		THIS TIME NEXT YEAR/		
		MY OLD GIRL FRIEND................	1.75	3.00
☐ 62444		ONCE A DAY/TING-A-LING-TING-TOY ...	1.75	3.00

DEMENSIONS—ALBUM

☐ 57430 (M)	**CORAL**	MY FOOLISH HEART	17.50	45.00

JOHN DENVER

☐ 74-0275	**RCA**	I WISH I KNEW/DAYDREAM	4.00	7.00
☐ 74-0305		ANTHEM (REVELATION)	3.00	6.00
☐ 74-0332		ISABEL/FOLLOW ME	3.00	6.00
☐ 74-0376		SAIL AWAY HOME/		
		I WISH I COULD HAVE BEEN THERE	4.00	7.00
☐ 74-0391		MR. BOJANGLES/		
		WHOSE GARDEN WAS THIS?	2.75	5.50
☐ 74-0445		TAKE ME HOME COUNTRY ROADS/		
		POEMS, PRAYERS, PROMISES	1.75	4.00
☐ 74-0567		STARWOOD IN ASPEN/FRIENDS WITH YOU ...	1.75	4.00

ISSUE #	LABEL		PRICE RANGE	
☐ 74-0647		CITY OF NEW ORLEANS/EVERYDAY	2.25	5.00
☐ 74-0737		THE EAGLE & THE HAWK/GOODBYE AGAIN	2.25	5.00
☐ 74-0829		ROCKY MOUNTAIN HIGH/SPRING	1.75	4.00
☐ APBO-0067		FAREWELL ANDROMEDA/		
		WHISKEY BASIN BLUES	1.75	4.00
☐ APBO-0182		ROCKY MOUNTAIN SUITE/PLEASE DADDY	1.75	4.00
☐ 74-0801		LATE WINTER, EARLY SPRING/		
		HARD LIFE, HARD TIMES	2.25	5.00
☐ 74-0955		SUNSHINE ON MY SHOULDERS/		
		I'D RATHER BE A COWBOY	3.00	6.50
☐ PB-10065		IT'S UP TO YOU/BACK HOME AGAIN	1.75	4.00
☐ PB-10148		SUMMER/SWEET SURRENDER	1.75	4.00
☐ APBO-0213		SUNSHINE ON MY SHOULDERS/		
		AROUND & AROUND	1.75	4.00
☐ APBO-0295		ANNIE'S SONG/COOL AN' GREEN	1.75	4.00

JOHN DENVER—ALBUMS

☐ 66 (S)	*HJD*	JOHN DENVER SINGS	17.50	60.00
☐ AQL1-3075 (S)	*RCA*	JOHN DENVER	3.00	9.00
☐ LSP-4207 (S)		RHYMES & REASONS	4.00	13.50
☐ LSP-4278 (S)		TAKE ME TO TOMORROW	4.00	13.50
☐ LSP-4414 (S)		WHOSE GARDEN WAS THIS?	3.50	10.00
☐ LSP-4499 (S)		POEMS, PRAYERS & PROMISES	4.00	13.50
☐ LSP-4607 (S)		AERIE	4.00	13.50
☐ LSP-4731 (S)		ROCKY MOUNTAIN HIGH	3.50	10.00
☐ RS-1050 (S)		LIVE IN LONDON	3.50	10.00
☐ APL1-1183 (S)		WINDSONG	4.00	12.00
☐ APL1-1201 (S)		ROCKY MOUNTAIN CHRISTMAS	3.50	10.00
☐ APL1-1694 (S)		SPIRIT	3.50	10.00
☐ APL2-1263 (S)		ROCKY MOUNTAIN CHRISTMAS/		
		WINDSONG	3.50	10.00

JACKIE DeSHANNON

☐ 416	*EDISON*			
	INTERNATIONAL	I WANNA GO HOME/SO WARM	3.75	6.50
☐ 418		PUT MY BABY DOWN/THE FOOLISH ONE	3.75	6.50
☐ 55288	*LIBERTY*	LONELY GIRL/TEACH ME	2.25	4.00
☐ 55342		THINK ABOUT YOU/		
		HEAVEN IS BEING WITH YOU	2.25	4.00
☐ 55358		WISH I COULD FIND A BOY/		
		I WON'T TURN YOU DOWN	2.25	4.00
☐ 55387		BABY (WHEN YA KISS ME)/		
		AIN'T THAT LOVE	2.25	4.00
☐ 55425		THE PRINCE/		
		I'LL DROWN IN MY OWN TEARS	2.25	4.00

ISSUE #	LABEL		PRICE RANGE	
☐ 55425		THE PRINCE/		
		THAT'S WHAT BOYS ARE MADE OF	2.00	3.50
☐ 55484		JUST LIKE IN THE MOVIES/GUESS WHO	2.25	3.50
☐ 55497		YOU WON'T FORGET ME/		
		I DON'T THINK SO MUCH OF MYSELF	2.25	4.00
☐ 55526		FADED LOVE/DANCING SILHOUETTES	2.25	4.00
☐ 55563		NEEDLES AND PINS/		
		DID HE CALL TODAY, MAMA?	2.25	4.00
☐ 55602		LITTLE YELLOW ROSES/		
		OH SWEET CHARIOT	2.25	4.00
☐ 55602		LITTLE YELLOW ROSES/500 MILES	2.25	4.00
☐ 55645		WHEN YOU WALK IN THE ROOM/		
		TILL YOU SAY YOU'RE MINE	2.25	4.00
☐ 55678		OH BOY!/		
		I'M LOOKIN' FOR SOMEONE TO LOVE	2.25	4.00
☐ 55705		SHE DON'T UNDERSTAND HIM LIKE		
		I DO/HOLD YOUR HEAD HIGH	2.25	4.00
☐ 55730		HE'S GOT THE WHOLE WORLD IN		
		IN HIS HANDS/IT'S LOVE BABY	2.25	4.00
☐ 55735		OVER YOU/WHEN YOU WALK IN THE ROOM	2.25	4.00
☐ 56187		IT'S SO NICE/MEDITERRANEAN SKY	2.25	4.00
☐ 13349	*MGM*	LOVE AND LEARN/I'M GLAD IT'S YOU	2.00	3.50
☐ 66110	*IMPERIAL*	WHAT THE WORLD NEEDS NOW IS LOVE/		
		REMEMBER THE BOY	1.75	3.00
☐ 66132		A LIFETIME OF LONELINESS/		
		DON'T TURN YOUR BACK ON ME	1.75	3.00
☐ 66171		COME AND GET ME/		
		SPLENDOR IN THE GRASS	1.75	3.00
☐ 66202		I CAN MAKE IT WITH YOU/TO BE MYSELF	1.75	3.00
☐ 66224		COME ON DOWN/FIND ME LOVE	1.75	3.00
☐ 66236		WHERE DOES THE SUN GO?/		
		THE WISHING DOLL	1.75	3.00

JACKIE DeSHANNON—ALBUMS

☐ 7320 (S)	*LIBERTY*	JACKIE DeSHANNON	10.00	25.00
☐ 7390 (S)		BREAKIN' IT UP ON THE BEATLES TOUR	10.00	25.00
☐ 7430 (S)		C'MON, LET'S LIVE A LITTLE	10.00	25.00
☐ 12286 (S)		THIS IS JACKIE DeSHANNON	7.00	18.00
☐ 12294 (S)		YOU WON'T FORGET ME	7.00	18.00
☐ 12296 (S)		IN THE WIND	6.00	15.00
☐ 12328 (S)		ARE YOU READY FOR THIS?	6.00	15.00
☐ 12344 (S)		NEW IMAGE	6.00	15.00
☐ 12352 (S)		FOR YOU	6.00	15.00
☐ 12386 (S)		ME ABOUT YOU	4.50	10.00
☐ 12404 (S)		WHAT THE WORLD NEEDS NOW IS LOVE	4.50	10.00
☐ 12415 (S)		LAUREL CANYON	4.50	10.00

ISSUE #	LABEL		PRICE RANGE	
☐ 12442 (S)		PUT A LITTLE LOVE IN YOUR HEART	4.50	10.00
☐ 12453 (S)		TO BE FREE	4.50	10.00

NEIL DIAMOND

☐ 42809	**COLUMBIA**	CLOWN TOWN/AT NIGHT	15.00	24.00
☐ 519	**BANG**	SOLITARY MAN/DO IT	2.00	3.50
☐ 528		CHERRY CHERRY/I'LL COME RUNNING	1.75	3.00
☐ 536		I GOT THE FEELIN' (OH NO NO)/ THE BOAT THAT I ROW	1.75	3.00
☐ 540		YOU GOT TO ME/SOMEDAY, BABY	1.75	3.00
☐ 542		GIRL, YOU'LL BE A WOMAN SOON/ YOU'LL FORGET	1.75	3.00
☐ 547		I THANK THE LORD FOR THE NIGHT TIME/ THE LONG WAY HOME	1.75	3.00
☐ 551		KENTUCKY WOMAN/THE TIME IS NOW	1.75	3.00
☐ 554		NEW ORLEANS/HANKY PANKY	1.75	3.00
☐ 556		RED RED WINE/RED RUBBER BALL	1.75	3.00
☐ 561		SHILO/LA BAMBA	1.75	3.00
☐ 575		SHILO/LA BAMBA	1.75	3.00
☐ 578		SOLITARY MAN/THE TIME IS NOW	1.75	3.00
☐ 580		DO IT/HANKY PANKY	1.75	3.00
☐ 586		I'M A BELIEVER/CROOKER STREET	1.75	3.00
☐ 703		MONDAY MONDAY/THE LONG WAY HOME	1.75	3.00
☐ 55065	**UNI**	BROOKLYN ROADS/HOLIDAY INN	1.50	2.50
☐ 55075		TWO BIT MANCHILD/BROAD OLD WOMAN	1.50	2.50
☐ 55084		SUNDAY SUN/HONEY DRIPPIN' TIME	1.50	2.50
☐ 55109		BROTHER LOVE'S TRAVELING SALVATION SHOW/MODERN DAY VERSION OF LOVE	1.50	2.50
☐ 55136		SWEET CAROLINE/DIG IN	1.50	2.50
☐ 55175		HOLLY HOLY/ HURTIN' YOU DON'T COME EASY	1.50	2.50
☐ 55204		UNTIL IT'S TIME FOR YOU TO GO/ THE SINGER SINGS HIS SONG	1.50	2.50
☐ 55224		SOOLAIMON/ AND THE GRASS WON'T PAY NO MIND	1.50	2.50
☐ 55250		CRACKLIN' ROSIE/LORDY	1.50	2.50
☐ 55264		HE AIN'T HEAVY, HE'S MY BROTHER/ FREE LIFE	1.50	2.50
☐ 55278		I AM . . . I SAID/DONE TOO SOON	1.50	2.50
☐ 55310		STONES/CRUNCHY GRANOLA SUITE	1.50	2.50
☐ 55326		SONG SUNG BLUE/GITCHY GOOMY	1.50	2.50
☐ 55346		PLAY ME/PORCUPINE PIE	1.50	2.50
☐ 55352		WALK ON WATER/HIGH ROLLING MAN	1.50	2.50
☐ 40017	**MCA**	CHERRY CHERRY/MORNINGSIDE	1.50	2.50

ISSUE #	LABEL		PRICE RANGE	

NEIL DIAMOND—ALBUMS

☐ 214 (S)	*BANG*	THE FEEL OF NEIL DIAMOND	8.00	22.50
☐ 217 (S)		JUST FOR YOU	7.00	18.00
☐ 219 (S)		GREATEST HITS	7.00	18.00
☐ 221 (S)		SHILO	5.00	13.50
☐ 224 (S)		DO IT!	5.00	13.50
☐ 73030 (S)	*UNI*	VELVET GLOVES AND SPIT	4.50	12.00
☐ 73047 (S)		BROTHER LOVE'S TRAVELING SALVATION SHOW	4.00	10.00
☐ 73071 (S)		TOUCHING YOU, TOUCHING ME	4.00	10.00
☐ 73084 (S)		NEIL DIAMOND - GOLD	4.00	10.00
☐ 73092 (S)		TAP ROOT MANUSCRIPT	4.00	10.00
☐ 93106 (S)		STONES	4.00	10.00
☐ 93136 (S)		MOODS	4.00	10.00

DICK AND DEEDEE

☐ 7778	*LAMA*	THE MOUNTAIN'S HIGH/I WANT SOMEONE . . .	10.00	18.00
☐ 7780		GOODBYE TO LOVE/SWING LOW	7.25	12.00
☐ 7783		TELL ME/WILL YOU ALWAYS LOVE ME?	8.50	15.00
☐ 55350	*LIBERTY*	THE MOUNTAIN'S HIGH/I WANT SOMEONE . . .	2.00	3.50
☐ 55382		GOODBYE TO LOVE/SWING LOW	2.00	3.50
☐ 55412		TELL ME/WILL YOU ALWAYS LOVE ME?	2.00	3.50
☐ 55478		ALL I WANT/LIFE'S JUST A PLAY	2.00	3.50
☐ 5320	*WARNER BROTHERS*	THE RIVER TOOK MY BABY/ MY LONELY SELF	2.00	3.50
☐ 5342		YOUNG AND IN LOVE/SAY TO ME	1.75	3.00
☐ 5364		LOVE IS A ONCE IN A LIFETIME THING/ CHUG-A-CHUG-A-CHOO-CHOO	1.75	3.00
☐ 5383		WHERE DID THE GOOD TIMES GO/ GUESS OUT LOVE MUST SHOW	1.75	3.00
☐ 5396		TURN AROUND/DON'T LEAVE ME	1.75	3.00
☐ 5411		ALL MY TRIALS/ DON'T THINK TWICE, IT'S ALL RIGHT	1.75	3.00
☐ 5426		THE GIFT/NOT FADE AWAY	1.75	3.00
☐ 5451		YOU WERE MINE/REMEMBER THEN	1.75	3.00
☐ 5470		WITHOUT YOUR LOVE/THE RIDDLE SONG . . .	1.75	3.00
☐ 5482		THOU SHALT NOT STEAL/ JUST 'ROUND THE RIVER BEND	1.75	3.00

DICK AND DEEDEE—ALBUMS

☐ 7236 (S)	*LIBERTY*	TELL ME	10.00	25.00
☐ 1500 (S)	*WARNER BROTHERS*	YOUNG AND IN LOVE	8.00	22.50

ISSUE #	LABEL		PRICE RANGE	
☐ 1538 (S)		TURN AROUND	8.00	22.50
☐ 1586 (S)		THOU SHALT NOT STEAL	8.00	22.50
☐ 1623 (S)		SONGS WE'VE SUNG ON SHINDIG	8.00	22.50

BO DIDDLEY

☐ 814	*CHECKER*	BO DIDDLEY/I'M A MAN	4.50	9.00
☐ 819		DIDDLEY DADDY/SHE'S FINE, SHE'S MINE . . .	4.00	7.00
☐ 827		PRETTY THING/BRING IT TO JEROME	4.00	7.00
☐ 832		DIDDY WAH DIDDY/		
		I'M LOOKING FOR A WOMAN	4.00	7.00
☐ 842		WHO DO YOU LOVE/I'M BAD	4.00	7.00
☐ 850		COPS AND ROBBERS/		
		DOWN HOME SPECIAL	4.00	7.00
☐ 860		HEY, BO DIDDLEY/MONA.	4.00	7.00
☐ 878		SAY, BOSS MAN/BEFORE YOU ACCUSE ME . . .	4.00	7.00
☐ 896		HUSH YOUR MOUTH/DEAREST DARLING	4.00	7.00
☐ 907		WILLIE AND LILLIE/		
		BO MEETS THE MONSTER	4.00	7.00
☐ 914		I'M SORRY/OH YEA	3.50	6.00
☐ 924		CRACKIN' UP/THE GREAT GRANDFATHER	3.50	6.00
☐ 931		SAY MAN/THE CLOCK STRIKES TWELVE	3.50	6.00
☐ 936		SAY MAN, BACK AGAIN/SHE'S ALRIGHT	3.50	6.00
☐ 942		ROAD RUNNER/MY STORY	3.50	6.00
☐ 951		WALKIN' AND TALKIN'/CRAWDAD	2.75	4.50
☐ 965		GUNSLINGER/SIGNIFYING	3.50	6.00
☐ 976		NOT GUILTY/AZTEC	2.75	4.50
☐ 985		CALL ME/PILLS	2.25	4.00
☐ 997		BO DIDDLEY/I'M A MAN	2.00	3.50
☐ 1019		YOU CAN'T JUDGE A BOOK BY ITS COVER/		
		I CAN TELL	2.00	3.50
☐ 1045		SURFER'S LOVE CALL/		
		GREATEST LOVER IN THE WORLD	2.00	3.50

BO DIDDLEY—ALBUMS

☐ 1431 (M)	*CHECKER*	BO DIDDLEY	15.00	35.00
☐ 1436 (M)		GO BO DIDDLEY	12.50	30.00
☐ 2974 (M)		HAVE GUITAR WILL TRAVEL	10.00	25.00
☐ 2976 (M)		IN THE SPOTLIGHT	10.00	25.00
☐ 2977 (M)		BO DIDDLEY IS A GUNSLINGER	10.00	25.00
☐ 2980 (M)		BO DIDDLEY IS A LOVER	10.00	25.00
☐ 2982 (M)		BO DIDDLEY IS A TWISTER	10.00	25.00
☐ 2984 (M)		BO DIDDLEY	8.00	22.50
☐ 2985 (M)		BO DIDDLEY AND COMPANY	7.00	18.00
☐ 2987 (M)		SURFIN' WITH BO DIDDLEY	7.00	18.00
☐ 2988 (M)		BO DIDDLEY'S BEACH PARTY	7.00	18.00

ISSUE #	LABEL		PRICE RANGE	
☐ 2989 (M)		16 ALL TIME GREATEST HITS.	8.00	22.50
☐ 2992 (M)		HEY GOOD LOOKIN'	7.00	18.00
☐ 2996 (M)		500% MORE MAN	7.00	18.00
☐ 3001 (M)		THE ORIGINATOR	6.00	15.00
☐ 3013 (M)		BLACK GLADIATOR	6.00	15.00

DION

ISSUE #	LABEL		PRICE RANGE	
☐ 3070	*LAURIE*	LONELY TEENAGER/LITTLE MISS BLUE	2.00	3.50
☐ 3081		HAVIN' FUN/		
		NORTHEAST END OF THE CORNER	2.00	3.50
☐ 3090		KISSIN' GAME/HEAVEN HELP ME	2.00	3.50
☐ 3101		SOMEBODY NOBODY WANTS/COULD		
		SOMEBODY TAKE MY PLACE TONIGHT? . . .	2.25	4.00
☐ 3110		RUNAROUND SUE/RUNAWAY GIRL	2.00	3.50
☐ 3115		THE WANDERER/THE MAJESTIC	2.00	3.50
☐ 3123		LOVERS WHO WANDER/		
		(I WAS) BORN TO CRY	2.00	3.50
☐ 3134		LITTLE DIANE/LOST FOR SURE	2.00	3.50
☐ 3145		LOVE CAME TO ME/LITTLE GIRL	2.00	3.50
☐ 3153		SANDY/FAITH	2.00	3.50
☐ 3171		COME GO WITH ME/		
		KING WITHOUT A QUEEN	2.00	3.50
☐ 3187		LONELY WORLD/TAG ALONG	2.25	4.00
☐ 3225		THEN I'LL BE TIRED OF YOU/		
		AFTER THE DANCE	2.25	4.00
☐ 3240		SHOUT/LITTLE GIRL . . . . :	2.25	4.00
☐ 3303		I GOT THE BLUES/(I WAS) BORN TO CRY	2.25	4.00
☐ 3464		ABRAHAM, MARTIN AND JOHN/		
		DADDY ROLLIN'	1.75	3.00
☐ 3478		PURPLE HAZE/THE DOLPHINS	1.75	3.00
☐ 3495		BOTH SIDES NOW/SUN FUN SONG	2.25	4.00
☐ 3504		LOVING YOU IS SWEETER THAN EVER/		
		HE LOOKS A LOT LIKE ME	2.25	4.00
☐ 42662	*COLUMBIA*	RUBY BABY/HE'LL ONLY HURT YOU	1.75	3.00
☐ 42776		THIS LITTLE GIRL/		
		THE LONELIEST MAN IN THE WORLD	2.00	3.50
☐ 42810		BE CAREFUL OF STONES THAT YOU		
		THROW/I CAN'T BELIEVE	2.00	3.50
☐ 42852		DONNA THE PRIMA DONNA/YOU'RE MINE . . .	2.00	3.50
☐ 42917		DRIP DROP/NO ONE'S WAITING FOR ME	2.00	3.50
☐ 42977		I'M YOU HOOCHIE COOCHI MAN/		
		THE ROAD I'M ON	2.00	3.50
☐ 43096		JOHNNY B. GOODE/CHICAGO BLUES	2.00	3.50
☐ 43213		UNLOVED, UNWANTED ME/		
		SWEET SWEET BABY	2.00	3.50

DION

ISSUE #	LABEL		PRICE RANGE	
☐ 43293		SPOONFUL/KICKIN' CHILD	2.00	3.50
☐ 43423		TOMORROW WON'T BRING THE RAIN/		
		YOU MOVE ME BABE	2.25	4.00
☐ 43483		TIME IN MY HEART FOR YOU/		
		WAKE UP BABY	2.00	3.50
☐ 43692		TWO TON FEATHER/SO MUCH YOUNGER	2.00	3.50
☐ 44719		SOUTHERN TRAIN/I CAN'T HELP		
		BUT WONDER WHERE I'M BOUND	2.00	3.50
☐ 7356	**WARNER BROTHERS**	NATURAL MAN/IF WE ONLY HAVE LOVE	2.00	3.50
☐ 7401		YOUR OWN BACK YARD/		
		SIT DOWN OLD FRIEND	1.75	3.00
☐ 7469		CLOSE TO IT ALL/LET IT BE	1.75	3.00
☐ 7491		JOSIE/SUNNILAND	1.75	3.00
☐ 7537		SANCTUARY/RRAND NEW MORNING	1.75	3.00
☐ 7663		RUNNING CLOSE BEHIND YOU/SEAGULL	1.75	3.00
☐ 7704		DOCTOR ROCK AND ROLL/SUNSHINE LADY . . .	1.75	3.00
☐ 7793		NEW YORK CITY SONG/		
		RICHER THAN A RICH MAN	1.75	3.00
☐ 8234		LOVER BOY SUPREME/HEY MY LOVE	1.75	3.00
☐ 8258		THE WAY YOU DO THE THINGS YOU DO/		
		LOVER BOY SUPREME	1.75	3.00
☐ 8293		THE QUEEN OF '59/OH, THE NIGHT	1.75	3.00
☐ 8406		YOUNG VIRGIN EYES/OH, THE NIGHT	1.75	3.00

DION—ALBUMS

ISSUE #		LABEL		PRICE RANGE	
☐ 2004	(M)	**LAURIE**	ALONE WITH DION	12.00	25.00
☐ 2009	(M)		RUNAROUND SUE	8.00	22.50
☐ 2012	(M)		LOVERS WHO WANDER	8.00	22.50
☐ 2013	(M)		DION SINGS HIS GREATEST HITS	8.00	22.50
☐ 2015	(M)		LOVE CAME TO ME	8.00	22.50
☐ 2017	(M)		DION SINGS TO SANDY	8.00	22.50
☐ 2019	(M)		DION SINGS THE 15 MILLION SELLERS	8.00	22.50
☐ 2022	(M)		MORE OF DION'S GREATEST HITS	8.00	22.50
☐ 2047	(S)		DION	6.00	15.00
☐ 8810	(S)	**COLUMBIA**	RUBY BABY	7.00	18.00
☐ 8907	(S)		DONNA THE PRIMA DONNA	7.00	18.00
☐ 9773	(S)		WONDER WHERE I'M BOUND	7.00	18.00
☐ 1826	(S)	**WARNER BROTHERS**	SIT DOWN OLD FRIEND	6.00	15.00
☐ 1872	(S)		YOU'RE NOT ALONE	5.00	10.50
☐ 1945	(S)		SANCTUARY	5.00	13.50
☐ 2642	(S)		SUITE FOR LATE SUMMER	5.00	13.50
☐ 2954	(S)		STREETHEART	4.00	10.00

ISSUE #	LABEL		PRICE RANGE	

DIXIE CUPS

☐ 10-001	*RED BIRD*	CHAPEL OF LOVE/AIN'T THAT NICE	2.00	3.50
☐ 10-006		PEOPLE SAY/GIRLS CAN TELL	2.00	3.50
☐ 10-012		YOU SHOULD HAVE SEEN THE WAY HE LOOKED AT ME/NO TRUE LOVE	2.00	3.50
☐ 10-017		LITTLE BELL/ANOTHER BOY LIKE MINE	2.00	3.50
☐ 10-024		IKO IKO/GEE BABY GEE	2.00	3.50
☐ 10-032		GEE THE MOON IS SHINING BRIGHT/ I'M GONNA GET YOU YET	2.00	3.50

DIXIE CUPS—ALBUMS

☐ 100 (S)	*RED BIRD*	CHAPEL OF LOVE	10.00	25.00
☐ 103 (S)		IKO IKO	8.00	22.50
☐ 525 (S)	*ABC-PARAMOUNT*	RIDING HIGH	8.00	22.50

FATS DOMINO

☐ 5058	*IMPERIAL*	THE FAT MAN/DETROIT CITY BLUES	24.00	42.00
☐ 5065		BOOGIE WOOGIE BABY/LITTLE BEE	24.00	42.00
☐ 5077		SHE'S MY BABY/HIDEAWAY BLUES	24.00	42.00
☐ 5085		HEY LA BAS BOOGIE/BRAND NEW BABY	24.00	42.00
☐ 5099		KOREA BLUES/ EVERY NIGHT ABOUT THIS TIME	30.00	44.00
☐ 5114		TIRED OF CRYING/ WHAT'S THE MATTER, BABY?	20.00	35.00
☐ 5123		DON'T YOU LIE TO ME/ SOMETIMES I WONDER	20.00	35.00
☐ 5138		NO, NO BABY/RIGHT FROM WRONG	20.00	30.00
☐ 5145		ROCKIN' CHAIR/CARELESS LOVE	30.00	30.00
☐ 5167		YOU KNOW I MISS YOU/I'LL BE GONE	15.00	25.00
☐ 5180		GOIN' HOME/REELING AND ROCKING	15.00	25.00
☐ 5197		POOR POOR ME/TRUST IN ME	15.00	25.00
☐ 5209		HOW LONG?/DREAMING	12.00	20.00
☐ 5220		NOBODY LOVES ME/CHEATIN'	10.00	18.00
☐ 5231		GOING TO THE RIVER/ MARDI GRAS IN NEW ORLEANS	10.00	18.00
☐ 5240		PLEASE DON'T LEAVE ME/THE GIRL I LOVE	8.50	15.00
☐ 5251		ROSE MARY/YOU SAID YOU LOVED ME	8.50	15.00
☐ 5262		DON'T LEAVE ME THIS WAY/ SOMETHING'S WRONG	8.50	15.00
☐ 5272		LITTLE SCHOOL GIRL/ YOU DONE ME WRONG	8.50	15.00
☐ 5283		BABY, PLEASE/WHERE DID YOU STAY?	8.50	15.00
☐ 5301		YOU CAN PACK YOUR SUITCASE/ I LIVED MY LIFE	8.50	15.00

ISSUE #	LABEL	PRICE RANGE	
☐5313	DON'T YOU HEAR ME CALLING YOU/		
	LOVE ME	7.25	12.00
☐5323	I KNOW/THINKING OF YOU	6.00	10.00
☐5340	DON'T YOU KNOW/HELPING HAND	4.50	9.00
☐5348	AIN'T IT A SHAME/LA LA	4.00	7.00
☐5357	ALL BY MYSELF/TROUBLES OF MY OWN	4.00	7.00
☐5369	POOR ME/I CAN'T GO ON	3.50	6.00
☐5375	BO WEEVIL/DON'T BLAME IT ON ME	3.50	6.00
☐5386	I'M IN LOVE AGAIN/MY BLUE HEAVEN	2.75	4.50
☐5396	WHEN MY DREAMBOAT COMES HOME/		
	SO-LONG	2.75	4.50
☐5407	BLUEBERRY HILL/HONEY CHILE	2.75	4.50
☐5417	BLUE MONDAY/WHAT'S THE REASON		
	I'M NOT PLEASING YOU	2.25	4.00
☐5428	I'M WALKIN'/I'M IN THE MOOD FOR LOVE	2.25	4.00
☐5442	VALLEY OF TEARS/IT'S YOU I LOVE	2.25	4.00
☐5454	WHEN I SEE YOU/		
	WHAT WILL I TELL MY HEART	2.25	4.00
☐5467	WAIT AND SEE/I STILL LOVE YOU	2.25	4.00
☐5477	THE BIG BEAT/I WANT YOU TO KNOW	2.00	3.50
☐5492	YES, MY DARLING/		
	DON'T YOU KNOW I LOVE YOU	2.00	3.50
☐5515	SICK AND TIRED/NO, NO	2.00	3.50
☐5526	LITTLE MARY/PRISONER'S SONG	2.00	3.50
☐5537	YOUNG SCHOOL GIRL/IT MUST BE LOVE	2.00	3.50
☐5553	WHOLE LOTTA LOVING/COQUETTE	2.00	3.50
☐5569	WHEN THE SAINTS GO MARCHING IN/		
	TELLING LIES	2.00	3.50
☐5585	I'M READY/MARGIE	2.00	3.50
☐5606	I WANT TO WALK YOU HOME/		
	I'M GONNA BE A WHEEL SOMEDAY	2.00	3.50
☐5629	BE MY GUEST/I'VE BEEN AROUND	2.00	3.50
☐5645	COUNTRY BOY/IF YOU NEED ME	2.00	3.50
☐5660	TELL ME THAT YOU LOVE ME/		
	BEFORE I GROW TOO OLD	2.00	3.50
☐5675	WALKING TO NEW ORLEANS/		
	DON'T COME KNOCKING	2.00	3.50
☐5687	THREE NIGHTS A WEEK/		
	PUT YOUR ARMS AROUND ME HONEY	2.00	3.50
☐5704	MY GIRL JOSEPHINE/		
	NATURAL BORN LOVER	2.00	3.50
☐5723	WHAT A PRICE/		
	AIN'T THAT JUST LIKE A WOMAN	2.00	3.50
☐5734	SHU RAH/FELL IN LOVE ON MONDAY	2.00	3.50
☐5753	IT KEEPS RAININ'/I JUST CRY	2.00	3.50

ISSUE #	LABEL		PRICE RANGE	
☐ 5764		LET THE FOUR WINDS BLOW/		
		GOOD HEARTED MAN	2.00	3.50
☐ 5779		WHAT A PARTY/ROCKIN' BICYCLE	2.00	3.50
☐ 5796		JAMBALAYA (ON THE BAYOU)/		
		I HEAR YOU KNOCKING	2.00	3.50
☐ 5816		YOU WIN AGAIN/IDA JANE	2.00	3.50
☐ 5833		MY REAL NAME/MY HEART IS BLEEDING	2.00	3.50
☐ 5863		NOTHING NEW (SAME OLD THING)/		
		DANCE WITH MR. DOMINO	2.00	3.50
☐ 5875		DID YOU EVER SEE A DREAM WALKING?/		
		STOP THE CLOCK	2.00	3.50
☐ 5895		WON'T YOU COME ON BACK/		
		HANDS ACROSS THE TABLE	2.00	3.50
☐ 5909		THOSE EYES/HUM DIDDY DOO	2.00	3.50
☐ 5937		YOU ALWAYS HURT THE ONE YOU LOVE/		
		TROUBLED BLUES	2.00	3.50
☐ 5959		ISLE OF CAPRI/I CAN'T GO ON THIS WAY	2.00	3.50
☐ 5980		ONE NIGHT/I CAN'T GO ON THIS WAY	2.00	3.50
☐ 66005		I CAN'T GIVE YOU ANYTHING BUT LOVE/		
		GOIN' HOME	2.00	3.50
☐ 66016		YOUR CHEATIN' HEART/		
		WHEN I WAS YOUNG	2.00	3.50

FATS DOMINO—EPs

☐ 127	*IMPERIAL*	FATS DOMINO	20.00	30.00
☐ 139		ROCK AND ROLLIN' WITH FATS DOMINO	15.00	25.00
☐ 141		FATS DOMINO: ROCK AND ROLLIN'	15.00	25.00
☐ 142		FATS DOMINO: ROCK AND ROLLIN'	15.00	25.00
☐ 143		FATS DOMINO: ROCK AND ROLLIN'	15.00	25.00
☐ 146		THIS IS FATS DOMINO	15.00	25.00
☐ 147		HERE COMES FATS	15.00	25.00
☐ 148		HERE STANDS FATS DOMINO	12.00	20.00
☐ 149		HERE STANDS FATS DOMINO	12.00	20.00
☐ 150		HERE STANDS FATS DOMINO	12.00	20.00
☐ 151		COOKIN' WITH FATS	10.00	18.00
☐ 152		ROCKIN' WITH FATS	10.00	18.00

FATS DOMINO—ALBUMS

☐ 9004 (M)	*IMPERIAL*	ROCK AND ROLLIN' WITH FATS DOMINO	25.00	60.00
☐ 9009 (M)		ROCK AND ROLLIN'	20.00	50.00
☐ 9028 (M)		THIS IS FATS DOMINO	20.00	50.00
☐ 9038 (M)		HERE STANDS FATS DOMINO	20.00	50.00
☐ 9040 (M)		THIS IS FATS	15.00	35.00
☐ 9055 (M)		THE FABULOUS MR. D.	15.00	35.00
☐ 9062 (M)		FATS DOMINO SWINGS	12.50	30.00
☐ 9065 (M)		LET'S PLAY	12.50	30.00

ISSUE #	LABEL		PRICE RANGE	
☐ 9103 (M)		FATS DOMINO SINGS	10.00	25.00
☐ 9138 (M)		A LOT OF DOMINOS	10.00	25.00
☐ 9153 (M)		LET THE FOUR WINDS BLOW	10.00	25.00
☐ 9164 (M)		WHAT A PARTY	10.00	25.00
☐ 9170 (M)		TWISTIN' THE STOMP	10.00	25.00
☐ 9195 (M)		MILLION SELLERS	8.00	22.50
☐ 9208 (M)		JUST DOMINO	8.00	22.50
☐ 9227 (M)		WALKING TO NEW ORLEANS	8.00	22.50
☐ 9239 (M)		LET'S DANCE WITH DOMINO	7.00	18.00
☐ 9248 (M)		HERE HE COMES AGAIN	7.00	18.00
☐ 455 (M)	*ABC-PARAMOUNT*	HERE COMES FATS DOMINO	6.00	15.00
☐ 455 (S)		HERE COMES FATS DOMINO	8.00	22.50
☐ 479 (S)		FATS ON FIRE	8.00	22.50
☐ 510 (S)		GETAWAY WITH FATS DOMINO	8.00	22.50
☐ 61039 (S)	*MERCURY*	FATS DOMINO '65	7.00	18.00
☐ 61065 (S)		SOUTHLAND U.S.A.	7.00	18.00
☐ 6304 (S)	*REPRISE*	FATS IS BACK	7.00	18.00
☐ 6439 (S)		FATS	7.00	18.00

DONOVAN

ISSUE #	LABEL		PRICE RANGE	
☐ 1309	*HICKORY*	CATCH THE WIND/ WHY DO YOU TREAT ME LIKE YOU DO	2.25	3.50
☐ 1324		COLOURS/JOSIE	2.25	3.50
☐ 1338		UNIVERSAL SOLDIER/ DO YOU HEAR ME NOW?	2.25	3.50
☐ 1402		TO TRY FOR THE SUN/TURQUOISE	2.25	3.50
☐ 1417		THE WAR DRAGS ON/HEY GYP	2.25	3.50
☐ 1470		SUNNY GOODGE STREET/ SUMMER DAY REFLECTION SONG	2.25	3.50
☐ 10045	*EPIC*	SUNSHINE SUPERMAN/THE TRIP	1.75	3.00
☐ 10098		MELLOW YELLOW/ SUNNY SOUTH KENSINGTON	1.75	3.00
☐ 10127		EPISTLE TO DIPPY/PREACHIN' LOVE	1.75	3.00
☐ 10212		THERE IS A MOUNTAIN/SAND AND FOAM	1.75	3.00
☐ 10253		WEAR YOUR LOVE LIKE HEAVEN/OH GOSH	1.75	3.00
☐ 10300		JENNIFER JUNIPER/POOR COW	1.75	3.00
☐ 10345		HURDY GURDY MAN/TEEN ANGEL	1.75	3.00
☐ 10393		LALENA/AYE MY LOVE	1.75	3.00
☐ 10434		ATLANTIS/TO SUSAN ON THE WEST COAST WAITING	1.75	3.00
☐ 10510		GOO GOO BARABAJAGAL/TRUDI	1.75	3.00
☐ 10649		RIKI TIKI TAVI/ROOTS OF OAK	1.75	3.00
☐ 10694		CELIA OF THE SEALS/ SONG OF THE WANDERING AENGUS	1.75	3.00

DOORS

ISSUE #	LABEL		PRICE RANGE	
☐ 10983		I LIKE YOU/EARTH SIGN MAN	1.75	3.00
☐ 11023		MARIA MAGENTA/		
		INTERGALACTIC LAXATIVE	1.75	3.00
☐ 11108		SAILING HOMEWARD/YELLOW STAR	1.75	3.00
☐ 50016		ROCK 'N ROLL WITH ME/		
		DIVINE DAZE OF DEATHLESS DELIGHT	1.75	3.00
☐ 50077		ROCK AND ROLL SOULIER/HOW SILLY	1.75	3.00

DONOVAN—ALBUMS

ISSUE #	LABEL		PRICE RANGE	
☐ 123 (M)	*HICKORY*	CATCH THE WIND	6.00	15.00
☐ 127 (S)		FAIRYTALES	6.00	15.00
☐ 135 (S)		THE REAL DONOVAN	6.00	15.00
☐ 143 (S)		LIKE IT IS, WAS AND EVERMORE SHALL BE	6.00	15.00
☐ 147 (S)		THE BEST OF DONOVAN	5.00	13.50
☐ 26217 (S)	*EPIC*	SUNSHINE SUPERMAN	6.00	15.00
☐ 26239 (S)		MELLOW YELLOW	6.00	15.00
☐ 26349 (S)		WEAR YOUR LOVE LIKE HEAVEN	6.00	15.00
☐ 26350 (S)		FOR LITTLE ONES	6.00	15.00
☐ 171 (S)		A GIFT FROM A FLOWER TO A GARDEN	6.00	15.00
☐ 26386 (S)		IN CONCERT	5.00	13.50
☐ 26420 (S)		THE HURDY GURDY MAN	5.00	13.50
☐ 26439 (S)		GREATEST HITS	5.00	13.50
☐ 26481 (S)		BARABAJAGAL	5.00	13.50
☐ 30125 (S)		OPEN ROAD	5.00	13.50
☐ 32156 (S)		COSMIC WHEELS	5.00	13.50
☐ 32800 (S)		ESSENCE TO ESSENCE	5.00	13.50
☐ 33245 (S)		7-TEASE	5.00	13.50
☐ 33945 (S)		SLOW DOWN WORLD	5.00	13.50

DOORS

ISSUE #	LABEL		PRICE RANGE	
☐ 45611	*ELEKTRA*	BREAK ON THROUGH/END OF THE NIGHT	3.50	6.00
☐ 45615		LIGHT MY FIRE/CRYSTAL SHIP	1.50	2.50
☐ 45621		PEOPLE ARE STRANGE/UNHAPPY GIRL	1.75	3.00
☐ 45624		LOVE ME TWO TIMES/STARLIGHT DRIVE	1.75	3.00
☐ 45628		UNKNOWN SOLDIER/		
		WE COULD BE SO GOOD TOGETHER	1.75	3.00
☐ 45635		HELLO, I LOVE YOU/LOVE STREET	1.75	3.00
☐ 45646		TOUCH ME/WILD CHILD	1.75	3.00
☐ 45656		WISHFUL, SINFUL/WHO SCARED YOU	1.75	3.00
☐ 45663		TELL ALL THE PEOPLE/EASY RIDE	1.75	3.00
☐ 45675		RUNNIN' BLUE/DO IT	1.75	3.00
☐ 45685		YOU MAKE ME REAL/ROADHOUSE BLUES	1.75	3.00
☐ 45726		LOVE HER MADLY/DON'T GO NO FURTHER	1.75	3.00
☐ 45738		RIDERS ON THE STORM/CHANGELING	1.75	3.00

ISSUE #	LABEL		PRICE RANGE	

DOORS—ALBUMS

☐ 74007 (S)	*ELEKTRA*	DOORS	5.00	13.50
☐ 74007 (S)		STRANGE DAYS	5.00	13.50
☐ 74024 (S)		WAITING FOR THE SUN	5.00	13.50
☐ 74079 (S)		13 (greatest hits)	4.50	12.00
☐ 9002 (S)		ABSOLUTELY LIVE	4.50	12.00
☐ 75005 (S)		SOFT PARADE	4.50	12.00
☐ 75007 (S)		MORRISON HOTEL	4.50	12.00
☐ 75011 (S)		L. A. WOMAN	4.50	12.00

DOVELLS

☐ 819	*PARKWAY*	NO NO NO/LETTERS OF LOVE	4.00	7.00
☐ 827		BRISTOL STOMP/OUT IN THE COLD AGAIN	3.50	6.00
☐ 827		BRISTOL STOMP/LETTERS OF LOVE	2.00	3.50
☐ 833		DOIN' THE NEW CONTINENTAL/		
		MOPE-ITTY MOPE STOMP	2.00	3.50
☐ 838		BRISTOL TWISTIN' ANNIE/THE ACTOR	2.00	3.50
☐ 845		HULLY GULLY BABY/YOUR LAST CHANCE	2.00	3.50
☐ 855		THE JITTERBUG/KISSIN' IN THE KITCHEN	2.00	3.50
☐ 861		YOU CAN'T RUN AWAY FROM YOURSELF/		
		HELP ME BABY	2.00	3.50
☐ 867		YOU CAN'T SIT DOWN/		
		STOMPIN' EVERYWHERE	2.00	3.50
☐ 867		YOU CAN'T SIT DOWN/WILDWOOD DAYS	2.00	3.50
☐ 882		BETTY IN BERMUDAS/DANCE THE FROOG	2.00	3.50
☐ 889		STOP MONKEYIN' AROUN'/NO NO NO	2.00	3.50
☐ 901		BE MY GIRL/DRAGSTER ON THE PROWL	2.00	3.50
☐ 911		HAPPY BIRTHDAY JUST THE SAME/		
		ONE POTATO, TWO POTATO	2.00	3.50
☐ 925		WATUSI WITH LUCY/WHAT IN THE		
		WORLD'S COME OVER YOU?	2.00	3.50
☐ 4231	*SWAN*	(HEY HEY HEY) ALRIGHT/HAPPY	2.00	3.50
☐ 1369	*JAMIE*	ONE WINTER LOVE/BLUE	2.00	3.50
☐ 13628	*MGM*	THERE'S A GIRL/LOVE IS EVERYWHERE	2.00	3.50
☐ 13946		HERE COMES THE JUDGE/GIRL	2.00	3.50
☐ 14568		MARY'S MAGIC SHOW/		
		DON'T VOTE FOR LUKE McCABE	2.00	3.50
☐ 3310	*EVENT*	ROLL OVER BEETHOVEN/		
		SOMETHING ABOUT YOU BOY	2.00	3.50
☐ 216		DANCING IN THE STREET/		
		BACK ON THE ROAD AGAIN	2.00	3.50

ISSUE #	LABEL		PRICE RANGE	

DOVELLS—ALBUMS

☐7006 (M)	*PARKWAY*	BRISTOL STOMP	8.00	22.50
☐7021 (M)		FOR YOUR HULLY GULLY PARTY	7.00	18.00
☐7025 (M)		YOU CAN'T SIT DOWN	7.00	18.00

DRIFTERS

☐1006	*ATLANTIC*	MONEY HONEY/THE WAY I FEEL	12.00	20.00
☐1019		SUCH A NIGHT/LUCILLE	12.00	20.00
☐1029		HONEY LOVE/WARM YOUR HEART	10.00	18.00
☐1043		BIP BAM/SOMEDAY YOU'LL WANT ME TO WANT YOU	8.00	15.00
☐1048		WHITE CHRISTMAS/ THE BELLS OF ST. MARY'S	7.25	12.00
☐1055		GONE/WHAT 'CHA GONNA DO?	7.25	12.00
☐1078		ADORABLE/STEAMBOAT	6.00	11.00
☐1089		RUBY BABY/YOUR PROMISE TO BE MINE	6.00	11.00
☐1101		SOLDIER OF FORTUNE/ I GOTTA GET MYSELF A WOMAN	6.00	11.00
☐1123		FOOLS FALL IN LOVE/IT WAS A TEAR	3.50	6.00
☐1141		HYPNOTIZED/DRIFTING AWAY FROM YOU	3.50	6.00
☐1161		I KNOW/YODEE YAKEE	3.50	6.00
☐1187		DRIP DROP/MOONLIGHT BAY	2.75	4.50
☐2025		THERE GOES MY BABY/OH MY LOVE	2.25	4.00
☐2038		THERE YOU GO/ YOU WENT BACK ON YOUR WORD	3.50	6.00
☐2040		DANCE WITH ME/TRUE LOVE, TRUE LOVE	2.25	4.00
☐2050		THIS MAGIC MOMENT/BALTIMORE	2.25	4.00
☐2062		LONELY WINDS/HEY SENORITA	2.25	4.00
☐2071		SAVE THE LAST DANCE FOR ME/ NOBODY BUT ME	2.25	4.00
☐2087		I COUNT THE TEARS/ SUDDENLY THERE'S A VALLEY	2.25	4.00
☐2096		SOME KIND OF WONDERFUL/HONEY BEE	2.25	4.00
☐2105		PLEASE STAY/NO SWEET LOVIN'	2.25	4.00
☐2117		SWEETS FOR MY SWEET/ LONELINESS OR HAPPINESS	2.00	3.50
☐2127		ROOM FULL OF TEARS/ SOMEBODY NEW DANCIN' WITH YOU	2.00	3.50
☐2134		WHEN MY LITTLE GIRL IS SMILING/ MEXICAN DIVORCE	2.00	3.50
☐2143		STRANGER ON THE SHORE/WHAT TO DO	2.00	3.50
☐2151		SOMETIMES I WONDER/JACKPOT	2.00	3.50
☐2162		UP ON THE ROOF/ ANOTHER NIGHT WITH THE BOYS	2.00	3.50

ISSUE #	LABEL		PRICE	RANGE
☐ 2182		ON BROADWAY/LET THE MUSIC PLAY	2.00	3.50
☐ 2191		RAT RACE/IF YOU DON'T COME BACK	2.00	3.50
☐ 2201		I'LL TAKE YOU HOME/		
		I FEEL GOOD ALL OVER	2.00	3.50
☐ 2216		VAYA CON DIOS/		
		IN THE LAND OF MAKE BELIEVE	2.00	3.50
☐ 2225		ONE WAY LOVE/DIDN'T IT	2.00	3.50
☐ 2237		UNDER THE BROADWALK/I DON'T WANT		
		TO GO ON WITHOUT YOU	2.00	3.50
☐ 2253		I'VE GOT SAND IN MY SHOES/		
		HE'S JUST A PLAYBOY	1.75	3.00
☐ 2260		SATURDAY NIGHT AT THE MOVIES/		
		SPANISH LACE	1.75	3.00
☐ 2261		THE CHRISTMAS SONG/		
		I REMEMBER CHRISTMAS	1.75	3.00
☐ 2268		AT THE CLUB/ANSWER THE PHONE	1.75	3.00
☐ 2285		COME ON OVER TO MY PLACE/		
		CHAINS OF LOVE	1.75	3.00
☐ 2292		FOLLOW ME/THE OUTSIDE WORLD	1.75	3.00
☐ 2298		I'LL TAKE YOU WHERE THE MUSIC'S		
		PLAYING/FAR FROM THE		
		MADDENING CROWD	1.75	3.00
☐ 2310		WE GOTTA SING/NYLON STOCKINGS	1.75	3.00

DRIFTERS—EPs

☐ 534	*ATLANTIC*	THE DRIFTERS FEATURING		
		CLYDE McPHATTER	10.00	18.00
☐ 592		THE DRIFTERS	8.50	15.00

DRIFTERS—ALBUMS

☐ 8003 (M)		CLYDE McPHATTER AND THE DRIFTERS	17.50	45.00
☐ 8022 (M)		ROCKIN' AND DRIFTIN'	15.00	35.00
☐ 8041 (M)		GREATEST HITS	15.00	35.00
☐ 8059 (S)		SAVE THE LAST DANCE FOR ME	12.50	30.00
☐ 8073 (S)		UP ON THE ROOF	12.50	30.00
☐ 8093 (S)		OUR BIGGEST HITS	10.00	25.00
☐ 8099 (S)		UNDER THE BOARDWALK	10.00	25.00
☐ 8102 (S)		THE GOOD LIFE WITH THE DRIFTERS	8.00	22.50
☐ 8113 (S)		I'LL TAKE YOU WHERE THE		
		MUSIC'S PLAYING	8.00	22.50
☐ 8153 (S)		THE DRIFTERS' GOLDEN HITS	8.00	22.50

DUPREES

☐ 569	*COED*	YOU BELONG TO ME/TAKE ME AS I AM	2.00	3.50
☐ 571		MY OWN TRUE LOVE/GINNY	2.00	3.50

ISSUE #	LABEL		PRICE RANGE	
☐574		I'D RATHER BE HERE IN YOU ARMS/		
		I WISH I COULD BELIEVE YOU	2.00	3.50
☐576		GONE WITH THE WIND/		
		LET'S MAKE LOVE AGAIN	2.00	3.50
☐580		I GOTTA TELL HER NOW/TAKE ME AS I AM . . .	2.00	3.50
☐584		WHY DON'T YOU BELIEVE ME/		
		THE THINGS I LOVE	2.25	4.00
☐584		WHY DON'T YOU BELIEVE ME/		
		MY DEAREST ONE	2.00	3.50
☐585		HAVE YOU HEARD?/LOVE EYES	2.00	3.50
☐587		(IT'S NO) SIN/THE SAND AND THE SEA	2.00	3.50
☐591		WHERE ARE YOU/PLEASE LET HER KNOW	2.00	3.50
☐593		SO MANY HAVE TOLD YOU/UNBELIEVABLE . . .	2.00	3.50
☐595		IT ISN'T FAIR/SO LITTLE TIME	2.00	3.50
☐596		I'M YOURS/WISHING RING	2.00	3.50

DUPREES—ALBUMS

☐905 (M)	*COED*	YOU BELONG TO ME	17.50	45.00
☐906 (M)		HAVE YOU HEARD?	15.00	35.00

BOB DYLAN

☐42656	*COLUMBIA*	MIXED UP CONFUSION/CORRINA CORRINA . . .	85.00	150.00
☐42856		BLOWIN' IN THE WIND/		
		DON'T THINK TWICE, IT'S ALL RIGHT	60.00	100.00
☐43242		SUBTERRANEAN HOMESICK BLUES/		
		SHE BELONGS TO ME	2.75	4.50
☐43346		LIKE A ROLLING STONE/GATES OF EDEN . . .	2.00	3.50
☐43389		POSITIVELY 4TH STREET/FROM A BUICK 6 . . .	2.00	3.50
☐43477		CAN YOU PLEASE CRAWL OUT YOUR		
		WINDOW?/HIGHWAY 61 REVISITED	2.75	4.50
☐43541		QUEEN JANE APPROXIMATELY/		
		ONE OF US MUST KNOW	4.00	7.00
☐43592		RAINY DAY WOMAN #12 AND 35/		
		PLEDGING MY TIME	2.00	3.50
☐43683		I WANT YOU/		
		JUST LIKE TOM THUMB'S BLUES	2.00	3.50
☐43792		JUST LIKE A WOMAN/		
		OBVIOUSLY 5 BELIEVERS	2.00	3.50
☐44069		LEOPARD SKIN PILL-BOX HAT/MOST		
		LIKELY YOU'LL GO YOUR WAY AND		
		I'LL GO MINE	2.75	4.50
☐44826		I THREW IT ALL AWAY/		
		DRIFTER'S ESCAPE	1.75	3.00
☐44926		LAY LADY LAY/PEGGY DAY	1.75	3.00

ISSUE #	LABEL		PRICE RANGE	
☐ 45004		TONIGHT I'LL BE STAYING HERE WITH YOU/COUNTRY PIE	1.75	3.00
☐ 45199		WIGWAM/COPPER KETTLE	1.75	3.00
☐ 45409		WATCHING THE RIVER FLOW/ SPANISH IS THE LOVING TONGUE	1.75	3.00
☐ 45516		GEORGE JACKSON/(PT. 2)	1.75	3.00
☐ 45913		KNOCKIN' ON HEAVEN'S DOOR/ TURKEY CHASE	1.75	3.00
☐ 45982		A FOOL SUCH AS I/LILY OF THE WEST	1.75	3.00
☐ 10106		TANGLED UP IN BLUE/ IF YOU SEE HER, SAY HELLO	1.75	3.00
☐ 10245		HURRICANE/(PT. 2)	1.75	3.00
☐ 10298		MOZAMBIQUE/OH SISTER	1.75	3.00
☐ 11033	*ASYLUM*	ON A NIGHT LIKE THIS/YOU ANGEL YOU	1.50	2.50
☐ 11035		GOING, GOING, GONE/ SOMETHING THERE IS ABOUT YOU	1.50	2.50
☐ 11043		MOST LIKELY YOU'LL GO YOUR WAY (AND I'LL GO MINE)/STAGE FRIGHT	1.25	2.50
☐ 45212		ALL ALONG THE WATCHTOWER/ IT AIN'T ME BABE	1.50	2.50

BOB DYLAN—ALBUMS

☐ 8579 (S)	*COLUMBIA*	BOB DYLAN	12.50	30.00
☐ 8786 (S)		FREEWHEELIN'	10.00	25.00
☐ 8905 (S)		THE TIMES ARE A-CHANGIN'	10.00	25.00
☐ 8993 (S)		ANOTHER SIDE OF BOB DYLAN	10.00	25.00
☐ 9128 (S)		BRINGING IT ALL BACK HOME	7.00	18.00
☐ 9189 (S)		HIGHWAY 61 REVISITED	7.00	18.00
☐ 9517 (S)		BLONDE ON BLONDE	6.00	15.00
☐ 9463 (S)		BOB DYLAN'S GREATEST HITS	6.00	15.00
☐ 9604 (S)		JOHN WESLEY HARDING	6.00	15.00
☐ 30050 (S)		SELF PORTRAIT	4.50	12.00
☐ 30290 (S)		NEW MORNING	4.50	12.00
☐ 31120 (S)		BOB DYLAN'S GREATEST HITS, VOL. II	4.50	12.00
☐ 32747 (S)		DYLAN	4.00	10.00
☐ 33235 (S)		BLOOD ON THE TRACKS	4.00	10.00
☐ 33682 (S)		BASEMENT TAPES	4.00	10.00
☐ 33893 (S)		DESIRE	4.00	10.00
☐ 1003	*ASYLUM*	PLANET WAVES	4.00	10.00
☐ 201 (S)		BEFORE THE FLOOD	4.00	10.00

— E —

ISSUE #	LABEL		PRICE RANGE	
DUANE EDDY				
☐ 500	*FORD*	RAMROD/CARAVAN	15.00	25.00
☐ 1101	*JAMIE*	MOVIN' 'N' GROOVIN'/UP AND DOWN	2.25	4.00
☐ 1104		REBEL-ROUSER/STALKIN'	2.00	3.50
☐ 1109		RAMROD/THE WALKER	2.00	3.50
☐ 1111		CANNONBALL/MASON DIXON LINE	2.00	3.50
☐ 1117		THE LONELY ONE/DETOUR	2.00	3.50
☐ 1122		YEP!/DETOUR	2.00	3.50
☐ 1126		FORTY MILES OF BAD ROAD/ THE QUIET THREE	2.00	3.50
☐ 1130		SOME KIND-A EARTHQUAKE/ FIRST LOVE, FIRST TEARS	2.00	3.50
☐ 1144		BONNIE CAME BACK/LOST ISLAND	2.00	3.50
☐ 1151		SHAZAM!/THE SECRET SEVEN	2.00	3.50
☐ 1156		BECAUSE THEY'RE YOUNG/REBEL WALK	2.00	3.50
☐ 1158		THE GIRL ON DEATH ROW/ WORDS MEAN NOTHING	2.00	3.50
☐ 1163		KOMOTION/THEME FOR MOON CHILDREN	2.00	3.50
☐ 1168		PETER GUNN/ALONG THE NAVAJO TRAIL	2.00	3.50
☐ 1175		PEPE/LOST FRIEND	2.00	3.50
☐ 1183		THEME FROM DIXIE/ GIDGET GOES HAWAIIAN	2.00	3.50
☐ 1187		RING OF FIRE/BOBBIE	2.00	3.50
☐ 1195		DRIVIN' HOME/TAMMY	2.00	3.50
☐ 1200		MY BLUE HEAVEN/ALONG CAME LINDA	2.00	3.50
☐ 1206		THE AVENGER/LONDONBERRY AIR	2.00	3.50
☐ 1209		THE BATTLE/TROMBONE	2.00	3.50
☐ 1224		RUNAWAY PONY/JUST BECAUSE	2.00	3.50
☐ 7999	*RCA*	DEEP IN THE HEART OF TEXAS/ SAINTS AND SINNERS	1.75	3.00
☐ 8047		THE BALLAD OF PALADIN/ THE WILD WESTERNERS	1.75	3.00
☐ 8087		(DANCE WITH THE) GUITAR MAN/ STRETCHIN' OUT	1.75	3.00
☐ 8131		BOSS GUITAR/THE DESERT RAT	1.75	3.00
☐ 8180		LONELY BOY, LONELY GUITAR/JOSHIN'	1.75	3.00
☐ 8214		YOUR BABY'S GONE SURFIN'/SHUCKIN'	1.75	3.00
☐ 8276		THE SON OF REBEL ROUSER/ THE STORY OF THREE LOVES	1.75	3.00
☐ 8335		GUITAR CHILD/JERKY JALOPY	1.75	3.00
☐ 8376		THEME FROM A SUMMER PLACE/ WATER SKIING	1.75	3.00
☐ 8442		GUITAR STAR/THE IGUANA	1.75	3.00

ISSUE #	LABEL		PRICE RANGE	
DUANE EDDY—EPs				
☐ 100	*JAMIE*	DUANE EDDY	7.25	12.00
☐ 301		DETOUR	4.50	9.00
☐ 302		YEP!	4.50	9.00
☐ 303		SHAZAM!	4.50	9.00
☐ 304		BECAUSE THEY'RE YOUNG	4.50	9.00
DUANE EDDY—ALBUMS				
☐ 3000 (S)	*JAMIE*	HAVE TWANGY GUITAR, WILL TRAVEL	17.50	30.00
☐ 3006 (S)		ESPECIALLY FOR YOU	15.00	25.00
☐ 3009 (S)		THE TWANG'S THE THING	15.00	25.00
☐ 3011 (S)		SONGS OF OUR HERITAGE	12.50	20.00
☐ 3014 (S)		$1,000,000 WORTH OF TWANG	12.50	20.00
☐ 3019 (S)		GIRLS, GIRLS, GIRLS	12.50	20.00
☐ 3021 (S)		$1,000,000 WORTH OF TWANG, VOL. II	10.00	17.50
☐ 3022 (S)		TWISTING WITH DUANE EDDY	8.00	22.50
☐ 3024 (S)		SURFIN'	8.00	22.50
☐ 3025 (S)		IN PERSON	8.00	22.50
☐ 3026 (S)		16 GREATEST HITS	7.00	18.00
☐ 2525 (S)	*RCA*	TWISTIN' AND TWANGIN'	7.00	18.00
☐ 2576 (S)		TWANGY GUITAR, SILKY STRINGS	7.00	18.00
☐ 2648 (S)		DANCE WITH THE GUITAR MAN	7.00	18.00
☐ 2681 (S)		TWANG A COUNTRY SONG	6.00	15.00
☐ 2700 (S)		TWANGIN' UP A STORM	6.00	15.00
☐ 2798 (S)		LONELY GUITAR	6.00	15.00
☐ 2918 (S)		WATER SKIING	6.00	15.00
☐ 2993 (S)		TWANGIN' THE GOLDEN HITS	6.00	15.00
☐ 3432 (S)		TWANGSVILLE	6.00	15.00
☐ 3477 (S)		THE BEST OF DUANE EDDY	6.00	15.00
☐ 490 (S)	*COLPIX*	A-GO-GO	6.00	15.00
☐ 490 (S)		DUANE EDDY DOES BOB DYLAN	6.00	15.00
☐ 6218 (S)	*REPRISE*	BIGGEST TWANG OF THEM ALL	6.00	15.00
☐ 6240 (S)		ROARING TWANGIES	6.00	15.00

CASS ELLIOT (MAMA CASS)

☐ 4145	*DUNHILL*	DREAM A LITTLE DREAM OF ME/ MIDNIGHT VOYAGE	1.75	4.00
☐ 4166		TALKIN' TO YOUR TOOTHBRUSH/ CALIFORNIA EARTHQUAKE	2.00	4.50
☐ 4184		ALL FOR ME/ MOVE IN A LITTLE CLOSER, BABY	2.00	4.50
☐ 4195		WHO'S TO BLAME/IT'S GETTING BETTER	1.75	4.00
☐ 4214		LADY LOVE/ MAKE YOUR OWN KIND OF MUSIC	1.75	4.00
☐ 4225		NEW WORLD COMING/BLOW ME A KISS	2.00	4.50

ISSUE #	LABEL		PRICE RANGE	
☐ 4226		NEXT TO YOU/		
		SOMETHING TO MAKE YOU HAPPY	1.75	4.00
☐ 4244		I CAN DREAM, CAN'T I?/		
		A SONG THAT NEVER COMES TRUE	1.75	4.00
☐ 4253		WELCOME TO THE WORLD/		
		GOOD TIMES ARE COMING	1.75	4.00
☐ 4264		DON'T LET THE GOOD LIFE PASS YOU BY/		
		SONG THAT NEVER COMES TRUE	1.75	4.00
☐ 0764	*RCA*	BREAK ANOTHER HEART/DISNEY GIRLS	1.75	4.00
☐ 0957		I THINK A LOT ABOUT YOU/		
		LISTEN TO THE WORLD	1.75	4.00

EMERSON, LAKE & PALMER

☐ 44106	*COTILLION*	KNIFE'S EDGE/LUCKY MAN	2.00	4.00
☐ 44131		A TIME & A PLACE/STONE OF YEARS	2.25	4.50
☐ 44151		GREAT GATES OF KIEV/NUTROCKER	1.75	3.50
☐ 44158		FROM THE BEGINNING/LIVING SIN	1.75	3.50
☐ 2003	*MANTICORE*	STILL YOU TURN ME ON/		
		BRAIN SALAD SURGERY	2.25	4.50
☐ 3405	*ATLANTIC*	JEREMY BENDER/C'EST LA VIE	1.75	3.50

ENGLAND DAN & JOHN FORD COLEY

☐ 1278	*A&M*	TELL HER HELLO/NEW JERSEY	2.00	4.00
☐ 1354		SIMONE/CASEY	2.50	5.00
☐ 1369		FREE THE PEOPLE/CAROLINA	2.50	5.00
☐ 1465		MISS YOU SONG/I HEAR THE MUSIC	2.00	4.00
☐ 16069	*BIG TREE*	IT'S NOT THE SAME/		
		I'D REALLY LOVE TO SEE YOU TONIGHT	1.75	3.50
☐ 16079		SHOWBOAT GAMBLER/		
		NIGHTS ARE FOREVER WITHOUT YOU	1.75	3.50
☐ 16088		THE TIME HAS COME/IT'S SAD TO BELONG ...	1.75	3.50
☐ 16102		WHERE DO I GO FROM HERE/		
		GONE TOO FAR	1.75	3.50
☐ 16110		CALLING FOR YOU/WE'LL NEVER HAVE		
		TO SAY GOODBYE AGAIN	1.75	3.50
☐ 16117		WANTING YOU DESPERATELY/		
		YOU CAN'T DANCE	1.75	3.50
☐ 16125		IF THE WORLD RAN OUT OF LOVE TONIGHT ...	1.75	3.50
☐ 16130		WESTWARD WIND/		
		SOME THINGS DON'T COME EASY	1.25	2.50
☐ 16131		LOVE IS THE ANSWER/		
		RUNNING AFTER YOU	1.25	2.50

ISSUE #	LABEL		PRICE RANGE	

ESSEX

☐ 4494	*ROULETTE*	EASIER SAID THAN DONE/		
		ARE YOU GOING MY WAY?	1.75	3.00
☐ 4515		A WALKIN' MIRACLE/		
		WHAT I DON'T KNOW WON'T HURT ME	1.75	3.00
☐ 4530		SHE'S GOT EVERYTHING/		
		OUT OF SIGHT, OUT OF MIND	1.75	3.00
☐ 4542		WHAT DID I DO?/CURFEW LOVER	1.75	3.00
☐ 537	*BANG*	MOONLIGHT, MUSIC AND YOU/THE EAGLE . . .	1.75	3.00

ESSEX—ALBUMS

☐ 25234 (S)				
	ROULETTE	EASIER SAID THAN DONE	8.00	22.50
☐ 25235 (S)		A WALKIN' MIRACLE	7.00	18.00

EVERLY BROTHERS

☐ 21496	*COLUMBIA*	KEEP A-LOVING ME/		
		THE SUN KEEPS SHINING	18.00	30.00
☐ 1315	*CADENCE*	BYE BYE LOVE/		
		I WONDER IF I CARE AS MUCH	2.25	4.00
☐ 1337		WAKE UP LITTLE SUZIE/		
		MAYBE TOMORROW	2.25	4.00
☐ 1342		THIS LITTLE GIRL OF MINE/		
		SHOULD WE TELL HIM?	2.25	4.00
☐ 1348		ALL I HAVE TO DO IS DREAM/CLAUDETTE	2.00	3.50
☐ 1350		BIRD DOG/DEVOTED TO YOU	2.00	3.50
☐ 1355		PROBLEMS/LOVE OF MY LIFE	2.00	3.50
☐ 1364		TAKE A MESSAGE TO MARY/POOR JENNY	2.00	3.50
☐ 1369		('TIL) I KISSED YOU/OH, WHAT A FEELING . . .	2.00	3.50
☐ 1376		LET IT BE ME/		
		SINCE YOU BROKE MY HEART	2.00	3.50
☐ 1380		WHEN WILL I BE LOVED?/BE BOP A LULA	2.00	3.50
☐ 1388		LIKE STRANGERS/		
		A BRAND NEW HEARTACHE	2.00	3.50
☐ 1429		I'M HERE TO GET MY BABY OUT OF JAIL/		
		LIGHTNING EXPRESS	2.25	4.00
☐ 5151	*WARNER BROTHERS*	CATHY'S CLOWN/ALWAYS IT'S YOU	2.00	3.50
☐ 5163		SO SAD/ LUCILLE	2.00	3.50
☐ 5199		EBONY EYES/WALK RIGHT BACK	2.00	3.50
☐ 5220		TEMPTATION/STICK WITH ME BABY	2.00	3.50
☐ 5250		CRYING IN THE RAIN/I'M NOT ANGRY	2.00	3.50
☐ 5273		THAT'S OLD FASHIONED/		
		HOW CAN I MEET HER?	2.00	3.50

ISSUE #	LABEL		PRICE RANGE	
☐ 5297		DON'T ASK ME TO BE FRIENDS/NO ONE		
		CAN MAKE MY SUNSHINE SMILE	1.75	3.00
☐ 346		NANCY'S MINUET/SO IT ALWAYS WILL BE	1.75	3.00
☐ 5362		IT'S BEEN NICE/I'M AFRAID	1.75	3.00
☐ 5389		THE GIRL SANG THE BLUES/LOVE HER	1.75	3.00
☐ 5422		HELLO AMY/		
		AIN'T THAT LOVING YOU BABY	1.75	3.00
☐ 5441		THE FERRIS WHEEL/		
		DON'T FORGET TO CRY	1.75	3.00
☐ 5466		YOU'RE THE ONE I LOVE/		
		RING AROUND MY ROSIE	1.75	3.00
☐ 5478		GONE, GONE, GONE/TORTURE	1.75	3.00
☐ 5600		YOU'RE MY GIRL/		
		DON'T LET THE WHOLE WORLD KNOW	1.75	3.00
☐ 5611		THAT'LL BE THE DAY/		
		GIVE ME A SWEETHEART	1.75	3.00
☐ 5628		THE PRICE OF LOVE/		
		IT ONLY COSTS A DIME	1.75	3.00
☐ 5639		FOLLOW ME/I'LL NEVER GET OVER YOU	1.75	3.00

EVERLY BROTHERS—EPs

☐ 104	CADENCE	THE EVERLY BROTHERS	8.50	15.00
☐ 105		THE EVERLY BROTHERS	8.50	15.00
☐ 107		THE EVERLY BROTHERS	8.50	15.00
☐ 108		SONGS OUR DADDY TAUGHT US	7.25	12.00
☐ 109		SONGS OUR DADDY TAUGHT US	7.25	12.00
☐ 110		SONGS OUR DADDY TAUGHT US	7.25	12.00
☐ 111		THE EVERLY BROTHERS	7.25	12.00
☐ 118		THE EVERLY BROTHERS	7.25	12.00
☐ 121		THE VERY BEST OF THE		
		EVERLY BROTHERS	6.00	11.00
☐ 333		ROCKIN' WITH THE EVERLY BROTHERS	6.00	11.00
☐ 334		DREAM WITH THE EVERLY BROTHERS	6.00	11.00
☐ 1381-1	WARNER BROTHERS	FOREVERLY YOURS	4.50	7.00
☐ 1381-2		ESPECIALLY FOR YOU	4.50	9.00
☐ 5501		THE EVERLY BROTHERS + TWO OLDIES	2.75	4.50

EVERLY BROTHERS—ALBUMS

☐ 3003 (M)	CADENCE	THE EVERLY BROTHERS	20.00	50.00
☐ 3016 (M)		SONGS OUR DADDY TAUGHT US	17.50	45.00
☐ 3025 (M)		THE EVERLY BROTHERS' BEST	15.00	35.00
☐ 3040 (M)		THE FABULOUS STYLE OF THE		
		EVERLY BROTHERS	15.00	35.00
☐ 25029 (S)		FOLK SONGS	15.00	35.00
☐ 25062 (S)		15 EVERLY HITS	12.50	30.00

ISSUE #	LABEL		PRICE RANGE	
☐ 1381 (S)	**WARNER BROTHERS**	IT'S EVERLY TIME	8.00	22.50
☐ 1395 (S)		A DATE WITH THE EVERLY BROTHERS	8.00	22.50
☐ 1418 (S)		THE EVERLY BROTHERS	8.00	22.50
☐ 1430 (S)		INSTANT PARTY	8.00	22.50
☐ 1471 (S)		GOLDEN HITS OF THE EVERLY BROTHERS	7.00	18.00
☐ 1483 (S)		CHRISTMAS WITH THE EVERLY BROTHERS	7.00	18.00
☐ 1513 (S)		THE EVERLY BROTHERS SING GREAT COUNTRY HITS	7.00	18.00
☐ 1554 (S)		THE VERY BEST OF THE EVERLY BROTHERS	6.00	15.00
☐ 1578 (S)		ROCK'N SOUL	6.00	15.00
☐ 1585 (S)		GONE, GONE, GONE	6.00	15.00
☐ 1605 (S)		BEAT'N SOUL	6.00	15.00
☐ 1620 (S)		IN OUR IMAGE	6.00	15.00
☐ 1646 (S)		TWO YANKS IN LONDON	6.00	10.50
☐ 1708 (S)		THE EVERLY BROTHERS SING	6.00	15.00
☐ 1752 (S)		ROOTS	5.00	13.50
☐ 1858 (S)		THE EVERLY BROTHERS SHOW	4.50	12.00

— F —

SHELLY FABARES

☐ 621	**COLPIX**	JOHNNY ANGEL/ WHERE'S IT GONNA GET ME	2.00	3.50
☐ 638		JOHNNY LOVES ME/I'M GROWING UP	2.00	3.50
☐ 654		THE THINGS WE DID LAST SUMMER/ BREAKING UP IS HARD TO DO	2.00	3.50
☐ 667		BIG STAR/TELEPHONE (WON'T YOU RING)	2.00	3.50
☐ 682		RONNIE, CALL ME WHEN YOU GET A CHANCE/I LEFT A NOTE TO SAY GOODBYE	2.00	3.50
☐ 705		WELCOME HOME/BILLY BOY	2.00	3.50
☐ 721		FOOTBALL SEASON'S OVER/ HE DON'T LOVE ME	2.00	3.50
☐ 632	**VEE JAY**	LOST SUMMER LOVE/ I KNOW YOU'LL BE THERE	2.75	4.50
☐ 4001	**DUNHILL**	MY PRAYER/PRETTY PLEASE	2.25	4.00

SHELLEY FABARES—ALBUMS

☐ 426 (M)	**COLPIX**	SHELLEY	8.50	15.00
☐ 431 (M)		THE THINGS WE DID LAST SUMMER	8.50	15.00

ISSUE #	LABEL		PRICE RANGE	

FABIAN

☐ 1020	*CHANCELLOR*	SHIVERS/I'M IN LOVE	4.50	9.00
☐ 1024		LILLY LOU/BE MY STEADY DATE	4.00	7.00
☐ 1029		I'M A MAN/HYPNOTIZED	2.25	4.00
☐ 1033		TURN ME LOOSE/STOP THIEF	2.00	3.50
☐ 1037		TIGER/MIGHTY COLD (TO A WARM, WARM HEART)	2.00	3.50
☐ 1041		COME ON AND GET ME/GOT THE FEELING	2.00	3.50
☐ 1044		HOUND DOG MAN/THIS FRIENDLY WORLD	2.00	3.50
☐ 1047		ABOUT THIS THING CALLED LOVE/ STRING ALONG	1.75	3.00
☐ 1051		STROLLIN' IN THE SPRINGTIME/ I'M GONNA SIT RIGHT DOWN AND WRITE MYSELF A LETTER	1.75	3.00
☐ 1055		TOMORROW/KING OF LOVE	2.00	3.50
☐ 1061		KISSIN' AND TWISTIN'/LONG BEFORE	1.75	3.00
☐ 1067		YOU KNOW YOU BELONG TO SOMEBODY ELSE/HOLD ON	1.75	3.00
☐ 1072		GRAPEVINE/DAVID AND GOLIATH	1.75	3.00
☐ 1079		THE LOVE THAT I'M GIVING TO YOU/ YOU'RE ONLY YOUNG ONCE	1.75	3.00
☐ 1084		A GIRL LIKE YOU/DREAM FACTORY	1.75	3.00
☐ 1086		KANSAS CITY/TONGUE-TIED	1.75	3.00
☐ 1092		WILD PARTY/THE GOSPEL TRUTH	1.75	3.00
☐ 1092		WILD PARTY/MADE YOU	1.75	3.00

FABIAN—EPs

☐ 5003	*CHANCELLOR*	HOLD THAT TIGER	7.25	12.00
☐ 5005		THE FABULOUS FABIAN	6.00	11.00
☐ 301		HOUND DOG MAN	6.00	11.00

FABIAN—ALBUMS

☐ 5003 (S)				
	CHANCELLOR	HOLD THAT TIGER	15.00	35.00
☐ 5005 (S)		THE FABULOUS FABIAN	15.00	35.00
☐ 5012 (S)		THE GOOD OLD SUMMERTIME	12.50	30.00
☐ 5019 (M)		ROCKIN' HOT	10.00	25.00
☐ 5024 (M)		FABIAN'S 16 FABULOUS HITS	10.00	25.00

MARIANNE FAITHFULL

☐ 9697	*LONDON*	AS TEARS GO BY/GLEENSLEEVES	2.00	3.50
☐ 9731		COME AND STAY WITH ME/ WHAT HAVE I DONE WRONG?	2.00	3.50
☐ 9759		THIS LITTLE BIRD/MORNING SUN	2.00	3.50
☐ 9780		SUMMER NIGHTS/THE SHA-LA-LA SONG	2.00	3.50

ISSUE #	LABEL		PRICE RANGE	
☐9802		GO AWAY FROM MY WORLD/		
		OH, LOOK AROUND YOU	2.00	3.50
☐1022		SISTER MORPHINE/SOMETHING BETTER	4.50	9.00

MARIANNE FAITHFULL—ALBUMS

☐3423 (M)	*LONDON*	MARIANNE FAITHFULL	6.00	15.00
☐423 (S)		MARIANNE FAITHFULL	8.00	22.50
☐3452 (M)		GO AWAY FROM MY WORLD	6.00	15.00
☐452 (S)		GO AWAY FROM MY WORLD	8.00	22.50
☐3482 (M)		FAITHFULL FOREVER	6.00	15.00
☐482 (S)		FAITHFULL FOREVER	8.00	22.50
☐3547 (M)		GREATEST HITS	6.00	15.00
☐547 (S)		GREATEST HITS	7.00	18.00

NARVEL FELTS

☐71140	*MERCURY*	KISS-A-ME BABY/FOOLISH THOUGHTS	4.25	8.00
☐71190		CRY BABY CRY/LONESOME FEELING	4.00	7.00
☐71249		DREAM WORLD/ROCKET RIDE	4.00	7.00

NARVEL FELTS—ALBUM

☐5000 (M)				
	CINNAMON	DRIFT AWAY	6.00	15.00
☐5000 (S)		DRIFT AWAY	7.00	18.00

FREDDY FENDER

☐1000	*DUNCAN*	MEAN WOMAN/HOLY ONE	4.50	9.00
☐1001		WASTED DAYS AND WASTED NIGHTS/		
		SAN ANTONIO ROCK	8.50	15.00
☐1002		CRAZY BABY/THE WILD SIDE OF LIFE	4.50	9.00
☐1004		SINCE I MET YOU BABY/LITTLE MAMA	6.00	11.00
☐5670	*IMPERIAL*	WASTED DAYS AND WASTED NIGHTS/		
		I CAN'T REMEMBER WHEN		
		(I DIDN'T LOVE YOU)	4.00	7.00
☐5375	*ARGO*	YOU'RE SOMETHING ELSE/		
		A MAN CAN CRY	4.00	7.00
☐100	*NORCO*	THE NEW STROLL/		
		LOVE'S LIGHT IS AN EMBER	3.50	6.00

FIFTH DIMENSION

☐752	*SOUL CITY*	I'LL BE LOVING YOU FOREVER/		
		TRAIN, KEEP ON MOVING	2.00	4.00
☐753		TOO POOR TO DIE/		
		GO WHERE YOU WANNA GO	2.00	4.00

ISSUE #	LABEL		PRICE RANGE	
☐ 755		ANOTHER DAY, ANOTHER HEADACHE/		
		ROSECRANS BLVD.	2.00	4.00
☐ 756		UP, UP & AWAY/		
		WHICH WAY TO NOWHERE	1.75	3.75
☐ 760		POOR SIDE OF TOWN/PAPER CUP	1.75	3.75
☐ 762		CARPET MAN/MAGIC GARDEN	1.75	3.75
☐ 766		STONED SOUL PICNIC/SAILBOAT SONG	1.75	3.75
☐ 768		SWEET BLINDNESS/BOBBY'S BLUES	1.75	3.75
☐ 770		CALIFORNIA SOUL/		
		IT'LL NEVER BE THE SAME	1.75	3.75

FIREBALLS

☐ 2008	*TOP RANK*	TORQUAY/CRY BABY	2.50	4.00
☐ 2026		BULLDOG/NEARLY SUNRISE	2.50	4.00
☐ 2038		FOOT PATTER/KISSIN'	2.50	4.00
☐ 2054		VAQUERO/CHIEF WHOOPEN KOFF	2.50	4.00
☐ 2081		ALMOST PARADISE/SWEET TALK	2.50	4.00
☐ 3003		RIK-A-TIK/YACKY DOO	2.50	4.00
☐ 248	*KAPP*	FIREBALL/I DON'T KNOW	2.00	3.50
☐ 630	*WARWICK*	RIK-A-TIK/YACKY DOO	2.00	3.50
☐ 644		QUITE A PARTY/GUNSHOT	2.00	3.50
☐ 16493	*DOT*	TORQUAY TWO/PEG LEG	2.00	3.50
☐ 16661		DUMBO/MR. REED	2.00	3.50
☐ 16715		MORE THAN I CAN SAY/		
		THE BEATING OF MY HEART	2.00	3.50
☐ 16745		CAMPUSOLOGY/AHHH, SOUL	2.00	3.50
☐ 16992		SHY GIRL/I THINK I'LL CATCH A BUG	2.00	3.50

FIREBALLS—EP

☐ 1000	*TOP RANK*	THE FIREBALLS	10.00	18.00

FIREBALLS—ALBUMS

☐ 324 (M)				
	TOP RANK	THE FIREBALLS	15.00	35.00
☐ 343 (M)		VAQUERO	12.50	30.00
☐ 2042 (M)	*WARWICK*	HERE ARE THE FIREBALLS	8.00	22.50
☐ 25512 (S)	*DOT*	TORQUAY	8.00	22.50
☐ 25709 (S)		CAMPUSOLOGY	8.00	22.50
☐ 25856 (S)		FIREWATER	8.00	22.50

FIVE AMERICANS

☐ 109	*ABNAK*	I SEE THE LIGHT/THE OUTCAST	2.75	4.50
☐ 118		WESTERN UNION/NOW THAT IT'S OVER	1.75	3.00
☐ 120		SOUND OF LOVE/SYMPATHY	1.75	3.00
☐ 123		ZIP CODE/SWEET BIRD OF YOUTH	1.75	3.00

5 SATINS

ISSUE #	LABEL		PRICE RANGE	
☐ 125		STOP LIGHT/TELL ANN I LOVE HER	1.75	3.00
☐ 126		7:30 GUIDED TOUR/SEE-SAW MAN	1.75	3.00
☐ 128		RAIN MAKER/NO COMMUNICATION	1.75	3.00
☐ 131		LOVIN' IS LOVIN'/CON MAN	1.75	3.00
☐ 132		GENERATION CAP/THE SOURCE.	1.75	3.00
☐ 142		SHE'S GOOD TO ME/MOLLY BLACK	1.75	3.00
☐ 454	*HBR*	I SEE THE LIGHT/THE OUTCAST	1.75	3.00
☐ 468		EVOL - NO LOVE/DON'T BLAME ME	1.75	3.00
☐ 483		THE LOSING GAME/GOOD TIMES	1.75	3.00

FIVE AMERICANS—ALBUMS

☐ 2067 (S)	*ABNAK*	WESTERN UNION	6.00	15.00
☐ 2069 (S)		PROGRESSIONS.	5.00	13.50
☐ 2071 (S)		NOW AND THEN	5.00	13.50
☐ 8503 (M)	*HBR*	I SEE THE LIGHT	5.00	13.50

FIVE SATINS

☐ 105	*STANDORD*	ALL MINE/ROSEMARIE	50.00	95.00
☐ 106		IN THE STILL OF THE NIGHT/ THE JONES GIRL	42.00	74.00
☐ 1005	*EMBER*	I'LL REMEMBER (IN THE STILL OF THE NITE)/THE JONES GIRL	10.00	18.00
☐ 1005		IN THE STILL OF THE NIGHT/ THE JONES GIRL	7.25	12.00
☐ 1008		WONDERFUL GIRL	7.25	12.00
☐ 1014		OH HAPPY DAY/OUR LOVE IS FOREVER	7.25	12.00
☐ 1019		TO THE AISLE/WISH I HAD MY BABY	4.50	9.00
☐ 1025		OUR ANNIVERSARY/PRETTY GIRL	4.50	9.00
☐ 1038		A NIGHT TO REMEMBER/SENORITA LOLITA . . .	4.50	9.00
☐ 1056		SHADOWS/TONI MY LOVE	4.50	9.00
☐ 1061		I'LL BE SEEING YOU/A NIGHT LIKE THIS	4.50	9.00
☐ 1066		CANDLELIGHT/THE TIME	4.50	9.00
☐ 1070		WISHING RING/TELL ME DEAR	4.50	9.00

FIVE SATINS—EPs

☐ 100	*EMBER*	THE FIVE SATINS SING	10.00	18.00
☐ 101		TO THE AISLE	8.50	15.00
☐ 102		OUR ANNIVERSARY	8.50	15.00

FIVE SATINS—ALBUMS

☐ 100 (M)	*EMBER*	THE FIVE SATINS SING	35.00	90.00
☐ 401 (M)		FIVE SATINS: ENCORE	25.00	60.00
☐ 108 (M)				
	MT. VERNON	THE FIVE SATINS SING	12.50	30.00

ISSUE #	LABEL		PRICE RANGE	

FLAMINGOS

☐ 1133	*CHANCE*	IF I CAN'T HAVE YOU/ SOMEDAY, SOMEWAY	95.00	180.00
☐ 1140		THAT'S MY DESIRE/HURRY HOME BABY	90.00	150.00
☐ 1140		THAT'S MY DESIRE/HURRY HOME BABY	120.00	200.00
☐ 1145		GOLDEN TEARDROPS/CARRIED AWAY	90.00	150.00
☐ 1145		GOLDEN TEARDROPS/CARRIED AWAY	120.00	200.00
☐ 1149		PLAN FOR LOVE/YOU AIN'T READY	120.00	200.00
☐ 1154		CROSS OVER THE BRIDGE/ LISTEN TO MY PLEA	120.00	200.00
☐ 1162		BLUES IN A LETTER/JUMP CHILDREN	120.00	200.00
☐ 808	*PARROT*	DREAM OF A LIFETIME/ ON MY MERRY WAY	60.00	135.00
☐ 808		DREAM OF A LIFETIME/ ON MY MERRY WAY	85.00	150.00
☐ 811		I REALLY DON'T WANT TO KNOW/ GET WITH IT	180.00	300.00
☐ 812		I'M YOURS/KO KO MO	72.00	120.00
☐ 384	*VEE JAY*	GOLDEN TEARDROPS/CARRIED AWAY	8.50	15.00
☐ 815	*CHECKER*	WHEN/THAT'S MY BABY	8.50	15.00
☐ 821		PLEASE COME BACK HOME/ I WANT TO LOVE	8.50	15.00
☐ 830		I'LL BE HOME/NEED YOUR LOVE	8.50	15.00
☐ 837		A KISS FROM YOUR LIPS/GET WITH IT	8.50	15.00
☐ 846		THE VOW/SILLY DILLY	8.50	15.00
☐ 853		WOULD I BE CRYING/JUST FOR A KICK	8.50	15.00
☐ 915		WHISPERING STARS/ DREAM OF A LIFETIME	7.25	12.00
☐ 1084		LOVER COME BACK TO ME/ YOUR LITTLE GUY	7.25	12.00
☐ 1091		GOODNIGHT SWEETHEART/ DOES IT REALLY MATTER?	7.25	12.00
☐ 30335	*DECCA*	THE LADDER OF LOVE/LET'S MAKE UP	6.00	11.00
☐ 30454		MY FAITH IN YOU/HELPLESSS	6.00	11.00
☐ 30687		WHERE DID MARY GO?/ ROCK N' ROLL MARCH	4.50	9.00
☐ 30880		EVER SINCE I MET LUCY/KISS-A-ME	4.50	9.00
☐ 30948		JERRI-LEE/HEY NOW	4.50	9.00
☐ 1035	*END*	LOVERS NEVER SAY GOODBYE/ THAT LOVE IS YOU	6.00	11.00
☐ 1040		BUT NOT FOR ME/ I SHED A TEAR AT YOUR WEDDING	6.00	11.00
☐ 1044		LOVE WALKED IN/AT THE PROM	6.00	11.00
☐ 1046		I ONLY HAVE EYES FOR YOU/ GOODNIGHT SWEETHEART	6.00	11.00

ISSUE #	LABEL		PRICE RANGE	
☐ 1046		I ONLY HAVE EYES FOR YOU/AT THE PROM ...	4.00	7.00
☐ 1055		LOVE WALKED IN/YOURS	4.00	7.00
☐ 1062		I WAS SUCH A FOOL/HEAVENLY ANGEL	4.00	7.00
☐ 1065		MIO AMORE/YOU, ME AND THE SEA	4.00	7.00
☐ 1068		NOBODY LOVES ME LIKE YOU/		
		BESAME MUCHO	4.00	7.00
☐ 1068		NOBODY LOVES ME LIKE YOU/		
		BESAME MUCHO	4.00	7.00
☐ 1070		BESAME MUCHO/YOU, ME AND THE SEA	3.50	6.00
☐ 1073		MIO AMORE/AT NIGHT	3.50	6.00
☐ 1079		WHEN I FALL IN LOVE/BESIDE YOU	3.50	6.00
☐ 1081		YOUR OTHER LOVE/LOVERS GOTTA CRY	3.50	6.00
☐ 1085		KOKOMO/THAT'S WHY I LOVE YOU	3.50	6.00

FLAMINGOS—EP
☐ 205	**END**	THE FLAMINGOS	10.00	18.00

FLAMINGOS—ALBUMS
☐ 304 (M)	**END**	FLAMINGO SERENADE	15.00	35.00
☐ 307 (M)		FLAMINGO FAVORITES	12.50	30.00
☐ 308 (M)		REQUESTFULLY YOURS	12.50	30.00
☐ 316 (M)		SOUND OF THE FLAMINGOS	12.50	30.00
☐ 1433 (M)	**CHECKER**	THE FLAMINGOS	10.00	25.00

FLEETWOOD MAC
☐ 10386	**EPIC**	STOP MESSIN' 'ROUND/		
		NEED YOUR LOVE SO BAD	2.75	4.50
☐ 10436		ALBATROSS/JIGSAW PUZZLE BLUES	2.75	4.50
☐ 11029		ALBATROSS/BLACK MAGIC WOMAN	2.25	4.00
☐ 0860	**REPRISE**	COMING YOUR WAY/RATTLESNAKE SHAKE ...	2.25	4.00
☐ 0883		OH WELL (PT. 1)/(PT. 2)	2.00	3.50
☐ 0925		WORLD IN HARMONY/GREEN MANALISHI	2.00	3.50
☐ 0984		JEWEL EYED JUDY/STATION MAN	2.00	3.50
☐ 1057		SANDS OF TIME/LAY IT ALL DOWN	2.00	3.50
☐ 1079		OH WELL/GREEN MANALISHI	2.00	3.50
☐ 1093		SENTIMENTAL LADY/SUNNY SIDE OF HEAVEN	2.25	4.00
☐ 1172		DID YOU EVER LOVE ME?/REVELATION	2.00	3.50

FLEETWOOD MAC—ALBUMS
☐ 26402 (S)	**EPIC**	FLEETWOOD MAC	5.00	13.50
☐ 26446 (S)		ENGLISH ROSE	4.50	12.00
☐ 2080 (S)	**REPRISE**	BARE TREES	4.00	10.00
☐ 2138 (S)		PENGUIN	4.00	10.00
☐ 2158 (S)		MYSTERY TO ME	4.00	10.00
☐ 2196 (S)		HEROES ARE HARD TO FIND	4.00	10.00
☐ 2225 (S)		FLEETWOOD MAC	4.00	10.00

ISSUE #	LABEL		PRICE RANGE	
☐6408 (S)		KILN HOUSE	4.00	10.00
☐6465 (S)		FUTURE GAMES	4.00	10.00

FLEETWOODS

☐55188	*LIBERTY*	COME SOFTLY TO ME/I CARE SO MUCH	3.50	6.00
☐3	*DOLPHIN*	GRADUATION'S HERE/OH LORD, LET IT BE	2.00	3.50
☐5	*DOLTON*	MR. BLUE/YOU MEAN EVERYTHING TO ME	2.00	3.50
☐15		OUTSIDE MY WINDOW/MAGIC STAR	1.75	3.00
☐22		RUNAROUND/TRULY DO	1.75	3.00
☐27		THE LAST ONE TO KNOW/DORMILONA	1.75	3.00
☐30		CONFIDENTIAL/I LOVE YOU SO	2.00	3.50
☐40		TRAGEDY/LITTLE MISS SAD ONE	1.75	3.00
☐45		(HE'S) THE GREAT IMPOSTER/ POOR LITTLE GIRL	1.75	3.00
☐49		BILLY OLD BUDDY/TROUBLE	1.75	3.00
☐62		LOVERS BY NIGHT, STRANGERS BY DAY/ THEY TELL ME IT'S SUMMER	1.75	3.00
☐74		YOU SHOULD HAVE BEEN THERE/ SURE IS LONESOME DOWNTOWN	1.75	3.00
☐75		GOODNIGHT MY LOVE/JIMMY BEWARE	1.75	3.00
☐86		WHAT'LL I DO?/BABY BYE-O	1.75	3.00
☐93		LONESOME TOWN/RUBY RED, BABY BLUE	1.73	3.00
☐97		TEN TIMES BLUE/SKA LIGHT, SKA BRIGHT	1.75	3.00
☐98		MR. SANDMAN/THIS IS MY PRAYER	1.75	3.00
☐302		BEFORE AND AFTER/ LONELY IS AS LONELY DOES	1.75	3.00
☐307		I'M NOT JIMMY/COME SOFTLY TO ME	1.75	3.00
☐310		RAINBOW/JUST AS I NEEDED YOU	1.75	3.00
☐315		FOR LOVIN' ME/THIS IS WHERE I SEE HER	1.75	3.00

FLEETWOODS—EP

☐502	*DOLTON*	RUNAROUND	5.00	9.00

FLEETWOODS—ALBUMS

☐8001 (S)	*DOLTON*	MR. BLUE	10.00	25.00
☐8002 (S)		THE FLEETWOODS	10.00	25.00
☐8005 (S)		SOFTLY	8.00	22.50
☐8007 (S)		DEEP IN A DREAM	8.00	22.50
☐8011 (S)		THE FLEETWOODS SING THE BEST OF THE OLDIES	8.00	22.50
☐8018 (S)		THE FLEETWOODS' GREATEST HITS	8.00	22.50
☐8020 (S)		THE FLEETWOODS SING FOR LOVERS BY NIGHT	7.00	18.00
☐8025 (S)		GOODNIGHT MY LOVE	7.00	18.00
☐8030 (S)		BEFORE AND AFTER	7.00	18.00
☐8039 (S)		FOLK ROCK	6.00	15.00

ISSUE #	LABEL		PRICE RANGE	

FONTANE SISTERS

☐ 3979	*RCA*	TENNESSEE WALTZ/I GUESS I'LL HAVE TO ...	2.25	4.00
☐ 5524		THE KISSING BRIDGE/SILVER BELLS	2.25	4.00
☐ 5612		TILL THEN/THE BEACON	2.25	4.00
☐ 15171	*DOT*	IF I DIDN'T HAVE YOU/		
		HAPPY DAYS AND LONELY NIGHTS	2.25	4.00
☐ 15265		HEARTS OF STONE/BLESS YOUR HEART	2.25	4.00
☐ 15333		ROCK LOVE/YOU'RE MINE	2.00	3.50
☐ 15352		MOST OF ALL/PUT ME IN THE MOOD	2.00	3.50
☐ 15370		ROLLIN' STONE/PLAYMATES	2.00	3.50
☐ 15386		SEVENTEEN/IF I COULD BE WITH YOU	2.00	3.50
☐ 15428		DADDY-O/ADORABLE....................	2.00	3.50
☐ 15434		NUTTIN' FOR CHRISTMAS/SILVER BELLS	2.00	3.50
☐ 15450		EDDIE MY LOVE/YUM YUM	2.00	3.50
☐ 15462		I'M IN LOVE AGAIN/YOU ALWAYS HURT		
		THE ONE YOU LOVE	1.75	3.00
☐ 15480		VOICES/LONESOME LOVER BLUES	1.75	3.00
☐ 15501		PLEASE DON'T LEAVE ME/STILL	1.75	3.00

FONTANE SISTERS—EPs

| ☐ 1019 | *DOT* | THE FONTANE SISTERS .... | 3.50 | 6.00 |
| ☐ 1020 | | THE FONTANE SISTERS .... | 3.50 | 6.00 |

FONTANE SISTERS—ALBUMS

☐ 3004 (M)	*DOT*	THE FONTANE SISTERS	6.00	15.00
☐ 3042 (M)		THE FONTANES SING	5.00	13.50
☐ 25531 (S)		TIPS OF MY FINGERS	6.00	15.00

FRANKIE FORD

☐ 549	*ACE*	CHEATIN' WOMAN/THE LAST ONE TO CRY ...	3.50	6.00
☐ 554		SEA CRUISE/ROBERTA	2.25	4.00
☐ 566		ALIMONY/		
		CAN'T TELL MY HEART (WHAT TO DO)	2.00	3.50
☐ 580		TIME AFTER TIME/		
		I WANT TO BE YOUR MAN	2.00	3.50
☐ 592		CHINATOWN/WHAT'S GOIN' ON?	2.00	3.50
☐ 8009		OCEAN FULL OF TEARS/HOURS OF NEED	1.75	3.00
☐ 5686	*IMPERIAL*	YOU TALK TOO MUCH/		
		IF YOU'VE GOT TROUBLES	1.75	3.00
☐ 5706		MY SOUTHERN BELLE/THE GROOM	1.75	3.00
☐ 5735		SEVENTEEN/DOGHOUSE	1.75	3.00
☐ 5749		SATURDAY NIGHT FISH FRY/		
		LOVE DON'T LOVE NOBODY	1.75	3.00
☐ 5775		WHAT HAPPENED TO YOU?/		
		LET THEM TALK......................	1.75	3.00

ISSUE #	LABEL		PRICE RANGE	
☐ 5819		A MAN ONLY DOES/		
		THEY SAID IT COULDN'T BE DONE	1.75	3.00

FRANKIE FORD—EP

| ☐ 105 | *ACE* | THE BEST OF FRANKIE FORD . . . . | 6.00 | 11.00 |

FRANKIE FORD—ALBUM

| ☐ 1005 (M) | *ACE* | ON A SEA CRUISE WITH FRANKIE FORD . . . . . | 10.00 | 25.00 |

FOUR SEASONS

☐ 5122	*GONE*	BERMUDA/SPANISH LACE	15.00	25.00
☐ 456	*VEE JAY*	SHERRY/I'VE CRIED BEFORE	2.00	3.50
☐ 465		BIG GIRLS DON'T CRY/CONNIE-O	2.00	3.50
☐ 478		SANTA CLAUS IS COMING TO TOWN/		
		CHRISTMAS TEARS	2.00	3.50
☐ 485		WALK LIKE A MAN/LUCKY LADYBUG	2.00	3.50
☐ 512		AIN'T THAT A SHAME/SOON	2.00	3.50
☐ 539		CANDY GIRL/MARLENA	2.00	3.50
☐ 562		NEW MEXICAN ROSE/		
		THAT'S THE ONLY WAY	2.00	3.50
☐ 576		PEANUTS/STAY	2.25	4.00
☐ 582		STAY/GOODNIGHT MY LOVE	2.00	3.50
☐ 597		ALONE/LONG LONELY NIGHTS	2.00	3.50
☐ 608		SINCERELY/ONE SONG	2.00	3.50
☐ 618		HAPPY, HAPPY BIRTHDAY BABY/		
		YOU'RE THE APPLE OF MY EYE	2.75	4.50
☐ 626		I SAW MOMMY KISSING SANTA CLAUS/		
		CHRISTMAS TEARS	2.75	4.50
☐ 639		NEVER ON SUNDAY/CONNIE-O	2.75	4.50
☐ 664		SINCE I DON'T HAVE YOU/TONITE, TONITE . . .	3.50	6.00
☐ 713		LITTLE BOY (IN GROWN-UP CLOTHES)/		
		SILVER WINGS	2.00	3.50
☐ 719		MY MOTHER'S EYES/STAY	2.00	3.50
☐ 40166	*PHILIPS*	DAWN/NO SURFIN' TODAY	1.75	3.00
☐ 40185		RONNIE/BORN TO WANDER	1.75	3.00
☐ 40211		RAG DOLL/SILENCE IS GOLDEN	1.75	3.00
☐ 40225		SAVE IT FOR ME/FUNNY FACE	1.75	3.00
☐ 40238		BIG MAN IN TOWN/LITTLE ANGEL	1.75	3.00
☐ 40260		BYE, BYE, BABY/SEARCHING WIND	1.75	3.00
☐ 40278		TOY SOLDIER/BETRAYED	1.75	3.00
☐ 40305		GIRL COME RUNNING/		
		CRY MYSELF TO SLEEP	1.75	3.00
☐ 40317		LET'S HANG ON/ON BROADWAY TONIGHT	1.75	3.00
☐ 40350		WORKING MY WAY BACK TO YOU/		
		TOO MANY MEMORIES	1.75	3.00

ISSUE #	LABEL		PRICE RANGE	
☐ 40370		OPUS 17/BEGGAR'S PARADISE	1.75	3.00
☐ 40393		I'VE GOT YOU UNDER MY SKIN/		
		HUGGIN' MY PILLOW	1.75	3.00
☐ 40412		TELL IT TO THE RAIN/SNOW GIRL	1.75	3.00
☐ 40433		BEGGIN'/DODY	1.75	3.00

FOUR SEASONS—EPs

☐ 1901	*VEE JAY*	THE FOUR SEASONS SING	5.00	10.00
☐ 1902		THE FOUR SEASONS SING	5.00	10.00

FOUR SEASONS—ALBUMS

☐ 1053 (S)	*VEE JAY*	SHERRY AND 11 OTHERS	10.00	25.00
☐ 1055 (S)		FOUR SEASONS' GREETINGS	12.50	30.00
☐ 1056 (S)		BIG GIRLS DON'T CRY	8.00	22.50
☐ 1059 (S)		AIN'T THAT A SHAME	8.00	22.50
☐ 1065 (S)		GOLDEN HITS OF THE FOUR SEASONS	8.00	22.50
☐ 1082 (S)		FOLK-NANNY	8.00	22.50
☐ 1082 (S)		STAY	7.00	18.00
☐ 1088 (S)		MORE GOLDEN HITS BY THE		
		FOUR SEASONS	7.00	18.00
☐ 1121 (S)		WE LOVE GIRLS	7.00	18.00
☐ 1154 (S)		RECORDED LIVE ON STAGE	7.00	18.00
☐ 600124 (S)		DAWN	6.00	15.00
☐ 600129 (S)		BORN TO WANDER	7.00	18.00
☐ 600146 (S)		RAG DOLL	6.00	15.00
☐ 600150 (S)		ALL THE SONG HITS OF THE		
		FOUR SEASONS	6.00	15.00
☐ 600164 (S)		THE FOUR SEASONS ENTERTAIN YOU	6.00	15.00
☐ 600193 (S)		BIG HITS BY BACHARACH-DAVID AND		
		BOB DYLAN	6.00	15.00
☐ 600196 (S)		GOLD VAULT OF HITS	6.00	15.00
☐ 600201 (S)		WORKING MY WAY BACK TO YOU	6.00	15.00
☐ 600221 (S)		2ND GOLD VAULT OF HITS	6.00	15.00
☐ 600222 (S)		LOOKIN' BACK	6.00	15.00
☐ 600223 (S)		CHRISTMAS ALBUM	6.00	15.00
☐ 600243 (S)		NEW GOLD HITS	6.00	15.00
☐ 600290 (S)		GENUINE IMITATION LIFE GAZETTE	5.00	13.50
☐ 600341 (S)		HALF AND HALF	5.00	13.50
☐ 6501 (S)		EDIZONE D'ORO	5.00	13.50
☐ 1081 (S)	*MOWEST*	CHAMELEON	4.50	12.00

FOUR TOPS

☐ 1623	*CHESS*	COULD IT BE YOU?/KISS ME BABY	24.00	42.00
☐ 4534	*RIVERSIDE*	PENNIES FROM HEAVEN/		
		WHERE ARE YOU?	12.00	20.00

ISSUE #	LABEL		PRICE RANGE	
☐ 41755	*COLUMBIA*	AIN'T THAT LOVE/LONELY SUMMER	7.00	12.00
☐ 43356		AIN'T THAT LOVE/LONELY SUMMER	3.50	6.00
☐ 1062	*MOTOWN*	BABY, I NEED YOUR LOVING/CALL ON ME	1.75	3.00
☐ 1069		WITHOUT THE ONE YOU LOVE/		
		LOVE HAS GONE	1.75	3.00
☐ 1073		ASK THE LONELY/WHERE DID YOU GO?	1.75	3.00
☐ 1076		I CAN'T HELP MYSELF/SAD SOUVENIRS	1.75	3.00
☐ 1081		IT'S THE SAME OLD SONG/		
		YOUR LOVE IS AMAZING	1.75	3.00
☐ 1084		SOMETHING ABOUT YOU/		
		DARLING, I HUM OUR SONG	1.75	3.00
☐ 1090		SHAKE ME, WAKE ME/		
		JUST AS LONG AS YOU NEED ME	1.75	3.00
☐ 1096		LOVING YOU IS SWEETER THAN EVER/		
		I LIKE EVERYTHING ABOUT YOU	1.75	3.00
☐ 1098		REACH OUT, I'LL BE THERE/		
		UNTIL YOU LOVE SOMEONE	1.75	3.00
☐ 1102		STANDING IN THE SHADOWS OF LOVE/		
		SINCE YOU'VE BEEN GONE	1.75	3.00
☐ 1104		BERNADETTE/I GOT A FEELING	1.75	3.00
☐ 1110		7 ROOMS OF GLOOM/I'LL TURN TO STONE	1.75	3.00
☐ 1113		YOU KEEP RUNNING AWAY/		
		IF YOU DON'T WANT MY LOVE	1.75	3.00
☐ 1119		WALK AWAY RENEE/		
		OUR LOVE IS WONDERFUL	1.75	3.00
☐ 1124		IF I WERE A CARPENTER/		
		WONDERFUL BABY	1.75	3.00
☐ 1127		YESTERDAY'S DREAMS/		
		FOR ONCE IN MY LIFE	1.75	3.00
☐ 1132		I'M IN A DIFFERENT WORLD/		
		REMEMBER WHEN	1.75	3.00
☐ 1147		WHAT IS A MAN/		
		DON'T BRING BACK MEMORIES	1.75	3.00
☐ 1159		DON'T LET HIM TAKE YOUR LOVE		
		FROM ME/THE KEY	1.75	3.00
☐ 1164		IT'S ALL IN THE GAME/		
		LOVE (IS THE ANSWER)	1.75	3.00
☐ 1170		STILL WATER (LOVE)/		
		STILL WATER (PEACE)	1.75	3.00
☐ 1175		JUST SEVEN NUMBERS/		
		I WISH I WERE YOUR MIRROR	1.75	3.00
☐ 1185		IN THESE CHANGING TIMES/		
		RIGHT BEFORE MY EYES	1.75	3.00
☐ 1189		MacARTHUR PARK/(PT. 2)	1.75	3.00
☐ 1196		A SIMPLE GAME/L. A. (MY TOWN)	1.75	3.00

ISSUE #	LABEL		PRICE RANGE	
☐1198		I CAN'T QUIT YOUR LOVE/		
		HAPPY (IS A BUMPY ROAD)	1.75	3.00
☐1210		(IT'S THE WAY) NATURE PLANNED IT/		
		I'LL NEVER CHANGE	1.75	3.00

FOUR TOPS—ALBUMS

☐622 (M)	*MOTOWN*	THE FOUR TOPS	10.00	25.00
☐634 (S)		FOUR TOPS, NO. 2	10.00	25.00
☐647 (S)		ON TOP	10.00	25.00
☐654 (S)		LIVE	7.00	18.00
☐669 (S)		YESTERDAY'S DREAMS	5.00	13.50
☐675 (S)		NOW	5.00	13.50
☐695 (S)		SOUL SPIN	5.00	13.50
☐704 (S)		STILL WATERS RUN DEEP	5.00	13.50
☐740 (S)		GREATEST HITS	4.50	12.00
☐748 (S)		NATURE PLANNED IT	4.50	12.00
☐764 (S)		BEST OF THE FOUR TOPS	4.50	12.00

PETER FRAMPTON

☐1379	*A & M*	JUMPING JACK FLASH/		
		OH, FOR ANOTHER DAY	2.00	3.50
☐1506		I WANNA GO TO THE SUN/		
		SOMETHING'S HAPPENING	2.00	3.50
☐1693		SHOW ME THE WAY/CRYING CLOWN	2.25	4.00
☐1738		BABY, I LOVE YOUR WAY/MONEY	2.25	4.00

CONNIE FRANCIS

☐12015	*MGM*	FREDDY/DIDN'T I LOVE YOU ENOUGH?	3.50	6.00
☐12056		MAKE HIM JEALOUS/GOODY GOODBYE	3.50	6.00
☐12122		ARE YOU SATISFIED?/MY TREASURE	3.50	6.00
☐12191		MY FIRST REAL LOVE/BELIEVE IN ME	3.50	6.00
☐12251		SEND FOR MY BABY/FORGETTING	3.50	6.00
☐12335		MY SAILOR BOY/		
		EVERYONE NEEDS SOMEONE	2.75	4.50
☐12375		I NEVER HAD A SWEETHEART/		
		LITTLE BLUE WREN	2.75	4.50
☐12440		NO OTHER ONE/I LEANED ON A MAN	2.75	4.50
☐12490		EIGHTEEN/FADED ORCHID	2.75	4.50
☐12555		YOU, MY DARLIN', YOU/		
		THE MAJESTY OF LOVE	2.75	4.50
☐12588		WHO'S SORRY NOW/		
		YOU WERE ONLY FOOLING	2.25	4.00
☐12647		I'M SORRY I MADE YOU CRY/		
		LOCK UP YOUR HEART	2.25	4.00

ISSUE #	LABEL		PRICE RANGE	
☐ 12683	STUPID CUPID/CAROLINA MOON		2.25	4.00
☐ 12713	FALLIN'/			
	HAPPY DAYS AND LONELY NIGHTS		2.25	4.00
☐ 12738	MY HAPPINESS/NEVER BEFORE		2.25	4.00
☐ 12769	IF I DIDN'T CARE/			
	TOWARD THE END OF THE DAY		2.25	4.00
☐ 12793	LIPSTICK ON YOUR COLLAR/FRANKIE		2.25	4.00
☐ 12824	YOU'RE GONNA MISS ME/			
	PLENTY GOOD LOVIN'		2.00	3.50
☐ 12841	AMONG MY SOUVENIRS/			
	GOD BLESS AMERICA		2.00	3.50
☐ 12878	MAMA/TEDDY		2.00	3.50
☐ 12899	EVERYBODY'S SOMEBODY'S FOOL/			
	JEALOUS OF YOU		2.00	3.50
☐ 12923	MY HEART HAS A MIND OF ITS OWN/			
	MALAGUENA		2.00	3.50
☐ 12964	MANY TEARS AGO/SENZA MAMA		2.00	3.50
☐ 12971	WHERE THE BOYS ARE/NO ONE		2.00	3.50
☐ 12995	BREAKIN' IN A BRAND NEW BROKEN			
	HEART/SOMEONE ELSE'S BOY		1.75	3.00
☐ 13005	SWANEE/ATASHI NO		1.75	3.00
☐ 13019	TOGETHER/TOO MANY RULES		1.25	2.50
☐ 13039	(HE'S MY) DREAMBOAT/HOLLYWOOD		1.50	2.50
☐ 13051	WHEN THE BOY IN YOUR ARMS/			
	BABY'S FIRST CHRISTMAS		1.25	2.50
☐ 13505	IT'S A DIFFERENT WORLD/EMPTY CHAPEL		1.50	2.50
☐ 13545	A LETTER FROM A SOLDIER/			
	SOMEWHERE, MY LOVE		1.50	2.50
☐ 13578	ALL THE LOVE IN THE WORLD/SO NICE		1.50	2.50
☐ 13610	SPANISH NIGHTS AND YOU/			
	GAMES THAT LOVERS PLAY		1.50	2.50
☐ 13665	ANOTHER PAGE/SOUVENIR D'ITALIE		1.50	2.50
☐ 13718	TIME ALONE WILL TELL/BORN FREE		1.50	2.50
☐ 13773	MY HEART CRIES OUT FOR YOU/			
	SOMEONE TOOK THE SWEETNESS OUT			
	OF SWEETHEART		1.50	2.50
☐ 13814	LONELY AGAIN/WHEN YOU CARE			
	A LOT FOR SOMEONE		1.50	2.50
☐ 13876	MY WORLD IS SLIPPING AWAY/			
	TILL WE'RE TOGETHER		1.50	2.50
☐ 13923	WHY SAY GOODBYE?/ADIOS MI AMORE		1.50	2.50
☐ 13948	SOMEBODY ELSE IS TAKING MY PLACE/			
	BROTHER, CAN YOU SPARE A DIME?		1.50	2.50
☐ 14004	I DON'T WANNA PLAY HOUSE/			
	THE WELFARE CHECK		1.50	2.50

ISSUE #	LABEL		PRICE RANGE	
☐ 14034		THE WEDDING CAKE/		
		OVER HILL, UNDER GROUND	1.50	2.50
☐ 14058		GONE LIKE THE WIND/AM I BLUE?	1.50	2.50
☐ 14089		INVIERNO TRISTE/		
		NOCHES ESPANOLAS Y TU	1.50	2.50
☐ 14091		MR. LOVE/ZINGARA	1.50	2.50

CONNIE FRANCIS—EPs

☐ 1599	*MGM*	CONNIE FRANCIS	6.00	10.00
☐ 1603		WHO'S SORRY NOW	4.50	9.00
☐ 1604		WHO'S SORRY NOW	4.50	9.00
☐ 1605		WHO'S SORRY NOW	4.50	9.00
☐ 1655		MY HAPPINESS	4.50	8.00
☐ 1662		IF I DIDN'T CARE	4.50	8.00
☐ 1663		EXCITING CONNIE FRANCIS	4.00	7.00
☐ 1664		EXCITING CONNIE FRANCIS	4.00	7.00
☐ 1665		EXCITING CONNIE FRANCIS	4.00	7.00
☐ 1687		CONNIE FRANCIS	3.50	6.00
☐ 1688		CONNIE'S GREATEST HITS	2.75	4.50
☐ 1689		CONNIE'S GREATEST HITS	2.75	4.50
☐ 1690		CONNIE'S GREATEST HITS	2.75	4.50
☐ 1691		ROCK 'N ROLL MILLION SELLERS	2.75	4.50
☐ 1692		ROCK 'N ROLL MILLION SELLERS	2.75	4.50
☐ 1693		ROCK 'N ROLL MILLION SELLERS	2.75	4.50
☐ 1694		COUNTRY AND WESTERN GOLDEN HITS	2.75	4.50
☐ 1695		COUNTRY AND WESTERN GOLDEN HITS	2.75	4.50
☐ 1696		COUNTRY AND WESTERN GOLDEN HITS	2.75	4.50
☐ 1703		CONNIE FRANCIS	2.75	4.50

CONNIE FRANCIS—ALBUMS

☐ 3686 (M)	*MGM*	WHO'S SORRY NOW	12.50	30.00
☐ 3761 (S)		EXCITING CONNIE FRANCIS	12.50	30.00
☐ 3776 (S)		MY THANKS TO YOU	12.50	30.00
☐ 3791 (S)		ITALIAN FAVORITES	10.00	25.00
☐ 3792 (S)		CHRISTMAS IN MY HEART	10.00	18.00
☐ 3793 (S)		CONNIE'S GREATEST HITS	10.00	18.00
☐ 3794 (S)		ROCK 'N ROLL MILLION SELLERS	8.00	22.50
☐ 3795 (S)		COUNTRY AND WESTERN GOLDEN HITS	8.00	22.50
☐ 3853 (S)		SPANISH AND LATIN AMERICAN		
		FAVORITES	8.00	22.50
☐ 3869 (S)		JEWISH FAVORITES	8.00	22.50
☐ 3871 (S)		MORE ITALIAN FAVORITES	8.00	22.50
☐ 3893 (S)		SONGS TO A SWINGIN' BAND	8.00	22.50
☐ 3913 (S)		AT THE COPA	8.00	22.50
☐ 3942 (S)		MORE GREATEST HITS	7.00	18.00
☐ 3965 (S)		CONNIE FRANCIS SINGS		
		"NEVER ON SUNDAY"	7.00	18.00

ISSUE #	LABEL		PRICE RANGE	
☐ 3969 (S)		FOLK SONG FAVORITES	7.00	18.00
☐ 4022 (S)		DO THE TWIST WITH CONNIE FRANCIS	7.00	18.00
☐ 4048 (S)		AWARD WINNING MOTION PICTURE HITS	7.00	18.00
☐ 4049 (S)		CONNIE FRANCIS SINGS	6.00	15.00
☐ 4079 (S)		COUNTRY MUSIC CONNIE STYLE	6.00	15.00

FREDDIE AND THE DREAMERS

☐ 5053	*CAPITOL*	I'M TELLIN' YOU NOW/ WHAT HAVE I DONE TO YOU?	4.00	7.00
☐ 5137		YOU WERE MADE FOR ME/ SEND A LETTER TO ME	3.50	6.00
☐ 127		YOU WERE MADE FOR ME/SO FINE	1.75	3.00
☐ 72327	*MERCURY*	DON'T DO THAT TO ME/JUST FOR YOU	2.00	3.50
☐ 72377		I UNDERSTAND/I WILL	1.75	3.00
☐ 72428		DO THE FREDDIE/TELL ME WHEN	1.75	3.00
☐ 72462		A LITTLE YOU/THINGS I'D LIKE TO SAY	1.75	3.00
☐ 72487		I DON'T KNOW/ WINDMILL IN OLD AMSTERDAM	1.75	3.00

BOBBY FREEMAN

☐ 835	*JOSIE*	DO YOU WANT TO DANCE?/ BIG FAT WOMAN	2.25	4.00
☐ 841		BETTY LOU GOT A NEW PAIR OF SHOES/ STARLIGHT	2.25	4.00
☐ 844		NEED YOUR LOVE/ SHAME ON YOU, MISS JOHNSON	2.00	3.50
☐ 855		WHEN YOU'RE SMILING/ A LOVE TO LAST A LIFETIME	2.00	3.50
☐ 872		EBB TIDE/SINBAD	2.00	3.50
☐ 879		I NEED SOMEONE/ THE FIRST DAY OF SPRING	1.75	3.00
☐ 886		BABY, WHAT WOULD YOU DO?/ I MISS YOU SO	1.75	3.00
☐ 887		MESS AROUND/SO MUCH TO DO	1.75	3.00
☐ 889		SHE SAID SHE WANTS TO DANCE/ PUT YOU DOWN	1.75	3.00
☐ 896		LITTLE GIRL DON'T UNDERSTAND/ LOVE ME	1.75	3.00
☐ 5373	*KING*	(I DO THE) SHIMMY SHIMMY/ YOU DON'T UNDERSTAND ME	2.00	3.50
☐ 1	*AUTUMN*	LET'S SURF AGAIN/COME TO ME	2.00	3.50
☐ 2		C'MON AND SWIM (PT. 1)/(PT. 2)	1.50	3.00
☐ 5		S-W-I-M/ THAT LITTLE OLD HEARTBREAKER ME	1.50	3.00

— G —

ISSUE #	LABEL		PRICE RANGE	

DAVID GATES

ISSUE #	LABEL		PRICE RANGE	
☐ 1008	ROBBINS	LOVIN' AT NIGHT/JO BABY	8.50	15.00
☐ 123	EAST WEST	SWINGIN' BABY DOLL/		
		WALKIN' AND TALKIN'	6.00	10.00
☐ 413	MALA	YOU'LL BE MY BABY/WHAT'S THIS I HEAR	4.50	9.00
☐ 418		THE HAPPIEST MAN ALIVE/		
		THE ROAD LEADS TO LOVE	4.50	9.00
☐ 427		TEARDROPS IN MY HEART/JO BABY	4.00	7.00
☐ 4206	DEL-FI	NO ONE REALLY LOVES A CLOWN/		
		YOU HAVE IT COMIN' TO YOU	4.00	7.00
☐ 108	PLANETARY	ONCE UPON A TIME/LET YOU GO	4.00	7.00

MARVIN GAYE

ISSUE #	LABEL		PRICE RANGE	
☐ 54041	TAMLA	LET YOUR CONSCIENCE BE YOUR GUIDE/		
		NEVER LET YOU GO	4.00	7.00
☐ 54055		I'M YOURS, YOU'RE MINE/SANDMAN	3.50	6.00
☐ 54063		SOLDIER'S PLEA/TAKING MY TIME	3.50	6.00
☐ 54068		STUBBORN KIND OF FELLOW/		
		IT HURTS ME TOO	2.00	3.50
☐ 54075		HITCH HIKE/HELLO THERE ANGEL	2.00	3.50
☐ 54079		PRIDE AND JOY/ONE OF THESE DAYS	1.75	3.00
☐ 54087		CAN I GET A WITNESS/		
		I'M CRAZY 'BOUT MY BABY	1.75	3.00
☐ 54093		YOU'RE A WONDERFUL ONE/		
		WHEN I'M ALONE I CRY	1.75	3.00
☐ 54095		TRY IT BABY/IF MY HEART COULD SING	1.75	3.00
☐ 54101		BABY DON'T YOU DO IT/		
		WALK ON THE WILD SIDE	1.75	3.00
☐ 54104		WHAT GOOD AM I WITHOUT YOU?/		
		I WANT YOU	1.75	3.00
☐ 54107		HOW SWEET IT IS (TO BE LOVED BY YOU)/		
		FOREVER	1.75	3.00
☐ 54112		I'LL BE DOGGONE/		
		YOU'VE BEEN A LONG TIME COMING	1.75	3.00
☐ 54117		PRETTY LITTLE BABY/		
		NOW THAT YOU'VE WON ME	1.75	3.00
☐ 54122		AIN'T THAT PECULIAR/		
		SHE'S GOT TO BE REAL	1.75	3.00
☐ 54129		ONE MORE HEARTACHE/		
		WHEN I HAD YOUR LOVE	1.75	3.00
☐ 54132		TAKE THIS HEART OF MINE/		
		NEED YOUR LOVIN'	1.75	3.00

ISSUE #	LABEL		PRICE RANGE	
☐54138		LITTLE DARLING, I NEED YOU/		
		HEY DIDDLE DIDDLE	1.75	3.00
☐54141		IT TAKES TWO/		
		IT'S GOT TO BE A MIRACLE	1.50	2.50
☐54149		AIN'T NO MOUNTAIN HIGH ENOUGH/		
		GIVE A LITTLE LOVE	1.50	2.50
☐54153		YOUR UNCHANGING LOVE/		
		I'LL TAKE CARE OF YOU	1.50	2.50
☐54156		YOUR PRECIOUS LOVE/		
		HOLD ME, OH MY DARLING	1.50	2.50
☐54160		YOU/CHANGE WHAT YOU CAN	1.50	2.50
☐54161		IF I COULD BUILD MY WHOLE WORLD		
		AROUND YOU/IF THIS WORLD		
		WERE MINE	1.50	2.50
☐54163		AIN'T NOTHING LIKE THE REAL THING/		
		LITTLE OLE BOY, LITTLE OLE GIRL	1.50	2.50

MARVIN GAYE—ALBUMS

☐221 (M)	*TAMLA*	SOULFUL MOODS OF MARVIN GAYE	15.00	35.00
☐239 (M)		THAT STUBBORN KINDA FELLA	8.00	22.50
☐242 (M)		MARVIN GAYE ON STAGE	7.00	18.00
☐251 (M)		WHEN I'M ALONE I CRY	7.00	18.00
☐252 (M)		MARVIN GAYE'S GREATEST HITS	7.00	18.00
☐258 (S)		HOW SWEET IT IS TO BE LOVED BY YOU	7.00	18.00
☐259 (S)		HELLO BROADWAY, THIS IS MARVIN	7.00	18.00
☐266 (S)		MOODS OF MARVIN GAYE	7.00	18.00
☐270 (S)		MARVIN GAYE AND KIM WESTON	7.00	18.00
☐278 (S)		GREATEST HITS, VOL. II	7.00	18.00
☐284 (S)		YOU'RE ALL I NEED	6.00	15.00
☐285 (S)		IN THE GROOVE	5.00	13.50
☐285 (S)		I HEARD IT THROUGH THE GRAPEVINE	5.00	13.50
☐299 (S)		THAT'S THE WAY LOVE IS	5.00	13.50

GERRY AND THE PACEMAKERS

☐3162	*LAURIE*	HOW DO YOU DO IT/AWAY FROM YOU	2.25	4.00
☐3196		I LIKE IT/IT HAPPENED TO ME	2.25	4.00
☐3218		IT'S ALL RIGHT/		
		YOU'LL NEVER WALK ALONE	2.25	4.00
☐3233		I'M THE ONE/YOU'VE GOT WHAT I LIKE	2.00	3.50
☐3251		DON'T LET THE SUN CATCH YOU CRYING/		
		I'M THE ONE	2.00	3.50
☐3251		DON'T LET THE SUN CATCH YOU CRYING/		
		AWAY FROM YOU	1.75	3.00
☐3261		HOW DO YOU DO IT/		
		YOU'LL NEVER WALK ALONE	1.75	3.00

ISSUE #	LABEL		PRICE RANGE	
☐ 3271		I LIKE IT/JAMBALAYA	1.75	3.00
☐ 3279		I'LL BE THERE/YOU, YOU, YOU	1.75	3.00
☐ 3284		FERRY ACROSS THE MERSEY/PRETEND	1.75	3.00
☐ 3293		IT'S GONNA BE ALRIGHT/SKINNY MINNIE	1.75	3.00
☐ 3302		YOU'LL NEVER WALK ALONE/ AWAY FROM YOU	1.75	3.00
☐ 3313		GIVE ALL YOUR LOVE TO ME/ YOU'RE THE REASON	1.75	3.00
☐ 3323		WALK HAND IN HAND/DREAMS	1.75	3.00
☐ 3337		LA LA LA/WITHOUT YOU	1.75	3.00
☐ 3354		GIRL ON A SWING/ THE WAY YOU LOOK TONIGHT	1.75	3.00
☐ 3370		LOOKING FOR MY LIFE/THE BIG BRIGHT GREEN PLEASURE MACHINE	1.75	3.00

GERRY AND THE PACEMAKERS—ALBUMS

☐ 2024 (S)	*LAURIE*	DON'T LET THE SUN CATCH YOU CRYING	8.00	22.50
☐ 2027 (S)		SECOND ALBUM	8.00	22.50
☐ 2030 (S)		I'LL BE THERE	8.00	22.50
☐ 2031 (S)		GREATEST HITS	7.00	18.00
☐ 2037 (S)		GIRL ON A SWING	7.00	18.00
☐ 90812 (S)		FERRY ACROSS THE MERSEY	7.00	18.00

PETER GOON

☐ 100	*POLEESE*	WHISTLER/SONG TITLES	12.00	36.00

LESLEY GORE

☐ 72119	*MERCURY*	IT'S MY PARTY/DANNY	1.75	3.00
☐ 72143		JUDY'S TURN TO CRY/JUST LET ME CRY	1.75	3.00
☐ 72180		SHE'S A FOOL/THE OLD CROWD	1.75	3.00
☐ 72206		YOU DON'T OWN ME/RUN, BOBBY, RUN	1.75	3.00
☐ 72245		JE NE SAIS PLUS/JE N'OSE PAS	1.75	3.00
☐ 72259		THAT'S THE WAY BOYS ARE/ THAT'S THE WAY THE BALL BOUNCES	1.75	3.00
☐ 72270		I DON'T WANNA BE A LOSER/ IT'S GOTTA BE YOU	1.75	3.00
☐ 72309		MAYBE I KNOW/WONDER BOY	1.75	3.00
☐ 72352		SOMETIMES I WISH I WERE A BOY/ HEY NOW	1.75	3.00
☐ 72372		THE LOOK OF LOVE/LITTLE GIRL, GO HOME	1.75	3.00
☐ 72412		ALL OF MY LIFE/ I CANNOT HOPE FOR ANYONE	1.75	3.00
☐ 72433		SUNSHINE, LOLLIPOPS AND ROSES/ YOU'VE COME BACK	1.75	3.00

ISSUE #	LABEL		PRICE RANGE	
☐ 72475		MY TOWN, MY GUY AND ME/		
		A GIRL IN LOVE	1.75	3.00
☐ 72513		I WON'T LOVE YOU ANYMORE (SORRY)/		
		NO MATTER WHAT YOU DID	1.75	3.00
☐ 72530		WE KNOW WE'RE IN LOVE/		
		THAT'S WHAT I'LL DO	1.75	3.00
☐ 72553		YOUNG LOVE/I JUST DON'T KNOW IF I CAN	1.75	3.00
☐ 72580		OFF AND RUNNING/I DON'T CARE	1.75	3.00
☐ 72611		TREAT ME LIKE A LADY/MAYBE NOW	1.75	3.00
☐ 72649		CALIFORNIA NIGHTS/I'M GOING OUT	1.75	3.00
☐ 72683		SUMMER AND SANDY/I'M FALLIN' DOWN	1.75	3.00
☐ 72726		BRINK OF DISASTER/ON A DAY LIKE THIS	1.75	3.00
☐ 72759		IT'S A HAPPENING WORLD/MAGIC COLORS	1.75	3.00
☐ 72787		SMALL TALK/SAY WHAT YOU SEE	1.75	3.00
☐ 72819		HE GIVES ME LOVE (LA LA LA)/		
		A BRAND NEW ME	1.75	3.00
☐ 72842		I CAN'T MAKE IT WITHOUT YOU/		
		WHERE CAN I GO?	1.75	3.00
☐ 72867		LOOK THE OTHER WAY/		
		I'LL BE STANDING BY	1.75	3.00
☐ 72892		TAKE GOOD CARE/		
		YOU SENT ME SILVER BELLS	1.75	3.00
☐ 72892		I CAN'T MAKE IT WITHOUT YOU/		
		TAKE GOOD CARE	1.75	3.00
☐ 72931		98.6 - SUMMER DAY/		
		SUMMER SYMPHONY	1.75	3.00
☐ 72969		WEDDING BELL BLUES/ONE BY ONE	1.75	3.00
☐ 338	*CREWE*	TOMORROW'S CHILREN/		
		WHY DOESN'T LOVE MAKE ME HAPPY?	1.75	3.00
☐ 343		COME SOFTLY TO ME/		
		BILLY 'N SUE'S LOVE SONG	2.00	3.50
☐ 344		WHEN YESTERDAY WAS TOMORROW/		
		WHY ME, WHY YOU?	1.75	3.00
☐ 5029	*MOWEST*	THE ROAD I WALK/SHE SAID THAT	1.75	3.00
☐ 1710	*A & M*	IMMORTALITY/		
		GIVE IT TO ME, SWEET THING	1.75	3.00

LESLEY GORE—ALBUMS

☐ 60805 (S)	*MERCURY*	I'LL CRY IF I WANT TO	10.00	25.00
☐ 60849 (S)		LESLEY GORE SINGS FOR MIXED UP		
		HEARTS	10.00	18.00
☐ 60901 (S)		BOYS, BOYS, BOYS	8.00	22.50
☐ 60943 (S)		GIRL TALK	8.00	22.50
☐ 61024 (S)		GOLDEN HITS OF LESLEY GORE	8.00	22.50
☐ 61042 (S)		MY TOWN, MY GUY, AND ME	7.00	18.00

ISSUE #	LABEL		PRICE RANGE	
☐ 61066 (S)		ALL ABOUT LOVE	7.00	18.00
☐ 61120 (S)		CALIFORNIA NIGHTS	7.00	18.00
☐ 61185 (S)		GOLDEN HITS OF LESLEY GORE, VOL. II	5.00	13.50
☐ 117 (S)	*MOWEST*	SOMEPLACE ELSE NOW	4.50	12.00

GRASS ROOTS

ISSUE #	LABEL		PRICE RANGE	
☐ 4013	*DUNHILL*	MR. JONES/YOU'RE A LONELY GIRL	2.25	4.00
☐ 4029		WHERE WERE YOU WHEN I NEEDED YOU?/		
		(THESE ARE) BAD TIMES	1.75	3.00
☐ 4043		ONLY WHEN YOU'RE LONELY/		
		THIS IS WHAT I WAS MADE FOR	2.00	3.50
☐ 4053		LOOK OUT, GIRL/TIP OF MY TONGUE	2.00	3.50
☐ 4084		LET'S LIVE FOR TODAY/		
		DEPRESSED FEELING ....:........	1.75	3.00
☐ 4094		THINGS I SHOULD HAVE SAID/		
		TIP OF MY TONGUE	1.75	3.00
☐ 4105		WAKE UP, WAKE UP/NO EXIT	1.75	3.00
☐ 4122		MELODY FOR YOU/HEY FRIEND	1.75	3.00
☐ 4129		FEELINGS/HERE'S WHERE YOU BELONG	1.75	3.00
☐ 4144		MIDNIGHT CONFESSIONS/		
		WHO WILL YOU BE TOMORROW?	1.75	3.00
☐ 4162		BELLA LINDA/HOT BRIGHT BLUES	1.75	3.00
☐ 4180		LOVIN' THINGS/		
		YOU AND LOVE ARE THE SAME	1.75	3.00
☐ 4187		THE RIVER IS WIDE/		
		(YOU GOTTA) LIVE FOR LOVE	1.75	3.00
☐ 4198		I'D WAIT A MILLION YEARS/		
		FLY ME TO HAVANA	1.75	3.00
☐ 4217		HEAVEN KNOWS/DON'T REMIND ME	1.75	3.00
☐ 4227		WALKING THROUGH THE COUNTRY/		
		TRUCK DRIVIN' MAN	1.75	3.00
☐ 4237		BABY HOLD ON/GET IT TOGETHER	1.75	3.00
☐ 4249		COME ON AND SAY IT/		
		SOMETHING'S COMIN' OVER ME	1.75	3.00
☐ 4263		TEMPTATION EYES/KEEPIN' ME DOWN	1.75	3.00
☐ 4279		SOONER OR LATER/		
		I CAN TURN OFF THE RAIN............	1.75	3.00
☐ 4289		TWO DIVIDED BY LOVE/LET IT GO	1.75	3.00
☐ 4302		GLORY BOUND/ONLY ONE	1.75	3.00
☐ 4316		THE RUNWAY/MOVE ALONG	1.75	3.00
☐ 4325		ANY WAY THE WIND BLOWS/		
		MONDAY BLUES	1.75	3.00
☐ 4335		LOVE IS WHAT YOU MAKE IT/		
		SOMEONE TO LOVE ....:.	1.75	3.00

ISSUE #	LABEL		PRICE RANGE	

GRASS ROOTS—ALBUMS

☐ 50020 (S)	*DUNHILL*	LET'S LIVE FOR TODAY	6.00	15.00
☐ 50027 (S)		FEELINGS	5.00	13.50
☐ 50047 (S)		GOLDEN GRASS	5.00	13.50
☐ 50052 (S)		LOVIN' THINGS	5.00	13.50
☐ 50067 (S)		LEAVING IT ALL BEHIND	5.00	13.50
☐ 50087 (S)		MORE GOLDEN GRASS	5.00	13.50
☐ 50107 (S)		THEIR 16 GREATEST HITS	4.00	10.00
☐ 50112 (S)		MOVE ALONG	4.00	10.00
☐ 50137 (S)		A LOTTA MILEAGE	4.00	10.00

GUESS WHO

☐ 1295	*SCEPTER*	SHAKIN' ALL OVER/TILL WE KISSED	2.00	3.50
☐ 12108		GOODNIGHT, GOODNIGHT/		
		HEY, HO, WHAT YOU DID TO ME	2.00	3.50
☐ 12188		HURTING EACH OTHER/BABY'S BIRTHDAY	2.00	3.50
☐ 12131		BABY FEELIN'/BELIEVE ME	2.00	3.50
☐ 12144		CLOCK ON THE WALL/ONE DAY	2.00	3.50
☐ 967	*AMY*	SHE'S ALL MINE/ALL RIGHT	2.00	3.50
☐ 976		HIS GIRL/IT'S MY PRIDE	2.00	3.50
☐ 1597	*FONTANA*	THIS TIME LONG AGO/		
		THERE'S NO GETTING AWAY FROM YOU	2.00	3.50
☐ 0102	*RCA*	THESE EYES/LIGHTFOOT	1.75	3.00
☐ 0195		LAUGHING/UNDUN	1.75	3.00
☐ 0223		FRIEND OF MINE/(PT. 2)	1.75	3.00
☐ 0300		NO TIME/PROPER STRANGER	1.75	3.00
☐ 0325		AMERICAN WOMAN/NO SUGAR TONIGHT	1.75	3.00
☐ 0367		HAND ME DOWN WORLD/		
		RUNNIN' DOWN THE STREET	1.75	3.00
☐ 0388		SHARE THE LAND/BUS RIDER	1.75	3.00
☐ 0414		HANG ON TO YOUR LIFE/		
		DO YOU MISS ME, DARLIN'	1.50	2.50

GUESS WHO—ALBUMS

☐ 533 (S)	*SCEPTER*	SHAKIN' ALL OVER	10.00	25.00
☐ 4141 (S)	*RCA*	WHEATFIELD SOUL	4.50	12.00
☐ 4157 (S)		CANNED WHEAT	4.50	12.00
☐ 4266 (S)		AMERICAN WOMAN	4.50	12.00
☐ 4359 (S)		SHARE THE LAND	4.50	12.00
☐ 4574 (S)		SO LONG BANNATYNE	4.50	12.00
☐ 4602 (S)		ROCKIN'	4.50	12.00
☐ 4779 (S)		LIVE AT THE PARAMOUNT	4.00	10.00
☐ 4830 (S)		ARTIFICIAL PARADISE	4.00	10.00
☐ 1004 (S)		BEST OF THE GUESS WHO	4.00	10.00
☐ 0130 (S)		NO. 10	4.00	10.00

ISSUE #	LABEL		PRICE RANGE	
☐ 0269 (S)		BEST OF THE GUESS WHO, VOL. II	4.00	10.00
☐ 0405 (S)		ROAD FOOD	4.00	10.00
☐ 0636 (S)		FLAVOURS	4.00	10.00

ARLO GUTHRIE

☐ PRO-304	*REPRISE*	MOTORCYCLE SONG/		
		THE PAUSE OF MR. CLAUS	3.00	6.50
☐ 0793		MOTORCYCLE SONG (PT. 1)/(PT. 2)	2.00	4.50
☐ 0877		ALICE'S RESTAURANT/COMING IN TO L.A. ...	2.00	4.50
☐ 0644		MOTORCYCLE SONG/NOW AND THEN	2.00	4.50
☐ 0951		VALLEY TO PRAY/GABRIEL'S MOTHER	2.00	4.50
☐ 1103		CITY OF NEW ORLEANS/DAYS ARE SHORT	1.25	2.50

— H —

BILL HALEY AND THE COMETS

☐ 303	*ESSEX*	ROCK THE JOINT/ICY HEART	18.00	30.00
☐ 305		DANCE WITH THE DOLLY/		
		ROCKING CHAIR ON THE MOON	18.00	30.00
☐ 310		REAL ROCK DRIVE/STOP BEATIN'		
		'ROUND THE MULBERRY BUSH	15.00	25.00
☐ 321		CRAZY MAN CRAZY/WHATCHA GONNA DO ...	10.00	18.00
☐ 327		FRACTURED/PAT-A-CAKE	10.00	18.00
☐ 332		LIVE IT UP/		
		FAREWELL, SO LONG, GOODBYE	8.50	15.00
☐ 340		I'LL BE TRUE/TEN LITTLE INDIANS	7.25	12.00
☐ 348		STRAIGHT JACKET/		
		CHATTANOOGA CHOO-CHOO	7.25	12.00
☐ 374		SUNDOWN BOOGIE/		
		JUKEBOX CANNONBALL	8.50	15.00
☐ 381		ROCKET 88/GREEN TREE BOOGIE	8.50	15.00
☐ 399		ROCK THE JOINT/		
		FAREWELL, SO LONG, GOODBYE	7.25	12.00
☐ 718	*TRANS WORLD*	REAL ROCK DRIVE/YES INDEED	7.25	12.00
☐ 29124	*DECCA*	ROCK AROUND THE CLOCK/		
		THIRTEEN WOMEN	3.50	6.00
☐ 29204		SHAKE, RATTLE AND ROLL/A.B.C. BOOGIE ...	3.50	6.00
☐ 29317		DIM, DIM THE LIGHTS/HAPPY BABY	3.00	4.50
☐ 29418		MAMBO ROCK/BIRTH OF THE BOOGIE	3.00	4.50
☐ 29552		RAZZLE-DAZZLE/TWO HOUND DOGS	3.00	4.50

ISSUE #	LABEL		PRICE RANGE	
☐ 29713		BURN THAT CANDLE/		
		ROCK-A-BEATIN' BOOGIE	3.00	4.50
☐ 29791		SEE YOU LATER ALLIGATOR/		
		THE PAPER BOY	3.00	4.50
☐ 29870		R-O-C-K/THE SAINTS ROCK 'N' ROLL	2.50	4.00
☐ 29948		HOT DOG BUDDY BUDDY/		
		ROCKIN' THROUGH THE RYE	2.50	4.00
☐ 30028		RIP IT UP/TEENAGER'S MOTHER	2.50	4.00
☐ 30085		RUDY'S ROCK/BLUE COMET BLUES	2.50	4.00
☐ 30148		DON'T KNOCK THE ROCK/		
		CHO CHO CH'BOOGIE	2.50	4.00
☐ 30214		FORTY CUPS OF COFFEE/		
		HOOK, LINE AND SINKER	2.00	3.50
☐ 30314		BILLY GOAT/ROCKIN' ROLLIN' ROVER	2.00	3.50
☐ 30394		THE DIPSY DOODLE/MISS YOU	2.00	3.50
☐ 30461		ROCK THE JOINT/HOW MANY	2.00	3.50
☐ 30530		MARY, MARY LOU/IT'S A SIN	2.00	3.50
☐ 30592		SKINNY MINNIE/SWAY WITH ME	2.00	3.50
☐ 30681		LEAN JEAN/DON'T NOBODY MOVE	2.00	3.50
☐ 30741		WHOA MABEL/CHIQUITA LINA	2.00	3.50
☐ 30781		CORRINE, CORRINA/ B. B. PLENTY	2.00	3.50
☐ 5145	*WARNER*			
	BROTHERS	CANDY KISSES/TAMIANI	1.75	3.00
☐ 5154		CHICK SAFARI/HAWK	1.75	3.00
☐ 5171		SO RIGHT TONIGHT/LET THE GOOD		
		TIMES ROLL, CREOLE	1.75	3.00
☐ 5228		FLIP, FLOP AND FLY/HONKY TONK	1.75	3.00
☐ 7124		ROCK AROUND THE CLOCK/		
		SHAKE, RATTLE AND ROLL	1.75	3.00

BILL HALEY AND THE COMETS—EPs

ISSUE #	LABEL		PRICE RANGE	
☐ 102	*ESSEX*	DANCE PARTY	20.00	35.00
☐ 117		ROCK WITH BILL HALEY AND THE COMETS . . .	18.00	30.00
☐ 118		ROCK WITH BILL HALEY AND THE COMETS . . .	18.00	30.00
☐ 2168	*DECCA*	SHAKE, RATTLE AND ROLL	12.00	20.00
☐ 2209		DIM, DIM THE LIGHTS	10.00	18.00
☐ 2322		ROCK AND ROLL	8.50	15.00
☐ 2398		HE DIGS ROCK AND ROLL	7.25	12.00
☐ 2416		ROCK AND ROLL STAGE SHOW	7.25	12.00
☐ 2417		ROCK AND ROLL STAGE SHOW	7.25	12.00
☐ 2418		ROCK AND ROLL STAGE SHOW	7.25	12.00
☐ 2532		ROCKIN' THE OLDIES	7.25	12.00
☐ 2533		ROCK AND ROLL PARTY	7.25	12.00
☐ 2534		ROCKIN' AND ROLLIN'	7.25	12.00
☐ 2564		ROCKIN' AROUND THE WORLD	7.25	12.00
☐ 2576		ROCKIN' AROUND EUROPE	6.00	11.00

ISSUE #	LABEL		PRICE RANGE	
☐ 2577		ROCKIN' AROUND THE AMERICAS	6.00	11.00
☐ 2615		ROCKIN' THE JOINT	4.50	9.00
☐ 2616		ROCKIN' THE JOINT	4.50	9.00
☐ 2638		BILL HALEY'S CHICKS	4.50	9.00
☐ 2670		BILL HALEY AND HIS COMETS	4.50	9.00
☐ 2671		STRICTLY INSTRUMENTAL	4.50	9.00

BILL HALEY AND THE COMETS—ALBUMS

ISSUE #	LABEL		PRICE RANGE	
☐ 202 (M)	**ESSEX**	ROCK WITH BILL HALEY AND HIS COMETS	50.00	135.00
☐ 202 (M)	**TRANS WORLD**	ROCK WITH BILL HALEY AND HIS COMETS	15.00	35.00
☐ 5560 (M)	**DECCA**	SHAKE RATTLE AND ROLL	40.00	110.00
☐ 8225 (M)		ROCK AROUND THE CLOCK	12.50	30.00
☐ 8315 (M)		HE DIGS ROCK AND ROLL	10.00	25.00
☐ 8345 (M)		ROCK AND ROLL STAGE SHOW	10.00	25.00
☐ 8569 (M)		ROCKIN' THE OLDIES	8.00	22.50
☐ 8692 (S)		ROCKIN' AROUND THE WORLD	10.00	25.00
☐ 8775 (S)		ROCKIN' THE JOINT	10.00	25.00
☐ 8821 (S)		BILL HALEY'S CHICKS	8.00	22.50
☐ 8964 (S)		STRICTLY INSTRUMENTAL	7.00	18.00
☐ 1378 (S)	**WARNER BROTHERS**	BILL HALEY AND HIS COMETS	7.00	18.00
☐ 1391 (S)		HALEY'S JUKE BOX	7.00	18.00

JIMI HENDRIX

ISSUE #	LABEL		PRICE RANGE	
☐ 167	**AUDIO FIDELITY**	NO SUCH ANIMAL (PT. 1)/(PT. 2)	8.50	15.00
☐ 0572	**REPRISE**	HEY JOE/51ST ANNIVERSARY	4.00	7.00
☐ 0597		PURPLE HAZE/THE WIND CRIES MARY	2.25	4.00
☐ 0641		FOXEY LADY/HEY JOE	2.25	4.00
☐ 0665		UP FROM THE SKIES/ONE RAINY WISH	2.25	4.00
☐ 0767		ALL ALONG THE WATCHTOWER/ BURNING OF THE MIDNIGHT LAMP	1.75	3.00
☐ 0792		CROSSTOWN TRAFFIC/GYPSY EYES	1.75	3.00
☐ 0853		IF 6 WAS 9/STONE FREE	2.00	3.50
☐ 1082		JOHNNY B. GOODE/LOVER MAN	2.00	3.50

JIMI HENDRIX—ALBUMS

ISSUE #	LABEL		PRICE RANGE	
☐ 6261 (S)	**REPRISE**	ARE YOU EXPERIENCED?	5.00	13.50
☐ 6281 (S)		AXIS: BOLD AS LOVE	5.00	13.50
☐ 6307 (S)		ELECTRIC LADYLAND	5.00	13.50
☐ 2025 (S)		SMASH HITS	5.00	13.50
☐ 2034 (S)		THE CRY OF LOVE	4.50	9.00
☐ 2049 (S)		HENDRIX IN THE WEST	4.50	9.00
☐ 2204 (S)		CRASH LANDING	4.50	9.00
☐ 2229 (S)		MIDNIGHT LIGHTNING	4.50	9.00

JIM HENDRIX

ISSUE #	LABEL		PRICE RANGE	

BUDDY HOLLY

ISSUE #	LABEL			
☐ 29854	*DECCA*	LOVE ME/BLUE DAYS, BLACK NIGHTS	24.00	42.00
☐ 30166		MODERN DON JUAN/		
		YOU ARE MY ONE DESIRE	20.00	36.00
☐ 61852	*CORAL*	WORDS OF LOVE/		
		MAILMAN, BRING ME NO MORE BLUES	48.00	90.00
☐ 61885		PEGGY SUE/EVERYDAY	4.00	7.00
☐ 61947		I'M GONNA LOVE YOU TOO/LISTEN TO ME	6.00	10.00
☐ 61985		RAVE ON/TAKE YOUR TIME	4.00	7.00
☐ 62006		EARLY IN THE MORNING/NOW WE'RE ONE	4.00	7.00
☐ 62051		HEARTBEAT/WELL . . . ALL RIGHT	4.00	7.00
☐ 62074		IT DOESN'T MATTER ANYMORE/		
		RAINING IN MY HEART	4.00	7.00
☐ 62134		PEGGY SUE GOT MARRIED/		
		CRYING, WAITING, HOPING	15.00	25.00
☐ 62210		TRUE LOVE WAYS/THAT MAKES IT TOUGH	15.00	25.00
☐ 62283		YOU'RE SO SQUARE/VALLEY OF TEARS	15.00	25.00
☐ 62329		REMINISCING/		
		WAIT TILL THE SUN SHINES NELLIE	8.50	15.00
☐ 62352		TRUE LOVE WAYS/BO DIDDLEY	6.00	10.00
☐ 62369		BROWN EYED HANDSOME MAN/WISHING	6.00	10.00
☐ 62390		I'M GONNA LOVE YOU TOO/		
		ROCK AROUND WITH OLLIE VEE	6.00	12.00
☐ 62448		SLIPPIN' AND SLIDIN'/WHAT TO DO	12.00	20.00
☐ 62554		RAVE ON/EARLY IN THE MORNING	8.50	15.00
☐ 62558		LOVE IS STRANGE/YOU'RE THE ONE	7.25	12.00

BUDDY HOLLY—EPs

ISSUE #	LABEL			
☐ 2575	*DECCA*	THAT'LL BE THE DAY	150.00	250.00
☐ 81169	*CORAL*	LISTEN TO ME	24.00	42.00
☐ 81182		THE BUDDY HOLLY STORY	20.00	36.00
☐ 81191		PEGGY SUE GOT MARRIED	20.00	36.00
☐ 81193		BROWN EYED HANDSOME MAN	20.00	36.00

BUDDY HOLLY—ALBUMS

ISSUE #	LABEL			
☐ 8707 (M)	*DECCA*	THAT'LL BE THE DAY	100.00	260.00
☐ 8707 (M)		THAT'LL BE THE DAY	70.00	185.00
☐ 57210 (M)	*CORAL*	BUDDY HOLLY	25.00	60.00
☐ 57279 (S)		THE BUDDY HOLLY STORY	15.00	35.00
☐ 57326 (S)		THE BUDDY HOLLY STORY, VOL. II	15.00	35.00
☐ 57405 (S)		BUDDY HOLLY AND THE CRICKETS	15.00	35.00
☐ 57426 (S)		REMINISCING	15.00	35.00
☐ 57450 (S)		SHOWCASE	12.50	30.00
☐ 57463 (S)		HOLLY IN THE HILLS	12.50	30.00
☐ 57492 (S)		GREATEST HITS	10.00	25.00

ISSUE #	LABEL		PRICE RANGE	

HOLLYWOOD ARGYLES

ISSUE #	LABEL	TITLE		
☐ 5905	*LUTE*	ALLEY-OOP/		
		SHO KNOW A LOT ABOUT LOVE	2.25	4.00
☐ 5908		GUN TOTIN' CRITTER NAMED JACK/		
		BUG EYE	2.25	4.00
☐ 6002		HULLY GULLY/SO FINE	2.25	4.00
☐ 752	*PAXLEY*	YOU'VE BEEN TORTURING ME/		
		THE GRUBBLE	2.00	3.50
☐ 691				
	CHATTAHOOCHIE	LONG HAIRED UNSQUARE DUDE		
		NAMED JACK/OLE'	2.00	3.50
☐ 8674	*FELSTED*	BOSSY NOVER/FIND ANOTHER WAY	2.00	3.50
☐ 105	*KAMMY*	ALLEY OOP '66/DO THE FUNKY FOOT	2.00	3.50

HOLLYWOOD ARGYLES—ALBUM

☐ 9001 (M)	*LUTE*	ALLEY-OOP	35.00	90.00

BRIAN HYLAND

☐ 801	*LEADER*	ROSEMARY/LIBRARY LOVE AFFAIR	4.50	9.00
☐ 805		ITSY BITSY TEENIE WEENIE YELLOW		
		POLKADOT BIKINI/		
		DON'T DILLY DALLY, SALLY	2.25	4.00
☐ 342	*KAPP*	ITSY BITSY TEENIE WEENIE YELLOW		
		POLKADOT BIKINI/		
		DON'T DILLY DALLY, SALLY	2.00	3.50
☐ 352		FOUR LITTLE HEELS/THAT'S HOW MUCH	2.00	3.50
☐ 363		I GOTTA GO/LOP-SIDED, OVERLOADED	2.00	3.50
☐ 401		LIPSTICK ON YOUR LIPS/		
		WHEN WILL I KNOW	2.00	3.50
☐ 10236	*ABC-*			
	PARAMOUNT	LET ME BELONG TO YOU/LET IT DIE	2.00	3.50
☐ 10262		I'LL NEVER STOP WANTING YOU/		
		THE NIGHT I CRIED	2.00	3.50
☐ 10294		GINNY COME LATELY/		
		I SHOULD BE GETTING BETTER	2.00	3.50
☐ 10336		SEALED WITH A KISS/SUMMER JOB	2.00	3.50
☐ 10359		WARMED OVER KISSES/		
		WALK A LONELY MILE	2.00	3.50
☐ 10374		I MAY NOT LIVE TO SEE TOMORROW/		
		IT AIN'T THAT WAY	2.00	3.50
☐ 10400		IF MARY'S THERE/REMEMBER ME	2.00	3.50
☐ 10427		SOMEWHERE IN THE NIGHT/		
		I WISH TODAY WAS YESTERDAY	2.00	3.50
☐ 10452		I'M AFRAID TO GO HOME/		
		SAVE YOUR HEART FOR ME	2.00	3.50

ISSUE #	LABEL		PRICE RANGE	
☐ 10494		NOTHING MATTERS BUT YOU/		
		LET US MAKE OUR OWN MISTAKES	2.00	3.50
☐ 10549		OUT OF SIGHT, OUT OF MIND/		
		ACT NATURALLY	2.00	3.50
☐ 40179	PHILIPS	HERE'S TO OUR LOVE/		
		TWO KINDS OF GIRLS	2.00	3.50
☐ 40203		DEVOTED TO YOU/PLEDGING MY LOVE	2.00	3.50
☐ 40221		NOW I BELONG TO YOU/		
		ONE STEP FORWARD, TWO STEPS BACK	2.00	3.50
☐ 40263		HE DON'T UNDERSTAND YOU/		
		LOVE WILL FIND A WAY	2.00	3.50
☐ 40306		STAY AWAY FROM HER/		
		I CAN'T KEEP A SECRET	2.00	3.50
☐ 40354		3,000 MILES/SOMETIMES THEY DO,		
		SOMETIMES THEY DON'T	2.00	3.50
☐ 40377		THE JOKER WENT WILD/		
		I CAN HEAR THE RAIN	1.75	3.00
☐ 40405		RUN, RUN, LOOK AND SEE/		
		WHY DID YOU DO IT?	1.75	3.00
☐ 40424		HUNG UP IN YOUR EYES/WHY MINE	1.75	3.00
☐ 40444		HOLIDAY FOR CLOWNS/		
		YESTERDAY I HAD A GIRL	1.75	3.00
☐ 40472		GET THE MESSAGE/KINDA GROOVY	1.75	3.00

BRIAN HYLAND—ALBUMS

☐ 1202 (M)	KAPP	THE BASHFUL BLONDE	7.00	18.00
☐ 400 (M)	ABC-PARAMOUNT	LET ME BELONG TO YOU	6.00	15.00
☐ 400 (S)		LET ME BELONG TO YOU	8.00	22.50
☐ 431 (S)		SEALED WITH A KISS	8.00	22.50
☐ 463 (S)		COUNTRY MEETS FOLK	7.00	18.00
☐ 136 (S)		HERE'S TO OUR LOVE	7.00	18.00
☐ 158 (S)		ROCKIN' FOLK	7.00	18.00
☐ 217 (S)		THE JOKER WENT WILD	7.00	18.00
☐ 25926 (S)	DOT	TRAGEDY	4.00	10.00
☐ 25954 (S)		STAY AND LOVE ME ALL SUMMER	4.00	10.00
☐ 73097 (S)	UNI	BRIAN HYLAND	4.00	10.00

— I —

ISSUE #	LABEL		PRICE RANGE	

JANIS IAN

☐ 5027	**VERVE**			
	FOLKWAYS	SOCIETY'S CHILD/LETTER TO JON	2.75	5.50
☐ 5041	**VERVE**			
	FORECASE	YOUNGER GENERATION BLUES/		
		I'LL GIVE YOU A STONE	2.75	5.50
☐ 5059		LADY OF THE NIGHT/FRIENDS AGAIN	2.75	5.50
☐ 5072		SUNFLAKES FALL/INSANITY	2.75	5.50
☐ 5079		SONG FOR ALL THE SEASONS/		
		LONELY ONE	2.75	5.50
☐ 5099		EVERYBODY KNOWS/JANEY'S BLUES	2.75	5.50
☐ 3107	**CAPITOL**	HERE IN SPAIN/HE'S A RAINBOW	2.25	4.50
☐ 10154	**COLUMBIA**	STARS/AT SEVENTEEN	1.25	2.50

FRANK IFIELD

☐ 457	**VEE JAY**	I REMEMBER YOU/I LISTEN TO MY HEART	2.00	3.50
☐ 477		LOVESICK BLUES/ANYTIME	2.00	3.50
☐ 499		THE WAYWARD WIND/I'M SMILING NOW . . .	2.00	3.50
☐ 525		UNCHAINED MELODY/		
		NOBODY'S DARLIN' BUT MINE	2.00	3.50
☐ 553		I'M CONFESSIN' (THAT I LOVE YOU)/		
		HEART AND SOUL	2.00	3.50
☐ 5032	**CAPITOL**	I'M CONFESSIN'/WALTZING MATILDA	1.75	3.00
☐ 5089		PLEASE/MULE TRAIN	1.75	3.00
☐ 5134		DON'T BLAME ME/SAY IT ISN'T SO	1.75	3.00
☐ 5170		YOU CAME A LONG WAY FROM ST. LOUIS/		
		SWEET LORRAINE	1.75	3.00

FRANK IFIELD—ALBUMS

☐ 1054 (S)	**VEE JAY**	I REMEMBER YOU	10.00	25.00
☐ 10356 (S)		I'M CONFESSIN' (THAT I LOVE YOU)	8.00	22.50

IMPALAS

☐ 50026	**HAMILTON**	FIRST DATE/I WAS A FOOL	7.25	12.00
☐ 9022	**CUB**	SORRY (I RAN ALL THE WAY HOME)/		
		FOOL FOOL FOOL	2.25	4.00
☐ 9033		OH, WHAT A FOOL/SANDY WENT AWAY	2.25	4.00
☐ 9053		PEGGY DARLING/BYE EVERYBODY	2.25	4.00
☐ 9066		WHEN MY HEART DOES ALL THE TALKING/		
		ALL ALONE	2.25	4.00

ISSUE #	LABEL		PRICE RANGE	

IMPALAS—EP

| ☐ 5000 | *CUB* | SORRY (I RAN ALL THE WAY HOME) . . . . | 10.00 | 18.00 |

IMPALAS—ALBUM

| ☐ 8003 (S) | *CUB* | SORRY (I RAN ALL THE WAY HOME) . . . . | 35.00 | 90.00 |

IMPRESSIONS

☐ 2504	*BANDERA*	LISTEN TO ME/SHORTY'S GOTTA GO	4.50	9.00
☐ 107	*SWIRL*	DON'T LEAVE ME/I NEED YOUR LOVE	4.00	7.00
☐ 280	*VEE JAY*	FOR YOUR PRECIOUS LOVE/		
		SWEET WAS THE WINE	70.00	120.00
☐ 424		SAY THAT YOU LOVE ME/		
		SENORITA, I LOVE YOU	4.00	7.00
☐ 575		THE GIFT OF LOVE/AT THE COUNTY FAIR	3.50	6.00
☐ 621		SAY THAT YOU LOVE ME/		
		SENORITA, I LOVE YOU	2.25	4.00
☐ 1013	*FALCON*	FOR YOUR PRECIOUS LOVE/		
		SWEET WAS THE WINE	7.25	12.00
☐ 1013	*ABNER*	FOR YOUR PRECIOUS LOVE/		
		SWEET WAS THE WINE	3.50	6.00

IMPRESSIONS—ALBUM

| ☐ 1075 (S) | *VEE JAY* | FOR YOUR PRECIOUS LOVE . . . . | 20.00 | 50.00 |

ISLEY BROTHERS

☐ 1004	*TEENAGE*	THE ANGELS CRIED/		
		THE COW JUMPED OVER THE MOON	36.00	60.00
☐ 3009	*CINDY*	DON'T BE JEALOUS/THIS IS THE END	18.00	30.00
☐ 5022	*GONE*	I WANNA KNOW/		
		EVERYBODY'S GONNA ROCK AND ROLL	10.00	18.00
☐ 5048		MY LOVE/THE DRAG	7.25	12.00
☐ 8000	*MARK X*	ROCKIN' MACDONALD/THE DRAG	5.00	9.00
☐ 7588	*RCA*	SHOUT (PT. 1)/(PT. 2)	2.25	4.00
☐ 7657		RESPECTABLE/WITHOUT A SONG	2.75	4.50
☐ 124	*WAND*	TWIST AND SHOUT/SPANISH TWIST	2.00	3.50
☐ 127		TWISTIN' WITH LINDA/		
		YOU BETTER COME HOME	2.00	3.50
☐ 501	*T NECK*	TESTIFY (PT. 1)/(PT. 2)	4.00	7.00
☐ 54128	*TAMLA*	THIS OLD HEART OF MINE/		
		THERE'S NO LOVE LEFT	2.00	3.50

ISLEY BROTHERS—ALBUMS

| ☐ 2156 (S) | *RCA* | SHOUT! . . . . | 20.00 | 50.00 |
| ☐ 269 (S) | *TAMLA* | THIS OLD HEART OF MINE . . . . | 7.00 | 18.00 |

— J —

ISSUE #	LABEL		PRICE RANGE	

JACKSON 5

☐ 681	*STEELTOWN*	YOU'VE CHANGED/BIG BOY	10.00	18.00
☐ 684		YOU DON'T HAVE TO BE OVER 21 TO FALL IN LOVE/SOME GIRLS WANT ME FOR THEIR LOVE	10.00	18.00
☐ 1157	*MOTOWN*	I WANT YOU BACK/WHO'S LOVING YOU	1.75	3.00
☐ 1163		ABC/IT'S ALL IN THE GAME	1.75	3.00
☐ 1166		THE LOVE YOU SAVE/I FOUND THAT GIRL	1.75	3.00
☐ 1171		I'LL BE THERE/ONE MORE CHANCE	1.75	3.00
☐ 1174		SANTA CLAUS IS COMING TO TOWN/ CHRISTMAS WON'T BE THE SAME THIS YEAR	2.25	4.00
☐ 1177		MAMA'S PEARL/DARLING DEAR	1.50	2.50
☐ 1179		NEVER CAN SAY GOODBYE/SHE'S GOOD	1.50	2.50
☐ 1186		MAYBE TOMORROW/I WILL FIND A WAY	1.50	2.50
☐ 1194		SUGAR DADDY/I'M SO HAPPY	1.50	2.50
☐ 1199		LITTLE BITTY PRETTY ONE/ IF I HAVE TO MORE A MOUNTAIN	1.50	2.50
☐ 1205		LOOKING THROUGH THE WINDOWS/ LOVE SONG	1.50	2.50
☐ 1214		CORNER OF THE SKY/TO KNOW	1.50	2.50
☐ 1224		HALLELUJAH DAY/ YOU MAKE ME WHAT I AM	1.50	2.50
☐ 1277		GET IT TOGETHER/TOUCH	1.50	2.50
☐ 1286		DANCING MACHINE/ IT'S TOO LATE TO CHANGE THE TIME	1.50	2.50
☐ 1308		WHATEVER YOU GOT, I WANT/ I CAN'T QUIT YOUR LOVE	1.50	2.50
☐ 1310		I AM LOVE (PT. 1)/(PT. 2)	1.50	2.50
☐ 1356		FOREVER CAME TODAY/ ALL I DO IS THINK OF YOU	1.50	2.50

CHUCK JACKSON

☐ 1005	*BELTONE*	MR. PRIDE/HULA HULA	2.75	4.50
☐ 106	*WAND*	I DON'T WANT TO CRY/JUST ONCE	2.00	3.50
☐ 108		(IT NEVER HAPPENS) IN REAL LIFE/ THE SAME OLD STORY	2.00	3.50
☐ 110		I WAKE UP CRYING/ EVERYBODY NEEDS LOVE	2.00	3.50
☐ 115		THE BREAKING POINT/MY WILLOW TREE	2.00	3.50

ISSUE #	LABEL		PRICE RANGE	
☐ 119		ANGEL OF ANGELS/		
		WHAT'CHA GONNA SAY TOMORROW?	2.00	3.50
☐ 122		ANY DAY NOW/THE PROPHET	2.00	3.50
☐ 126		I KEEP FORGETTIN'/		
		WHO'S GONNA PICK UP THE PIECES?	1.75	3.00
☐ 128		GETTING READY FOR THE HEARTBREAK/		
		IN BETWEEN TEARS	1.75	3.00
☐ 132		TELL HIM I'M NOT HOME/LONELY AM I	1.75	3.00
☐ 138		TEARS OF JOY/I WILL NEVER		
		TURN MY BACK ON YOU	1.75	3.00
☐ 141		ANY OTHER WAY/BIG NEW YORK	1.75	3.00
☐ 149		HAND IT OVER/		
		LOOK OVER YOUR SHOULDER	1.75	3.00
☐ 154		BEG ME/FOR ALL TIME	1.75	3.00
☐ 161		SOMEBODY NEW/STAND BY ME	1.75	3.00
☐ 169		SINCE I DON'T HAVE YOU/HAND IT OVER	1.75	3.00
☐ 179		I NEED YOU/SOUL BROTHER'S TWIST	1.75	3.00
☐ 188		IF I DIDN'T LOVE YOU/		
		JUST A LITTLE BIT OF YOUR SOUL	1.75	3.00
☐ 1105		GOOD THINGS COME TO THOSE		
		WHO WAIT/YEAH	1.75	3.00
☐ 1119		ALL IN MY MIND/THAT'S SAYING A LOT	1.75	3.00

CHUCK JACKSON—ALBUMS

ISSUE #	LABEL		PRICE RANGE	
☐ 650 (M)	*WAND*	I DON'T WANT TO CRY	8.00	22.50
☐ 654 (M)		ANY DAY NOW	7.00	18.00
☐ 665 (M)		ENCORE	6.00	15.00
☐ 667 (S)		MR. EVERYTHING	7.00	18.00
☐ 673 (S)		TRIBUTE TO RHYTHM AND BLUES	7.00	18.00
☐ 676 (S)		TRIBUTE TO RHYTHM AND BLUES, VOL. II	7.00	18.00
☐ 680 (S)		DEDICATED TO THE KING	7.00	18.00
☐ 683 (S)		CHUCK JACKSON'S GREATEST HITS	6.00	15.00

WANDA JACKSON

ISSUE #	LABEL		PRICE RANGE	
☐ 3485	*CAPITOL*	I GOTTA KNOW/HALF AS GOOD A GIRL	3.50	6.00
☐ 3575		HOT DOG, THAT MADE HIM MAD!/		
		SILVER THREADS AND GOLDEN NEEDLES ...	3.50	6.00
☐ 3637		CRYIN' THROUGH THE NIGHT/		
		BABY LOVES HIM	2.75	4.50
☐ 3683		LET ME EXPLAIN/DON'A WANNA	2.75	4.50
☐ 3764		COOL LOVE/DID YOU MISS ME?	3.50	5.50
☐ 3843		FUJIYAMA MAMA/		
		NO WEDDING BELLS FOR JOE	3.50	5.50
☐ 3941		HONEY BOP/JUST A QUEEN FOR A DAY	3.50	5.50
☐ 4026		MEAN MEAN MAN/OUR SONG	3.50	5.50

WANDA JACKSON

ISSUE #	LABEL		PRICE RANGE	
☐ 4081		ROCK YOUR BABY/SINFUL HEART	3.50	5.50
☐ 4142		SAVIN' MY LOVE/I WANNA WALTZ	2.75	4.50
☐ 4398		LET'S HAVE A PARTY/COOL LOVE	2.75	4.50
☐ 4553		RIGHT OR WRONG/TUNNEL OF LOVE	2.25	4.00
☐ 4635		IN THE MIDDLE OF A HEARTACHE/		
		I'D BE ASHAMED	2.25	4.00
☐ 4681		A LITTLE BITTY TEAR/I DON'T WANTA GO	2.25	4.00
☐ 4723		IF I CRIED EVERY TIME YOU HURT ME/		
		LET MY LOVE WALK IN	2.25	4.00

WANDA JACKSON—ALBUMS

☐ 1041 (M)	*CAPITOL*	WANDA JACKSON	25.00	60.00
☐ 1384 (M)		ROCKIN' WITH WANDA	20.00	50.00
☐ 1511 (S)		THERE'S A PARTY GOIN' ON	20.00	50.00
☐ 1596 (S)		RIGHT OR WRONG	15.00	35.00
☐ 1776 (S)		WONDERFUL WANDA	12.50	30.00
☐ 1911 (S)		LOVE ME FOREVER	12.50	30.00

TOMMY JAMES
AND THE SHONDELLS

☐ 102	*SNAP*	HANKY PANKY/THUNDERBOLT	10.00	18.00
☐ 110	*RED FOX*	HANKY PANKY/THUNDERBOLT	8.50	15.00
☐ 4686	*ROULETTE*	HANKY PANKY/THUNDERBOLT	1.75	3.00
☐ 4695		SAY I AM (WHAT I AM)/		
		LOTS OF PRETTY GIRLS	1.75	3.00
☐ 4710		IT'S ONLY LOVE/		
		DON'T LET MY LOVE PASS YOU BY	1.75	3.00
☐ 4720		I THINK WE'RE ALONE NOW/		
		GONE GONE GONE	1.75	3.00
☐ 4736		MIRAGE/RUN RUN RUN	1.75	3.00
☐ 4756		I LIKE THE WAY/I CAN'T TAKE IT NO MORE . . .	1.75	3.00
☐ 4762		GETTIN' TOGETHER/REAL GIRL	1.75	3.00
☐ 4775		OUT OF THE BLUE/		
		LOVE'S CLOSIN' IN ON ME	1.75	3.00
☐ 7000		GET OUT NOW/WISH IT WERE YOU	1.75	3.00
☐ 7008		MONY MONY/		
		ONE, TWO, THREE AND I FELL	1.50	2.50
☐ 7016		SOMEBODY CARES/DO UNTO ME	1.50	2.50
☐ 7024		DO SOMETHING TO ME/		
		GINGERBREAD MAN	1.50	2.50
☐ 7028		CRIMSON AND CLOVER/(I'M) TAKEN	1.50	2.50
☐ 7039		SWEET CHERRY WINE/BREAKAWAY	1.50	2.50
☐ 7050		CRYSTAL BLUE PERSUASION/I'M ALIVE	1.50	2.50
☐ 7060		BALL OF FIRE/MAKIN' GOOD TIME	1.50	2.50

ISSUE #	LABEL		PRICE RANGE	
☐ 7066		SHE/LOVED ONE	1.50	2.50
☐ 7071		GOTTA GET BACK TO YOU/RED ROVER	1.50	2.50
☐ 7076		COME TO ME/LOVED ONE	1.50	2.50

TOMMY JAMES
AND THE SHONDELLS—ALBUMS

☐ 25336 (S)				
	ROULETTE	HANKY PANKY	7.00	18.00
☐ 25344 (S)		IT'S ONLY LOVE	7.00	18.00
☐ 25353 (S)		I THINK WE'RE ALONE NOW	7.00	18.00
☐ 25355 (S)		SOMETHING SPECIAL	6.00	15.00
☐ 25357 (S)		GETTIN' TOGETHER	5.00	13.50
☐ 42023 (S)		CRIMSON AND CLOVER	4.50	12.00
☐ 42040 (S)		THE BEST OF TOMMY JAMES		
		AND THE SHONDELLS	4.50	12.00
☐ 42044 (S)		TRAVELIN'	4.50	12.00

JAN AND DEAN

☐ 522	*DORE*	BABY TALK/JEANETTE, GET YOUR HAIR DONE .	45.00	90.00
☐ 522		BABY TALK/		
		JEANETTE GET YOUR HAIR DONE	3.50	6.00
☐ 531		THERE'S A GIRL/MY HEART SINGS	4.00	7.00
☐ 539		CLEMENTINE/YOU'RE ON MY MIND	4.00	7.00
☐ 548		WHITE TENNIS SNEAKERS/CINDY	4.50	9.00
☐ 555		WE GO TOGETHER/ROSIE LANE	3.50	6.00
☐ 555		WE GO TOGETHER/ROSILANE	3.50	6.00
☐ 576		GEE/SUCH A GOOD NIGHT FOR DREAMING	3.50	6.00
☐ 583		BAGGY PANTS/JUDY'S AN ANGEL	4.50	9.00
☐ 610		JULIE/DON'T FLY AWAY	7.25	12.00
☐ 9111	*CHALLENGE*	HEART AND SOUL/THOSE WORDS	10.00	18.00
☐ 9111		HEART AND SOUL/		
		MIDSUMMER NIGHT'S DREAM	2.25	4.00
☐ 9120		WANTED, ONE GIRL/		
		SOMETHING A LITTLE BIT DIFFERENT	3.50	6.00
☐ 55397	*LIBERTY*	A SUNDAY KIND OF LOVE/		
		POOR LITTLE PUPPET	3.50	6.50
☐ 55454		TENNESSEE/		
		YOUR HEART HAS CHANGED ITS MIND	2.75	4.50
☐ 55496		WHO PUT THE BOMP/		
		MY FAVORITE DREAM	4.50	9.00
☐ 55522		SHE'S STILL TALKING BABY TALK/		
		FROSTY THE SNOWMAN	10.00	18.00
☐ 55531		LINDA/WHEN I LEARN HOW TO CRY	2.00	3.50
☐ 55580		SURF CITY/SHE'S MY SUMMER GIRL	1.75	3.50

ISSUE #	LABEL		PRICE RANGE	
☐ 55849		FOLK CITY/BEGINNING TO AN END	2.25	4.00
☐ 55860		BATMAN/BUCKET "T"	2.00	3.50
☐ 55886		POPSICLE/NORWEGIAN WOOD	1.75	3.00
☐ 55905		FIDDLE AROUND/A SURFER'S DREAM	2.00	3.50
☐ 55923		SCHOOL DAY/THE NEW GIRL IN SCHOOL	2.00	3.50
☐ 10	*JAN AND DEAN*	HAWAII/TIJUANA	30.00	48.00
☐ 11		FAN TAN/LOVE AND HATE	30.00	48.00
☐ 001	*J & D*	SUMMERTIME, SUMMERTIME/ CALIFORNIA LULLABY	30.00	48.00
☐ 401		SUMMERTIME, SUMMERTIME/ CALIFORNIA LULLABY	7.25	12.00
☐ 402		LIKE A SUMMER RAIN/LOUISIANA MAN ...	8.50	15.00
☐ 401	*MAGIC LAMP*	SUMMERTIME, SUMMERTIME/ CALIFORNIA LULLABY	7.25	12.00
☐ 44036	*COLUMBIA*	YELLOW BALLOON/TASTE OF RAIN	7.25	12.00
☐ 7151	*WARNER BROTHERS*	ONLY A BOY/LOVE AND HATE	12.00	20.00
☐ 7219		LAUREL AND HARDY/I KNOW MY MIND	10.00	18.00

JAN AND DEAN—ALBUMS

☐ 101 (M)	*DORE*	JAN AND DEAN	50.00	135.00
☐ 7248 (S)		JAN AND DEAN'S GREATEST HITS	12.50	30.00
☐ 7294 (S)		JAN AND DEAN TAKE LINDA SURFING	10.00	25.00
☐ 7314 (S)		SURF CITY	8.00	22.50
☐ 7339 (S)		DRAG CITY	8.00	22.50
☐ 7361 (S)		DEAD MAN'S CURVE/ NEW GIRL IN SCHOOL	10.00	25.00
☐ 7368 (S)		RIDE THE WILD SURF	10.00	25.00
☐ 7377 (S)		LITTLE OLD LADY FROM PASADENA	8.00	22.50
☐ 7403 (S)		COMMAND PERFORMANCE	8.00	22.50
☐ 7414 (S)		JAN AND DEAN'S POP SYMPHONY NO. 1	10.00	25.00
☐ 7417 (S)		JAN AND DEAN'S GOLDEN HITS, VOL. II	7.00	18.00
☐ 7431 (S)		FOLK 'N' ROLL	6.00	15.00
☐ 7441 (S)		FILET OF SOUL	6.00	15.00
☐ 7444 (S)		JAN AND DEAN MEET BATMAN	6.00	15.00
☐ 7458 (S)		POPSICLE	6.00	15.00
☐ 7460 (S)		JAN AND DEAN'S GOLDEN HITS, VOL. III	6.00	15.00

JAY AND THE AMERICANS

☐ 353	*UNITED ARTISTS*	TONIGHT/THE OTHER GIRLS	2.75	4.50
☐ 415		SHE CRIED/DAWNING	2.00	3.50
☐ 479		THIS IS IT/IT'S MY TURN TO CRY	2.25	4.00
☐ 504		TOMORROW/YES	2.25	4.00

JAN AND DEAN

ISSUE #	LABEL		PRICE RANGE	
☐566		WHAT'S THE USE/		
		STRANGERS TOMORROW	2.25	4.00
☐626		ONLY IN AMERICA/MY CLAIR DE LUNE	1.75	3.00
☐669		COME DANCE WITH ME/		
		LOOK IN MY EYES, MARIE	1.75	3.00
☐693		TO WAIT FOR LOVE/FRIDAY.	1.75	3.00
☐759		COME A LITTLE BIT CLOSER/		
		GOODBYE, BOYS, GOODBYE	1.75	3.00
☐805		LET'S LOCK THE DOOR/		
		I'LL REMEMBER YOU	1.75	3.00
☐845		THINK OF THE GOOD TIMES/		
		IF YOU WERE MINE, GIRL	1.75	3.00
☐881		CARA MIA/WHEN IT'S ALL OVER	1.75	3.00
☐919		SOME ENCHANTED EVENING/GIRL	1.75	3.00
☐948		SUNDAY AND ME/		
		THROUGH THIS DOORWAY	1.75	3.00
☐992		WHY CAN'T YOU BRING ME HOME?/		
		BABY, STOP YOUR CRYIN'	1.75	3.00
☐50016		CRYING/I DON'T NEED A FRIEND	1.75	3.00
☐50046		LIVIN' ABOVE YOUR HEAD/		
		LOOK AT ME, WHAT DO YOU SEE?	1.75	3.00
☐50086		STOP THE CLOCK/BABY, COME HOME	1.75	3.00
☐50094		HE'S RAINING IN MY SUNSHINE/		
		THE REASON FOR LIVING	1.75	3.00

JAY AND THE AMERICANS—ALBUMS

☐6222 (S)	*UNITED*			
	ARTISTS	SHE CRIED	10.00	25.00
☐6300 (S)		JAY AND THE AMERICANS AT THE		
		CAFE WHA?	8.00	22.50
☐6417 (S)		BLOCKBUSTERS	8.00	22.50
☐6453 (S)		GREATEST HITS	7.00	18.00
☐6474 (S)		SUNDAY AND ME	7.00	18.00
☐6534 (S)		LIVIN' ABOVE YOUR HEAD	6.00	15.00
☐6555 (S)		GREATEST HITS, VOL. II	6.00	15.00
☐6562 (S)		TRY SOME OF THIS	4.50	12.00
☐6671 (S)		SANDS OF TIME	4.50	12.00
☐6719 (S)		WAX MUSEUM	4.50	12.00
☐6751 (S)		WAX MUSEUM, VOL. II	4.50	12.00
☐6762 (S)		CAPTURE THE MOMENT	4.50	12.00

JEFFERSON AIRPLANE

☐8769	*RCA*	RUNNIN' AROUND THIS WORLD/		
		IT'S NO SECRET.	2.25	4.00

ISSUE #	LABEL		PRICE RANGE	
☐ 8848		COME UP THE YEARS/		
		BLUES FROM AN AIRPLANE	2.25	4.00
☐ 8967		BRINGING ME DOWN/LET ME IN	2.25	4.00
☐ 9063		MY BEST FRIEND/HOW DO YOU FEEL?	2.25	4.00
☐ 9140		SOMEBODY TO LOVE/		
		SHE HAS FUNNY CARS	1.75	3.00
☐ 9248		WHITE RABBIT/		
		PLASTIC FANTASTIC LOVER	1.75	3.00
☐ 9297		BALLAD OF YOU AND ME AND POONEIL/		
		TWO HEADS	1.75	3.00
☐ 9389		WATCH HER RIDE/MARTHA	1.75	3.00
☐ 9496		GREASY HEART/SHARE A LITTLE JOKE	1.75	3.00
☐ 9644		CROWN OF CREATION/LATHER	1.75	3.00
☐ 0245		VOLUNTEERS/WE CAN BE TOGETHER	1.75	3.00
☐ 0150		THE OTHER SIDE OF THIS LIFE/		
		PLASTIC FANTASTIC LOVER	1.75	3.00

WAYLON JENNINGS

ISSUE #	LABEL		PRICE RANGE	
☐ 55130	*BRUNSWICK*	JOLE BLON/WHEN SIN STOPS	45.00	90.00
☐ 121639	*BAT*	CRYING/DREAM BABY	8.50	15.00
☐ 722	*A & M*	RAVE ON/LOVE DENIED	5.00	10.00

BILLY JOEL

ISSUE #	LABEL		PRICE RANGE	
☐ 0900	*FAMILY*	EVERYBODY LOVES YOU NOW/		
		SHE'S GOT A WAY	2.75	4.50
☐ 0906		TOMORROW IS TODAY/		
		EVERYBODY LOVES YOU NOW	2.25	4.00
☐ 45963	*COLUMBIA*	PIANO MAN/YOU'RE MY HOME	1.75	3.00
☐ 46055		WORSE COMES TO WORST/		
		SOMEWHERE ALONG THE LINE	1.75	3.00
☐ 10064		THE ENTERTAINER/		
		THE MEXICAN CONNECTION	1.75	3.00
☐ 10412		SUMMER HIGHLAND FALLS/JAMES	1.75	3.00
☐ 10562		SAY GOODBYE TO HOLLYWOOD/		
		I'VE LOVED THESE DAYS	2.00	3.50

BILLY JOEL—ALBUM

☐ 2700 (S)	*FAMILY*	COLD SPRING HARBOR	12.50	30.00

ELTON JOHN

☐ 1643	*PHILIPS*	I'VE BEEN LOVING YOU/		
		HERE'S TO THE NEXT TIME	24.00	42.00

ISSUE #	LABEL		PRICE RANGE	
☐70-008	*DJM*	LADY SAMANTHA/		
		ALL ACROSS THE HEAVENS	18.00	30.00
☐6017	*CONGRESS*	LADY SAMANTHA/		
		IT'S ME THAT YOU NEED	18.00	30.00
☐6022		BORDER SONG/BAD SIDE OF THE MOON	10.00	18.00
☐55246	*UNI*	BORDER SONG/BAD SIDE OF THE MOON	2.00	3.50
☐55265		YOUR SONG/TAKE ME TO THE PILOT	1.75	3.00
☐55277		FRIENDS/HONEY ROLL	1.75	3.00
☐55314		LEVON/GOODBYE	1.75	3.00
☐55318		TINY DANCER/RAZOR FACE	1.75	3.00
☐55328		ROCKET MAN/SUZIE (DRAMAS)	1.75	3.00
☐55343		HONKY CAT/SLAVE	1.75	3.00

ELTON JOHN—ALBUMS

☐73090 (S)	*UNI*	ELTON JOHN	7.00	18.00
☐73096 (S)		TUMBLEWOOD CONNECTION	7.00	18.00
☐93105 (S)		11-17-70	7.00	18.00
☐93120 (S)		MADMAN ACROSS THE WATER	7.00	18.00
☐93135 (S)		HONKY CHATEAU	7.00	18.00

JANIS JOPLIN

☐45023	*COLUMBIA*	KOZMIC BLUES/LITTLE GIRL BLUE	2.00	3.50
☐45080		ONE GOOD MAN/		
		TRY (A LITTLE BIT HARDER)	2.25	4.00
☐45128		MAYBE/WORK ME, LORD	2.25	4.00
☐45284		KEEP ON/HOME ON THE STRANGER	2.25	4.00
☐45314		ME AND BOBBY McGEE	1.25	2.50
☐45379		CRY BABY/MERCEDES BENZ	1.50	2.50
☐45433		GET IT WHILE YOU CAN/MOVE OVER	1.50	2.50
☐45630		DOWN MON ME/BYE BYE BABY	1.50	2.50

JANIS JOPLIN—ALBUMS

☐9913 (S)	*COLUMBIA*	I GOT DEM OLD KOZMIC BLUES		
		AGAIN MAMA	4.00	10.00
☐30322 (S)		PEARL	4.00	10.00
☐32168 (S)		JANIS JOPLIN'S GREATEST HITS	4.50	12.00
☐33160 (S)		JOPLIN IN CONCERT	4.00	9.50
☐33345 (S)		JANIS	4.00	9.50
☐713 (S)	*MEMORY*	WICKED WOMAN	4.50	12.00

JUMPIN' TONES

☐8004	*RAVEN*	I HAD A DREAM/I WONDER	12.00	20.00
☐8005		THAT ANGEL IS YOU/		
		GRANDMA'S HEARING AID	18.00	30.00

— K —

ISSUE #	LABEL		PRICE RANGE	
KEITH				
☐ 72596	*MERCURY*	AIN'T GONNA LIE/		
		IT STARTED ALL OVER AGAIN	1.75	3.00
☐ 72639		98.6/TEENIE BOPPER SONG	1.50	3.00
☐ 72652		TELL ME TO MY FACE/		
		PRETTY LITTLE SHY ONE	1.75	3.00
☐ 72695		DAYLIGHT SAVIN' TIME/		
		HAPPY WALKING AROUND	1.75	3.00
☐ 72715		SUGAR MAN/EASY AS PIE	1.75	3.00
☐ 72746		CANDY, CANDY/I'M SO PROUD	1.75	3.00
☐ 72794		THE PLEASURE OF YOUR COMPANY/		
		HURRY	1.75	3.00
KEITH—ALBUMS				
☐ 61102 (S)				
	MERCURY	98.6/AIN'T GONNA LIE	5.00	13.50
☐ 61129 (S)		OUT OF CRANK	5.00	13.50
CAROLE KING				
☐ 9921	*ABC-*			
	PARAMOUNT	GOIN' WILD/THE RIGHT GIRL	18.00	30.00
☐ 9986		BABY SITTIN'/UNDER THE STARS	18.00	30.00
☐ 7560	*RCA*	QUEEN OF THE BEACH/SHORT MORT	18.00	30.00
☐ 57	*ALPINE*	OH NEIL!/A VERY SPECIAL BOY	30.00	42.00
☐ 2000	*COMPANION*	IT MIGHT AS WELL RAIN UNTIL		
		SEPTEMBER/NOBODY'S PERFECT	24.00	42.00
☐ 2000	*DIMENSION*	IT MIGHT AS WELL RAIN UNTIL		
		SEPTEMBER/NOBODY'S PERFECT	2.00	3.50
☐ 1004		SCHOOL BELLS ARE RINGING/		
		I DIDN'T HAVE ANY	4.50	9.00
☐ 1009		HE'S A BAD BOY/WE GROW UP TOGETHER	3.50	6.00
☐ 7502	*TOMORROW*	A ROAD TO NOWHERE/		
		SOME OF YOUR LOVIN'	6.00	11.00
KINGSMEN				
☐ 108	*JALYNNE*	LADY'S CHOICE/DIG THIS	4.00	7.00
☐ 712	*JERDEN*	LOUIE LOUIE/HAUNTED CASTLE	18.00	30.00
☐ 150		MONEY/BENT SCEPTER	1.75	3.00
☐ 157		LITTLE LATIN LUPE LU/DAVID'S MOOD	1.75	3.00
☐ 164		DEATH OF AN ANGEL/		
		SEARCHING FOR LOVE	1.75	3.00

ISSUE #	LABEL		PRICE RANGE	
☐ 172		THE JOLLY GREEN GIANT/LONG GREEN	1.75	3.00
☐ 183		THE CLIMB/I'M WAITING	1.75	3.00
☐ 189		ANNIE FANNY/GIVE HER LOVIN'	1.75	3.00
☐ 1107		THE GAMMA GOOCHEE/		
		IT'S ONLY THE DOG	1.75	3.00
☐ 1115		KILLER JOE/LITTLE GREEN THING	1.75	3.00

KINGSMEN—ALBUMS

☐ 657	(M)	*WAND*	IN PERSON	5.00	10.00
☐ 659	(M)		VOLUME 2	5.00	10.00
☐ 662	(M)		VOLUME 3	5.90	10.00
☐ 670	(M)		ON CAMPUS	5.90	10.00
☐ 674	(M)		16 GREATEST HITS	4.50	9.00

KINGSTON TRIO

☐ 3970	*CAPITOL*	SCARLET RIBBONS/		
		THREE JOLLY COACHMEN	3.50	6.00
☐ 4049		TOM DOOLEY/RUBY RED	2.25	4.00
☐ 4114		RASPBERRIES, STRAWBERRIES/SALLY	2.25	4.00
☐ 4167		TIJUANA JAIL/OH, CINDY	2.00	3.50
☐ 4221		M.T.A./ALL MY SORROWS	2.00	3.50
☐ 4271		A WORRIED MAN/SAN MIGUEL	2.00	3.50
☐ 4303		COO COO-U/GREEN GRASSES	2.25	4.00
☐ 4338		EL MATADOR/HOME FROM THE HILL	2.00	3.50
☐ 4379		BAD MAN BLUNDER/		
		THE ESCAPE OF OLD JOHN WEBB	2.00	3.50
☐ 4441		EVERGLADES/		
		THIS MORNIN' THIS EVENIN' SO SOON	2.00	3.50
☐ 4536		YOU'RE GONNA MISS ME/EN EL AGUA	2.00	3.50
☐ 4671		WHERE HAVE ALL THE FLOWERS GONE/		
		O KEN KARANGA	1.75	3.00
☐ 4740		SCOTCH AND SODA/JANE, JANE, JANE	1.75	3.00
☐ 4808		OLD JOE CLARK/C'MON HOME BETTY	2.00	3.50
☐ 4842		ONE MORE TOWN/SHE WAS GOOD TO ME	1.75	3.00
☐ 4898		GREENBACK DOLLAR/THE NEW FRONTIER	1.75	3.00
☐ 4951		REVEREND MR. BLACK/ONE MORE ROUND	1.75	3.00
☐ 5005		DESERT PETE/BALLAD OF THE THRESHER	1.75	3.00
☐ 5078		ALLY ALLY OXEN FREE/		
		MARCELLE VAHINE	1.75	3.00
☐ 5138		LAST NIGHT I HAD THE STRANGEST		
		DREAM/THE PATRIOT GAME	2.00	3.50
☐ 5166		SEASONS IN THE SUN/		
		IF YOU DON'T LOOK AROUND	2.00	3.50

ISSUE #	LABEL		PRICE RANGE	

KINGSTON TRIO—ALBUMS

☐ 996 (M)	*CAPITOL*	THE KINGSTON TRIO	7.00	18.00
☐ 1107 (M)		FROM THE HUNGRY I	7.00	18.00
☐ 1199 (S)		THE KINGSTON TRIO AT LARGE	7.00	18.00
☐ 1258 (S)		HERE WE GO AGAIN	7.00	18.00
☐ 1352 (S)		SOLD OUT	7.00	18.00
☐ 1407 (S)		STRING ALONG	7.00	18.00
☐ 1183 (S)		STEREO CONCERT	6.00	15.00
☐ 1446 (S)		THE LAST MONTH OF THE YEAR	6.00	15.00
☐ 1474 (S)		MAKE WAY	6.00	15.00
☐ 1564 (S)		GOIN' PLACES	6.00	15.00
☐ 1642 (S)		THE KINGSTON TRIO CLOSE UP	6.00	15.00
☐ 1658 (S)		COLLEGE CONCERT	6.00	15.00
☐ 1705 (S)		THE BEST OF THE KINGSTON TRIO	5.00	13.50
☐ 1747 (S)		SOMETHING SPECIAL	5.00	13.50
☐ 1809 (S)		NEW FRONTIER	5.00	13.50
☐ 1871 (S)		KINGSTON TRIO #16	5.00	13.50
☐ 1935 (S)		SUNNY SIDE!	5.00	13.50
☐ 2005 (S)		SING A SONG WITH THE KINGSTON TRIO	6.00	15.00
☐ 2011 (S)		TIME TO THINK	5.00	13.50
☐ 2081 (S)		BACK IN TOWN	5.00	13.50

KINKS

☐ 308	*CAMEO*	LONG TALL SALLY/I TOOK MY BABY HOME	42.00	75.00
☐ 345		LONG TALL SALLY/I TOOK MY BABY HOME	30.00	48.00
☐ 348		YOU STILL WANT ME/		
		YOU DO SOMETHING TO ME	30.00	48.00
☐ 0306	*REPRISE*	YOU REALLY GOT ME/IT'S ALL RIGHT	3.25	4.00
☐ 0334		ALL DAY AND ALL OF THE NIGHT/		
		I GOTTA MOVE	3.25	4.00
☐ 0347		TIRED OF WAITING FOR YOU/		
		COME ON NOW	3.25	4.00
☐ 0366		WHO'LL BE THE NEXT IN LINE?/		
		EVERYBODY'S GONNA BE HAPPY	2.00	3.50
☐ 0379		SET ME FREE/I NEED YOU	2.00	3.50
☐ 0409		SEE MY FRIENDS/		
		NEVER MET A GIRL LIKE YOU BEFORE	2.25	4.00
☐ 0420		A WELL RESPECTED MAN/SUCH A SHAME	2.00	3.50
☐ 0454		TILL THE END OF THE DAY/WHERE HAVE		
		ALL THE GOOD TIMES GONE	2.00	3.50
☐ 0471		DEDICATED FOLLOWER OF FASHION/		
		SITTING ON MY SOFA	2.00	3.50
☐ 0497		SUNNY AFTERNOON/		
		I'M NOT LIKE EVERYONE ELSE	2.00	3.50

ISSUE #	LABEL		PRICE RANGE	
☐ 0540		DEADEND STREET/BIG BLACK SMOKE	2.00	3.50
☐ 0587		MR. PLEASANT/HARRY RAG	2.00	3.50
☐ 0612		WATERLOO SUNSET/TWO SISTERS	2.00	3.50
☐ 0647		AUTUMN ALMANAC/DAVID WAITS	2.00	3.50
☐ 0691		WONDERBOY/POLLY	2.00	3.50
☐ 0743		LOLA/APEMAN	3.50	6.00

KINKS—ALBUMS

ISSUE #	LABEL		PRICE RANGE	
☐ 6143 (S)	REPRISE	YOU REALLY GOT ME	12.50	30.00
☐ 6158 (S)		KINKS SIZE	12.50	30.00
☐ 6173 (S)		KINDA KINKS	12.50	30.00
☐ 6184 (S)		KINKS KINGDOM	12.50	30.00
☐ 6197 (S)		KINK KONTROVERSY	12.50	30.00
☐ 6217 (S)		THE KINKS' GREATEST HITS	8.00	22.50
☐ 6280 (S)		LIVE KINKS	7.00	18.00
☐ 6279 (S)		SOMETHING ELSE	7.00	18.00
☐ 6327 (S)		THE VILLAGE GREEN PRESERVATION		
		SOCIETY	6.00	15.00
☐ 6366 (S)		ARTHUR	6.00	15.00
☐ 6423 (S)		LOLA VERSUS THE POWERMAN	6.00	15.00
☐ 6454 (S)		KINK KRONIKLES	6.00	15.00
☐ 2127 (S)		THE GREAT LOST KINKS ALBUM	6.00	15.00

KISS

ISSUE #	LABEL		PRICE RANGE	
☐ 931	BELL	HEY, MR. HOLY MAN/KIDS ARE CRYING	2.75	4.50
☐ 0004	CASABLANCA	LOVE THEME FROM KISS/		
		NOTHIN' TO LOSE	2.75	4.00
☐ 0011		KISSIN' TIME/NOTHIN' TO LOSE	2.00	3.50
☐ 0015		STRUTTER/100,000 YEARS	2.00	3.50
☐ 823		HOTTER THAN HELL/		
		LET ME GO, ROCK AND ROLL	2.00	3.50
☐ 829		ROCK AND ROLL ALL NITE/GETAWAY	1.75	3.00
☐ 841		C'MON AND LOVE ME/GETAWAY	1.75	3.00
☐ 850		ROCK AND ROLL ALL NITE/		
		ROCK AND ROLL ALL NITE (LIVE)	1.50	2.50

KNICKERBOCKERS

ISSUE #	LABEL		PRICE RANGE	
☐ 59268	CHALLENGE	BITE BITE BARRACUDA/ALL I NEED IS YOU . . .	2.25	4.00
☐ 59293		JERKTOWN/ROOM FOR ONE MORE	2.25	4.00
☐ 59321		LIES/THE COMING GENERATION	2.00	3.50
☐ 59326		ONE TRACK MIND/		
		I MUST BE DOING SOMETHING RIGHT	1.75	3.00
☐ 59332		HIGH ON LOVE/STICK WITH ME	1.75	3.00
☐ 59335		CHAPEL IN THE FIELDS/JUST ONE GIRL	1.75	3.00

ISSUE #	LABEL		PRICE RANGE	
☐ 59341		RUMORS, GOSSIP, WORDS UNTRUE/		
		LOVE IS A BIRD	1.75	3.00
☐ 59348		CAN YOU HELP ME/		
		PLEASE DON'T LOVE HIM	1.75	3.00
☐ 59359		SWEET GREEN FIELDS/		
		WHAT DOES THAT MAKE YOU?	1.75	3.00
☐ 59366		COME AND GET IT/WISHFUL THINKING	1.75	3.00
☐ 59380		YOU'LL NEVER WALK ALONE/		
		I CAN DO IT BETTER	1.75	3.00
☐ 59384		THEY RAN FOR THEIR LIVES/		
		AS A MATTER OF FACT	1.75	3.00

KNICKERBOCKERS—ALBUMS

☐ 621 (S)				
	CHALLENGE	JERK AND TWINE TIME	10.00	25.00
☐ 622 (S)		LIES	10.00	25.00
☐ 12664 (S)		LLOYD THAXTON PRESENTS		
		THE KNICKERBOCKERS	8.00	22.50

GLADYS KNIGHT AND THE PIPS

☐ 55048	*BRUNSWICK*	CHING CHONG/WHISTLE MY LOVE	18.00	30.00
☐ 2510	*HUNTOM*	EVERY BEAT OF MY HEART/		
		ROOM IN YOUR HEART	12.00	20.00
☐ 386	*VEE JAY*	EVERY BEAT OF MY HEART/		
		ROOM IN YOUR HEART	2.25	4.00
☐ 545		QUEEN OF TEARS/A LOVE LIKE MINE	2.00	3.50
☐ 2012	*ENJOY*	LOVE CALL/WHAT SHALL I DO	2.00	3.50
☐ 5035	*EVERLAST*	I HAD A DREAM LAST NIGHT/HAPPINESS	2.00	3.50
☐ 1050	*FURY*	EVERY BEAT OF MY HEART/		
		ROOM IN YOUR HEART	2.00	3.50
☐ 1052		GUESS WHO/STOP RUNNING AROUND	2.00	3.50
☐ 1054		LETTER FULL OF TEARS/YOU BROKE		
		YOUR PROMISE	1.75	3.00
☐ 1064		OPERATOR/I'LL TRUST IN YOU	1.75	3.00
☐ 1067		DARLING/LINDA	1.75	3.00
☐ 1073		COME SEE ABOUT ME/I WANT THAT		
		KIND OF LOVE	1.75	3.00
☐ 326	*MAXX*	GIVING UP/MAYBE MAYBE BABY	1.75	3.00
☐ 329		LOVERS ALWAYS FORGIVE/		
		ANOTHER LOVE	1.75	3.00
☐ 331		EITHER WAY I LOSE/		
		GO AWAY, STAY AWAY	1.75	3.00
☐ 334		STOP AND THINK IT OVER/WHO KNOWS	1.75	3.00

ISSUE #	LABEL		PRICE RANGE	

GLADYS KNIGHT AND THE PIPS—ALBUMS

☐ 1003 (M)	**FURY**	LETTER FULL OF TEARS	15.00	35.00
☐ 3000 (M)	**MAXX**	GLADYS KNIGHT AND THE PIPS	8.00	22.50

KRIS KRISTOFFERSON

☐ 8525	**MONUMENT**	LOVING HER WAS EASIER (THAN ANYTHNG I'LL EVER DO AGAIN)/EPITAPH	1.75	3.00
☐ 8531		THE PILGRIM, CHAPTER 33/(DJ)	2.00	3.50
☐ 8536		JOSIE/BORDER LORD	1.75	3.00
☐ 8558		JESUS WAS A CAPRICORN/ ONLY IN A MOMENT	2.00	3.50
☐ 8564		JESSE YOUNG/GIVE IT TIME TO BE TENDER	2.00	3.50
☐ 8571		WHY ME?/HELP ME	1.50	3.00
☐ 8618		THE LIGHTS OF MAGDALA/ I MAY SMOKE TO MUCH	1.75	3.00
☐ 8658		EASY, COME ON/ROCKET TO STARDOM	1.75	3.00
☐ 8679		THE YEAR 2000 MINUS 25/(DJ)	1.75	3.00
☐ 8707		IT'S NEVER GONNA BE THE SAME AGAIN/ (DJ)	1.75	3.00

— L —

LED ZEPPELIN

☐ 2613	**ATLANTIC**	GOOD TIMES BAD TIMES/ COMMUNICATION BREAKDOWN	2.25	4.00
☐ 2690		WHOLE LOTTA LOVE/LIVING LOVING MAID	1.75	3.00
☐ 2777		IMMIGRANT SONG/ HEY HEY, WHAT CAN I DO	2.25	4.00
☐ 2849		BLACK DOG/MISTY MOUNTAIN HOP	1.75	3.00
☐ 2865		ROCK AND ROLL/FOUR STICKS	1.75	3.00
☐ 2970		OVER THE HILLS AND FAR AWAY/ DANCING DAYS	1.75	3.00
☐ 2986		D'YER MAKER/THE CRUNGE	1.75	3.00
☐ 70102	**SWAN SONG**	TRAMPLED UNDER FOOT/ BLACK COUNTRY WOMAN	1.75	3.00
☐ 70110		ROYAL ORLEANS/CANDY STORE ROCK	2.00	3.50

BRENDA LEE

☐ 30050	**DECCA**	JAMBALAYA/BIGELOW-6200	4.50	9.00

ISSUE #	LABEL		PRICE RANGE	
☐30107	CHRISTY CHRISTMAS/			
	I'M GONNA LASSO SANTA CLAUS		4.00	7.00
☐30198	ONE STEP AT A TIME/FAIRYLAND		3.50	6.00
☐30333	DYNAMITE/LOVE YOU 'TIL I DIE		3.50	6.00
☐30411	AIN'T THAT LOVE/			
	ONE TEENAGER TO ANOTHER		2.75	4.50
☐30535	ROCK THE BOP/ROCK-A-BYE BABY BLUES		2.75	4.50
☐30673	RING-A MY PHONE/LITTLE JONAH		3.50	6.00
☐30776	ROCKIN' AROUND THE CHRISTMAS TREE/			
	PAPA NOEL		2.00	3.50
☐30806	BILL BAILEY WON'T YOU PLEASE COME			
	HOME/HUMMIN' THE BLUES		2.75	4.50
☐30885	LET'S JUMP THE BROOMSTICK/			
	SOME OF THESE DAYS		2.75	4.50
☐30967	SWEET NOTHIN'S/			
	WEEP NO MORE MY BABY		2.00	3.50
☐31093	I'M SORRY/THAT'S ALL YOU GOTTA DO		2.00	3.50
☐31149	I WANT TO BE WANTED/JUST A LITTLE		2.00	3.50
☐31195	EMOTIONS/I'M LEARNING ABOUT LOVE		1.75	3.00
☐31231	YOU CAN DEPEND ON ME/			
	IT'S NEVER TOO LATE		1.75	3.00
☐31272	DUM DUM/EVENTUALLY		1.75	3.00
☐31309	FOOL NO. 1/ANYBODY BUT ME		1.75	3.00
☐31348	BREAK IT TO ME GENTLY/SO DEEP		1.75	3.00
☐31379	EVERYBODY LOVES ME BUT YOU/			
	HERE COMES THAT FEELIN'		1.75	3.00
☐31407	HEART IN HAND/			
	IT STARTED ALL OVER AGAIN		1.75	3.00
☐31424	ALL ALONE AM I/			
	SAVE ALL YOUR LOVIN' FOR ME		1.75	3.00
☐31454	YOUR USED-TO-BE/SHE'LL NEVER KNOW		1.75	3.00
☐31478	LOSING YOU/HE'S SO HEAVENLY		1.75	3.00
☐31510	MY WHOLE WORLD IS FALLING DOWN/			
	I WONDER		1.75	3.00
☐31539	THE GRASS IS GREENER/			
	SWEET IMPOSSIBLE YOU		1.75	3.00
☐31570	AS USUAL/LONELY LONELY LONELY ME		1.75	3.00
☐31599	THINK/THE WAITING GAME		1.75	3.00
☐31628	ALONE WITH YOU/MY DREAMS		1.75	3.00
☐31654	WHEN YOU LOVED ME/			
	HE'S SURE TO REMEMBER ME		1.75	3.00
☐31687	JINGLE BELL ROCK/WINTER WONDERLAND		1.75	3.00
☐31688	THIS TIME OF THE YEAR/CHRISTMAS			
	WILL BE JUST ANOTHER DAY		1.75	3.00
☐31690	IS IT TRUE?/JUST BEHIND THE RAINBOW		1.75	3.00

ISSUE #	LABEL		PRICE RANGE	
☐31728		THANKS A LOT/THE CRYING GAME	1.75	3.00
☐31762		TRULY, TRULY, TRUE/		
		I STILL MISS SOMEONE	1.75	3.00
☐31792		TOO MANY RIVERS/NO ONE	1.75	3.00
☐31849		RUSTY BELLS/IF YOU DON'T	1.75	3.00
☐31917		TOO LITTLE TIME/TIME AND TIME AGAIN	1.75	3.00
☐31970		AIN'T GONNA CRY NO MORE/IT TAKES ONE		
		TO KNOW ONE	1.75	3.00
☐32018		COMING ON STRONG/YOU KEEP COMING		
		BACK TO ME	1.75	3.00

BRENDA LEE—EPs

☐2661	*DECCA*	BRENDA LEE	7.25	12.00
☐2678		SWEET NOTHIN'S	6.00	12.00
☐2682		BRENDA LEE	4.50	8.00
☐2683		I'M SORRY	4.50	8.00
☐2702		BRENDA LEE	4.50	8.00
☐2704		LOVER, COME BACK TO ME	4.50	8.00
☐2712		BRENDA LEE	4.00	7.00
☐2716		BRENDA LEE	4.00	7.00
☐2725		EVERYBODY LOVES ME BUT YOU	4.00	7.00
☐2730		BRENDA LEE	3.25	6.00
☐2738		BRENDA LEE	3.25	6.00
☐2745		BRENDA LEE	3.25	6.00
☐2764		BRENDA LEE	3.25	6.00
☐2755		BRENDA LEE	3.25	6.00

BRENDA LEE—ALBUMS

☐74039 (S)	*DECCA*	BRENDA LEE	15.00	35.00
☐74082 (S)		THIS IS BRENDA	15.00	35.00
☐74104 (S)		EMOTIONS	12.50	30.00
☐74176 (S)		ALL THE WAY	12.50	30.00
☐74216 (S)		SINCERELY, BRENDA LEE	10.00	25.00
☐74326 (S)		THAT'S ALL	10.00	25.00
☐74370 (S)		ALL ALONE AM I	10.00	25.00
☐74439 (S)		LET ME SING	7.00	18.00
☐74509 (S)		BY REQUEST	7.00	18.00
☐74583 (S)		MERRY CHRISTMAS FROM BRENDA LEE	7.00	18.00
☐74626 (S)		TOP TEEN HITS	7.00	18.00
☐74661 (S)		THE VERSATILE BRENDA LEE	7.00	18.00
☐74684 (S)		TOO MANY RIVERS	7.00	18.00
☐74755 (S)		BYE BYE BLUES	6.00	15.00
☐74757 (S)		10 GOLDEN YEARS	6.00	15.00

ISSUE #	LABEL		PRICE RANGE	

DICKIE LEE

☐ 131	*TAMPA*	STAY TRUE BABY/DREAM BOY	8.50	15.00
☐ 16087	*DOT*	WHY DON'T YOU WRITE ME?/		
		LIFE IN A TEENAGE WORLD	4.00	7.00
☐ 1758	*SMASH*	PATCHES/MORE OR LESS	2.00	3.50
☐ 1791		I SAW LINDA YESTERDAY/		
		THE GIRL I CAN'T FORGET	2.00	3.50
☐ 1808		DON'T WANNA THINK ABOUT PAULA/		
		JUST A FRIEND	2.00	3.50
☐ 1822		I GO LONELY/TEN MILLION FACES	2.00	3.50
☐ 1844		SHE WANTS TO BE BOBBY'S GIRL/		
		THE DAY THE SAWMILL CLOSED DOWN	2.00	3.50
☐ 1871		TO THE AISLE/MOTHER NATURE	2.00	3.50
☐ 1913		ME AND MY TEARDROPS/		
		ONLY TRUST IN ME	2.00	3.50
☐ 102	*TCF HALL*	LAURIE (STRANGE THINGS HAPPEN)/		
		PARTY DOLL	1.75	3.00
☐ 111		THE GIRL FROM PEYTON PLACE/THE GIRL		
		I USED TO KNOW	1.75	3.00
☐ 118		GOOD GIRL GOIN' BAD/		
		PRETTY WHITE DRESS	1.75	3.00
☐ 188		STAY TRUE BABY/DREAM BOY	1.75	3.00

DICKIE LEE—ALBUMS

☐ 67020 (S)	*SMASH*	THE TALE OF PATCHES	8.00	22.60
☐ 8001 (S)		LAURIE AND THE GIRL FROM		
		PEYTON PLACE	7.00	18.00

LEFT BANKE

☐ 2041	*SMASH*	WALK AWAY RENEE/		
		I HAVEN'T GOT THE NERVE	1.75	3.00
☐ 2074		PRETTY BALLERINA/LAZY DAY	1.75	3.00
☐ 2089		AND SUDDENLY/IVY, IVY	1.75	3.00
☐ 2119		DESIREE/		
		I'VE GOT SOMETHING ON MY MIND	1.75	3.00
☐ 2197		BARTENDERS AND THEIR WIVES/		
		SHE MAY CALL YOU UP TONIGHT	1.75	3.00

LEFT BANKE—ALBUMS

☐ 67088 (S)	*SMASH*	WALK AWAY RENEE	8.00	22.50
☐ 67113 (S)		TOO	7.00	18.00

ISSUE #	LABEL		PRICE RANGE	

JOHN LENNON

☐ 1809	*APPLE*	GIVE PEACE A CHANCE/REMEMBER LOVE	1.75	3.00
☐ 1813		COLD TURKEY/DON'T WORRY, YOKO	1.75	3.00
☐ 1818		INSTANT KARMA/		
		WHO HAS SEEN THE WIND?	1.75	3.50
☐ 1827		MOTHER/WHY	1.75	3.50
☐ 1830		POWER TO THE PEOPLE/TOUCH ME	1.75	3.50
☐ 1840		IMAGINE/IT'S SO BAD	1.75	3.50
☐ 1846		HAPPY XMAS (WAR IS OVER)/		
		LISTEN, THE SNOW IS FALLING	3.00	4.50
☐ 1848		WOMAN IS THE NIGGER OF THE WORLD/		
		SISTERS, OH SISTERS	2.00	3.00
☐ 1868		MIND GAMES/MEAT CITY	1.75	3.50
☐ 1874		WHATEVER GETS YOU THROUGH THE		
		NIGHT/BEEF JERKY	1.75	3.50
☐ 1878		#9 DREAM/WHAT YOU GOT	1.75	3.50
☐ 1881		STAND BY ME/MOVE OVER, MRS. L.	1.75	3.50

JOHN LENNON—ALBUMS

☐ 8018 (S)	*ADAM VIII*	JOHN LENNON SINGS THE GREAT		
		ROCK & ROLL HITS	25.00	65.00
☐ 5001 (S)	*APPLE*	TWO VIRGINS/UNFINISHED MUSIC NO. 1	25.00	65.00
☐ 3361 (S)		WEDDING ALBUM	30.00	80.00
☐ 3362 (S)		LIVE PEACE IN TORONTO	10.00	25.00
☐ 3372 (S)		PLASTIC ONO BAND	7.00	18.00
☐ 3379 (S)		IMAGINE	6.00	18.00
☐ 3392 (S)		SOME TIME IN NEW YORK CITY	6.00	18.00
☐ 3414 (S)		MIND GAMES	6.00	18.00
☐ 3416 (S)		WALLS AND BRIDGES	6.00	18.00
☐ 3419 (S)		ROCK 'N' ROLL	6.00	18.00
☐ 3421 (S)		SHAVED FISH	6.00	18.00

GARY LEWIS AND THE PLAYBOYS

☐ 55756	*LIBERTY*	THIS DIAMOND RING/HARD TO FIND	1.75	3.00
☐ 55756		THIS DIAMOND RING/TIJUANA WEDDING	1.75	3.00
☐ 55778		COUNT ME IN/LITTLE MISS GO-GO	1.75	3.00
☐ 55809		SAVE YOUR HEART FOR ME/		
		WITHOUT A WORD OF WARNING	1.75	3.00
☐ 55818		EVERYBODY LOVES A CLOWN/		
		TIME STANDS STILL	1.75	3.00
☐ 55846		SHE'S JUST MY STYLE/ I WON'T MAKE		
		THAT MISTAKE AGAIN	1.75	3.00
☐ 55865		SURE GONNA MISS HER/		
		I DON'T WANNA SAY GOODNIGHT	1.75	3.00

JOHN LENNON

ISSUE #	LABEL		PRICE RANGE	
☐ 55880		GREEN GRASS/		
		I CAN READ BETWEEN THE LINES	1.75	3.00
☐ 55898		MY HEART'S SYMPHONY/TINA	1.75	3.00
☐ 55914		(YOU DON'T HAVE TO) PAINT ME A		
		PICTURE/LOOKING FOR THE STARS	1.75	3.00
☐ 55933		WHERE WILL THE WORDS COME FROM?/		
		MAY THE BEST MAN WIN	1.75	3.00
☐ 55949		THE LOSER (WITH A BROKEN HEART)/		
		ICE MELTS IN THE SUN	1.75	3.00
☐ 55971		GIRLS IN LOVE/		
		LET'S BE MORE THAN FRIENDS	1.75	3.00
☐ 55985		JILL/NEW IN TOWN	1.75	3.00
☐ 56011		HAPPINESS/		
		HAS SHE GOT THE NICEST EYES	1.75	3.00
☐ 56037		SEALED WITH A KISS/SARA JANE	1.75	3.00

GARY LEWIS AND THE PLAYBOYS—ALBUMS

ISSUE #	LABEL		PRICE RANGE	
☐ 7408 (S)	*LIBERTY*	THIS DIAMOND RING	7.00	18.00
☐ 7419 (S)		A SESSION WITH GARY LEWIS		
		AND THE PLAYBOYS	7.00	18.00
☐ 7428 (S)		EVERYBODY LOVES A CLOWN	7.00	18.00
☐ 7435 (S)		SHE'S JUST MY STYLE	6.00	15.00
☐ 7453 (S)		HITS AGAIN	6.00	15.00
☐ 7468 (S)		GOLDEN GREATS	6.00	15.00
☐ 7519 (S)		NEW DIRECTIONS	5.00	13.50
☐ 7524 (S)		LISTEN	5.00	13.50
☐ 7568 (S)		NOW	5.00	13.50
☐ 7606 (S)		CLOSE COVER BEFORE PLAYING	5.00	13.50
☐ 7623 (S)		RHYTHM OF THE RAIN	5.00	13.50
☐ 7633 (S)		I'M ON THE RIGHT ROAD NOW	5.00	13.50

JERRY LEE LEWIS

ISSUE #	LABEL		PRICE RANGE	
☐ 259	*SUN*	CRAZY ARMS/END OF THE ROAD	7.25	12.00
☐ 267		WHOLE LOT OF SHAKIN' GOING ON/		
		IT'LL BE ME	3.50	6.00
☐ 281		GREAT BALLS OF FIRE/YOU WIN AGAIN	3.50	6.00
☐ 288		BREATHLESS/DOWN THE LINE	3.00	4.50
☐ 296		HIGH SCHOOL CONFIDENTIAL/		
		FOOLS LIKE ME	3.00	4.50
☐ 301		THE RETURN OF JERRY LEE/LEWIS BOOGIE . . .	3.50	6.00
☐ 303		BREAK-UP/I'LL MAKE IT ALL UP TO YOU . . .	2.25	4.00
☐ 312		I'LL SAIL MY SHIP ALONE/IT HURT ME SO . . .	2.25	4.00
☐ 317		LOVIN' UP A STORM/BIG BLON' BABY	2.25	4.00
☐ 324		LET'S TALK ABOUT US/		
		BALLAD OF BILLY JOE	2.25	4.00

JERRY LEE LEWIS

ISSUE #	LABEL		PRICE RANGE	
☐330		LITTLE QUEENIE/		
		I COULD NEVER BE ASHAMED OF YOU	2.25	4.00
☐337		OLD BLACK JOE/BABY, BABY BYE BYE	2.25	4.00
☐344		HANG UP MY ROCK AND ROLL SHOES/		
		JOHN HENRY	2.25	4.00
☐352		WHEN I GET PAID/		
		LOVE MADE A FOOL OF ME	2.25	4.00
☐356		WHAT'D I SAY/LIVIN' LOVIN' WRECK	2.00	3.50
☐364		IT WON'T HAPPEN WITH ME/		
		COLD, COLD HEART	2.00	3.50
☐367		SAVE THE LAST DANCE FOR ME/		
		AS LONG AS I LIVE	2.00	3.50
☐371		MONEY/BOBBIE B	2.00	3.50
☐374		I'VE BEEN TWISTIN'/RAMBLIN' ROSE	2.00	3.50
☐379		SWEET LITTLE SIXTEEN/HOW'S MY EX		
		TREATING YOU?	2.00	3.50
☐382		GOOD GOLLY, MISS MOLLY/I CAN'T		
		TRUST ME (IN YOUR ARMS)	2.00	3.50
☐384		TEENAGE LETTER/SEASONS OF MY HEART ...	2.00	3.50
☐396		CARRY ME BACK TO OLD VIRGINIA/I KNOW		
		WHAT IT MEANS	2.00	3.50
☐1101		INVITATION TO YOUR PARTY/I COULD		
		NEVER BE ASHAMED OF YOU	2.00	3.50
☐1107		ONE MINUTE PAST ETERNITY/		
		FRANKIE AND JOHNNY	2.00	3.50
☐1115		I CAN'T SEEM TO SAY GOODBYE/		
		GOODNIGHT IRENE	2.00	3.50
☐1119		BIG LEGGED WOMAN/		
		WAITING FOR A TRAIN	2.00	3.50
☐1125		MATCHBOX/LOVE ON BROADWAY	2.00	3.50
☐1128		YOUR LOVING WAYS/I CAN'T TRUST ME IN		
		YOUR ARMS ANYMORE	2.00	3.50
☐1130		GOOD ROCKIN' TONIGHT/I CAN'T TRUST		
		ME IN YOUR ARMS ANYMORE	2.00	3.50
☐1857	*SMASH*	HIT THE ROAD JACK/PEN AND PAPER	1.75	3.00
☐1886		I'M ON FIRE/BREAD AND BUTTER MAN	1.75	3.00
☐1906		SHE WAS MY BABY, HE WAS MY FRIEND/		
		THE HOME HE SAID HE BUILT FOR ME	1.75	3.00
☐1930		HIGH HEEL SNEAKERS/YOU WENT BACK		
		ON YOUR WORD	1.75	3.00
☐1969		I BELIEVE IN YOU/BABY, HOLD ME CLOSE	1.75	3.00
☐1992		ROCKIN' PNEUMONIA AND THE BOOGIE		
		WOOGIE FLU/THIS MUST BE THE PLACE ...	2.00	3.50
☐2006		YOU'VE GOT WHAT IT TAKES/		
		THE GREEN, GREEN GRASS OF HOME	1.75	3.00

ISSUE #	LABEL		PRICE RANGE	

JERRY LEE LEWIS—EPs

□ 107	*SUN*	THE GREAT BALL OF FIRE	10.00	18.00
□ 108		JERRY LEE LEWIS	8.50	15.00
□ 109		JERRY LEE LEWIS	8.50	15.00
□ 110		JERRY LEE LEWIS	8.50	15.00

JERRY LEE LEWIS—ALBUMS

□ 1230 (M)	*SUN*	JERRY LEE LEWIS	15.00	35.00
□ 1265 (M)		JERRY LEE'S GREATEST!	20.00	50.00
□ 27010 (M)	*SMASH*	COUNTRY SONGS FOR CITY FOLKS	6.00	15.00
□ 67010 (S)		COUNTRY SONGS FOR CITY FOLKS	7.00	18.00
□ 67040 (S)		GOLDEN HITS OF JERRY LEE LEWIS	7.00	18.00
□ 67056 (S)		THE GREATEST LIVE SHOW ON EARTH	7.00	18.00
□ 67063 (S)		THE RETURN OF ROCK	6.00	15.00
□ 67079 (S)		MEMPHIS BEAT	6.00	15.00
□ 67086 (S)		BY REQUEST	6.00	15.00
□ 67097 (S)		SOUL MY WAY	6.00	15.00
□ 67104 (S)		ANOTHER PLACE, ANOTHER TIME	4.50	12.00
□ 67112 (S)		SHE STILL COMES AROUND	4.50	12.00
□ 67118 (S)		COUNTRY HITS, VOL. I	4.50	13.50
□ 67126 (S)		TOGETHER WITH LINDA GAIL LEWIS	4.50	12.00
□ 67128 (S)		SHE EVEN WOKE ME UP TO SAY GOODBYE	4.50	12.00
□ 67131 (S)		THE BEST OF JERRY LEE LEWIS	4.50	12.00

LITTLE EVA

□ 1000	*DIMENSION*	THE LOCO-MOTION/HE IS THE BOY	2.00	3.50
□ 1003		KEEP YOUR HANDS OFF MY BABY/		
		WHERE DO I GO?	2.00	3.50
□ 1006		LET'S TURKEY TROT/DOWN HOME	2.00	3.50
□ 1011		OLD SMOKEY LOCOMOTION/		
		JUST A LITTLE GIRL	2.00	3.50
□ 1013		THE TROUBLE WITH BOYS/		
		WHAT I GOTTA DO	2.00	3.50
□ 1019		PLEASE HURT ME/		
		LET'S START THE PARTY AGAIN	2.00	3.50
□ 1021		THE CHRISTMAS SONG/		
		I WISH YOU A MERRY CHRISTMAS	2.00	3.50
□ 1035		RUN TO HER/MAKIN' WITH THE MAGILLA	2.00	3.50
□ 1042		WAKE UP JOHN/TAKIN' BACK WHAT I SAID	2.00	3.50
□ 943	*AMY*	STAND BY ME/THAT'S MY MAN	2.00	3.50

LITTLE EVA—ALBUM

| □ 6000 (S) | | | | |
| | *DIMENSION* | L-L-L-LOCOMOTION | 12.50 | 30.00 |

ISSUE #	LABEL		PRICE RANGE	

LITTLE RICHARD

☐4392	*RCA*	TAXI BLUES/EVERY HOUR	72.00	120.00
☐4582		GET RICH QUICK/		
		THINKIN' ABOUT MY MOTHER	60.00	120.00
☐4722		WHY DID YOU LEAVE ME?/		
		AIN'T NOTHIN' HAPPENIN'	60.00	120.00
☐5025		PLEASE HAVE MERCY ON ME/		
		I BROUGHT IT ALL ON MYSELF	48.00	90.00
☐1616	*PEACOCK*	FOOL AT THE WHEEL/		
		AIN'T THAT GOOD NEWS	24.00	42.00
☐1628		RICE, RED BEANS AND TURNIP GREENS/		
		ALWAYS	20.00	36.00
☐1658		LITTLE RICHARD'S BOOGIE/		
		DIRECTLY FROM MY HEART	18.00	30.00
☐1673		MAYBE I'M RIGHT/I LOVE MY BABY	15.00	25.00
☐561	*SPECIALTY*	TUTTI FRUTTI/I'M JUST A LONELY GUY	3.50	6.00
☐572		LONG TALL SALLY/SLIPPIN' AND SLIDIN'	3.50	6.00
☐579		RIP IT UP/REDDY TEDDY	3.50	6.00
☐584		SHE'S GOT IT/HEEBIE JEEBIES	4.50	9.00
☐591		THE GIRL CAN'T HELP IT/		
		ALL AROUND THE WORLD	4.00	7.00
☐598		LUCILLE/SEND ME SOME LOVIN'	2.75	4.50
☐606		JENNY JENNY/MISS ANN	2.25	4.00
☐611		KEEP A KNOCKIN'/		
		CAN'T BELIEVE YOU WANNA LEAVE	2.25	4.00
☐624		GOOD GOLLY MISS MOLLY/		
		HEY HEY HEY HEY	2.25	4.00
☐660		BY THE LIGHT OF THE SILVERY MOON/		
		WONDERIN'	2.00	3.50
☐664		KANSAS CITY/LONESOME AND BLUE	2.00	3.50
☐670		SHAKE A HAND/ALL NIGHT LONG	2.00	3.50
☐680		WHOLE LOTTA SHAKIN' GOING ON/		
		MAYBE I'M RIGHT	2.00	3.50
☐681		I GOT IT/BABY	2.00	3.50
☐686		DIRECTLY FROM MY HEART/		
		THE MOST I CAN OFFER	2.00	3.50
☐692		BAMA LAMA BAMA LOO/ANNIE'S BACK	2.00	3.50

LITTLE RICHARD—EPs

☐400	*SPECIALTY*	HERE'S LITTLE RICHARD, VOL. I	10.00	18.00
☐401		HERE'S LITTLE RICHARD, VOL. II	10.00	18.00
☐402		HERE'S LITTLE RICHARD, VOL. III	10.00	18.00
☐403		LITTLE RICHARD, VOL. I	8.50	15.00
☐404		LITTLE RICHARD, VOL. II	8.50	15.00
☐405		LITTLE RICHARD, VOL. III	8.50	15.00

ISSUE #	LABEL		PRICE RANGE	

LITTLE RICHARD—ALBUMS

☐SP-100 (M)				
	SPECIALTY	HERE'S LITTLE RICHARD	15.00	35.00
☐2100 (M)		HERE'S LITTLE RICHARD	7.00	18.00
☐2103 (M)		LITTLE RICHARD, VOL. II	8.00	22.50
☐2104 (M)		THE FABULOUS LITTLE RICHARD	8.00	22.50

LOVIN' SPOONFUL

☐201	*KAMA*			
	SUTRA	DO YOU BELIEVE IN MAGIC?/		
		ON THE ROAD AGAIN	1.75	3.00
☐205		YOU DIDN'T HAVE TO BE SO NICE/MY GAL . . .	1.75	3.00
☐209		DID YOU EVER HAVE TO MAKE UP YOUR		
		MIND?/DIDN'T WANT TO HAVE TO DO IT . . .	1.75	3.00
☐211		SUMMER IN THE CITY/BUTCHIE'S TUNE	1.75	3.00
☐211		SUMMER IN THE CITY/FISHIN' BLUES	1.75	3.00
☐216		RAIN ON THE ROOF/POW!	1.75	3.00
☐219		NASHVILLE CATS/FULL MEASURE	1.75	3.00
☐220		DARLING BE HOME SOON/		
		DARLIN' COMPANION	1.75	3.00
☐225		SIX O'CLOCK/THE FINALE	1.75	3.00
☐231		YOU'RE A BIG BOY NOW/		
		LONELY (AMY'S THEME)	2.00	3.50
☐239		SHE IS STILL A MYSTERY/ONLY PRETTY,		
		WHAT A PITY	1.50	2.50
☐241		MONEY/CLOSE YOUR EYES	1.50	2.50
☐250		NEVER GOING BACK/FOREVER	1.50	2.50
☐251		RUN WITH YOU/		
		REVELATION: REVOLUTION '69	1.50	2.50
☐255		ME ABOUT YOU/AMAZING AIR	1.50	2.50

LOVIN' SPOONFUL—ALBUMS

☐8050 (S)	*KAMA*			
	SUTRA	DO YOU BELIEVE IN MAGIC?	7.00	18.00
☐8051 (S)		DAYDREAM	7.00	18.00
☐8054 (M)		HUMS OF THE LOVIN' SPOONFUL	4.50	12.00
☐8054 (S)		HUMS OF THE LOVIN' SPOONFUL	6.00	15.00
☐8056 (S)		BEST OF THE LOVIN' SPOONFUL	4.50	12.00
☐8061 (S)		EVERYTHING PLAYING	4.00	10.00
☐8064 (S)		BEST OF THE LOVIN' SPOONFUL, VOL. II	4.00	10.00
☐8073 (S)		REVELATION REVOLUTION '69	4.00	10.00
☐2608-2 (S)		BEST OF THE LOVIN' SPOONFUL	4.00	10.00

ISSUE #	LABEL		PRICE RANGE	

FRANKIE LYMON
AND THE TEENAGERS

☐ 1002	*GEE*	WHY DO FOOLS FALL IN LOVE/		
		PLEASE BE MINE	3.50	6.00
☐ 1012		I WANT YOU TO BE MY GIRL/		
		I'M NOT A KNOW IT ALL	3.50	6.00
☐ 1018		I PROMISE TO REMEMBER/		
		WHO CAN EXPLAIN	3.50	6.00
☐ 1022		THE ABC'S OF LOVE/SHARE	3.50	6.00
☐ 1026		I'M NOT A JUVENILE DELINQUENT/		
		BABY BABY	4.00	7.00
☐ 1032		TEENAGE LOVE/PAPER CASTLES	4.00	7.00

FRANKIE LYMON
AND THE TEENAGERS—ALBUM

☐ 701 (S)	*GEE*	THE TEENAGERS FEATURING		
		FRANKIE LYMON	4.50	12.00

— M —

MAMAS AND PAPAS

☐ 4020	*DUNHILL*	CALIFORNIA DREAMIN'/		
		SOMEDAY GROOVY	1.75	3.00
☐ 4026		MONDAY MONDAY/GOT A FEELING	1.75	3.00
☐ 4031		I SAW HER AGAIN/EVEN IF I COULD	1.75	3.00
☐ 4050		LOOK THROUGH MY WINDOW/		
		ONCE WAS A TIME I THOUGHT	1.75	3.00
☐ 4057		WORDS OF LOVE/DANCIN' IN THE STREET	1.75	3.00
☐ 4077		DEDICATED TO THE ONE I LOVE/		
		FREE ADVICE	1.75	3.00
☐ 4083		CREEQUE ALLEY/		
		DID YOU EVER WANT TO CRY?	1.75	3.00
☐ 4099		TWELVE THIRTY/STRAIGHT SHOOTER	1.50	2.50
☐ 4107		GLAD TO BE UNHAPPY/HEY GIRL	1.50	2.50
☐ 4113		DANCING BEAR/JOHN'S MUSIC BOX	1.50	2.50
☐ 4125		SAFE IN MY GARDEN/TOO LATE	1.50	2.50
☐ 4150		FOR THE LOVE OF IVY/		
		STRANGE YOUNG GIRLS	1.50	2.50
☐ 4171		DO YOU WANNA DANCE?/MY GIRL	1.50	2.50
☐ 4301		STEP OUT/SHOOTING STAR	1.50	2.50

ISSUE #	LABEL		PRICE RANGE	

MAMAS AND PAPAS—ALBUMS

ISSUE #	LABEL			
☐50006 (S)	*DUNHILL*	IF YOU CAN BELIEVE YOUR EYES AND EARS	5.00	13.50
☐50010 (S)		CASS, JOHN, MICHELLE, DENNY	5.00	13.50
☐50014 (S)		DELIVER	5.00	13.50
☐50025 (S)		FAREWELL TO THE FIRST GOLDEN ERA	4.00	10.00
☐50031 (S)		THE MAMAS AND THE PAPAS	4.00	10.00
☐50038 (S)		GOLDEN ERA, VOL. II	4.00	10.00

MANFRED MANN

☐2157	*ASCOT*	DO WAH DIDDY DIDDY/ WHAT YOU GONNA DO?	2.00	3.50
☐2165		SHA LA LA/JOHN HARDY	2.00	3.50
☐2170		COME TOMORROW/ WHAT DID I DO WRONG?	2.00	3.50
☐2184		MY LITTLE RED BOOK/ WHAT AM I DOING WRONG?	2.25	4.00
☐2194		IF YOU GOTTA GO, GO NOW/ ONE IN THE MIDDLE	2.00	3.50
☐2210		SHE NEEDS COMPANY/HI LILI, HI LO	2.00	3.50
☐2241		I CAN'T BELIEVE WHAT YOU SAY/ MY LITTLE RED BOOK	2.00	3.50
☐55040	*UNITED ARTISTS*	PRETTY FLAMINGO/YOU'RE STANDING BY	2.00	3.50
☐55066		WHEN WILL I BE LOVED?/ DO YOU HAVE TO DO THAT?	2.00	3.50

MANFRED MANN—ALBUMS

☐16015 (S)	*ASCOT*	THE MANFRED MANN ALBUM	8.00	22.50
☐16018 (S)		THE FIVE FACES OF MANFRED MANN	8.00	22.50
☐16021 (S)		MY LITTLE RED BOOK OF WINNERS	8.00	22.50
☐16024 (S)		MANN MADE	7.00	18.00
☐6549 (S)	*UNITED ARTISTS*	PRETTY FLAMINGO	8.00	22.50
☐6551 (S)		MANFRED MANN'S GREATEST HITS	7.00	18.00

MARTHA AND THE VANDELLAS

☐7011	*GORDY*	I'LL HAVE TO LET HIM GO/ MY BABY WON'T COME BACK	3.50	6.00
☐7014		COME AND GET THESE MEMORIES/ JEALOUS LOVER	2.00	3.50
☐7022		HEAT WAVE/A LOVE LIKE YOURS	2.00	3.50
☐7025		QUICKSAND/DARLING, I HUM OUR SONG	2.00	3.50
☐7027		LIVE WIRE/OLD LOVE	2.00	3.50

ISSUE #	LABEL		PRICE RANGE	
☐ 7031		IN MY LONELY ROOM/		
		A TEAR FOR THE GIRL	2.00	3.50
☐ 7033		DANCING IN THE STREET/THERE HE IS	2.00	3.50
☐ 7036		WILD ONE/DANCING SLOW	2.00	3.50
☐ 7039		NOWHERE TO RUN/MOTORING	2.00	3.50
☐ 7045		YOU'VE BEEN IN LOVE TOO LONG/LOVE	1.75	3.00
☐ 7048		MY BABY LOVES ME/NEVER, NEVER		
		LEAVE YOUR BABY'S SIDE	1.75	3.00
☐ 7053		WHAT AM I GOING TO DO WITHOUT YOUR		
		LOVE?/GO AHEAD AND LAUGH	1.75	3.00
☐ 7056		I'M READY FOR LOVE/		
		HE DOESN'T LOVE HER ANYMORE	1.75	3.00
☐ 7058		JIMMY MACK/THIRD FINGER, LEFT HAND	1.75	3.00
☐ 7062		LOVE BUG, LEAVE MY HEART ALONE/		
		THE WAY OUT	1.75	3.00
☐ 7067		HONEY CHILE/SHOW ME THE WAY	1.75	3.00
☐ 7070		I PROMISE TO WAIT, MY LOVE/		
		FORGET-ME-NOT	1.75	3.00
☐ 7075		I CAN'T DANCE TO THAT MUSIC YOU'RE		
		PLAYIN'/I TRIED	1.75	3.00

MARTHA AND THE VANDELLAS—ALBUMS

☐ 902 (M)	*GORDY*	COME AND GET THESE MEMORIES	10.00	25.00
☐ 907 (M)		HEAT WAVE	8.00	22.50
☐ 915 (M)		DANCE PARTY	8.00	22.50
☐ 917 (M)		GREATEST HITS	7.00	18.00
☐ 920 (M)		WATCH OUT	6.00	15.00
☐ 925 (M)		LIVE	6.00	15.00

MARVELETTES

☐ 54046	*TAMLA*	PLEASE MR. POSTMAN/SO LONG BABY	2.00	3.50
☐ 54054		TWISTIN' POSTMAN/I WANT A GUY	2.00	3.50
☐ 54060		PLAYBOY/ALL THE LOVE I'VE GOT	2.00	3.50
☐ 54065		BEECHWOOD 4-5789/		
		SOMEDAY, SOMEWAY	2.00	3.50
☐ 54072		STRANGE I KNOW/		
		TOO STRUNG OUT TO BE STRUNG ALONG	1.75	3.00
☐ 54077		LOCKING UP MY HEART/FOREVER	1.75	3.00
☐ 54082		MY DADDY KNOWS BEST/		
		TIE A STRING AROUND MY FINGER	1.75	3.00
☐ 54088		AS LONG AS I KNOW HE'S MINE/		
		LITTLE GIRL BLUE	1.75	3.00
☐ 54091		HE'S A GOOD GUY/GODDESS OF LOVE	1.75	3.00
☐ 54097		YOU'RE MY REMEDY/A LITTLE BIT OF		
		SYMPATHY, A LITTLE BIT OF LOVE	1.75	3.00

ISSUE #	LABEL		PRICE RANGE	
☐54105		TOO MANY FISH IN THE SEA/		
		A NEED FOR TEARS	1.75	3.00
☐54116		I'LL KEEP HOLDING ON/		
		NO TIME FOR TEARS	1.75	3.00
☐54120		DANGER HEARTBREAK AHEAD/		
		YOUR CHEATING WAYS	1.75	3.00
☐54126		DON'T MESS WITH BILL/		
		ANYTHING YOU WANNA DO	1.75	3.00
☐54131		YOU'RE THE ONE/PAPER BOY	1.75	3.00
☐54143		THE HUNTER GETS CAPTURED BY THE		
		GAME/I THINK I CAN CHANGE YOU	1.75	3.00
☐54150		WHEN YOU'RE YOUNG AND IN LOVE/		
		THE DAY YOU TAKE ONE, YOU HAVE TO		
		TAKE THE OTHER	1.75	3.00
☐54158		MY BABY MUST BE A MAGICIAN/		
		I NEED SOMEONE	1.75	3.00
☐54166		HERE I AM BABY/		
		KEEP OFF, NO TRESPASSING	1.75	3.00
☐54171		DESTINATION: ANYWHERE/WHAT'S EASY		
		FOR TWO IS SO HARD FOR ONE	1.75	3.00

MARVELETTES—ALBUMS

☐228 (M)	*TAMLA*	PLEASE MR. POSTMAN	12.50	30.00
☐228 (M)		THE MARVELETTES SING	10.00	25.00
☐231 (M)		PLAYBOY	8.00	22.50
☐237 (M)		MARVELOUS	8.00	22.50
☐243 (M)		ON STAGE	7.00	18.00
☐253 (M)		GREATEST HITS	7.00	18.00
☐274 (M)		THE MARVELETTES	6.00	15.00

MC-5

☐1000	*AMG*	I CAN ONLY GIVE YOU EVERYTHING/		
		I JUST DON'T KNOW	10.00	17.50
☐1001		I CAN ONLY GIVE YOU EVERYTHING/		
		ONE OF THE GUYS	10.00	17.50
☐333	*A-SQUARE*	LOOKING AT YOU/BORDERLINE	7.00	12.50
☐45648	*ELEKTRA*	KICK OUT THE JAMS/		
		MOTOR CITY IS BURNING	2.25	4.00
☐2724		AMERICAN RUSH/SHAKIN' STREET	2.00	3.50

MC-5—ALBUMS

☐74072 (S)	*ELEKTRA*	KICKIN' OUT THE JAMS	7.00	18.00
☐8247 (S)	*ATLANTIC*	BACK IN THE U.S.A.	4.50	12.00
☐8285 (S)		HIGH TIME	4.50	12.00

ISSUE #	LABEL		PRICE RANGE	

PAUL McCARTNEY

☐ 1829	*APPLE*	ANOTHER DAY/OH WOMAN, OH WHY	1.75	3.00
☐ 1837		UNCLE ALBERT-ADMIRAL HALSEY/		
		TOO MANY PEOPLE	1.75	3.00
☐ 1847		GIVE IRELAND BACK TO THE IRISH (PT. 2)	1.75	3.00
☐ 1851		MARY HAD A LITTLE LAMB/		
		LITTLE WOMAN LOVE	1.75	3.00
☐ 1857		HI HI HI/C MOON	1.50	2.50
☐ 1861		MY LOVE/THE MESS	1.50	2.50
☐ 1863		LIVE AND LET DIE/I LIE AROUND	1.50	2.50
☐ 1869		HELEN WHEELS/COUNTRY DREAMER	1.50	2.50
☐ 1871		JET/MAMUNIA	2.00	3.50
☐ 1871		JET/LET ME ROLL IT	1.50	2.50
☐ 1873		BAND ON THE RUN/		
		NINETEEN HUNDRED AND EIGHTY-FIVE	1.50	2.50
☐ 1875		JUNIOR'S FARM/SALLY G.	1.50	2.50

PAUL McCARTNEY AND WINGS—ALBUMS

☐ 3363 (S)	*APPLE*	McCARTNEY	4.00	10.00
☐ 3375 (S)		RAM	4.00	10.00
☐ 3386 (S)		WILD LIFE	4.00	10.00
☐ 3409 (S)		RED ROSE SPEEDWAY	4.00	10.00
☐ 3415 (S)		BAND ON THE RUN	4.00	10.00

McCOYS

☐ 506	*BANG*	HANG ON SLOOPY/I CAN'T EXPLAIN IT	1.75	3.00
☐ 511		FEVER/SORROW	1.75	3.00
☐ 516		UP AND DOWN/IF I TELL YOU A LIE	1.75	3.00
☐ 522		COME ON LET'S GO/LITTLE PEOPLE	1.75	3.00
☐ 527		(YOU MAKE ME FEEL) SO GOOD/		
		RUNAWAY	1.75	3.00
☐ 532		DON'T WORRY, MOTHER, YOUR SON'S		
		HEART IS PURE/KO-KO	1.75	3.00
☐ 538		I GOT TO GO BACK/DYNAMITE	1.75	3.00
☐ 543		BEAT THE CLOCK/LIKE YOU DO TO ME	1.75	3.00
☐ 549		SAY THOSE MAGIC WORDS/		
		I WONDER IF SHE REMEMBERS ME	1.75	3.00

McCOYS—ALBUMS

☐ 212 (M)	*BANG*	HANG ON SLOOPY	7.00	18.00
☐ 213 (M)		YOU MAKE ME FEEL SO GOOD	6.00	15.00

PAUL McCARTNEY

ISSUE #	LABEL		PRICE RANGE	

GENE McDANIELS

☐ 55231	*LIBERTY*	IN TIMES LIKE THESE/ONCE BEFORE	2.00	3.50
☐ 55265		FACTS OF LIFE/THE GREEN DOOR	2.00	3.50
☐ 55308		A HUNDRED POUNDS OF CLAY/		
		TAKE A CHANCE ON LOVE	1.75	3.00
☐ 55344		A TEAR/SHE'S COME BACK	1.75	3.00
☐ 55371		TOWER OF STRENGTH/THE SECRET	1.75	3.00
☐ 55405		CHIP CHIP/ANOTHER TEAR FALLS	1.75	3.00
☐ 55444		FUNNY/CHAPEL OF TEARS	1.75	3.00
☐ 55480		POINT OF NO RETURN/		
		WARMER THAN A WHISPER	1.75	3.00
☐ 55510		SPANISH LACE/SOMEBODY'S WAITING	1.75	3.00
☐ 55541		CRY BABY CRY/THE PUZZLE	1.75	3.00
☐ 55597		IT'S A LONELY TOWN/FALSE FRIENDS	1.75	3.00

GENE McDANIELS—EP

☐ 1014	*LIBERTY*	GENE McDANIELS	3.00	5.00

GENE McDANIELS—ALBUMS

☐ 7146 (S)	*LIBERTY*	IN TIMES LIKE THESE	10.00	25.00
☐ 7175 (S)		SOMETIMES I'M HAPPY		
		(SOMETIMES I'M BLUE)	8.00	22.50
☐ 7191 (S)		100 LBS. OF CLAY	7.00	18.00
☐ 7204 (S)		GENE McDANIELS SINGS		
		MOVIE MEMORIES	7.00	18.00
☐ 7258 (S)		HIT AFTER HIT	7.00	18.00
☐ 7275 (S)		SPANISH LACE	7.00	18.00
☐ 7311 (S)		THE WONDERFUL WORLD OF		
		GENE McDANIELS	6.00	15.00

DON McLEAN

☐ 50856	*UNITED ARTISTS*	AMERICAN PIE (PT. 1)/(PT. 2)	1.50	3.00
☐ 50887		CASTLES IN THE AIR/VINCENT	1.50	3.00
☐ 51100		BRONCO BILL'S LAMENT/DREIDEL	1.50	3.00
☐ 541		SITTING ON TOP OF THE WORLD/		
		MULE SKINNER BLUES	1.50	3.00
☐ 579		LA LA LOVE YOU/HOMELESS BROTHER . . .	1.50	3.00
☐ 614		BIRTHDAY SONG/WONDERFUL BABY	1.50	3.00
☐ 0284	*ARISTA*	THE STATUE/PRIME TIME	1.50	3.00

MELLO-KINGS

☐ 502	*HERALD*	TONITE-TONITE/DO BABY DO	20.00	36.00
☐ 502		TONITE-TONITE/DO BABY DO	4.00	7.00
☐ 507		CHAPEL ON THE HILL/SASSAFRASS	3.50	6.00

ISSUE #	LABEL		PRICE RANGE	
☐511		BABY TELL ME/ONLY GIRL	3.50	6.00
☐518		VALERIE/SHE'S REAL COOL	3.50	6.00
☐536		RUNNING TO YOU/CHIP CHIP	3.50	6.00

MELLO-KINGS—EP

☐451	*HERALD*	THE FABULOUS MELLO KINGS	12.00	20.00

MELLO-KINGS—ALBUM

☐1013 (M)	*HERALD*	TONIGHT, TONIGHT	30.00	75.00

MICKEY AND SYLVIA

☐102	*CAT*	FINE LOVE/SPEEDY LIFE	10.00	18.00
☐316	*RAINBOW*	I'M SO GLAD/SE DEE BOOM RUN DUN	7.25	12.00
☐318		FOREVER AND A DAY/RISE SALLY RISE	7.25	12.00
☐330		WHERE IS MY HONEY?/		
		SEEMS JUST LIKE YESTERDAY	7.25	12.00
☐0164	*GROOVE*	WALKING IN THE RAIN/NO GOOD LOVER	4.50	9.00
☐0175		LOVE IS STRANGE/I'M GOING HOME	4.00	7.00
☐0267	*VIK*	THERE OUGHT TO BE A LAW/DEAREST	2.25	4.00
☐0280		LOVE WILL MAKE YOU FAIL IN SCHOOL/		
		TWO SHADOWS ON YOUR WINDOW	2.25	4.00
☐0290		LET'S HAVE A PICNIC/		
		LOVE IS A TREASURE	2.25	4.00
☐0297		WHERE IS MY HONEY?/		
		THERE'LL BE NO BACKING OUT	2.25	4.00
☐0324		BEWILDERED/ROCK AND STROLL ROOM	2.25	4.00
☐0334		IT'S YOU I LOVE/TRUE, TRUE LOVE	2.25	4.00
☐7403	*RCA*	OH YEAH! UH HUH/TO THE VALLEY	2.00	3.50
☐7774		SWEETER AS THE DAY GOES BY/		
		MOMMY OUT DE LIGHT	2.00	3.50
☐7811		WHAT SHOULD I DO?/THIS IS MY STORY	2.00	3.50
☐7877		LOVE LESSON/LOVE IS THE ONLY THING	2.00	3.50
☐8517		GYPSY/LET'S SHAKE SOME MORE	2.00	3.50
☐8582		FROM THE BEGINNING OF TIME/		
		FALLING IN LOVE	2.00	3.50
☐23000	*WILLOW*	BABY, YOU'RE SO FINE/LOVEDROPS	2.00	3.50
☐23002		DARLING, I MISS YOU/I'M GUILTY	2.00	3.50
☐23004		SINCE I FELL FOR YOU/		
		HE GAVE ME EVERYTHING	2.00	3.50
☐23006		LOVE IS STRANGE/WALKING IN THE RAIN	1.75	3.00

MICKEY AND SYLVIA—EPS

☐18	*GROOVE*	LOVE IS STRANGE	8.50	15.00
☐262	*VIK*	MICKEY AND SYLVIA	7.25	12.00

ISSUE #	LABEL		PRICE RANGE	

MICKEY AND SYLVIA—ALBUMS

☐1102 (M)	VIK	NEW SOUNDS	12.50	30.00
☐0327 (M)	RCA	MICKEY AND SYLVIA DO IT AGAIN	8.00	22.50
☐863 (S)	CAMDEN	LOVE IS STRANGE	8.00	22.50

MIDNIGHTERS

☐12169	FEDERAL	WORK WITH ME ANNIE/SINNER'S PRAYER	8.50	15.00
☐12177		GIVE IT UP/THAT WOMAN	7.25	12.00
☐12185		SEXY WAYS/ DON'T SAY YOUR LAST GOODBYE	7.25	12.00
☐12195		ANNIE HAD A BABY/SHE'S THE ONE	7.25	12.00
☐12200		ANNIE'S AUNT FANNIE/CRAZY LOVING	6.00	11.00
☐12202		STINGY LITTLE THING/TELL THEM	4.50	9.00
☐12205		MOONRISE/SHE'S THE ONE	4.50	9.00
☐12210		RING-A-LING-A-LING/ ASHAMED OF MYSELF	4.50	9.00
☐12220		SWITCHIE WITCHIE TICHIE/ WHY ARE WE APART?	4.00	7.00
☐12224		HENRY'S GOT FLAT FEET/ WHATSOEVER YOU DO	4.00	7.00
☐12227		LOOK-A-HERE/IT'S LOVE BABY	4.00	7.00
☐12230		GIVE IT UP/THAT WOMAN	4.00	7.00
☐12240		THAT HOUSE ON THE HILL/ ROCK AND ROLL WEDDING	4.00	7.00
☐12243		DON'T CHANGE YOUR PRETTY WAYS/ WE'LL NEVER MEET AGAIN	4.00	7.00
☐12251		SWEET MAMA DO RIGHT/ PARTNERS FOR LIFE	4.00	7.00
☐12260		ROCK GRANNY ROLL/ OPEN UP THE BACK DOOR	4.00	7.00
☐12270		TORE UP OVER YOU/EARLY ONE MORNING	4.00	7.00
☐12285		COME ON AND GET IT/ I'LL BE HOME SOMEDAY	4.00	7.00
☐12288		LET ME HOLD YOUR HAND/OOH BAH BABY	4.00	7.00
☐12293		IN THE DOORWAY CRYING/E BASTI COSI	4.00	7.00
☐12299		IS YOUR LOVE SO REAL?/OH, SO HAPPY	4.00	7.00
☐12305		LET 'EM ROLL/ WHAT MADE YOU CHANGE YOUR MIND?	4.00	7.00
☐12317		DADDY'S LITTLE BABY/STAY BY MY SIDE	4.00	7.00
☐12339		BABY PLEASE/OW-WOW-OO-WEE	4.00	7.00
☐12345		THE TWIST/TEARDROPS ON YOUR LETTER	10.00	18.00

MIDNIGHTERS—EP

☐333	FEDERAL	THE MIDNIGHTERS SING THEIR GREATEST HITS	7.25	12.00

ISSUE #	LABEL		PRICE RANGE	
MIDNIGHTERS—ALBUMS				
☐ 541 (M)	***FEDERAL***	THE MIDNIGHTERS	40.00	100.00
☐ 581 (M)		THE MIDNIGHTERS, VOL. II	35.00	90.00

RONNIE MILSAP

☐ 5405	***WARNER BROTHERS***	IT WENT TO YOUR HEAD/TOTAL DISASTER . . .	4.00	7.00
☐ 12109	***SCEPTER***	LET'S GO GET STONED/ NEVER HAD IT SO GOOD	3.50	6.00
☐ 12127		WHEN IT COMES TO MY BABY/ A THOUSAND MILES FROM NOWHERE . . .	2.75	4.50
☐ 12145		END OF THE WORLD/ I SAW PITY IN THE FACE OF A FRIEND	2.75	4.50
☐ 12161		ANOTHER BRANCH FROM THE OLD TREE/ AIN'T NO SOLE IN THESE OLD SHOES	2.25	4.00
☐ 12228		DO WHAT YOU GOTTA DO/MR. MAILMAN	2.25	4.00
☐ 12246		NOTHING IS AS GOOD AS IT USED TO BE/ DENVER.	2.25	4.00
☐ 12272		WHAT'S YOUR NAME/ LOVE WILL NEVER PASS US BY	2.75	4.50
☐ 2889	***CHIPS***	LOVING YOU IS A NATURAL THING/ SO HUNG UP ON SYLVIA	2.75	4.50
☐ 2987		A ROSE BY ANY OTHER NAME/ SERMONETTE	2.25	4.00

MINDBENDERS

☐ 1541	***FONTANA***	A GROOVY KIND OF LOVE/LOVE IS GOOD	1.75	3.00
☐ 1555		ASHES TO ASHES/ YOU DON'T KNOW ABOUT LOVE	1.75	3.00
☐ 1620		BLESSED ARE THE LONELY/ YELLOW BRICK ROAD.	1.75	3.00

MINDBENDERS—ALBUM

☐ 67554 (S)	***FONTANA***	A GROOVY KIND OF LOVE.	7.00	18.00

JONI MITCHELL

☐ 0906	***REPRISE***	BIG YELLOW TAXI/WOODSTOCK	2.25	4.50
☐ 1049		CASE OF YOU/CALIFORNIA	2.25	4.50
☐ 1154		CHELSEA MORNING/BOTH SIDES NOW	2.25	4.50
☐ 11010	***ASYLUM***	URGE FOR GOING/YOU TURN ME ON	1.75	3.50
☐ 11029		COURT & SPARK/RAISED ON ROBBERY	1.75	3.50
☐ 11034		JUST LIKE THIS TRAIN/HELP ME.	1.75	3.50

ISSUE #	LABEL		PRICE RANGE	
☐ 11041		FREE MAN IN PARIS/PEOPLE'S PARTIES	1.75	3.50
☐ 45244		CAREY/JERICHO	1.50	3.25
☐ 45298		BOHO DANCE/IN FRANCE		
		THEY DANCE ON MAIN STREET	1.50	3.25
☐ 45377		BLUE MOTEL ROOM/COYOTE	1.50	3.25
☐ 45467		JERICHO/DREAMLAND	1.50	3.25
☐ 46506		DRY CLEANER FROM DES MOINES/		
		GOD MUST BE A BOOGIE MAN	1.50	3.25
☐ 54221		BIG YELLOW TAXI/RAINY NIGHT HOUSE	1.25	2.50

MONKEES

☐ 1001	*COLGEMS*	LAST TRAIN TO CLARKSVILLE/		
		TAKE A GIANT STEP	1.75	3.00
☐ 1002		I'M A BELIEVER/		
		(I'M NOT YOUR) STEPPING STONE	1.75	3.00
☐ 1004		A LITTLE BIT ME, A LITTLE BIT YOU/		
		THE GIRL I KNEW SOMEWHERE	1.75	3.00
☐ 1007		PLEASANT VALLEY SUNDAY/WORDS	1.75	3.00
☐ 1012		DAYDREAM BELIEVER/GOIN' DOWN	1.75	3.00
☐ 1019		VALLERI/TAPIOCA TUNDRA	1.75	3.00
☐ 1023		D.W. WASHBURN/		
		IT'S NICE TO BE WITH YOU	1.75	3.00
☐ 1031		PORPOISE SONG/AS WE GO ALONG	1.75	3.00
☐ 5000		TEAR DROP CITY/		
		A MAN WITHOUT A DREAM	1.75	3.00
☐ 5004		LISTEN TO THE BAND/SOMEDAY MAN	1.75	3.00
☐ 5005		GOOD CLEAN FUN/MOMMY DADDY	1.75	3.00
☐ 5011		OH MY MY/I LOVE YOU BETTER	1.75	3.00

MONKEES—ALBUMS

☐ 101 (S)	*COLGEMS*	MEET THE MONKEES	7.00	18.00
☐ 102 (S)		MORE OF THE MONKEES	7.00	18.00
☐ 103 (S)		HEADQUARTERS	7.00	18.00
☐ 104 (S)		PISCES, AQUARIUS, CAPRICORN AND		
		JONES, LTD	6.00	15.00
☐ 104 (S)		THE BIRDS, THE BEES, AND THE MONKEES . . .	6.00	15.00
☐ 113 (S)		INSTANT REPLAY	5.00	13.50
☐ 115 (S)		GREATEST HITS	6.00	15.00
☐ 117 (S)		THE MONKEES PRESENT	8.00	22.50
☐ 5008 (S)		HEAD	12.50	30.00
☐ 1001 (S)		A BARREL FULL OF MONKEES	8.00	22.50

MOODY BLUES

☐ 9726	*LONDON*	GO NOW!/LOSE YOUR MONEY	2.00	3.50

ISSUE #	LABEL		PRICE RANGE	
☐9764		FROM THE BOTTOM OF MY HEART/		
		MY BABY'S GONE	2.00	3.50
☐9799		YOU DON'T/EV'RY DAY	2.00	3.50
☐9810		STOP!/BYE BYE BIRD	2.00	3.50
☐20030		FLY ME HIGH/		
		I REALLY HAVEN'T GOT THE TIME	2.00	3.50
☐85023	*DERAM*	NIGHTS IN WHITE SATIN/CITIES	1.75	3.00
☐85028		TUESDAY AFTERNOON (FOREVER		
		AFTERNOON) ANOTHER MORNING	1.75	3.00

MOODY BLUES—ALBUMS

☐428 (S)	*LONDON*	GO NOW!-MOODY BLUES #1	12.50	30.00
☐18012 (S)		DAYS OF FUTURE PASSED	6.00	15.00
☐18017 (S)		IN SEARCH OF THE LOST CHORD	4.50	12.00
☐18025 (S)		ON THE THRESHOLD OF A DREAM	4.50	12.00
☐18051 (S)		IN THE BEGINNING	4.50	12.00
☐1 (S)	*THRESHOLD*	TO OUR CHILDREN'S CHILDREN'S		
		CHILDREN	4.50	12.00
☐3 (S)		A QUESTION OF BALANCE	4.50	12.00
☐5 (S)		EVERY GOOD BOY DESERVES FAVOUR ...	4.50	12.00
☐7 (S)		SEVENTH SOJOURN	4.50	12.00
☐12/13 (S)		THIS IS THE MOODY BLUES	4.50	12.00

MOONGLOWS

☐7500	*CHAMPAGNE*	I JUST CAN'T TELL YOU NO LIE/		
		I'VE BEEN YOUR DOG	70.00	120.00
☐1147	*CHANCE*	WHISTLE MY LOVE/BABY PLEASE	100.00	180.00
☐1150		JUST A LONELY CHRISTMAS/		
		HEY SANTA CLAUS	150.00	250.00
☐1152		SECRET LOVE/REAL GONE MAMA	100.00	180.00
☐1156		I WAS WRONG/OOH ROCKING DADDY	70.00	120.00
☐1161		219 TRAIN/MY GAL	150.00	250.00
☐1581	*CHESS*	SINCERELY/TEMPTING	8.50	15.00
☐1589		MOST OF ALL/SHE'S GONE	8.50	15.00
☐1598		FOOLISH ME/SLOW DOWN	7.25	12.00
☐1605		STARLITE/IN LOVE	7.25	12.00
☐1611		IN MY DIARY/LOVER, LOVE ME	7.25	12.00
☐1619		WE GO TOGETHER/CHICKIE UM BAH	7.25	12.00
☐1629		SEE SAW/WHEN I'M WITH YOU	4.50	9.00
☐1646		OVER AND OVER AGAIN/		

MOONGLOWS—ALBUMS

☐1430 (M)	*CHESS*	LOOK	15.00	35.00
☐1471 (M)		THE BEST OF BOBBY LESTER		
		AND THE MOONGLOWS	12.50	30.00

ISSUE #	LABEL		PRICE RANGE	

MARIA MULDAUR

☐ 1183	*REPRISE*	MIDNIGHT AT THE OASIS/ANY OLD TIME	1.75	3.50
☐ 1319		COOL RIVER/I'M A WOMAN	1.75	3.50
☐ 1331		OH PAPA/GRINGO EN MEXICO	1.75	3.50
☐ 1362		JON THE GENERATOR/SWEET HARMONY	1.75	3.50
☐ 8580	*WARNER BROTHERS*	I'LL KEEP MY LIGHT/ MAKE LOVE TO THE MUSIC	1.25	2.50
☐ 49058		BIRDS FLY SOUTH	1.25	2.50

MUSIC EXPLOSION

☐ 1404	*ATTACK*	LITTLE BLACK EGG/STAY BY MY SIDE	3.50	6.00
☐ 3380	*LAURIE*	LITTLE BIT O' SOUL/I SEE THE LIGHT	1.75	3.00
☐ 3400		SUNSHINE GAMES/CAN'T STOP NOW	1.75	3.00
☐ 3414		HEARTS AND FLOWERS/ WE GOTTA GO HOME	1.75	3.00
☐ 3429		ROAD RUNNER/WHAT YOU WANT	1.75	3.00
☐ 3440		FLASH/WHERE ARE WE GOING?	1.75	3.00
☐ 3454		YES SIR/DAZZLING	1.75	3.00
☐ 3466		JACK IN THE BOX/REWIND	1.75	3.00

MUSIC EXPLOSION—ALBUM

☐ 2040 (S)	*LAURIE*	LITTLE BIT O'SOUL	6.00	15.00

— N —

NASHVILLE TEENS

☐ 9689	*LONDON*	TOBACCO ROAD/I LIKE IT LIKE THAT	1.75	3.00
☐ 9712		T.N.T./GOGGLE EYE	1.75	3.00
☐ 9736		FIND MY WAY BACK HOME/DEVIL-IN-LAW . . .	1.75	3.00
☐ 13357	*MGM*	LITTLE BIRD/WATCHA GONNA DO	1.50	3.00
☐ 13406		I KNOW HOW IT FEELS TO BE LOVED/ SOON FORGOTTEN	1.75	3.00
☐ 13483		THE HARD WAY/UPSIDE DOWN	1.75	3.00

NASHVILLE TEENS—ALBUMS

☐ 407 (S)	*LONDON*	TOBACCO ROAD	7.00	18.00

ISSUE #	LABEL		PRICE RANGE	

RICKY NELSON

ISSUE #	LABEL		PRICE	RANGE
☐ 10047	*VERVE*	A TEENAGER'S ROMANCE/I'M WALKIN'	3.50	6.00
☐ 10070		YOU'RE MY ONE AND ONLY LOVE/		
		HONEY ROCK	4.00	7.00
☐ 5463	*IMPERIAL*	BE BOP BABY/HAVE I TOLD YOU LATELY		
		THAT I LOVE YOU?	2.25	4.00
☐ 5463		BE BOP BABY/HAVE I TOLD YOU LATELY		
		THAT I LOVE YOU?	3.50	6.00
☐ 5483		STOOD UP/WAITIN' IN SCHOOL	2.25	4.00
☐ 5503		BELIEVE WHAT YOU SAY/		
		MY BUCKET'S GOT A HOLE IN IT	2.25	4.00
☐ 5528		POOR LITTLE FOOL/		
		DON'T LEAVE ME THIS WAY	2.25	4.00
☐ 5545		LONESOME TOWN/I GOT A FEELING	2.25	4.00
☐ 5565		NEVER BE ANYONE ELSE BUT YOU/		
		IT'S LATE	2.25	4.00
☐ 5595		SWEETER THAN YOU/		
		JUST A LITTLE TOO MUCH	2.25	4.00
☐ 5614		I WANNA BE LOVED/MIGHTY GOOD	2.00	3.50
☐ 5663		YOUNG EMOTIONS/RIGHT BY MY SIDE	2.00	3.50
☐ 5685		I'M NOT AFRAID/		
		YES SIR, THAT'S MY BABY	2.00	3.50
☐ 5707		YOU ARE THE ONLY ONE/		
		MILK COW BLUES	2.00	3.50
☐ 5741		TRAVELIN' MAN/HELLO MARY LOU	2.00	3.50
☐ 5770		A WONDER LIKE YOU/EVERLOVIN'	2.00	3.50
☐ 5805		YOUNG WORLD/SUMMERTIME	2.00	3.50
☐ 5864		TEEN AGE IDOL/I'VE GOT MY EYES ON YOU	2.00	3.50
☐ 5901		IT'S UP TO YOU/I NEED YOU	2.00	3.50
☐ 5910		THAT'S ALL/I'M IN LOVE AGAIN	2.00	3.50
☐ 5935		OLD ENOUGH TO LOVE/		
		IF YOU CAN'T ROCK ME	2.00	3.50
☐ 5958		A LONG VACATION/MAD, MAD WORLD	2.00	3.50
☐ 5985		TIME AFTER TIME/THERE'S NOT A MINUTE	2.00	3.50
☐ 66004		TODAY'S TEARDROPS/		
		THANK YOU DARLIN'	2.00	3.50
☐ 66017		CONGRATULATIONS/ONE MINUTE TO ONE	2.00	3.50
☐ 66039		LUCKY STAR/EVERYBODY BUT ME	2.00	3.50
☐ 31475	*DECCA*	YOU DON'T LOVE ME ANYMORE/		
		I GOT A WOMAN	2.00	3.50
☐ 31495		STRING ALONG/GYPSY WOMAN	1.75	3.00
☐ 31533		FOOLS RUSH IN/DOWN HOME	1.75	3.00
☐ 31574		FOR YOU/THAT'S ALL SHE WROTE	1.75	3.00
☐ 31612		THE VERY THOUGHT OF YOU/I WONDER	1.75	3.00
☐ 31656		THERE'S NOTHING I CAN SAY/		
		LONELY CORNER	1.75	3.00

ISSUE #	LABEL		PRICE RANGE	
RICKY NELSON—EPs				
☐ 5048	*VERVE*	RICKY	15.00	25.00
☐ 153	*IMPERIAL*	RICKY	8.50	15.00
☐ 154		RICKY	8.50	15.00
☐ 155		RICKY	8.50	15.00
☐ 156		RICKY NELSON	7.25	12.00
☐ 157		RICKY NELSON	7.25	12.00
☐ 158		RICKY NELSON	7.25	12.00
☐ 159		RICKY SINGS AGAIN	6.00	11.00
☐ 160		RICKY SINGS AGAIN	6.00	11.00
☐ 161		RICKY SINGS AGAIN	6.00	11.00
☐ 162		SONGS BY RICKY	5.00	10.00
☐ 163		SONGS BY RICKY	5.00	10.00
☐ 164		SONGS BY RICKY	5.00	10.00
☐ 165		RICKY SINGS SPIRITUALS	4.50	9.00
RICKY NELSON—ALBUMS				
☐ 2083 (M)	*VERVE*	TEEN TIME	25.00	60.00
☐ 9048 (M)	*IMPERIAL*	RICKY	15.00	35.00
☐ 9050 (M)		RICKY NELSON	10.00	25.00
☐ 9061 (M)		RICKY SINGS AGAIN	10.00	25.00
☐ 9082 (M)		SONGS BY RICKY	10.00	25.00
☐ 9122 (M)		MORE SONGS BY RICKY	8.00	22.50
☐ 9152 (M)		RICK IS 21	8.00	22.50
☐ 9167 (M)		ALBUM SEVEN BY RICK	8.00	22.50
☐ 9218 (M)		BEST SELLERS	7.00	18.00
☐ 9223 (M)		IT'S UP TO YOU	7.00	18.00
☐ 9232 (M)		MILLION SELLERS	7.00	18.00
☐ 9244 (M)		A LONG VACATION	7.00	18.00
☐ 9251 (M)		RICK NELSON SINGS FOR YOU	7.00	18.00
☐ 74419 (S)	*DECCA*	FOR YOUR SWEET LOVE	7.00	18.00
☐ 74479 (S)		RICK NELSON SINGS FOR YOU	7.00	18.00
☐ 74459 (S)		THE VERY THOUGHT OF YOU	7.00	18.00
☐ 74608 (S)		SPOTLIGHT ON RICK	7.00	18.00
☐ 74660 (S)		BEST ALWAYS	7.00	18.00
☐ 74678 (S)		LOVE AND KISSES	7.00	18.00
☐ 74779 (S)		BRIGHT LIGHTS AND COUNTRY MUSIC	7.00	18.00
☐ 74837 (S)		COUNTRY FEVER	7.00	18.00
☐ 74944 (S)		ANOTHER SIDE OF RICK	7.00	18.00
☐ 75014 (S)		PERSPECTIVE	6.00	15.00
☐ 75162 (S)		RICK NELSON IN CONCERT	5.00	13.50
☐ 75236 (S)		RICK SINGS NELSON	5.00	13.50
☐ 75297 (S)		RUDY THE FIFTH	5.00	13.50
☐ 75391 (S)		GARDEN PARTY	5.00	13.50
☐ 3830 (S)	*MCA*	WINDFALL	5.00	13.50
☐ 4004 (S)		RICK NELSON COUNTRY	5.00	13.50

RICKY NELSON

— O —

ISSUE #	LABEL		PRICE RANGE	

ROY ORBISON

ISSUE #	LABEL		PRICE RANGE	
☐ 101	**JE-WEL**	OOBY DOOBY/TRYING TO GET TO YOU	150.00	250.00
☐ 7381	**RCA**	SWEET AND INNOCENT/SEEMS TO ME	7.25	12.00
☐ 7447		ALMOST EIGHTEEN/JOLIE	7.25	12.00
☐ 409	**MONUMENT**	PAPER BOY/WITH THE BUG	3.50	6.00
☐ 412		UP TOWN/PRETTY ONE	2.25	4.00
☐ 421		ONLY THE LONELY/		
		HERE COMES THAT SONG AGAIN	2.00	3.50
☐ 425		BLUE ANGEL/TODAY'S TEARDROPS	2.00	3.50
☐ 433		I'M HURTIN'/I CAN'T STOP LOVING YOU	2.00	3.50
☐ 438		RUNNING SCARED/LOVE HURTS	1.75	3.30
☐ 447		CRYING/CANDY MAN	1.75	3.70
☐ 456		DREAM BABY/THE ACTRESS	1.75	3.50
☐ 461		THE CROWD/MAMA	1.75	3.50
☐ 467		LEAH/WORKIN' FOR THE MAN	1.75	3.50
☐ 806		IN DREAMS/SHAHDAROBA	1.75	3.50
☐ 815		FALLING/DISTANT DRUMS	1.75	3.50
☐ 824		MEAN WOMAN BLUES/BLUE BAYOU	1.75	3.50
☐ 830		PRETTY PAPER/BEAUTIFUL DREAMER	1.75	3.50
☐ 837		IT'S OVER/INDIAN WEDDING	1.75	3.50
☐ 861		OH, PRETTY WOMAN/YO TE AMO MARIA	1.75	3.50
☐ 873		GOODNIGHT/ONLY WITH YOU	1.75	3.50
☐ 891		(SAY) YOU'RE MY GIRL/SLEEPY HOLLOW	1.75	3.50
☐ 906		LET THE GOOD TIMES ROLL/		
		DISTANT DRUMS	1.75	3.50
☐ 939		LANA/OUR SUMMER SONG	1.75	3.50
☐ 8690		BELINDA/NO CHAIN AT ALL	1.75	3.50
☐ 200		(I'M A) SOUTHERN MAN/		
		BORN TO LOVE ME	1.75	3.50
☐ 215		DRIFTING AWAY/UNDER SUSPICION	1.75	3.50
☐ 11386	**MGM**	RIDE AWAY/WONDERING	1.50	2.50
☐ 13410		CRAWLING BACK/		
		IF YOU CAN'T SAY SOMETHING NICE	1.50	2.50
☐ 13446		BREAKIN' UP IS BREAKIN' MY HEART/		
		WAIT	1.50	2.50
☐ 13498		TWINKLE TOES/WHERE IS TOMORROW?	1.50	2.50
☐ 13549		TOO SOON TO KNOW/		
		YOU'LL NEVER BE SIXTEEN AGAIN	1.50	2.50
☐ 13634		COMMUNICATION BREAKDOWN/		
		GOING BACK TO GLORIA	1.50	2.50
☐ 13685		MEMORIES/SO GOOD	1.50	2.50
☐ 13759		SWEET DREAMS/GOING BACK TO GLORIA	1.50	2.50

ISSUE #	LABEL		PRICE RANGE	

ROY ORBISON—ALBUMS

☐ 1260 (M)	*SUN*	ROY ORBISON AT THE ROCKHOUSE	30.00	60.00
☐ 14007 (S)				
	MONUMENT	CRYING	17.50	35.00
☐ 14009 (S)		GREATEST HITS	15.00	35.00
☐ 18003 (S)		IN DREAMS	15.00	35.00
☐ 18023 (S)		EARLY ORBISON	12.50	30.00
☐ 18024 (S)		MORE OF ROY ORBISON'S GREATEST HITS	12.50	30.00
☐ 18035 (S)		ORBISONGS	12.50	30.00
☐ 18045 (S)		THE VERY BEST OF ROY ORBISON	10.00	25.00
☐ 4308 (S)		THERE IS ONLY ONE ROY ORBISON	8.00	22.50
☐ 4322 (S)		THE ORBISON WAY	8.00	22.50
☐ 4379 (S)		CLASSIC ROY ORBISON	6.00	15.00
☐ 4424 (S)		ROY ORBISON SINGS DON GIBSON	6.00	15.00
☐ 4514 (S)		CRY SOFTLY, LONELY ONE	6.00	15.00
☐ 4683 (S)		HANK WILLIAMS THE ROY ORBISON WAY	4.50	12.00
☐ 4835 (S)		ROY ORBISON SINGS	4.50	12.00
☐ 4934 (S)		MILESTONES	4.50	12.00

TONY ORLANDO

☐ 101	*MILO*	DING DONG/YOU AND ONLY YOU	15.00	25.00
☐ 9441	*EPIC*	HALFWAY TO PARADISE/ LONELY TOMORROWS	2.00	3.50
☐ 9452		BLESS YOU/AM I THE GUY	2.00	3.50
☐ 9476		HAPPY TIMES ARE HERE TO STAY/ LONELY AM I	2.00	3.50
☐ 9491		MY BABY'S A STRANGER/ TALKIN' ABOUT YOU	2.00	3.50
☐ 9502		LOVE ON YOUR LIPS/ I'D NEVER FIND ANOTHER YOU	2.00	3.50
☐ 9519		CHILLS/AT THE EDGE OF TEARS	2.00	3.50
☐ 9562		THE LONELIEST/BEAUTIFUL DREAMER	2.00	3.50
☐ 9570		SHIRLEY/JOANIE	2.00	3.50
☐ 9622		I'LL BE THERE/WHAT AM I GONNA DO?	2.00	3.50
☐ 9668		SHE DOESN'T KNOW ME/ TELL ME, WHAT CAN I DO?	2.00	3.50
☐ 9715		TO WAIT FOR LOVE/ACCEPTED	2.00	3.50
☐ 6376	*ATCO*	THINK BEFORE YOU ACT/SHE LOVES ME (FOR WHAT I AM)	2.00	3.50
☐ 471	*CAMEO*	SWEET, SWEET/MANUELITO	2.00	3.50

TONY ORLANDO—ALBUM

☐ 611 (S)	*EPIC*	BLESS YOU	15.00	35.00

— P —

ISSUE #	LABEL		PRICE RANGE	

DOLLY PARTON

☐ 1086	**GOLDBAND**	PUPPY LOVE/GIRL LEFT ALONE	15.00	25.00
☐ 71982	**MERCURY**	IT'S SURE GONNA HURT/		
		THE LOVE YOU GAVE	10.00	18.00
☐ 869	**MONUMENT**	I WASTED MY TEARS/		
		WHAT DO YOU THINK ABOUT LOVIN'	4.00	7.00
☐ 897		HAPPY, HAPPY BIRTHDAY BABY/		
		OLD ENOUGH TO KNOW BETTER	4.00	7.00
☐ 913		BUSY SIGNAL/I TOOK HIM FOR GRANTED	4.00	7.00
☐ 922		CONTROL YOURSELF/DON'T DROP OUT	4.00	7.00
☐ 948		LITTLE THINGS/		
		I'LL PUT IT OFF UNTIL TOMORROW	4.00	7.00
☐ 982		DUMB BLONDE/		
		THE GIVING AND THE TAKING	3.50	6.00
☐ 1007		SOMETHING FISHY/I'VE LIVED MY LIFE	3.50	6.00
☐ 1032		I COULDN'T WAIT FOREVER/		
		WHY, WHY, WHY	3.50	6.00
☐ 1047		I'M NOT WORTH THE TEARS/PING PONG	3.50	6.00

DOLLY PARTON—ALBUMS

☐ 8085 (S)				
	MONUMENT	HELLO, I'M DOLLY!	10.00	25.00
☐ 8136 (S)		AS LONG AS I LOVE	10.00	25.00

PAUL AND PAULA

☐ 40084	**PHILIPS**	HEY PAULA/BOBBY IS THE ONE	1.75	3.00
☐ 40096		YOUNG LOVERS/BA-HAY-BE	1.75	3.00
☐ 40114		FIRST QUARREL/SCHOOL IS THRU	1.75	3.00
☐ 40130		SOMETHING OLD, SOMETHING, NEW/		
		FLIPPED OVER YOU	1.75	3.00
☐ 40158		HOLIDAY FOR TEENS/		
		HOLIDAY HOOTENANNY	1.75	3.00
☐ 40168		CRAZY LITTLE THINGS/		
		WE'LL NEVER BREAK UP FOR GOOD	1.75	3.00
☐ 40209		DARLIN'/THE YOUNG YEARS	1.75	3.00
☐ 40234		NO OTHER BABY/TOO DARK TO SEE	1.75	3.00
☐ 40268		TRUE LOVE/ANY WAY YOU WANT ME	1.75	3.00
☐ 40296		DEAR PAUL/ALL THE LOVE	1.75	3.00
☐ 40352		ALL I WANT IS YOU/		
		THE BEGINNING OF LOVE	1.75	3.00

ISSUE #	LABEL		PRICE RANGE	

PAUL AND PAULA—ALBUMS

☐ 600078 (S)	*PHILIPS*	PAUL AND PAULA SING FOR YOUNG LOVERS	8.00	22.50
☐ 600101 (S)		HOLIDAY FOR TEENS	8.00	22.50

CARL PERKINS

☐ 501	*FLIP*	MOVIE MAGG/TURN AROUND	180.00	300.00
☐ 224	*SUN*	LET THE JUKE BOX KEEP ON PLAYING/ GONE GONE GONE	30.00	48.00
☐ 234		BLUE SUEDE SHOES/HONEY DON'T	4.00	7.00
☐ 243		BOPPIN' THE BLUES/ ALL MAMA'S CHILDREN	3.50	6.00
☐ 249		DIXIE FRIED/I'M SORRY I'M NOT SORRY	3.50	6.00
☐ 261		YOUR TRUE LOVE/MATCHBOX	3.50	6.00
☐ 274		FOREVER YOURS/THAT'S RIGHT	3.50	6.00
☐ 287		GLAD ALL OVER/LEND ME YOUR COMB	3.50	6.00
☐ 41131	*COLUMBIA*	PINK PEDAL PUSHERS/JIVE AFTER FIVE	3.50	6.00
☐ 41207		LEVI JACKET/POP, LET ME HAVE THE CAR	3.50	6.00
☐ 41296		Y-O-U/THIS LIFE I LEAD	3.50	6.00
☐ 41379		POINTED TOE SHOES/HIGHWAY OF LOVE	3.50	6.00
☐ 41449		ONE TICKET TO LONELINESS/I DON'T SEE ME IN YOUR ARMS ANYMORE	2.75	4.50
☐ 41651		L-O-V-E-V-I-L-L-E/TOO MUCH FOR A MAN TO UNDERSTAND	2.75	4.50
☐ 41825		JUST FOR YOU/ HONEY, 'CAUSE I LOVE YOU	2.75	4.50
☐ 42061		ANY WAY THE WIND BLOWS/ THE UNHAPPY GIRLS	2.75	4.50
☐ 42405		HOLLYWOOD CITY/THE FOOL I USED TO BE	2.75	4.50
☐ 42514		TWISTER SISTER/HAMBONE	2.25	4.00
☐ 42753		FORGET ME NEXT TIME AROUND/ I JUST GOT BACK FROM THERE	2.25	4.00
☐ 44883		FOR YOUR LOVE/FOUR LETTER WORD	2.25	4.00
☐ 45107		ALL MAMA'S CHILDREN/STEP ASIDE	2.00	3.50
☐ 45253		WHAT EVERY LITTLE BOY OUGHT TO KNOW/JUST AS LONG	2.00	3.50
☐ 45347		ME WITHOUT YOU/RED HEADED WOMAN	2.00	3.50
☐ 45466		COTTON TOP/ ABOUT ALL I CAN GIVE YOU IS LOVE	2.00	3.50
☐ 45582		TAKE ME BACK TO MEMPHIS/ HIGH ON LOVE	2.00	3.50
☐ 45694		SOMEDAY/THE TRIP	2.00	3.50
☐ 31548	*DECCA*	HELP ME FIND MY BABY/ FOR A LITTLE WHILE	2.00	3.50

ISSUE #	LABEL		PRICE	RANGE
☐ 31591		AFTER SUNDOWN/I WOULDN'T HAVE YOU ...	2.00	3.50
☐ 31709		LET MY BABY BE/THE MONKEYSHINE	2.00	3.50
☐ 31786		ONE OF THESE DAYS/MAMA OF MY SONG	2.00	3.50
☐ 505	*DOLLIE*	COUNTRY BOY'S DREAM/		
		IF I COULD COME BACK	2.25	4.00
☐ 508		SHINE, SHINE, SHINE/ALMOST LOVE	2.25	4.00
☐ 512		WITHOUT YOU/YOU CAN TAKE THE BOY		
		OUT OF THE COUNTRY	2.25	4.00
☐ 514		BACK TO TENNESSEE/		
		MY OLD HOME TOWN	2.25	4.00

CARL PERKINS—EPs

☐ 115	*SUN*	CARL PERKINS	20.00	36.00
☐ 12341	*COLUMBIA*	WHOLE LOTTA SHAKIN'	18.00	30.00

CARL PERKINS—ALBUMS

☐ 1225 (M)	*SUN*	DANCE ALBUM	80.00	180.00
☐ 1225 (M)		TEEN BEAT-THE BEST OF CARL PERKINS	60.00	150.00
☐ 1234 (M)				
	COLUMBIA	WHOLE LOTTA SHAKIN'	35.00	90.00
☐ 4001 (M)	*DOLLIE*	COUNTRY BOY'S DREAM	8.00	22.50
☐ 1691 (S)	*MERCURY*	MY KIND OF COUNTRY	4.50	12.00

PETER AND GORDON

☐ 5175	*CAPITOL*	A WORLD WITHOUT LOVE/IF I WERE YOU	1.75	3.00
☐ 5211		NOBODY I KNOW/		
		YOU DON'T HAVE TO TELL ME	1.75	3.00
☐ 5272		I DON'T WANT TO SEE YOU AGAIN/		
		I WOULD BUY YOU PRESENTS	1.75	3.00
☐ 5335		I GO TO PIECES/LOVE ME BABY	1.75	3.00
☐ 5406		TRUE LOVE WAYS/IF YOU WISH	1.75	3.00
☐ 5461		TO KNOW YOU IS TO LOVE YOU/		
		I TOLD YOU SO	1.75	3.00
☐ 5532		DON'T PITY ME/CRYING IN THE RAIN	1.75	3.00
☐ 5579		WOMAN/WRONG FROM THE START	1.75	3.00
☐ 5650		THERE'S NO LIVING WITHOUT YOUR		
		LOVING/STRANGER WITH A		
		BLACK DOVE	1.75	3.00
☐ 5684		TO SHOW I LOVE YOU/		
		START TRYING SOMEONE ELSE	1.75	3.00
☐ 5740		LADY GODIVA/YOU'VE HAD BETTER TIMES ..	1.75	3.00
☐ 5808		KNIGHT IN RUSTY ARMOR/FLOWER LADY	1.75	3.00
☐ 5864		SUNDAY FOR TEA/HURTIN' IS LOVIN'	1.75	3.00
☐ 5919		THE JOKERS/RED, CREAM AND VELVET	1.75	3.00
☐ 2071		NEVER EVER/GREENER DAYS	1.75	3.00

CARL PERKINS

ISSUE #	LABEL		PRICE RANGE	
☐ 2214		SIPPIN' MY WINE/		
		YOU'VE HAD BETTER DAYS	1.75	3.00
☐ 2544		I CAN REMEMBER/		
		HARD TIMES, RAINY DAY	1.75	3.00

PETER AND GORDON—ALBUMS

☐ 2115 (S)	*CAPITOL*	A WORLD WITHOUT LOVE	7.00	18.00
☐ 2220 (S)		I DON'T WANT TO SEE YOU AGAIN	7.00	18.00
☐ 2324 (S)		I GO TO PIECES	7.00	18.00
☐ 2368 (S)		TRUE LOVE WAYS	7.00	18.00
☐ 2430 (S)		PETER AND GORDON SING AND PLAY THE		
		HITS OF NASHVILLE, TENNESSEE	7.00	18.00
☐ 2477 (S)		WOMAN	6.00	15.00
☐ 2549 (S)		THE BEST OF PETER AND GORDON	6.00	15.00
☐ 2664 (S)		LADY GODIVA	6.00	15.00
☐ 2729 (S)		KNIGHT IN RUSTY ARMOR	6.00	15.00
☐ 2747 (S)		IN LONDON FOR TEA	5.00	13.50
☐ 2882 (S)		HOT, COLD AND CUSTARD	4.50	12.00

WILSON PICKETT

☐ 501	*CORRECTONE*	MY HEART BELONGS TO YOU/		
		LET ME BE YOUR BOY	7.25	12.00
☐ 9113	*CUB*	MY HEART BELONGS TO YOU/		
		LET ME BE YOUR BOY	4.50	9.00
☐ 713	*DOUBLE L*	IF YOU NEED ME/BABY CALL ON ME	2.25	4.00
☐ 717		IT'S TOO LATE/I'M GONNA LOVE YOU	2.25	4.00
☐ 724		I'M DOWN TO MY LAST HEARTBREAK/		
		I CAN'T STOP	2.25	4.00

WILSON PICKETT—ALBUM

☐ 2300 (M)	*DOUBLE L*	IT'S TOO LATE	8.00	22.50

PINK FLOYD

☐ 333	*TOWER*	ARNOLD LAYNE/		
		CANDY AND A CURRANT BUN	3.50	6.00
☐ 356		SEE EMILY PLAY/SCARECROW	3.50	6.00
☐ 378		THE GNONE/FLAMING	3.50	6.00
☐ 440		LET THERE BE MORE LIGHT/		
		REMEMBER A DAY	3.50	6.00
☐ 3391	*CAPITOL*	STAY/FREE FOUR	2.75	4.50
☐ 3609	*HARVEST*	MONEY/ANY COLOUR YOU LIKE	1.75	3.00
☐ 3832		US AND THEM/TIME	1.75	3.00

ISSUE #	LABEL		PRICE RANGE	

ELVIS PRESLEY

☐ 209	*SUN*	THAT'S ALL RIGHT/		
		BLUE MOON OF KENTUCKY	180.00	300.00
☐ 210		GOOD ROCKIN' TONIGHT/I DON'T CARE		
		IF THE SUN DON'T SHINE	150.00	250.00
☐ 215		MILKCOW BLUES BOOGIE/		
		YOU'RE A HEARTBREAKER	225.00	350.00
☐ 217		BABY LET'S PLAY HOUSE/		
		I'M LEFT, YOUR RIGHT, SHE'S GONE	120.00	220.00
☐ 223		MYSTERY TRAIN/		
		I FORGOT TO REMEMBER TO FORGET	120.00	220.00
☐ 6357	*RCA*	MYSTERY TRAIN/		
		I FORGOT TO REMEMBER TO FORGET	12.00	20.00
☐ 6380		THAT'S ALL RIGHT/		
		BLUE MOON OF KENTUCKY	12.00	20.00
☐ 6381		GOOD ROCKIN' TONIGHT/I DON'T CARE		
		IF THE SUN DON'T SHINE	12.00	20.00
☐ 6382		MILKCOW BLUES BOOGIE/		
		YOU'RE A HEARTBREAKER	12.00	20.00
☐ 6383		BABY LET'S PLAY HOUSE/		
		I'M LEFT, YOU'RE RIGHT, SHE'S GONE	12.00	20.00
☐ 6420		HEARTBREAK HOTEL/I WAS THE ONE	4.00	7.00
☐ 6540		I WANT YOU, I NEED YOU, I LOVE YOU/		
		MY BABY LEFT ME	4.00	7.00
☐ 6604		DON'T BE CRUEL/HOUND DOG	4.00	7.00
☐ 6636		BLUE SUEDE SHOES/TUTTI FRUITTI	12.00	20.00
☐ 6637		I GOT A WOMAN/I'M COUNTIN' ON YOU	12.00	20.00
☐ 6638		I'M GONNA SIT RIGHT DOWN AND CRY		
		OVER YOU/I'LL NEVER LET YOU GO	12.00	20.00
☐ 6639		TRYIN' TO GET TO YOU/		
		I LOVE YOU BECAUSE	12.00	20.00
☐ 6640		BLUE MOON/JUST BECAUSE	12.00	20.00
☐ 6641		MONEY HONEY/ONE-SIDED LOVE AFFAIR	12.00	20.00
☐ 6642		SHAKE, RATTLE AND ROLL/		
		LAWDY MISS CLAWDY	12.00	20.00
☐ 6643		LOVE ME TENDER/ANYWAY YOU WANT ME ...	3.50	6.00
☐ 6800		TOO MUCH/PLAYING FOR KEEPS	3.50	6.00
☐ 6870		ALL SHOOK UP/THAT'S WHEN		
		YOUR HEARTACHES BEGIN	3.50	6.00
☐ 7000		TEDDY BEAR/LOVING YOU	3.50	6.00
☐ 7035		JAILHOUSE ROCK/TREAT ME NICE	3.50	6.00
☐ 7150		DON'T/I BEG OF YOU	3.50	6.00
☐ 7240		WEAR MY RING AROUND YOUR NECK/		
		DONCHA THINK IT'S TIME	3.50	6.00

ISSUE #	LABEL	PRICE RANGE	
☐7280	HARD HEADED WOMAN/		
	DON'T ASK ME WHY	3.50	6.00
☐7410	ONE NIGHT/I GOT STUNG	3.50	6.00
☐7506	A FOOL SUCH AS I/		
	I NEED YOUR LOVE TONIGHT	2.75	4.50
☐7600	A BIG HUNK O' LOVE/		
	MY WISH CAME TRUE	2.75	4.50
☐7740	STUCK ON YOU/FAME AND FORTUNE	2.25	4.00
☐7740	STUCK ON YOU/FAME AND FORTUNE	60.00	110.00
☐7777	IT'S NOW OR NEVER/A MESS OF BLUES	2.25	4.00
☐7777	IT'S NOW OR NEVER/A MESS OF BLUES	60.00	110.00
☐7810	ARE YOU LONESOME TONIGHT?/		
	I GOTTA KNOW	2.25	4.00
☐7810	ARE YOU LONESOME TONIGHT?/		
	I GOTTA KNOW	60.00	110.00
☐7850	SURRENDER/LONELY MAN	2.25	4.00
☐7850	SURRENDER/LONELY MAN	85.00	150.00
☐7880	I FEEL SO BAD/WILD IN THE COUNTRY	2.25	4.00
☐7880	I FEEL SO BAD/WILD IN THE COUNTRY	85.00	150.00
☐098	HIS LATEST FLAME/LITTLE SISTER	2.00	3.50
☐7968	CAN'T HELP FALLING IN LOVE/		
	ROCK-A-HULA-BABY	2.00	3.50
☐7992	GOOD LUCK CHARM/		
	ANYTHING THAT'S A PART OF YOU	2.00	3.50
☐8041	SHE'S NOT YOU/		
	JUST TELL HER JIM SAID HELLO	2.00	3.50
☐8100	RETURN TO SENDER/		
	WHERE DO YOU COME FROM?	2.00	3.50
☐8134	ONE BROKEN HEART FOR SALE/		
	THEY REMIND ME TOO MUCH OF YOU	2.00	3.50
☐8188	DEVIL IN DISGUISE/PLEASE		
	DON'T DRAG THAT STING AROUND	2.00	3.50
☐8234	KISSIN' COUSINS/IT HURTS ME	2.00	3.50
☐8360	WHAT'D I SAY/VIVA LAS VEGAS	2.00	3.50
☐8400	SUCH A NIGHT/NEVER ENDING	2.00	3.50
☐8440	ASK ME/AIN'T THAT LOVING YOU BABY	2.00	3.50
☐8500	DO THE CLAM/YOU'LL BE GONE	2.00	3.50
☐8585	(SUCH AN) EASY QUESTION/		
	IT FEELS SO RIGHT	2.00	3.50
☐8740	TELL ME WHY/BLUE RIDER	2.00	3.50
☐8780	FRANKIE AND JOHNNY/		
	PLEASE DON'T STOP LOVING ME	2.00	3.50
☐8870	LOVE LETTERS/COME WHAT MAY	2.00	3.50
☐8941	IF EVERY DAY WAS LIKE CHRISTMAS/		
	HOW WOULD YOU LIKE TO BE	3.50	6.00

ELVIS PRESLEY

ISSUE #	LABEL		PRICE RANGE	
☐ 9056		INDESCRIBABLY BLUE/		
		FOOLS FALL IN LOVE	2.00	3.50
☐ 9115		LONG LEGGED GIRL/		
		THAT'S SOMEONE YOU NEVER FORGET	2.00	3.50
☐ 9287		THERE'S ALWAYS ME/JUDY	2.00	3.50
☐ 9341		BIG BOSS MAN/YOU DON'T KNOW ME	2.00	3.50
☐ 94258		GUITAR MAN/HIGH HEELED SNEAKERS	2.00	3.50
☐ 9465		U.S. MALE/STAY AWAY JOE	2.00	3.50
☐ 9547		LET YOURSELF GO/		
		YOUR TIME HASN'T COME YET BABY	2.00	3.50
☐ 9600		YOU'LL NEVER WALK ALONE/		
		WE CALL ON HIM	2.00	3.50
☐ 9610		A LITTLE LESS CONVERSATION/		
		ALMOST IN LOVE	2.00	3.50

ELVIS PRESLEY—EPs

☐ 1254	*RCA*	ELVIS PRESLEY	85.00	150.00
☐ 747		ELVIS PRESLEY	10.00	18.00
☐ 821		HEARTBREAK HOTEL	12.00	20.00
☐ 830		ELVIS PRESLEY	12.00	20.00
☐ 940		THE REAL ELVIS	12.00	20.00
☐ 965		ANYWAY YOU WANT ME	12.00	20.00
☐ 4006		LOVE ME TENDER	10.00	18.00
☐ 992		ELVIS, VOL. I	10.00	18.00
☐ 993		ELVIS, VOL. II	12.00	20.00
☐ 994		STRICTLY ELVIS	12.00	20.00
☐ 1-1515		LOVING YOU, VOL. I	12.00	20.00
☐ 2-1515		LOVING YOU, VOL. II	12.00	20.00
☐ 4041		JUST FOR YOU	12.00	20.00
☐ 4054		PEACE IN THE VALLEY	10.00	18.00
☐ 4108		ELVIS SINGS CHRISTMAS SONGS	12.00	20.00
☐ 4114		JAILHOUSE ROCK	12.00	20.00
☐ 4319		KING CREOLE, VOL. I	12.00	20.00
☐ 4321		KING CREOLE, VOL. II	12.00	20.00
☐ 4325		ELVIS SAILS	24.00	42.00
☐ 4340		CHRISTMAS WITH ELVIS	12.00	20.00
☐ 4368		FOLLOW THAT DREAM	7.25	12.00
☐ 4371		KID GALAHAD	7.25	12.00
☐ 4382		EASY COME, EASY GO	8.50	15.00
☐ 4383		TICKLE ME	8.50	15.00
☐ 5088		A TOUCH OF GOLD, VOL. I	30.00	48.00
☐ 5088		A TOUCH OF GOLD, VOL. I	10.00	18.00
☐ 5120		THE REAL ELVIS	30.00	48.00
☐ 5120		THE REAL ELVIS	8.50	12.00
☐ 5121		PEACE IN THE VALLEY	30.00	48.00
☐ 5151		PEACE IN THE VALLEY	8.50	12.00

ISSUE #	LABEL		PRICE RANGE	
☐ 5122		KING CREOLE, VOL. I	30.00	48.00
☐ 5122		KING CREOLE, VOL. I	8.50	12.00
☐ 5101		A TOUCH OF GOLD, VOL. II	30.00	48.00
☐ 5101		A TOUCH OF GOLD, VOL. II	10.00	18.00
☐ 5141		A TOUCH OF GOLD, VOL. III	30.00	48.00
☐ 5141		A TOUCH OF GOLD, VOL. III	10.00	18.00
☐ 5157		ELVIS SAILS	36.00	60.00
☐ 5157		ELVIS SAILS	10.00	18.00

ELVIS PRESLEY-ALBUMS

ISSUE #	LABEL		PRICE RANGE	
☐ 1254 (M)	*RCA*	ELVIS PRESLEY	20.00	50.00
☐ 1382 (M)		ELVIS	20.00	50.00
☐ 1515 (M)		LOVING YOU	15.00	35.00
☐ 1035 (M)		ELVIS' CHRISTMAS ALBUM	70.00	180.00
☐ 1707 (M)		ELVIS' GOLDEN RECORDS	15.00	35.00
☐ 1884 (M)		KING CREOLE	15.00	35.00
☐ 1951 (M)		ELVIS' CHRISTMAS ALBUM	15.00	35.00
☐ 1990 (M)		FOR LP FANS ONLY	20.00	50.00
☐ 2011 (M)		A DATE WITH ELVIS	30.00	75.00
☐ 2011 (M)		A DATE WITH ELVIS	15.00	35.00
☐ 2075 (M)		ELVIS' GOLDEN RECORDS, VOL. II	15.00	35.00
☐ 2231 (M)		ELVIS IS BACK	15.00	35.00
☐ 2256 (M)		G.I. BLUES	15.00	35.00
☐ 2328 (M)		HIS HAND IN MINE	10.00	25.00
☐ 2370 (M)		SOMETHING FOR EVERYBODY	15.00	35.00
☐ 2436 (M)		BLUE HAWAII	15.00	35.00
☐ 2523 (M)		POT LUCK	15.00	35.00
☐ 2621 (M)		GIRLS! GIRLS! GIRLS!	15.00	35.00
☐ 2697 (M)		IT HAPPENED AT THE WORLD'S FAIR	15.00	35.00
☐ 2697 (M)		FUN IN ACAPULCO	12.50	30.00
☐ 2765 (M)		ELVIS' GOLDEN RECORDS, VOL. III	12.50	30.00
☐ 2894 (M)		KISSIN' COUSINS	12.50	30.00
☐ 2999 (M)		ROUSTABOUT	12.50	30.00
☐ 3338 (M)		GIRL HAPPY	12.50	30.00
☐ 3450 (M)		ELVIS FOR EVERYONE	12.50	30.00
☐ 3468 (M)		HARUM SCARUM	17.50	45.00
☐ 3553 (M)		FRANKIE AND JOHNNY	15.00	35.00
☐ 3643 (M)		PARADISE, HAWAIIAN STYLE	12.50	30.00
☐ 3702 (M)		SPINOUT	15.00	35.00
☐ 3758 (M)		HOW GREAT THOU ART	12.50	30.00
☐ 3787 (M)		DOUBLE TROUBLE	12.50	30.00
☐ 3893 (M)		CLAMBAKE	35.00	90.00
☐ 3893 (S)		CLAMBAKE	15.00	35.00
☐ 3921 (M)		ELVIS' GOLDEN RECORDS, VOL. IV	80.00	225.00
☐ 3921 (S)		ELVIS' GOLDEN RECORDS, VOL. IV	15.00	35.00
☐ 3989 (M)		SPEEDWAY	300.00	750.00

— Q —

ISSUE #	LABEL		PRICE	RANGE

SUZI QUATRO

ISSUE #	LABEL		PRICE	RANGE
☐ 4512	*RAK*	ROLLING STONE/BRAIN CONFUSION	6.00	11.00
☐ 45477		ALL SHOOK UP/GLYCERINE QUEEN	2.00	3.50
☐ 45609		DEVIL GATE DRIVE/IN THE MORNING	2.25	4.00
☐ 16053	*BIG TREE*	CAN THE CAN/DON'T MESS AROUND	2.00	3.50
☐ 0106	*ARISTA*	YOUR MAMA WON'T LIKE ME/		
		PETER, PETER	2.00	3.50

SUZI QUATRO—ALBUMS

☐ 1302 (S)	*BELL*	SUZI QUATRO	6.00	15.00
☐ 1313 (S)		QUATRO	6.00	15.00
☐ 4035 (S)	*ARISTA*	YOUR MAMA WON'T LIKE ME	5.00	13.50

? AND THE MYSTERIANS

☐ 102	*PA-GO-GO*	96 TEARS/MIDNIGHT HOUR...........	24.00	42.00
☐ 441		I NEED SOMEBODY/"8" TEEN	8.50	15.00
☐ 467		CAN'T GET ENOUGH OF YOU, BABY/		
		SMOKES	4.50	9.00
☐ 479		GIRL (YOU CAPTIVATE ME)/GOT TO ...	4.50	9.00
☐ 496		DO SOMETHING TO ME/LOVE ME BABY	4.50	9.00
☐ 428	*CAMEO*	96 TEARS/MIDNIGHT HOUR	1.75	3.00
☐ 441		I NEED SOMEBODY/"8" TEN	1.75	3.00
☐ 467		CAN'T GET ENOUGH OF YOU, BABY/		
		SMOKES	1.75	3.00
☐ 479		GIRL (YOU CAPTIVATE ME)/GOT TO ...	1.75	3.00
☐ 496		DO SOMETHING TO ME/LOVE ME BABY	1.75	3.00

? AND THE MYSTERIANS—ALBUMS

☐ 2004 (S)	*CAMEO*	96 TEARS	7.00	18.00
☐ 2006 (S)		ACTION	7.00	18.00

— R —

LOU RAWLS

☐ 702	*SHAR-DEE*	MY HEART BELONGS TO YOU/		
		LOVE, LOVE, LOVE	2.75	4.50
☐ 705		KIDDIO/WALKIN' (FOR MILES)	2.75	4.50
☐ 305	*CANDIX*	IN MY LITTLE BLACK BOOK/		
		JUST THOUGHT YOU'D LIKE TO KNOW	2.25	4.00

ISSUE #	LABEL		PRICE RANGE	

PAUL REVERE AND THE RAIDERS

☐ 106	*GARDENA*	BEATNIK STICKS/ORBIT	8.50	15.00
☐ 115		PAUL REVERE'S RIDE/UNFINISHED 5TH	7.25	12.00
☐ 116		LIKE LONG HAIR/SHARON	4.50	9.00
☐ 118		LIKE CHARLESTON/MIDNIGHT RIDE	4.00	7.00
☐ 124		ALL NIGHT LONG/GROOVY	4.00	7.00
☐ 127		LIKE BLUEGRASS/LEATHERNECK	4.00	7.00
☐ 131		SHAKE IT UP (PT. 1)(PT. 2)	4.00	7.00
☐ 137		TALL COOL ONE/ROAD RUNNER	4.00	7.00
☐ 807	*JERDEN*	SO FINE/BLUES STAY AWAY	10.00	18.00
☐ 101	*SANDE*	LOUIE LOUIE/NIGHT TRAIN	7.25	15.00
☐ 42813	*COLUMBIA*	LOUIE LOUIE/NIGHT TRAIN	2.25	4.00
☐ 43008		HAVE LOVE, WILL TRAVEL/ LOUIE GO HOME	2.25	4.00
☐ 43114		OVE YOU/SWIM	2.25	4.00
☐ 43273		OO POO PAH DO/SOMETIMES	2.25	4.00
☐ 43375		STEPPIN' OUT/BLUE FOX	2.00	3.50
☐ 43461		JUST LIKE ME/B.F.D.R.F. BLUES	1.75	3.00
☐ 43356		KICKS/SHAKE IT UP	1.75	3.00
☐ 43678		HUNGRY/THERE SHE GOES	1.75	3.00
☐ 43810		THE GREAT AIRPLANE STRIKE/ IN MY COMMUNITY	1.75	3.00
☐ 43907		GOOD THING/UNDECIDED MAN	1.75	3.00
☐ 44018		UPS AND DOWNS/LESLIE	1.75	3.00
☐ 44094		HIM OR ME-WHAT'S IT GONNA BE/ LEGEND OF PAUL REVERE	1.75	3.00
☐ 44227		I HAD A DREAM/UPON YOUR LEAVING	1.75	3.00
☐ 44335		PEACE OF MIND/DO UNTO OTHERS	1.75	3.00
☐ 44444		TOO MUCH TALK/HAPPENING '68	1.75	3.00

PAUL REVERE AND THE RAIDERS—ALBUMS

☐ 1000 (M)	*GARDENA*	LIKE LONG HAIR	35.00	90.00
☐ 7004 (M)	*JERDEN*	IN THE BEGINNING	8.00	22.50
☐ 1001 (M)	*SANDE*	PAUL REVERE AND THE RAIDERS	45.00	120.00
☐ 9107 (S)		HERE THEY COME	8.00	22.50
☐ 2451 (M)		JUST LIKE US	5.00	13.50
☐ 9251 (S)		JUST LIKE US	8.50	15.00
☐ 9308 (S)		MIDNIGHT RIDE	8.50	15.00
☐ 9395 (S)		THE SPIRIT OF '67	8.50	15.00
☐ 9462 (S)		GREATEST HITS	7.25	12.00
☐ 9521 (S)		REVOLUTION	6.00	11.00
☐ 9555 (S)		A CHRISTMAS PRESENT AND PAST	5.00	9.00
☐ 9605 (S)		GOIN' TO MEMPHIS	5.00	9.00
☐ 9665 (S)		SOMETHING HAPPENING	4.50	9.00
☐ 9753 (S)		HARD AND HEAVY WITH MARSHMALLOW	4.50	9.00
☐ 9905 (S)		ALIAS PINK FUZZ	4.50	9.00

ISSUE #	LABEL		PRICE RANGE	

CHARLIE RICH

☐ 3532	PHILLIPS			
	INTERNATIONAL	WHIRLWIND/PHILADELPHIA BABY	6.00	11.00
☐ 3542		BIG MAN/REBOUND	4.00	7.00
☐ 3552		LONELY WEEKENDS/		
		EVERYTHING I DO IS WRONG	2.25	4.00
☐ 3560		GONNA BE WAITING/SCHOOL DAYS	2.75	4.50
☐ 3562		STAY/ON MY KNEES	2.75	4.50
☐ 3566		WHO WILL THE NEXT FOOL BE?/		
		CAUGHT IN THE MIDDLE	2.75	4.50
☐ 3572		JUST A LITTLE SWEET/IT'S TOO LATE	2.75	4.50
☐ 3584		THERE'S ANOTHER PLACE I CAN'T GO/		
		I NEED YOUR LOVE	2.75	4.50
☐ 580020	GROOVE	SHE LOVED EVERYBODY BUT ME/		
		THE GRASS IS ALWAYS GREENER	2.00	3.50
☐ 580035		THE WAYS OF A WOMAN IN LOVE/		
		MOUNTAIN DEW	2.00	3.50

CHARLIE RICH—ALBUMS

☐ 1970 (M)	PHILLIPS			
	INTERNATIONAL	LONELY WEEKENDS	35.00	90.00
☐ 67070 (S)	SMASH	MANY NEW SIDES OF CHARLIE RICH	7.00	18.00

ROLLING STONES

☐ 9657		NOT FADE AWAY/I WANNA BE YOUR MAN	3.30	5.50
☐ 9682		TELL ME/		
		I JUST WANT TO MAKE LOVE TO YOU	3.50	6.00
☐ 9687		IT'S ALL OVER NOW/		
		GOOD TIMES, BAD TIMES	3.50	6.00
☐ 9708		TIME IS ON MY SIDE/CONGRATULATIONS	2.75	4.50
☐ 9725		HEART OF STONE/WHAT A SHAME	2.75	4.50
☐ 9741		THE LAST TIME/PLAY WITH FIRE	2.75	4.50
☐ 9766		SATISFACTION/UNDER ASSISTANT		
		WEST COAST PROMOTION MAN	2.00	3.50
☐ 9792		GET OFF MY CLOUD/I'M FREE	2.00	3.50
☐ 9808		AS TEARS GO BY/GOTTA GET AWAY	2.00	3.50
☐ 9823		19TH NERVOUS BREAKDOWN/SAD DAY	2.00	3.50
☐ 901		PAINT IT, BLACK/STUPID GIRL	2.00	3.50
☐ 902		MOTHER'S LITTLE HELPER/LADY JANE	2.00	3.50
☐ 903		HAVE YOU SEEN YOUR MOTHER, BABY,		
		STANDING IN THE SHADOW/		
		WHO'S DRIVING YOUR PLANE	2.00	3.50
☐ 904		RUBY TUESDAY/		
		LET'S SPEND THE NIGHT TOGETHER	2.00	3.50
☐ 905		DANDELION/WE LOVE YOU	2.00	3.50

LINDA RONSTADT

ISSUE #	LABEL		PRICE RANGE	

ROLLING STONES—ALBUMS

☐ 3375 (M)	*LONDON*	THE ROLLING STONES	12.00	20.00
☐ 3402 (M)		12x5	10.00	18.00
☐ 3420 (M)		THE ROLLING STONES NOW	10.00	18.00
☐ 3429 (M)		OUT OF OUR HEADS	10.00	18.00
☐ 3451 (M)		DECEMBER'S CHILDREN	10.00	18.00
☐ 3476 (M)		AFTERMATH	8.50	15.00
☐ 3493 (M)		GOT LIVE IF YOU WANT IT	8.50	15.00
☐ 3499 (M)		BETWEEN THE BUTTONS	8.50	15.00
☐ 3509 (M)		FLOWERS	8.50	15.00
☐ NPS-1 (S)		BIG HITS	8.50	15.00
☐ NPS-2 (S)		THEIR SATANIC MAJESTIES' REQUEST	15.00	25.00
☐ NPS-3 (S)		THROUGH THE PAST DARKLY	7.25	12.00

LINDA RONSTADT

☐ 937	*SIDEWALK*	EVERYBODY HAS THEIR OWN IDEAS/ SO FINE	8.50	15.00
☐ 5838	*CAPITOL*	ALL THE BEAUTIFUL THINGS/ SWEET SUMMER BLUE AND GOLD	4.00	7.00
☐ 5910		EVERGREEN/ONE FOR ALL	4.00	7.00
☐ 2004		DIFFERENT DRUM/I'VE GOT TO KNOW	2.00	3.50
☐ 2110		UP TO MY NECK IN MUDDY WATER/ CARNIVAL BEAT	2.25	4.00
☐ 2195		SOME OF SHELLY'S BLUES/ HOBO (MORNING GLORY)	2.00	3.50
☐ 2438		DOLPHINS/LONG WAY AROUND	2.00	3.50
☐ 2767		WILL YOU LOVE ME TOMORROW/ LOVESICK BLUES	2.00	3.50
☐ 2846		LONG LONG TIME/NOBODYS	1.75	3.00
☐ 3021		(SHE'S A) VERY LOVELY WOMAN/ LONG WAY AROUND	1.75	3.00
☐ 3210		I FALL TO PIECES/CAN IT BE TRUE	1.75	3.00
☐ 3273		ROCK ME ON THE WATER/CRAZY ARMS	1.75	3.00

TODD RUNDGREN

☐ 0003	*BEARSVILLE*	I SAW THE LIGHT/MARLENE	7.25	18.00
☐ 0003		I SAW THE LIGHT/MARLENE	1.50	3.00
☐ 0007		WOLFMAN JACK/ COULDN'T I JUST TELL YOU	1.75	3.50
☐ 0009		COLD MORNING LIGHT/HELLO IT'S ME	1.75	3.50
☐ 0015		SOMETIMES/DOES ANYBODY LOVE YOU	1.75	3.50
☐ 0020		HEAVY METAL KIDS/ A DREAM GOES ON FOREVER	1.75	3.50

— S —

ISSUE #	LABEL		PRICE RANGE	

SAM THE SHAM
AND THE PHAROAHS

☐ 2982	*TUPELO*	BETTY AND DUPREE/MAN CHILD	8.50	15.00
☐ 001	*DINGO*	HAUNTED HOUSE/		
		HOW DOES A CHEATING WOMAN FEEL?	7.25	12.00
☐ 905	*XL*	THE SIGNIFYING MONKEY/JUIMONOS	7.25	12.00
☐ 906		WOOLY BULLY/AIN'T GONNA MOVE	18.00	30.00
☐ 13322	*MGM*	WOOLY BULLY/AIN'T GONNA MOVE	2.00	3.50
☐ 13364		JU JU HAND/BIG CITY LIGHTS	2.00	3.50
☐ 13397		RING DANG DOO/DON'T TRY IT	2.00	3.50
☐ 13452		RED HOT/A LONG LONG WAY	2.00	3.50
☐ 13506		LIL' RED RIDING HOOD/		
		LOVE ME LIKE BEFORE	1.75	3.00

SAM THE SHAM
AND THE PHAROAHS—ALBUMS

☐ 4297 (S)	*MGM*	WOOLY BULLY	8.00	22.50
☐ 4314 (S)		THEIR SECOND ALBUM	8.00	22.50
☐ 4347 (S)		ON TOUR	7.00	18.00
☐ 4407 (S)		LIL' RED RIDING HOOD	7.00	18.00
☐ 4422 (S)		THE BEST OF SAM THE SHAM		
☐ 4526 (S)		TEN OF PENTACLES	5.00	13.50
☐ 8271 (S)	*ATLANTIC*	HARD AND HEAVY	6.00	15.00

BOB SEGER

☐ 1013	*HIDEOUT*	EAST SIDE STORY/EAST SIDE STORY	7.00	12.00
☐ 438	*CAMEO*	EAST SIDE STORY/EAST SIDE STORY	2.75	4.50
☐ 444		SOCK IT TO ME, SANTA/FLORIDA TIME	2.75	4.50
☐ 1117	*REPRISE*	TURN ON YOUR LOVE LIGHT/		
		WHO DO YOU LOVE?	2.00	3.50
☐ 1143		ROSALIE/NEON SKY	2.00	3.50

BOB SEGER—ALBUMS

☐ 1106 (S)				
	PALLADIUM	SMOKIN' O.P.'S	6.00	15.00
☐ 2126 (S)		BACK IN '72	6.00	15.00

BOB SEGER SYSTEM

☐ 2143	*CAPITOL*	2 PLUS 2 EQUALS WHAT?/DEATH ROW	2.25	4.00
☐ 2297		RAMBLIN' GAMBLIN' MAN/		
		TALES OF LUCY BLUE	2.00	3.50

ISSUE #	LABEL		PRICE	RANGE
☐ 2640		LONELY MAN/INNERVENUS EYES	1.75	3.00
☐ 2748		LUCIFER/BIG RIVER	1.75	3.00
☐ 3187		LOOKIN' BACK/HIGHWAY CHILD	1.75	3.00
☐ 4062		BEAUTIFUL LOSER/FINE MEMORY	1.75	3.00
☐ 4116		KATMANDU/BLACK NIGHT	1.75	3.00

BOB SEGER SYSTEM—ALBUMS

☐ 172 (S)	*CAPITOL*	RAMBLIN' GAMBLIN' MAN	5.00	13.50
☐ 236 (S)		NOAH	4.50	12.00
☐ 499 (S)		MONGREL	4.50	12.00
☐ 731 (S)		BRAND NEW DAY	4.50	12.00

SHANGRI-LAS

☐ 1866	*SMASH*	SIMON SAYS/SIMON SPEAKS	3.50	6.00
☐ 4006	*SPOKANE*	WISHING WELL/		
		HATE TO SAY I TOLD YOU SO	4.00	7.00
☐ 1291	*SCEPTER*	WISHING WELL/		
		HATE TO SAY I TOLD YOU SO	2.75	4.50
☐ 10-008	*RED BIRD*	REMEMBER (WALKIN' IN THE SAND)/		
		IT'S EASIER TO CRY	2.00	3.50
☐ 10-014		LEADER OF THE PACK/WHAT IS LOVE	2.00	3.50
☐ 10-018		GIVE HIM A GREAT BIG KISS/		
		TWIST AND SHOUT	2.00	3.50
☐ 10-019		MAYBE/SHOUT	2.00	3.50
☐ 10-025		OUT IN THE STREETS/THE BOY	2.00	3.50
☐ 10-030		GIVE US YOUR BLESSINGS/		
		ONLY HEAVEN KNOWS	2.00	3.50
☐ 10-036		RIGHT NOW AND NOT LATER/		
		TRAIN FROM KANSAS CITY	2.00	3.50
☐ 10-043		I CAN NEVER GO HOME ANYMORE/		
		BULLDOG	2.00	3.50
☐ 10-048		LONG LIVE OUR LOVE/		
		SOPHISTICATED BOOM BOOM	2.00	3.50
☐ 10-053		HE CRIED/DRESSED IN BLACK	2.00	3.50
☐ 10-068		PAST, PRESENT AND FUTURE/PARADISE	2.00	3.50

SHANGRI-LAS—ALBUMS

☐ 101 (M)	*RED BIRD*	LEADER OF THE PACK	7.00	18.00
☐ 104 (M)		SHANGRI-LAS '65	10.00	25.00
☐ 104 (M)		I CAN NEVER GO HOME ANYMORE	7.00	18.00
☐ 61099 (S)				
	MERCURY	GOLDEN HITS OF THE SHANGRI-LAS	7.00	18.00

ISSUE #	LABEL		PRICE RANGE	

DEL SHANNON

ISSUE #	LABEL		PRICE	RANGE
☐ 3067	*BIG TOP*	RUNAWAY/JODY	2.00	3.50
☐ 3075		HATS OFF TO LARRY/		
		DON'T GILD THE LILY, LILY	2.00	3.50
☐ 3083		SO LONG BABY/		
		THE ANSWER TO EVERYTHING	2.00	3.50
☐ 3091		HEY! LITTLE GIRL/		
		I WON'T CARE ANYMORE	2.00	3.50
☐ 3098		GINNY IN THE MIRROR/I WON'T BE THERE	2.00	3.50
☐ 3112		CRY MYSELF TO SLEEP/		
		I'M GONNA MOVE ON	2.25	4.00
☐ 3117		THE SWISS MAID/		
		YOU NEVER TALKED ABOUT ME	2.00	3.50
☐ 3131		LITTLE TOWN FLIRT/THE WAMBOO	2.00	3.50
☐ 3143		TWO KINDS OF TEARDROPS/KELLY	2.00	3.50
☐ 3152		FROM ME TO YOU/TWO SILHOUETTES	4.00	7.00
☐ 501	*BERLEE*	SUE'S GOTTA BE MINE/NOW SHE'S GONE	2.25	4.00
☐ 502		THAT'S THE WAY LOVE IS/		
		TIME OF THE DAY	2.25	4.00
☐ 897	*AMY*	STAINS ON MY LETTER/MARY JANE	2.25	4.00
☐ 905		HANDY MAN/GIVE HER LOTS OF LOVIN'	2.00	3.50
☐ 911		DO YOU WANT TO DANCE/		
		THIS IS ALL I HAVE TO GIVE	2.00	3.50
☐ 915		KEEP SEARCHIN'/BROKEN PROMISES	2.00	3.50
☐ 919		STRANGER IN TOWN/OVER YOU	2.00	3.50
☐ 925		BREAK UP/WHY DON'T YOU TELL HIM	2.25	4.00
☐ 937		SHE STILL REMEMBERS TONY/		
		MOVE IT OVER	2.25	4.00
☐ 55866	*LIBERTY*	THE BIG HURT/I GOT IT BAD	2.00	3.50
☐ 55889		FOR A LITTLE WHILE/HEY LITTLE STAR	2.00	3.50
☐ 55894		SHOW ME/NEVER THOUGHT I COULD	2.00	3.50
☐ 55904		UNDER MY THUMB/SHE WAS MINE	2.00	3.50
☐ 55939		WHAT MAKES YOU RUN/SHE	2.00	3.50

DEL SHANNON—ALBUMS

ISSUE #	LABEL		PRICE	RANGE
☐ 1303 (M)	*BIG TOP*	RUNAWAY	15.00	35.00
☐ 1308 (M)		LITTLE TOWN FLIRT	10.00	25.00
☐ 8003 (S)		HANDY MAN	12.50	30.00
☐ 8004 (S)		DEL SHANNON SINGS HANK WILLIAMS	8.00	22.50
☐ 8006 (S)		1,661 SECONDS OF DEL SHANNON	8.00	22.50
☐ 7453 (S)	*LIBERTY*	THIS IS MY BAG	7.00	18.00
☐ 7479 (S)		TOTAL COMMITMENT	7.00	18.00
☐ 8539 (S)		THE FURTHER ADVENTURES OF		
		CHARLES WESTOVER	4.50	12.00
☐ 25824 (S)	*DOT*	THE BEST OF DEL SHANNON	4.50	12.00

ISSUE #	LABEL		PRICE RANGE	

SIMON AND GARFUNKEL

☐ 43396	*COLUMBIA*	SOUNDS OF SILENCE/WE'VE GOT A GROOVY THING GOIN'	1.75	3.00
☐ 43511		HOMEWARD BOUND/ LEAVES THAT ARE GREEN	1.75	3.00
☐ 43617		I AM A ROCK/FLOWERS NEVER BEND WITH THE RAINFALL	1.75	3.00
☐ 43728		DANGLING CONVERSATION/BIG BRIGHT GREEN PLEASURE MACHINE	1.75	3.00
☐ 43873		A HAZY SHADE OF WINTER/FOR EMILY, WHEREVER I MAY FIND HER	1.75	3.00
☐ 44046		AT THE ZOO/59TH STREET BRIDGE SONG (FEELIN' GROOVY)	1.75	3.00
☐ 45663		FOR EMILY, WHEREVER I MAY FIND HER/ AMERICA	1.75	3.00
☐ 10230		MY LITTLE TOWN/RAG DOLL-YOU'RE KIND	1.50	2.50

SIMON AND GARFUNKEL—ALBUMS

☐ 3059 (S)	*PICKWICK*	HIT SOUNDS OF SIMON AND GARFUNKEL	15.00	35.00
☐ 2249 (M)		WEDNESDAY MORNING, 3 A.M.	5.00	13.50
	COLUMBIA			
☐ 9049 (S)		WEDNESDAY MORNING, 3 A.M.	7.00	18.00
☐ 9269 (S)		SOUNDS OF SILENCE	6.00	15.00
☐ 9363 (S)		PARSLEY, SAGE, ROSEMARY & THYME	6.00	15.00
☐ 9529 (S)		BOOKENDS	4.50	12.00
☐ 9914 (S)		BRIDGE OVER TROUBLED WATER	4.50	12.00
☐ 31350 (S)		GREATEST HITS	4.50	12.00

SONNY AND CHER

☐ 6345	*ATCO*	JUST YOU/SING C'EST LA VIE	1.75	3.00
☐ 6359		I GOT YOU BABE/IT'S GONNA RAIN	1.75	3.00
☐ 6381		BUT YOU'RE MINE/HELLO	1.75	3.00
☐ 6395		WHAT NOW MY LOVE/I LOOK FOR YOU	1.75	3.00
☐ 6420		HAVE I STAYED TOO LONG/LEAVE ME BE	1.75	3.00
☐ 6440		LITTLE MAN/MONDAY	1.75	3.00
☐ 6461		THE BEAT GOES ON/LOVE DON'T COME	1.75	3.00
☐ 6480		A BEAUTIFUL STORY/PODUNK	1.75	3.00
☐ 6486		PLASTIC MAN/IT'S THE LITTLE THINGS	1.75	3.00
☐ 6507		IT'S THE LITTLE THINGS/ DON'T TALK TO STRANGERS	1.75	3.00
☐ 6541		GOOD COMBINATION/YOU AND ME	1.75	3.00
☐ 6555		I WOULD MARRY YOU TODAY/CIRCUS	1.75	3.00
☐ 6605		YOU GOTTA HAVE A THING OF YOUR OWN/ I GOT YOU BABE	1.75	3.00

ISSUE #	LABEL		PRICE RANGE	
☐6683		YOU'RE A FRIEND OF MINE/I WOULD MARRY YOU TODAY	1.75	3.00
☐6758		GET IT TOGETHER/HOLD ME TIGHTER	1.75	3.00

SONNY AND CHER—ALBUMS

☐6177 (S)	*REPRISE*	BABY DON'T GO	7.00	18.00
☐177 (S)	*ATCO*	LOOK AT US	5.00	13.50
☐183 (S)		THE WONDROUS WORLD OF SONNY AND CHER	5.00	13.50
☐203 (S)		IN CASE YOU'RE IN LOVE	5.00	13.50
☐214 (S)		GOOD TIMES	5.00	13.50
☐219 (S)		THE BEST OF SONNY AND CHER	5.00	13.50

BRUCE SPRINGSTEEN

☐45805	*COLUMBIA*	BLINDED BY THE LIGHT/THE ANGEL	24.00	42.00
☐45864		FOR YOU/SPIRIT IN THE NIGHT	20.00	36.00
☐10209		BORN TO RUN/ MEETING ACROSS THE RIVER	2.00	3.50
☐10274		TENTH AVENUE FREEZE-OUT/ SHE'S THE ONE	2.25	4.00
☐10763		PROVE IT ALL NIGHT/FACTORY	1.75	3.00
☐10801		BADLANDS/STREETS OF FIRE	1.75	3.00

TERRY STAFFORD

☐101	*CRUSADE*	SUSPICION/JUDY	2.00	3.50
☐105		I'LL TOUCH A STAR/PLAYING WITH FIRE	2.00	3.50
☐109		FOLLOW THE RAINBOW/ ARE YOU A FOOL LIKE ME?	2.00	3.50
☐110		A LITTLE BIT BETTER/HOPING	2.00	3.50
☐914	*SIDEWALK*	THE JOKE'S ON ME/ A STEP OR TWO BEHIND YOU	2.25	4.00

TERRY STAFFORD—ALBUM

☐1001 (S)	*CRUSADE*	SUSPICION	12.50	30.00

STEPPENWOLF

☐4109	*DUNHILL*	A GIRL I KNOW/THE OSTRICH	2.25	4.00
☐4123		SOOKIE SOOKIE/TAKE WHAT YOU NEED	2.25	4.00
☐4138		BORN TO BE WILD/ EVERYBODY'S NEXT ONE	1.75	3.00
☐4160		MAGIC CARPET RIDE/SOOKIE SOOKIE	1.75	3.00
☐4182		ROCK ME/JUPITER CHILD	1.50	2.50
☐4192		IT'S NEVER TOO LATE/HAPPY BIRTHDAY	1.50	2.50

ISSUE #	LABEL		PRICE RANGE	
☐ 4205		MOVE OVER/POWER PLAY	1.50	2.50
☐ 4221		MONSTER/BERRY RIDES AGAIN	1.50	2.50
☐ 4234		HEY LAWDY MAMA/TWISTED	1.50	2.50

STEPPENWOLF—ALBUMS

☐ 50029 (S)	*DUNHILL*	STEPPENWOLF	4.50	10.00
☐ 50037 (S)		STEPPENWOLF THE SECOND	4.50	10.00
☐ 50053 (S)		AT YOUR BIRTHDAY PARTY	4.50	10.00
☐ 50060 (S)		EARLY STEPPENWOLF	4.50	10.00
☐ 50066 (S)		MONSTER	4.50	10.00
☐ 50075 (S)		STEPPENWOLF LIVE	4.50	10.00
☐ 50090 (S)		STEPPENWOLF 7	4.50	10.00
☐ 50099 (S)		STEPPENWOLF GOLD—THEIR GREATEST HITS	4.50	10.00

CAT STEVENS

☐ 5872	*DERAM*	PORTOBELLO ROAD/I LOVE MY DOG	2.25	4.00
☐ 7505 .		MATTHEW AND SON/GRANNY	2.25	4.00
☐ 85006		SCHOOL IS OUT/ I'M GONNA GET ME A GUN	2.25	4.00
☐ 85015		BAD NIGHT/LAUGHING APPLE	2.25	4.00

CAT STEVENS—ALBUMS

☐ 18005 (S)	*DERAM*	MATTHEW AND SON/NEW MASTERS	7.00	18.00
☐ 18061 (S)		VERY YOUNG AND EARLY SONGS	6.00	15.00

CONNIE STEVENS

☐ 5092	*WARNER BROTHERS*	WHY DO I CRY FOR JOEY?/APOLLO	2.75	4.50
☐ 5137		SIXTEEN REASONS/LITTLE SISTER	2.00	3.50
☐ 5159		TOO YOUNG TO GO STEADY/A LITTLE KISS	2.00	3.50
☐ 5232		THE GREENWOOD TREE/IF YOU DON'T SOMEBODY ELSE WILL	2.00	3.50
☐ 5217		MAKE-BELIEVE LOVER/AND THIS IS MINE	2.00	3.50
☐ 5265		WHY'D YOU WANNA MAKE ME CRY/ JUST ONE KISS	2.00	3.50
☐ 5289		MR. SONGWRITER/I COULDN'T SAY NO	2.00	3.50
☐ 5318		NOBODY'S LONESOME FOR ME/ HEY GOOD LOOKIN'	2.00	3.50
☐ 5380		THERE GOES YOUR GUY/ LITTLE MISSUNDERSTOOD	2.00	3.50

CONNIE STEVENS—ALBUMS

☐ 1208 (M)	*WARNER BROTHERS*	CONCHETTA	8.00	22.50
☐ 1431 (S)		CONNIE STEVENS	10.00	25.00
☐ 1460 (S)		THE HANK WILLIAMS SONG BOOK	8.00	22.50

ISSUE #	LABEL		PRICE RANGE	
SUPREMES				
☐ 54038	*TAMLA*	I WANT A GUY/NEVER AGAIN	15.00	25.00
☐ 54045		BUTTERED POPCORN/WHO'S LOVING YOU	12.00	20.00
☐ 1027	*MOTOWN*	YOUR HEART BELONGS TO ME/		
		(HE'S) SEVENTEEN	3.50	6.00
☐ 1034		LET ME GO THE RIGHT WAY/		
		TIME CHANGES THINGS	3.50	6.00
☐ 1040		YOU BRING BACK MEMORIES/		
		MY HEART CAN'T TAKE IT NO MORE	2.75	4.50
☐ 1044		A BREATH-TAKING GUY/		
		ROCK AND ROLL BANJO BAND	2.25	4.00
☐ 1051		WHEN THE LOVELIGHT STARTS SHINING		
		THROUGH HIS EYES/STANDING AT THE		
		CROSSROADS OF LOVE	2.00	3.50
☐ 1054		RUN, RUN, RUN/		
		I'M GIVING YOU YOUR FREEDOM	2.00	3.50
☐ 1060		WHERE DID OUR LOVE GO?/		
		HE MEANS THE WORLD TO ME	1.75	3.00
☐ 1097		YOU CAN'T HURRY LOVE/		
		PUT YOURSELF IN MY PLACE	1.75	3.00
☐ 1101		YOU KEEP ME HANGIN' ON/		
		REMOVE THIS DOUBT	1.75	3.00
☐ 1103		LOVE IS HERE AND NOW YOU'RE GONE/		
		THERE'S NO STOPPING US NOW	1.75	3.00
☐ 1107		THE HAPPENING/ALL I KNOW ABOUT YOU	1.75	3.00
☐ 1111		REFLECTIONS/		
		GOING DOWN FOR THE THIRD TIME	1.75	3.00
☐ 1116		IN AND OUT OF LOVE/		
		I GUESS I'LL ALWAYS LOVE YOU	1.75	3.00
☐ 1122		FOREVER CAME TODAY/		
		TIME CHANGES THINGS	1.75	3.00
☐ 1126		SOME THINGS YOU NEVER GET USED TO/		
		YOU'VE BEEN SO WONDERFUL TO ME	1.75	3.00
☐ 1139		I'M LIVIN' IN SHAME/		
		I'M SO GLAD I GOT SOMEBODY	1.75	3.00
☐ 1146		THE COMPOSER/		
		THE BEGINNING OF THE END	1.75	3.00
☐ 1148		NO MATTER WHAT SIGN YOU ARE/		
		THE YOUNG FOLKS	1.75	3.00
☐ 1156		SOMEDAY WE'LL BE TOGETHER/		
		HE'S MY SUNNY BOY	1.75	3.00
SUPREMES—ALBUMS				
☐ 606 (M)	*MOTOWN*	MEET THE SUPREMES	30.00	75.00
☐ 606 (M)		MEET THE SUPREMES	17.50	30.00
☐ 621 (M)		WHERE DID OUR LOVE GO?	6.00	15.00

ISSUE #	LABEL		PRICE RANGE	
☐ 623 (M)		A BIT OF LIVERPOOL	6.00	15.00
☐ 625 (S)		THE SUPREMES SING COUNTRY, WESTERN AND POP	8.00	22.50
☐ 627 (S)		MORE HITS BY THE SUPREMES	7.00	18.00
☐ 629 (S)		WE REMEMBER SAM COOKE	7.00	18.00
☐ 636 (S)		AT THE COPA	6.00	15.00
☐ 638 (S)		MERRY CHRISTMAS	6.00	15.00
☐ 643 (S)		I HEAR A SYMPHONY	4.50	12.00
☐ 649 (S)		SUPREMES A-GO-GO	4.50	12.00
☐ 659 (S)		THE SUPREMES SING ROGERS AND HART	4.50	12.00
☐ 663 (S)		GREATEST HITS	4.00	10.00
☐ 665 (S)		REFLECTIONS	4.00	10.00

— T —

JAMES TAYLOR

☐ 1805	**APPLE**	CAROLINA IN MY MIND/ SOMETHING'S WRONG..............	1.75	3.00
☐ 201	**EUPHORIA**	BRIGHTEN YOUR DAY WITH MY DAY/ THE ZOO	1.75	3.00
☐ 45880	**ELEKTRA**	GROWNUP/MOCKINGBIRD...............	1.25	3.00
☐ 7135	**WARNER BROTHERS**	SWEET BABY JAMES/ LONG AGO & FAR AWAY	1.25	3.00
☐ 7387		SWEET BABY JAMES/SUITE FOR 20G	1.25	3.00
☐ 7423		FIRE & RAIN/ANYWHERE LIKE HEAVEN	1.25	3.00

TEDDY BEARS

☐ 503	**DORE**	TO KNOW HIM, IS TO LOVE HIM/ DON'T YOU WORRY MY PRETTY PET	2.75	4.50
☐ 520		WONDERFUL, LOVEABLE YOU/ TILL YOU'LL BE MINE	4.00	7.00
☐ 5562	**IMPERIAL**	OH WHY/I DON'T NEED YOU ANYMORE	3.50	6.00
☐ 5581		IF YOU ONLY KNEW/YOU SAID GOODBYE	3.50	6.00
☐ 5594		DON'T GO AWAY/SEVEN LONELY DAYS	3.50	6.00

TEDDY BEARS—ALBUM

☐ 9067 (M)	**IMPERIAL**	TEDDY BEARS	25.00	60.00
☐ 12067 (S)		TEDDY BEARS	60.00	150.00

ISSUE #	LABEL		PRICE RANGE	

TEMPTATIONS

☐5	*MIRACLE*	OH MOTHER OF MINE/ ROMANCE WITHOUT FINANCE	7.25	12.00
☐12		YOUR WONDERFUL LOVE/ CHECK YOURSELF	6.00	11.00
☐7001	*GORDY*	DREAM COME TRUE/ISN'T SHE PRETTY	2.75	4.50
☐7010		PARADISE/SLOW DOWN HEART	2.75	4.50
☐7015		THE FURTHER YOU LOOK/ I WANT A LOVE I CAN SEE	2.75	4.50
☐7020		MAY I HAVE THIS DANCE?/ FAREWELL MY LOVE	2.75	4.50
☐7028		THE WAY YOU DO THE THINGS YOU DO/ JUST LET ME KNOW	1.75	3.00
☐7030		KEEP ME/MIDNIGHT JOURNEY	2.00	3.50
☐7032		I'LL BE IN TROUBLE/ THE GIRL'S ALRIGHT WITH ME	1.75	3.00
☐7035		GIRL (WHY YOU WANNA MAKE ME BLUE?)/BABY, BABY, I NEED YOU	1.75	3.00
☐7038		MY GIRL/NOBODY BUT MY BABY	1.75	3.00
☐7040		IT'S GROWING/ WHAT LOVE HAS JOINED TOGETHER	1.75	3.00
☐7043		SINCE I LOST MY BABY/ YOU'VE GOT TO EARN IT	1.75	3.00
☐7047		MY BABY/DON'T LOOK BACK	1.75	3.00
☐7049		GET READY/FADING AWAY	1.75	3.00
☐7054		AIN'T TOO PROUD TO BEG/ YOU'LL LOSE A PRECIOUS LOVE	1.75	3.00
☐7055		BEAUTY IS ONLY SKIN DEEP/ YOU'RE NOT AN ORDINARY GIRL	1.75	3.00
☐7057		(I KNOW) I'M LOSING YOU/ I COULDN'T CRY IF I WANTED TO	1.75	3.00
☐7061		ALL I NEED/SORRY IS A SORRY WORD	1.75	3.00
☐7063		YOU'RE MY EVERYTHING/ I'VE BEEN GOOD TO YOU	1.75	3.00
☐7065		(LONELINESS MADE ME REALIZE) IT'S YOU THAT I NEED/DON'T SEND ME AWAY	1.75	3.00
☐7068		I WISH IT WOULD RAIN/ I TRULY TRULY BELIEVE	1.75	3.00
☐7072		I COULD NEVER LOVE ANOTHER (AFTER LOVING YOU)/GONNA GIVE HER ALL THE LOVE I GOT	1.75	3.00
☐7074		PLEASE RETURN YOUR LOVE TO ME/ HOW CAN I FORGET	1.75	3.00
☐7081		CLOUD NINE/ WHY DID SHE HAVE TO LEAVE ME?	1.75	3.00

ISSUE #	LABEL		PRICE RANGE	
☐ 7082		RUDOLPH THE RED NOSED REINDEER/ SILENT NIGHT	1.75	3.00
☐ 7084		RUNAWAY CHILD, RUNNING WILD/ I NEED YOUR LOVE	1.75	3.00
☐ 7086		DON'T LET THE JONESES GET YOU DOWN/ SINCE I'VE LOST YOU	1.75	3.00
☐ 7093		I CAN'T GET NEXT TO YOU/RUNNING AWAY AIN'T GONNA HELP YOU	1.75	3.00
☐ 7096		PSYCHEDELIC SHACK/ THAT'S THE WAY LOVE IS	1.75	3.00
☐ 7099		BALL OF CONFUSION/IT'S SUMMER	1.75	3.00
☐ 7102		UNGENA ZA ULIMWENGU (UNITE THE WORLD)/HUM ALONG AND DANCE	1.75	3.00
☐ 7015		JUST MY IMAGINATION (RUNNING AWAY WITH ME)/YOU MAKE YOUR OWN HEAVEN AND HELL RIGHT HERE ON EARTH	1.75	3.00
☐ 7109		IT'S SUMMER/ I'M THE EXCEPTION TO THE RULE	1.75	3.00
☐ 7111		SUPERSTAR (REMEMBER HOW YOU GOT WHERE YOU ARE)/ GONNA KEEP ON TRYIN' TILL I WIN YOUR LOVE	1.75	3.00
☐ 7115		TAKE A LOOK AROUND/ SMOOTH SAILING (FROM NOW ON)	1.75	3.00
☐ 7119		MOTHER NATURE/FUNKY MUSIC SHONUFF TURNS ME ON	1.75	3.00

TEMPTATIONS—ALBUMS

☐ 911 (S)	*GORDY*	MEET THE TEMPTATIONS	10.00	25.00
☐ 912 (S)		THE TEMPTATIONS SING SMOKEY	8.00	22.50
☐ 914 (S)		TEMPTIN' TEMPTATIONS	7.00	18.00
☐ 918 (S)		GETTIN' READY	7.00	18.00
☐ 919 (S)		GREATEST HITS	6.00	15.00
☐ 921 (S)		LIVE	6.00	15.00
☐ 922 (S)		WITH A LOT O' SOUL	5.00	13.50
☐ 924 (S)		IN A MELLOW MOOD	4.50	12.00
☐ 927 (S)		THE TEMPTATIONS WISH IT WOULD RAIN	4.50	12.00
☐ 933 (S)		TV SHOW	4.00	10.00
☐ 938 (S)		LIVE AT THE COPA	4.00	10.00
☐ 939 (S)		CLOUD NINE	4.00	10.00
☐ 947 (S)		PSYCHEDELIC SHACK	4.00	10.00
☐ 949 (S)		PUZZLE PEOPLE	4.00	10.00
☐ 953 (S)		LIVE AT LONDON'S TALK OF THE TOWN	4.00	10.00
☐ 954 (S)		GREATEST HITS, VOL. II	4.00	10.00

ISSUE #	LABEL		PRICE RANGE	

IKE AND TINA TURNER

☐730	**SUE**	A FOOL IN LOVE/THE WAY YOU LOVE ME	2.25	4.00
☐735		I IDOLIZE YOU/LETTER FROM TINA	2.25	4.00
☐749		IT'S GONNA WORK OUT FINE/		
		WON'T YOU FORGIVE ME	2.25	4.00
☐753		POOR FOOL/YOU CAN'T BLAME ME	2.25	4.00
☐757		TRA LA LA LA LA/PUPPY LOVE	2.25	4.00
☐760		PRANCING/IT'S GONNA WORK OUT FINE	2.25	4.00
☐765		YOU SHOULD-A TREATED ME RIGHT/		
		SLEEPLESS	2.25	4.00
☐772		THE ARGUMENT/MIND IN A WHIRL	2.25	4.00
☐774		PLEASE DON'T HURT ME/		
		WORRIED AND HURTIN' INSIDE	2.25	4.00
☐135		TWO IS A COUPLE/TIN TOP HOUSE	2.25	4.00
☐138		THE NEW BREED (PT. 1)/(PT. 11)	2.25	4.00
☐139		CAN'T CHANCE A BREAKUP/		
		STAGGER LEE AND BILLY	2.25	4.00
☐146		I MADE A PROMISE UP ABOVE/DEAR JOHN . . .	2.25	4.00
☐402	**KENT**	I CAN'T BELIEVE WHAT YOU SAY/		
		MY BABY NOW	2.00	3.50
☐409		PLEASE PLEASE PLEASE/		
		AM I A FOOL IN LOVE?	2.00	3.50
☐418		CHICKEN SHACK/HE'S THE ONE	2.00	3.50
☐457		I WISH MY DREAM WOULD COME TRUE/		
		FLEE FLEE FLEA	2.00	3.50
☐1007	**MODERN**	GOODBYE, SO LONG/		
		HURT IS ALL YOU GAVE ME	2.00	3.50
☐1012		GONNA HAVE FUN/I DON'T NEED	2.00	3.50
☐135		I'LL NEVER NEED MORE THAN THIS/		
		THE CASHBOX BLUES	3.50	6.00
☐136		A LOVE LIKE YOURS/HOLD ON BABY	3.50	6.00
☐1118	**A&M**	RIVER DEEP-MOUNTAIN HIGH/		
		I'LL KEEP YOU HAPPY	2.25	4.00

IKE AND TINA TURNER—ALBUMS

☐2001 (M)	**SUE**	THE SOUND OF IKE AND TINA TURNER	12.50	30.00
☐2003 (M)		DANCE	10.00	25.00
☐2004 (M)		DYNAMITE	10.00	25.00
☐2005 (M)		DON'T PLAY ME CHEAP	10.00	25.00
☐2007 (M)		IT'S GONNA WORK OUT FINE	10.00	25.00
☐1038 (M)		THE GREATEST HITS OF		
		IKE AND TINA TURNER	10.00	25.00
☐538 (M)	**KENT**	FESTIVAL OF LIVE PERFORMANCES	6.00	15.00
☐550 (M)		PLEASE PLEASE PLEASE	6.00	15.00

ISSUE #	LABEL		PRICE	RANGE
☐5014 (M)		LIVE	6.00	15.00
☐5019 (S)		THE SOUL OF IKE AND TINA TURNER	7.00	18.00
☐4001 (S)	*PHILLES*	RIVER DEEP-MOUNTAIN HIGH	35.00	90.00
☐4178 (S)	*A&M*	RIVER DEEP-MOUNTAIN HIGH	7.00	18.00

CONWAY TWITTY

☐71086	*MERCURY*	I NEED YOUR LOVIN'/		
		BORN TO SING THE BLUES	8.50	15.00
☐71384		DOUBLE TALK BABY/		
		WHY CAN'T I GET THROUGH TO YOU	10.00	18.00
☐12677	*MGM*	IT'S ONLY MAKE BELIEVE/I'LL TRY	2.25	4.00
☐12748		THE STORY OF MY LOVE/		
		MAKE ME KNOW YOU'RE MINE	2.25	4.00
☐12785		HEY LITTLE LUCY/		
		WHEN I'M NOT WITH YOU	2.25	4.00
☐12804		MONA LISA/HEAVENLY	2.25	4.00
☐12826		DANNY BOY/HALFWAY TO HEAVEN	2.25	4.00
☐12857		LONELY BLUE BOY/		
		STAR SPANGLED HEAVEN	2.25	4.00
☐12886		WHAT AM I LIVING FOR?/		
		THE HURT IN MY HEART	2.25	4.00
☐12918		TELL ME ONE MORE TIME/WHAT A DREAM ...	2.25	4.00
☐12911		IS A BLUE BIRD BLUE/SHE'S MINE	2.25	4.00
☐12943		I NEED YOU SO/TEASIN'	2.00	3.50
☐12962		WHOLE LOT OF SHAKIN' GOING ON/		
		THE FLAME	2.00	3.50
☐12969		C'EST SI BON/DON'T YOU DARE		
		LET ME DOWN	2.00	3.50
☐12998		THE NEXT KISS (IS THE LAST GOODBYE)/		
		MAN ALONE	2.00	3.50
☐13011		A MILLION TEARDROPS/		
		I'M IN A BLUE, BLUE MOOD	2.00	3.50
☐13034		IT'S DRIVIN' ME WILD/SWEET SORROW	2.00	3.50
☐13050		TOWER OF TEARS/PORTRAIT OF A FOOL	2.00	3.50
☐13072		COMFY 'N COZY/		
		A LITTLE PIECE OF MY HEART	2.00	3.50
☐13089		THERE'S SOMETHING ON YOUR MIND/		
		UNCHAINED MELODY	2.00	3.50
☐13112		THE PICKUP/I HOPE, I THINK/I WISH	2.00	3.50
☐13149		GOT MY MOJO WORKING/		
		SHE AIN'T NO ANGEL	2.00	3.50

CONWAY TWITTY

ISSUE #	LABEL		PRICE RANGE	

CONWAY TWITTY—EPs

☐ 1623	*MGM*	IT'S ONLY MAKE BELIEVE	8.50	15.00
☐ 1640		CONWAY TWITTY SINGS	7.25	12.00
☐ 1641		CONWAY TWITTY SINGS	7.25	12.00
☐ 1642		CONWAY TWITTY SINGS	7.25	12.00
☐ 1678		SATURDAY NIGHT WITH CONWAY TWITTY	6.00	11.00
☐ 1679		SATURDAY NIGHT WITH CONWAY TWITTY	6.00	11.00
☐ 1680		SATURDAY NIGHT WITH CONWAY TWITTY	6.00	11.00
☐ 1071		LONELY BLUE BOY	6.00	11.00

CONWAY TWITTY—ALBUMS

☐ 3744 (S)	*MGM*	CONWAY TWITTY SINGS	20.00	45.00
☐ 3786 (S)		SATURDAY NIGHT WITH CONWAY TWITTY	15.00	35.00
☐ 3818 (S)		LONELY BLUE BOY	15.00	35.00
☐ 3849 (S)		CONWAY TWITTY'S GREATEST HITS	15.00	35.00
☐ 3907 (S)		ROCK AND ROLL STORY	12.50	30.00
☐ 3943 (S)		THE CONWAY TWITTY TOUCH	10.00	25.00
☐ 4019 (S)		CONWAY TWITTY SINGS	10.00	25.00
☐ 4089 (S)		R & B '63	8.00	22.50
☐ 4217 (S)		CONWAY TWITTY HITS THE ROAD	7.00	18.00

— V —

RITCHIE VALENS

☐ 4106	*DEL-FI*	COME ON, LET'S GO/FRAMED	4.00	7.00
☐ 4110		DONNA/LA BAMBA	2.75	4.50
☐ 4114		THAT'S MY LITTLE SUZIE/		
		IN A TURKISH TOWN	2.75	4.50
☐ 4117		LITTLE GIRL/WE BELONG TOGETHER	3.50	6.00
☐ 4128		STAY BESIDE ME/BIG BABY BLUES	3.50	6.00
☐ 4133		CRY, CRY, CRY/PADDIWACK SONG	3.50	6.00

RITCHIE VALENS—EPs

☐ 101	*DEL-FI*	RITCHIE VALENS	12.00	20.00
☐ 111		RITCHIE VALENS	12.00	20.00

RITCHIE VALENS—ALBUMS

☐ 1201 (M)	*DEL-FI*	RITCHIE VALENS	17.50	45.00
☐ 1206 (M)		RITCHIE	20.00	50.00
☐ 1214 (M)		IN CONCERT AT PACOIMA JR. HIGH	35.00	90.00
☐ 1225 (M)		HIS GREATEST HITS	10.00	25.00
☐ 1247 (M)		GREATEST HITS, VOL. II	20.00	50.00

ISSUE #	LABEL		PRICE RANGE	

VENTURES

☐ 100	*BLUE HORIZON*	THE REAL McCOY/COOKIES AND COKE	4.50	9.00
☐ 101		WALK-DON'T RUN/HOME	7.25	12.00
☐ 25	*DOLTON*	WALK-DON'T RUN/HOME	1.75	3.00
☐ 28		PERFIDIA/NO TRESPASSING	1.75	3.00
☐ 32		RAM-BUNK-SHUSH/LONELY HEART	1.75	3.00
☐ 41		LULLABY OF THE LEAVES/GINCHY	1.50	2.50
☐ 44		(THEME FROM) SILVER CITY/		
		BLUER THAN BLUE	1.50	2.50
☐ 47		BLUE MOON/LADY OF SPAIN	1.50	2.50
☐ 50		YELLOW JACKET/GENESIS	1.50	2.50
☐ 55		INSTANT MASHED/MY BONNIE	1.50	2.50
☐ 60		LOLITA YA-YA/LUCILLE	1.50	2.50
☐ 67		THE 2,000 POUND BEE (PT. 1)/(PT. 2)	1.50	2.50
☐ 68		SKIP TO M'LIMBO/EL CUMBANCHERO	1.50	2.50
☐ 78		THE NINTH WAVE/DAMAGED GOODS	1.50	2.50
☐ 85		THE CHASE/THE SAVAGE	1.50	2.50
☐ 91		JOURNEY TO THE STARS/		
		WALKIN' WITH PLUTO	1.50	2.50
☐ 94		FUGITIVE/SCRATCHIN'	1.50	2.50
☐ 96		WALK-DON'T RUN '64/THE CRUEL SEA	1.50	2.50

VENTURES—EP

☐ 503	*DOLTON*	WALK-DON'T RUN	4.50	9.00

VENTURES—ALBUMS

☐ 8003 (S)	*DOLTON*	WALK-DON'T RUN	10.00	25.00
☐ 8004 (S)		THE VENTURES	10.00	25.00
☐ 8006 (S)		ANOTHER SMASH	8.00	22.50
☐ 8008 (S)		THE COLORFUL VENTURES	8.00	22.50
☐ 8010 (S)		TWIST WITH THE VENTURES	7.00	18.00
☐ 8010 (S)		DANCE!	6.00	15.00
☐ 8014 (S)		THE VENTURE'S TWIST PARTY, VOL. II	7.00	18.00
☐ 8014 (S)		DANCE WITH THE VENTURES	6.00	15.00
☐ 8016 (S)		MASHED POTATOES AND GRAVY	7.00	18.00
☐ 8016 (S)		THE VENTURES' BEACH PARTY	6.00	15.00
☐ 8017 (S)		GOING TO THE VENTURES' DANCE PARTY	7.00	18.00
☐ 8019 (S)		THE VENTURES PLAY TELSTAR		
		(THE LONELY BULL)	6.00	15.00
☐ 8022 (S)		SURFING	6.00	15.00
☐ 8023 (S)		THE VENTURES PLAY THE		
		COUNTRY CLASSICS	6.00	15.00
☐ 8024 (S)		LET'S GO!	6.00	15.00
☐ 8027 (S)		THE VENTURES IN SPACE	6.00	15.00
☐ 8029 (S)		THE FABULOUS VENTURES	6.00	15.00
☐ 8031 (S)		WALK, DON'T RUN, VOL. II	5.00	13.50

ISSUE #	LABEL		PRICE RANGE	
☐ 8033 (S)		THE VENTURES KNOCK ME OUT	5.00	13.50
☐ 8035 (S)		ON STAGE	5.00	13.50
☐ 8037 (S)		THE VENTURES A GO-GO	5.00	13.50
☐ 8038 (S)		THE VENTURES' CHRISTMAS ALBUM	5.00	13.50
☐ 8040 (S)		WHERE THE ACTION IS	4.50	12.00
☐ 8042 (S)		VENTURES	4.50	12.00
☐ 8042 (S)		BATMAN THEME	4.00	10.00
☐ 8045 (S)		GO WITH THE VENTURES!	4.00	10.00
☐ 8047 (S)		WILD THINGS!	4.00	10.00
☐ 8050 (S)		GUITAR FREAKOUT	4.00	10.00

GENE VINCENT

3450	CAPITOL	BE-BOP-A-LULU/WOMAN LOVE	3.50	6.50
☐ 3530		RACE WITH THE DEVIL/		
		GONNA BACK UP BABY	4.50	9.00
☐ 3558		BLUEJEAN BOP/WHO SLAPPED JOHN	4.00	7.00
☐ 3617		CRAZY LEGS/IMPORTANT WORDS	4.00	7.00
☐ 3678		FIVE DAYS, FIVE DAYS/		
		BI-BICKEY-BI-BO-BO-GO	4.00	7.00
☐ 3763		LOTTA LOVIN'/WEAR MY RING	4.00	7.00
☐ 3839		DANCE TO THE BOP/I GOT IT	3.50	6.00
☐ 3874		WALKIN' HOME FROM SCHOOL/		
		I GOT A BABY	3.50	6.00
☐ 3959		BABY BLUE/TRUE TO YOU	3.50	6.00
☐ 4010		ROCKY ROAD BLUES/		
		YES, I LOVE YOU BABY	3.50	6.00
☐ 4051		LITTLE LOVER/GIT IT	3.50	6.00
☐ 4105		BE BOP BOOGIE BABY/SAY MAMA	3.50	6.00
☐ 4153		WHO'S PUSHIN' YOUR SWING?/		
		OVER THE RAINBOW	3.50	6.00
☐ 4237		RIGHT NOW/THE NIGHT IS SO LONELY	3.50	6.00
☐ 4313		WILD CAT/RIGHT HERE ON EARTH	3.50	6.00
☐ 4442		ANNA-ANNABELLE/		
		PISTOL PACKIN' MAMA	3.50	6.00
☐ 4525		IF YOU WANT MY LOVIN'/		
		MISTER LONELINESS	3.50	6.00
☐ 4665		LUCKY STAR/BABY DON'T BELIEVE HIM	3.50	6.00

GENE VINCENT—EPs

☐ 1-764	CAPITOL	BLUEJEAN BOP	12.00	20.00
☐ 2-764		BLUEJEAN BOP	13.00	20.00
☐ 3-764		BLUEJEAN BOP	13.00	20.00
☐ 1-811		GENE VINCENT AND HIS BLUE CAPS	12.00	20.00
☐ 2-811		GENE VINCENT AND HIS BLUE CAPS	12.00	20.00
☐ 3-811		GENE VINCENT AND HIS BLUE CAPS	12.00	20.00

GENE VINCENT

ISSUE #	LABEL		PRICE RANGE	
☐ 1-970		GENE VINCENT ROCKS...................	12.00	20.00
☐ 2-970		GENE VINCENT ROCKS/	12.00	20.00
☐ 3-970		GENE VINCENT ROCKS/	12.00	20.00
☐ 985		HOT ROD GANG	24.00	42.00
☐ 1-1059		A GENE VINCENT RECORD DATE..........	12.00	20.00
☐ 2-1059		A GENE VINCENT RECORD DATE	12.00	20.00
☐ 3-1059		A GENE VINCENT RECORD DATE	12.00	20.00

GENE VINCENT—ALBUMS

☐ 764 (M)	*CAPITOL*	BLUEJEAN BOP	40.00	100.00
☐ 811 (M)		GENE VINCENT AND HIS BLUE CAPS	30.00	75.00
☐ 970 (M)		GENE VINCENT ROCKS AND THE BLUE CAPS ROLL	30.00	75.00
☐ 1059 (M)		A GENE VINCENT RECORD DATE	30.00	75.00
☐ 1207 (M)		SOUNDS LIKE GENE VINCENT	20.00	50.00
☐ 1342 (S)		CRAZY TIMES	30.00	75.00
☐ 102 (S)	*DANDELION*	I'M BACK AND I'M PROUD	6.00	15.00
☐ 2019 (S)	*KAMA SUTRA*	GENE VINCENT	6.00	15.00
☐ 2027 (S)		THE DAY THE WORLD TURNED BLUE	6.00	15.00

— W —

WALKER BROTHERS

☐ 1952	*SMASH*	PRETTY GIRLS EVERYWHERE/ DOIN' THE JERK......................	2.00	3.50
☐ 1976		SEVENTH DAWN/LOVE HER..............	2.00	3.50
☐ 2000		MAKE IT EASY ON YOURSELF/ DO THE JERK	2.00	3.50
☐ 2009		MAKE IT EASY ON YOURSELF/BUT I DO	1.75	3.00
☐ 2016		MY SHIP IS COMIN' IN/ YOU'RE ALL AROUND ME	1.75	3.00
☐ 2032		THE SUN AIN'T GONNA SHINE (ANYMORE)/AFTER THE LIGHTS GO OUT ...	1.75	3.00
☐ 2048		YOU DON'T HAVE TO TELL ME BABY/ THE YOUNG MAN CRIED..............	1.75	3.00
☐ 2063		ANOTHER TEAR FALLS/ SADDEST NIGHT IN THE WORLD	1.75	3.00

WALKER BROTHERS—ALBUMS

☐ 67076 (S)	*SMASH*	INTRODUCING THE WALKER BROTHERS	7.00	18.00
☐ 67082 (S)		THE SUN AIN'T GONNA SHINE ANYMORE	7.00	18.00

ISSUE #	LABEL		PRICE RANGE	

IAN WHITCOMB

☐ 120	*TOWER*	THIS SPORTING LIFE/FIZZ	2.25	4.00
☐ 134		YOU TURN ME ON/POOR BUT HONEST	2.00	3.50
☐ 155		N-E-R-V-O-U-S/THE END	2.00	3.50
☐ 170		18 WHITCOMB STREET/FIZZ	2.00	3.50
☐ 192		HIGH BLOOD PRESSURE/GOOD HARD ROCK . . .	2.00	3.50
☐ 251		YOU WON'T SEE ME/		
		PLEASE DON'T LEAVE ME ON THE SHELF . . .	2.00	3.50
☐ 274		WHERE DID ROBINSON CRUSOE GO WITH		
		FRIDAY ON SATURDAY NIGHT/		
		POOR LITTLE BIRD	2.00	3.50

IAN WHITCOMB—ALBUMS

☐ 5004 (S)	*TOWER*	YOU TURN ME ON	8.00	22.50
☐ 5042 (S)		IAN WHITCOMB'S MOD, MOD MUSIC HALL . . .	7.00	18.00
☐ 5071 (S)		YELLOW UNDERGROUND	6.00	15.00
☐ 5100 (S)		ROCK ME SOME ROCK	7.00	18.00

WHO

☐ 31725	*DECCA*	I CAN'T EXPLAIN/BALD HEADED WOMAN	3.50	6.00
☐ 31801		ANYWAY, ANYWHERE, ANYHOW/		
		DADDY ROLLING STONE	4.00	7.00
☐ 31801		ANYWAY, ANYWHERE, ANYHOW/		
		ANYTIME YOU WANT ME	3.50	6.00
☐ 31877		MY GENERATION/OUT IN THE STREET	2.25	4.00
☐ 31988		THE KIDS ARE ALRIGHT/A LEGAL MATTER	2.75	4.50
☐ 32058		I'M A BOY/IN THE CITY	2.75	4.50
☐ 32114		HAPPY JACK/WHISKEY MAN	1.75	3.00
☐ 32156		PICTURES OF LILY/DOCTOR, DOCTOR	1.75	3.00
☐ 32206		I CAN SEE FOR MILES/		
		MARY-ANNE WITH THE SHAKEY HANDS . . .	1.75	3.00
☐ 32288		CALL ME LIGHTNING/		
		DR. JEKYLL AND MR. HYDE	2.00	3.50
☐ 32362		MAGIC BUS/SOMEONE'S CRYING	1.75	3.00
☐ 32465		PINBALL WIZARD/DOGS, (PT. 1)	1.75	3.00

WHO—ALBUMS

☐ 74664 (S)	*DECCA*	THE WHO SINGS "MY GENERATION"	10.00	25.00
☐ 74892 (S)		HAPPY JACK	8.00	22.50
☐ 74950 (S)		THE WHO SELL OUT	7.00	18.00
☐ 75064 (S)		MAGIC BUS	5.00	13.50
☐ 79175 (S)		LIVE AT LEEDS	5.00	13.50
☐ 79182 (S)		WHO'S NEXT	5.00	13.50
☐ 79184 (S)		MEATY, BEATY, BIG & BOUNCY	5.00	13.50
☐ 7205 (S)		TOMMY	5.00	13.50

ISSUE #	LABEL		PRICE RANGE	

CHUCK WILLIS

☐ 1098	*ATLANTIC*	KANSAS CITY WOMAN/IT'S TOO LATE	4.00	7.00
☐ 1112		JUANITA/WHATCHA GONNA DO WHEN		
		YOUR BABY LEAVE YOU	4.00	7.00
☐ 1130		C. C. RIDER/EASE THE PAIN	2.75	4.50

CHUCK WILLIS—EPs

☐ 591	*ATLANTIC*	CHUCK WILLIS	6.00	11.00
☐ 608		ROCK WITH CHUCK WILLIS	6.00	11.00
☐ 609		ROCK WITH CHUCK WILLIS	6.00	11.00

CHUCK WILLIS—ALBUMS

☐ 8018 (M)	*ATLANTIC*	CHUCK WILLIS-THE KING OF THE STROLL	15.00	35.00
☐ 8079 (M)		I REMEMBER CHUCK WILLIS	10.00	25.00

(LITTLE) STEVIE WONDER

☐ 54061	*TAMLA*	I CALL IT PRETTY MUSIC (BUT OLD PEOPLE CALL IT THE BLUES) (PT. 1)/(PT. 2)	4.50	9.00
☐ 54070		LA LA LA LA LA/LITTLE WATER BOY	4.00	7.00
☐ 54074		CONTRACT ON LOVE/SUNSET	4.00	7.00
☐ 54080		FINGERTIPS (PT. 1)/(PT. 2)	2.00	3.50
☐ 54086		WORKOUT STEVIE, WORKOUT/ MONKEY TALK	2.00	3.50
☐ 54090		CASTLES IN THE SAND/TO THANK YOU	2.00	3.50
☐ 54096		HEY HARMONICA MAN/THIS LITTLE GIRL	2.00	3.50
☐ 54103		SAD BOY/HAPPY STREET	2.00	3.50
☐ 54114		TEARS IN VAIN/KISS ME, BABY	2.00	3.50
☐ 54119		HIGH HEEL SNEAKERS/MUSIC NOTES	2.00	3.50
☐ 54124		UPTIGHT (EVERYTHING'S ALRIGHT)/ PURPLE RAINDROPS	1.75	3.00
☐ 54130		NOTHING'S TOO GOOD FOR MY BABY/ WITH A CHILD'S HEART	1.75	3.00
☐ 54136		BLOWIN' IN THE WIND/ AIN'T THAT ASKING FOR TROUBLE	1.75	3.00
☐ 54139		A PLACE IN THE SUN/SYLVIA	1.75	3.00
☐ 54142		SOMEDAY AT CHRISTMAS/ THE MIRACLE OF CHRISTMAS	2.25	4.00
☐ 54147		TRAVELIN' MAN/HEY LOVE	1.75	3.00
☐ 54157		I'M WONDERING/EVERY TIME I SEE YOU I GO WILD	1.50	2.50
☐ 54165		SHOO-BE-DOO-BE-DOO-DA-DAY/ WHY DON'T YOU LEAVE ME TO LOVE?	1.50	2.50
☐ 54168		YOU MET YOUR MATCH/MY GIRL	1.50	2.50
☐ 54174		FOR ONCE IN MY LIFE/ANGIE GIRL	1.50	2.50
☐ 54180		MY CHERIE AMOUR/I DON'T KNOW WHY	1.50	2.50

ISSUE #	LABEL		PRICE RANGE	
☐54188		YESTER-ME, YESTER-YOU, YESTERDAY/		
		I'D BE A FOOL RIGHT NOW	1.50	2.50
☐54191		NEVER HAD A DREAM COME TRUE/		
		SOMEBODY KNOWS, SOMEBODY CARES ...	1.50	2.50
☐54196		SIGNED, SEALED, DELIVERED, I'M YOURS/		
		I'M MORE THAN HAPPY	1.50	2.50

(LITTLE) STEVIE WONDER—ALBUMS

☐232 (M)	*TAMLA*	TRIBUTE TO UNCLE RAY	8.00	22.50
☐233 (M)		JAZZ SOUL	8.00	22.50
☐240 (M)		THE 12-YEAR-OLD GENIUS	7.00	18.00
☐248 (M)		WORKOUT STEVIE, WORKOUT	6.00	15.00
☐250 (M)		WITH A SONG IN MY HEART	6.00	15.00
☐255 (M)		STEVIE AT THE BEACH	6.00	15.00
☐268 (S)		UPTIGHT	8.00	22.50
☐272 (S)		DOWN TO EARTH	8.00	22.50
☐279 (S)		I WAS MADE TO LOVE HER	7.00	18.00
☐282 (S)		GREATEST HITS	6.00	15.00
☐291 (S)		FOR ONCE IN MY LIFE	5.00	13.50
☐296 (S)		MY CHERIE AMOUR	5.00	13.50
☐298 (S)		STEVIE WONDER LIVE	5.00	13.50
☐304 (S)		SIGNED, SEALED AND DELIVERED	4.50	12.00
☐308 (S)		WHERE I'M COMING FROM	4.50	12.00
☐313 (S)		GREATEST HITS, VOL. II	4.50	12.00

— Y —

YARDBIRDS

☐9709	*EPIC*	I WISH YOU WOULD/A CERTAIN GIRL	10.00	18.00
☐9709		I WISH YOU WOULD/I AIN'T GOT YOU	10.00	18.00
☐9790		FOR YOUR LOVE/GOT TO HURRY	2.25	4.00
☐9823		HEART FULL OF SOUL/STEELED BLUES	2.25	4.00
☐9857		I'M A MAN/STILL I'M SAD	2.25	4.00
☐9891		SHAPES OF THINGS/I'M NOT TALKING	4.50	9.00
☐10006		SHAPES OF THINGS/		
		NEW YORK CITY BLUES	2.25	4.00
☐10006		SHAPES OF THINGS/		
		YOU'RE A BETTER MAN THAN I	2.25	4.00
☐10035		OVER UNDER SIDEWAYS DOWN/		
		JEFF'S BOOGIE	2.25	4.00

ISSUE #	LABEL		PRICE RANGE	

YARDBIRDS—ALBUMS

☐ 26167 (S)	*EPIC*	FOR YOUR LOVE	10.00	25.00
☐ 26177 (S)		HAVING A RAVE-UP WITH THE YARDBIRDS	10.00	25.00
☐ 26210 (S)		OVER UNDER SIDEWAYS DOWN	10.00	25.00
☐ 26246 (S)		GREATEST HITS	10.00	·25.00
☐ 26313 (S)		LITTLE GAMES	12.50	30.00
☐ 30615 (S)		LIVE YARDBIRDS FEATURING JIMMY PAGE	20.00	50.00

YOUNG RASCALS

☐ 2312	*ATLANTIC*	I AIN'T GONNA EAT OUT MY HEART		
		ANYMORE/SLOW DOWN	1.75	3.00
☐ 2321		GOOD LOVIN'/MUSTANG SALLY	1.75	3.00
☐ 2338		YOU BETTER RUN/		
		LOVE IS A BEAUTIFUL THING	1.75	3.00
☐ 2353		COME ON UP/WHAT IS THE REASON?	1.75	3.00
☐ 2377		I'VE BEEN LONELY TOO LONG/		
		IF YOU KNEW	1.75	3.00
☐ 2401		GROOVIN'/SUENO	1.75	3.00
☐ 2424		A GIRL LIKE YOU/IT'S LOVE	1.75	3.00
☐ 2428		GROOVIN'/GROOVIN'	2.00	3.50
☐ 2438		HOW CAN I BE SURE?/I'M SO HAPPY	1.75	3.00
☐ 2463		IT'S WONDERFUL/OF COURSE	1.75	3.00

YOUNG RASCALS—ALBUMS

☐ 8123 (S)	*ATLANTIC*	THE YOUNG RASCALS	6.00	15.00
☐ 8134 (S)		COLLECTIONS	6.00	15.00
☐ 8148 (S)		GROOVIN'	5.00	13.50
☐ 8169 (S)		ONCE UPON A DREAM	4.00	10.00
☐ 8190 (S)		TIME PEACE-THE RASCALS'		
		GREATEST HITS (1)	4.00	10.00

— Z —

FRANK ZAPPA

☐ 889	*BIZARRE*	LITTLE UMBRELLAS/		
		PEACHES EN REGALIA	2.25	4.00
☐ 967		WOULD YOU GO ALL THE WAY FOR THE		
		U.S.A./TELL ME YOU LOVE ME	2.25	4.00
☐ 58057	*UNITED ARTISTS*	MAGIC FINGERS/ DADDY, DADDY, DADDY	2.25	4.00

ISSUE #	LABEL		PRICE RANGE	
☐1312	*DISCREET*	DON'T EAT THE YELLOW SNOW/		
		COSMIK DEBRIS	3.50	6.00
☐214		SHE'S MINE/BICYCLE RIDE	3.50	6.00
☐215		DON'T MISS THE BOAT/YES MY LOVE	3.50	6.00
☐5006	*ROTATE*	THERE'S SOMETHING ABOUT YOU/		
		SHE'S LOST YOU	3.50	6.00
☐5009		WONDER WHAT I'M GONNA DO/		
		LET ME LOVE YOU BABY	3.50	6.00

FRANK ZAPPA— ALBUMS

☐8741 (S)	*VERVE*	LUMPY GRAVY	8.00	22.50
☐6356 (S)	*BIZARRE*	HOT RATS	7.00	18.00
☐2030 (S)		CHUNGA'S REVENGE	7.00	18.00
☐2094 (S)		WAKA/JAWAKA-HOT RATS	6.00	15.00
☐2175 (S)	*DISCREET*	APOSTROPHE (')	4.50	12.00
☐2202 (S)		ROXY AND ELSEWHERE	4.50	12.00
☐2216 (S)		ONE SIZE FITS ALL	4.50	12.00
☐2234 (S)		BONGO FURY	4.50	12.00
☐2289 (S)		APOSTROPHE (')	4.50	12.00
☐2290 (S)		ZAPPA IN NEW YORK	4.50	12.00
☐2291 (S)		STUDIO TAN	4.50	12.00

ZOMBIES

☐9695	*PARROT*	SHE'S NOT THERE/		
		YOU MAKE ME FEEL SO GOOD	2.00	3.50
☐9723		TELL HER NO/LEAVE ME BE	2.00	3.50
☐9747		SHE'S COMING HOME/I MUST MOVE	2.00	3.50
☐9769		I WANT YOU BACK AGAIN/		
		ONCE UPON A TIME	2.00	3.50
☐9797		JUST OUT OF REACH/REMEMBER YOU	2.00	3.50
☐9821		DON'T GO AWAY/IS THIS THE DREAM?	2.00	3.50
☐3004		HOW WE WERE BEFORE/INDICATION	2.00	3.50

For More Information . . .

The Official Collector's Price Guide to Records was designed as a basic introduction course for the beginning collector and flea market shopper, as well as a handy, tote-along reference book for the more seasoned hobbyist.

This guide offers the beginner a general overview of collecting techniques, tips, and prices for the collectibles most commonly bought and sold on the market today. Sufficient information on how to start a collection and how to avoid costly blunders can aid the novice in "getting off on the right foot."

You can slip this price guide into a pocket or a purse and take along your own "official" expert on your next shopping excursion. By flipping to the sections on the items you're planning to buy, you can feel more confident about the type of articles you purchase and the prices you pay, whether you're just learning or merely need to refresh your memory.

As your interest in collecting grows, you may want to start a reference library for other types of articles. For the collector who needs a more extensive coverage of the collectibles market, The House of Collectibles publishes a complete line of comprehensive companion guides to many of the pocket-sized books. These larger price guides, which are itemized at the back of this book, contain full coverage on buying, selling, and caring of valuable articles, plus listings with thousands of prices for rare, unusual, and common antiques and collectibles.

The House of Collectibles recommends *The Official Price Guide to Records*, fourth edition, as the companion to this pocket book.

- NEW, REVISED, FULLY UPDATED EDITION ... *more than 31,000 current collector prices* for all categories of old, rare, modern records ... 45 rpm singles ... extended plays ... LP albums ... from 1953 to 1980! A massive encyclopedia of music nostalgia.
- Rock 'n Roll • Hard Rock • Rockabilly • Punk Rock • Elvis • The Beatles • Country and Western • Pop • Easy Listening, *all* the stars, *all* the hits from *nearly 30 years of music* ... lists more than *1,100 artists* ... more than *20,000 song titles* ... including many rare, obscure labels.
- EXCLUSIVE PHOTOS AND BIOGRAPHIES OF NEARLY 200 RECORDING STARS, with information never before in print!
- EXPERT COLLECTING ADVICE on all aspects of the record collecting hobby ... including CONDITION, CARE, STORAGE and much more.
- COMPLETE DISCOGRAPHIES FOR MOTOWN AND PHILLES RECORDS ... including the rare early Elvis singles!

$9.95-4th Edition, 544 pgs., Order 356-2
Available from your local dealer or order direct from:
THE HOUSE OF COLLECTIBLES, see order blank

There is only one . . .

THE OFFICIAL
PRICE GUIDE®

THE MULTIPURPOSE REFERENCE GUIDE!!

THE OFFICIAL PRICE GUIDE SERIES has gained the reputation as the standard barometer of values on collectors' items. When you need to check the market price of a collectible, turn first to the OFFICIAL PRICE GUIDES . . . for impartial, unbiased, current information that is presented in an easy-to-follow format.

• **CURRENT VALUES FOR BUYING AND SELLING.** ACTUAL SALES that have occurred in all parts of the country are CAREFULLY EVALUATED and COMPUTERIZED to arrive at the most ACCURATE PRICES AVAILABLE.

• **CONCISE REFERENCES.** Each OFFICIAL PRICE GUIDE is designed primarily as a *guide to current market values.* They also include a useful summary of the information most readers are seeking: a history of the item; how it's manufactured; how to begin and maintain a collection; how and where to sell; addresses of periodicals and clubs.

• **INDEXED FORMAT.** • **FULLY ILLUSTRATED.**

Over 21 years of experience has made
THE HOUSE OF COLLECTIBLES
the most respected price guide authority!

PRICE GUIDE SERIES

American Silver & Silver Plate
Today's silver market offers excellent opportunities *to gain big profits* — if you are well informed. *Over 15,000 current market values* are listed for 19th and 20th century American-made Sterling, Coin and Silverplated flatware and holloware. Special souvenir spoon section. *ILLUSTRATED.*
$9.95-2nd Edition, 576 pgs., 5⅜" x 8", paperback, Order #: 184-5

Antique Clocks
A pictorial price reference for all types of American made clocks. Over *10,000 detailed listings* insure positive identification. *Includes histories of companies and line drawings. ILLUSTRATED.*
$9.95-1st Edition, 576 pgs., 5⅜" x 8", paperback, Order #: 364-3

Antique & Modern Dolls
More than *6,000 current retail selling prices* for antique dolls in wax, carved wood, china and bisque; modern and semi-modern dolls in celluloid, chalk, plastic, composition, and cloth. Advice on where and how to buy, condition, care and display, and selling dolls. *ILLUSTRATED.*
9.95-1st Edition, 544 pgs., 5⅜" x 8", paperback, Order #: 381-3

Antique & Modern Firearms
This unique book is an encyclopedia of gun lore featuring over *20,500 listings* with histories of American and foreign manufacturers *plus a special section on collector cartridge values. Advice on the investment potential of old and modern guns. ILLUSTRATED.*
$9.95-3rd Edition, 544 pgs., 5⅜" x 8", paperback, Order #: 363-5

Antique Jewelry
Over *8,200 current collector values* for the most extensive listing of antique jewelry ever published, Georgian, Victorian, Art Nouveau, Art Deco. A complete description of style and pattern. *Plus a special full color gem identification guide. ILLUSTRATED.*
$9.95-2nd Edition, 672 pgs., 5⅜" x 8", paperback, Order #: 354-6

Antiques & Other Collectibles
Introduces TODAY'S world of antiques with *over 100,000 current market values* for the most complete listing of antiques and collectibles IN PRINT! In this *new — 832 PAGE edition*, many new *categories have been added to keep fully up-to-date with the latest collecting trends. ILLUSTRATED.*
$9.95-4th Edition, 832 pgs., 5⅜" x 8", paperback, Order #: 374-0

Bottles Old & New
Over *22,000 current buying and selling prices* of both common and rare collectible bottles . . . ale, soda, bitters, flasks, medicine, perfume, poison, milk and more. Current production bottles. *Plus expanded sections on Avon and Jim Beam. ILLUSTRATED.*
$9.95-6th Edition, 576 pgs., 5⅜" x 8", paperback, Order #: 350-3

Collectible Cameras
More than *5,000 up-to-the-minute selling prices* for all types of popular collector cameras. An encyclopedia of American and foreign camera brands and models. Information on manufacturer, models, specifications, and date. Advice on buying and building a collection. *ILLUSTRATED.*
$9.95-1st Edition, 320 pgs., 5⅜" x 8", paperback, Order #: 383-X

Collectible Toys
Over *25,000 current values* for trains, windups, autos, soldiers, boats, banks, guns, musical toys, Disneyana, comic characters, Star Trek, Star Wars, and more. Valuable collecting tips. *ILLUSTRATED.*
$9.95-1st Edition, 576 pgs., 5⅜" x 8", paperback, Order #: 384-8

Collector Cars
Over *37,000 actual current prices* for 4000 models of antique and classic automobiles — U.S. and foreign. U.S. production figures — 1897 to date. Complete with engine specifications. *Special sections on auto memorabilia values and restoration techniques. ILLUSTRATED.*
$9.95-4th Edition, 544 pgs., 5⅜" x 8", paperback, Order #: 357-0

For your convenience use the handy order form.

PRICE GUIDE SERIES

Collector Handguns
Over *5,000 current values* for antique and modern handguns of all styles and all calibers. Plus the most up-to-date listing of current production handguns. *ILLUSTRATED.*
$9.95-1st Edition, 544 pgs., 5⅜" x 8", paperback, Order #: 367-8

Collector Knives
Over *13,000 buying and selling prices* on U.S. and foreign pocket and sheath knives. *Special sections on bicentennial, commemorative, limited edition, and handmade knives. Includes Case, Ka-Bar.* By J. Parker & B. Voyles. *ILLUSTRATED.*
$9.95-6th Edition, 736 pgs., 5⅜" x 8", paperback, Order #: 389-9

Collector Plates
Destined to become the ''PLATE COLLECTORS' BIBLE.'' This unique price guide offers the most comprehensive listing of collector plate values — *in Print! Special information includes: histories of companies; and helpful tips on buying, selling and displaying a collection. ILLUSTRATED.*
$9.95-1st Edition, 672 pgs., 5⅜" x 8", paperback, Order #: 349-X

Collector Prints
Over *14,750 detailed listings* representing over 400 of the most famous collector print artists from Audubon and Currier & Ives, to modern day artists. Information on buying, selling, storing, and caring for prints. *Special feature includes gallery/artist reference chart. ILLUSTRATED.*
$9.95-4th Edition, 544 pgs., 5⅜" x 8", paperback, Order #: 189-6

Comic & Science Fiction Books
Over *31,000 listings with current values* for comic and science fiction publications *from 1903-to-date. Special sections on Tarzan, Big Little Books, original and newspaper comic art, Science Fiction publications and paperbacks. Plus important collecting advice. ILLUSTRATED.*
$9.95-6th Edition, 544 pgs., 5⅜" x 8", paperback, Order #: 353-8

Glassware
Over *60,000 listings* for all types of American-made glassware, art, pressed and pattern, depression, cut, carnival and more. Collecting advice. Compendium of references. *ILLUSTRATED.*
$9.95-1st Edition, 608 pgs., 5⅜" x 8", paperback, Order #: 125-X

Hummel Figurines & Plates
The most complete guide ever published on every type of Hummel — including the most recent trademarks and size variations, with *6,100 up-to-date prices. A complete guide to trademarks and variations. Plus tips on buying, selling and investing. ILLUSTRATED.*
$9.95-3rd Edition, 448 pgs., 5⅜" x 8", paperback, Order #: 352-X

Kitchen Collectibles
This beautiful pictorial guide has *hundreds of illustrations* - truly a MASTERPIECE of reference. This first really complete *History of America in the Kitchen* describes hundreds of implements and lists *28,000 current market values.* China, glassware, silver, copper, iron, wood. *ILLUSTRATED.*
$9.95-1st Edition, 544 pgs., 5⅜" x 8", paperback, Order #: 371-6

Military Collectibles
This detailed historical reference price guide covers the largest accumulation of military objects — 15th century-to-date — listing over *12,500 accurate prices. Armor, weapons, uniforms, bayonets, and rare objects. Special expanded Samurai sword and headdress sections. ILLUSTRATED.*
$9.95-3rd Edition, 608 pgs., 5⅜" x 8", paperback, Order #: 398-8

Music Machines
Virtually every music-related collectible is included in this guide — over *11,000 current prices.* 78 recordings, mechanical musical machines and U.S. and foreign instruments. *ILLUSTRATED.*
$9.95-2nd Edition, 544 pgs., 5⅜" x 8", paperback, Order #: 187-X

For your convenience use the handy order form.

Old Books & Autographs

Descriptions of the finest literary collectibles available, with over *11,000 prices for all types of books from the 15th to the 20th century*: Americana, bibles, medicine, cookbooks, novels, children's, and more. *Plus an updated autograph section. ILLUSTRATED.*
$9.95-4th Edition, 512 pgs., 5⅜" x 8", paperback, Order #: 351-1

Oriental Collectibles

Over *10,000 detailed listings and values* for all types of Chinese, Japanese, and Asian collectibles, pottery, rugs, statues, porcelain, cloisonne, metalware. netsuke. *ILLUSTRATED.*
$9.95-1st Edition, 512 pgs., 5⅜" x 8", paperback, Order #: 375-9

Paper Collectibles

Old Checks, Invoices, Books, Magazines, Newspapers, Ticket Stubs and even Matchbooks — any paper items that reflect America's past — are gaining collector value. This book contains *over 26,000 current values* and descriptions for all types of paper collectibles. *ILLUSTRATED.*
$9.95-3rd Edition, 608 pgs., 5⅜" x 8", paperback, Order #: 394-5

Pottery & Porcelain

Over *10,000 current prices and listings* of fine pottery and porcelain of all types and periods from the 18th century to date, plus an extensive Lenox china section. *Special sections on histories of manufacturers and identifying china trademarks. ILLUSTRATED.*
$9.95-2nd Edition, 576 pgs., 5⅜" x 8", paperback, Order #: 188-8

Records

Over *31,000 current prices* of collectible singles, EPs, albums, plus 20,000 memorable song titles recorded by over 1100 artists. *Rare biographies and photos are provided for many well-known artists.* Complete discographies for Motown and Philles records. *ILLUSTRATED.*
$9.95-4th Edition, 544 pgs., 5⅜" x 8", paperback, Order #: 356-2

Royal Doulton

This authoritative guide to Royal Doulton porcelains contains over *5,500 detailed listings* on figurines, plates and Toby jugs. Includes tips on buying, selling and displaying. The history of the Royal Doulton factory. *Plus an exclusive numerical reference index. ILLUSTRATED.*
$9.95-2nd Edition, 544 pgs., 5⅜" x 8", paperback, Order #: 355-4

Wicker

You could be sitting on a *fortune!* Decorators and collectors are driving wicker values to unbelievable highs! This pictorial price guide *positively identifies all types* of Victorian, Turn of the Century and Art Deco wicker furniture. *A special illustrated section on wicker repair is included. ILLUSTRATED.*
$9.95-1st Edition, 416 pgs., 5⅜" x 8", paperback, Order #: 348-1

Encyclopedia of Antiques

A total of more than *10,000 definitions, explanations, concise factual summaries of names, dates, histories, confusing terminology* . . . for every popular field of collecting. An exclusive appendix includes many trademark and pattern charts, conversion tables for precious metals, and furniture. styles as well as a categorized list of museums and reference publications.
$9.95-1st Edition, 704 pgs., 5⅜" x 8", paperback, Order #: 365-1

Buying & Selling Guide to Antiques

Covers every phase of collecting, from beginning a collection to its ultimate sale . . . examines in detail the collecting potential of *over 200 different catagories of items in all price ranges.* Special features include a dealer directory, a condition grading report, list of museums and reference publications, plus a discussion of buying, selling and investment techniques. *ILLUSTRATED.*
$9.95-1st Edition, 608 pgs., 5⅜" x 8", paperback, Order #: 369-4

NUMISMATIC SERIES

THE BLACKBOOKS are more than just informative books, they are the most highly-regarded authority on the nation's most popular hobbies.

1984 Blackbook Price Guide of United States Coins

A coin collector's guide to current market values for all U.S. coins from 1616 to date—over *16,500 prices*. **THE OFFICIAL BLACKBOOK OF COINS** has gained the reputation as the most reliable, up-to-date guide to U.S. Coin values. This new edition features an exclusive gold and silver identification guide. Learn how to test, weigh and calculate the value of any item made of gold or silver. Proven professional techniques revealed for the first time. Detecting altered coins section. Take advantage of the current ''BUYERS' MARKET'' in gold and silver. *ILLUSTRATED.*
$2.95-22nd Edition, 288 pgs., 4″ x 5½″, paperback, Order #: 385-6

1984 Blackbook Price Guide of United States Paper Money

Over *9,000 buying and selling prices* covering U.S. currency from 1861 to date. Every note issued by the U.S. government is listed and priced, including many Confederate States notes. Error Notes are described and priced, and there are detailed articles on many phases of the hobby for beginners and advanced collectors alike. Comprehensive grading section. *ILLUSTRATED.*
$2.95-16th Edition, 240 pgs., 4″ x 5½″, paperback, Order #: 387-2

1984 Blackbook Price Guide of United States Postage Stamps

Featuring all U.S. stamps from 1847 to date pictured in full color. Over *19,000 current selling prices*. General issues, airmails, United Nations, first day covers, more. You will find new listings for the most current commemorative and regular issue stamps, a feature not offered in any other price guide, at any price! There were numerous important developments in the fast moving stamp market during the past year and they are all included in this *NEW REVISED EDITION. ILLUSTRATED.*
$2.95-6th Edition, 240 pgs., 4″ x 5½″, paperback, Order #: 386-4

INVESTORS SERIES

The Official Investors Guide Series shows you, *step by step*, how to select the right items for your investment program, how to avoid the many pitfalls that can foil new investors, with full instructions on when to sell and *How And Where To Sell* in order to realize the *Highest Possible Profit.*

Investors Guide to Gold, Silver, Diamonds

All you need to know about making money trading in the precious metals and diamond markets. This practical, easy-to-read investment guide is for everyone in all income brackets. *ILLUSTRATED.*
$6.95-1st Edition, 208 pgs., 5⅜″ x 8″, paperback, Order #: 171-3

Investors Guide to Gold Coins

The first complete book on investing in gold coins. Exclusive price performance charts trace all U.S. gold coin values from *1955 to date. Forcasts price trends. ILLUSTRATED.*
$6.95-1st Edition, 288 pgs., 5⅜″ x 8″, paperback, Order #: 300-7

Investors Guide to Silver Coins

The most extensive listing of all U.S. silver coins. Detailed price performance charts trace actual sales figures from *1955 to date. Learn how to figure investment profit. ILLUSTRATED.*
$6.95-1st Edition, 288 pgs., 5⅜″ x 8″, paperback, Order #: 301-5

Investors Guide to Silver Dollars

Regardless of your income, you can *become a successful silver dollar investor.* Actual sales figures for every U.S. silver dollar *1955 to date. Comprehensive grading section. ILLUSTRATED.*
$6.95-1st Edition, 192 pgs., 5⅜″ x 8″, paperback, Order #: 302-3

For your convenience use the handy order form.